THE CAMBRIDGE COMPANION TO JAMES JOYCE

Third Edition

The Cambridge Companion to James Joyce is an indispensable scholarly guide to one of the world's most important and influential writers. Fifteen chapters, each written by a leading Joyce scholar, address each of Joyce's major works, key contexts, and important themes, resulting in both an accessible introduction for students and a lively resource for teachers and researchers.

In this much revised and expanded third edition, featuring eleven entirely new and four revised chapters, the editorial matter (chronology and guide to further reading) has been written from scratch. The third edition creates more space for Joyce's fascination with gender, sex, and bodies, and provides renewed attention to his engagement with Irish history. Scholarship on ecocriticism, serialization, editing, and publishing is also represented for the first time. Joyce's most influential work, *Ulysses*, has two dedicated chapters covering different aspects and perspectives, as well as a chapter on its serialization.

JOHN NASH is Professor of English at Durham University and an internationally recognized authority on the work of James Joyce. He is the author of *James Joyce and the Act of Reception* (Cambridge University Press, 2006), editor of *James Joyce in the Nineteenth Century* (Cambridge University Press, 2013) and *Joyce's Audiences* (Rodopi, 2002), and co-editor of *Modernism and Non-Translation* (Oxford University Press, 2019).

A complete list of books in the series is at the back of this book.

THE CAMBRIDGE COMPANION TO
JAMES JOYCE

Third Edition

EDITED BY
JOHN NASH
Durham University

CAMBRIDGE
UNIVERSITY PRESS

Shaftesbury Road, Cambridge CB2 8EA, United Kingdom

One Liberty Plaza, 20th Floor, New York, NY 10006, USA

477 Williamstown Road, Port Melbourne, VIC 3207, Australia

314–321, 3rd Floor, Plot 3, Splendor Forum, Jasola District Centre, New Delhi – 110025, India

103 Penang Road, #05-06/07, Visioncrest Commercial, Singapore 238467

Cambridge University Press is part of Cambridge University Press & Assessment, a department of the University of Cambridge.

We share the University's mission to contribute to society through the pursuit of education, learning and research at the highest international levels of excellence.

www.cambridge.org
Information on this title: www.cambridge.org/9781009636407

DOI: 10.1017/9781009636414

© Cambridge University Press & Assessment 1990, 2004 and 2025

This publication is in copyright. Subject to statutory exception and to the provisions of relevant collective licensing agreements, no reproduction of any part may take place without the written permission of Cambridge University Press & Assessment.

When citing this work, please include a reference to the DOI 10.1017/9781009636414

First published 1990
Second edition 2004
Third edition 2025

A catalogue record for this publication is available from the British Library

A Cataloging-in-Publication data record for this book is available from the Library of Congress

ISBN 978-1-009-63640-7 Hardback
ISBN 978-1-009-63639-1 Paperback

Cambridge University Press & Assessment has no responsibility for the persistence or accuracy of URLs for external or third-party internet websites referred to in this publication and does not guarantee that any content on such websites is, or will remain, accurate or appropriate.

For EU product safety concerns, contact us at Calle de José Abascal, 56, 1°, 28003 Madrid, Spain, or email eugpsr@cambridge.org.

CONTENTS

List of Figures		*page* vii
Notes on Contributors		viii
Note on the Cambridge Companion to James Joyce, *Third Edition*		xi
Chronology of Joyce's Life		xii
List of Abbreviations		xvii
	Introduction: Placing Joyce JOHN NASH	1
1	*Dubliners*: Narration, Church, and Revival JOHN NASH	12
2	*Stephen Hero* and *A Portrait of the Artist as a Young Man*: Recursion, Time, Emergence, and the Nation JOHN PAUL RIQUELME	31
3	*Ulysses*: Form of Forms SCARLETT BARON	47
4	Reading *Ulysses* Historically: Modes and Methods ANDREW GIBSON	64
5	De-Confusing Confession at *Finnegans Wake* FINN FORDHAM	84
6	Joyce's Shorter Works VICKI MAHAFFEY	102
7	Joyce the Irishman SEAMUS DEANE	120

CONTENTS

8 Joyce the European 136
   JEAN-MICHEL RABATÉ

9 Joyce, Colonialism, and Nationalism 153
   MARJORIE HOWES

10 Gender Politics 169
   MARIAN EIDE

11 Sex and Sexuality 184
   KATHERINE MULLIN

12 Joyce and the Everyday 200
   SEAN LATHAM

13 Joyce and Nature 216
   JIM FAIRHALL

14 Periodical Publication and Modernism: The Case of *Ulysses* 232
   CLARE HUTTON

15 Writing, Reading, Revising, Editing, Archiving: The Sociology of Joyce's Writing 251
   DIRK VAN HULLE

Further Reading 266
Index 279

FIGURES

14.1 Advertisement for *The Egoist*, published in *The Little Review*, April 1918 *page* 233
14.2 Contents page of *The Little Review*, April 1918 236
14.3 Masthead and contents of *The Egoist*, January–February 1919 238
14.4 *The Egoist*, January–February 1919 240
14.5 A full page of *Ulysses* as it appeared in *The Egoist*, January–February 1919 242

All images reproduced from The Modernist Journals Project (searchable database). Brown and Tulsa Universities, ongoing, at modjourn.org.

CONTRIBUTORS

SCARLETT BARON is Associate Professor in Twentieth- and Twenty-First-Century Literature at University College London. She is the author of *'Strandentwining Cable': Joyce, Flaubert, and Intertextuality* (Oxford University Press, 2012) and *The Birth of Intertextuality: The Riddle of Creativity* (Routledge, 2019). She has written a number of essays on Joyce and his relations to other twentieth-century authors.

SEAMUS DEANE (d. 2021) was Keough Professor of Irish Studies at the University of Notre Dame. His publications included the novel *Reading in the Dark* (Vintage, 1996) and *Strange Country: Modernity and Nationhood in Irish Writing since 1790* (Clarendon, 1997). He was General Editor of *The Field Day Anthology of Irish Writing*, 3 vols. (1991), the Penguin Joyce (1991–1992), and the series Critical Conditions: Field Day Essays and Monographs (1996–2002). A collection of his essays, *Small World*, appeared with Cambridge University Press in 2021.

MARIAN EIDE is Professor of English and Women's and Gender Studies at Texas A&M University. She is the author of *Ethical Joyce* (Cambridge University Press, 2002) and *Terrible Beauty: The Violent Aesthetic and Twentieth-Century Literature* (University of Virginia Press, 2019).

JIM FAIRHALL teaches modern literature and environmental studies at DePaul University in Chicago. He has published *James Joyce and the Question of History* (Cambridge University Press, 1993) and, more recently, articles on Joyce and ecocriticism. He is also an award-winning writer of fiction, creative nonfiction, and poetry.

FINN FORDHAM is Professor of Twentieth-Century Literature at Royal Holloway, University of London. He is the author of *Lots of Fun at 'Finnegans Wake'* (2007) and *I do I undo I redo: The Textual Genesis of Modernist Selves* (2010), both for Oxford University Press. He is currently working on a cultural history focusing on the day Britain and France declared war on Germany.

LIST OF CONTRIBUTORS

ANDREW GIBSON is Professor Emeritus at Royal Holloway, University of London, where he was Research Professor of Modern Literature and Theory. His books include *Joyce's Revenge: History, Politics and Aesthetics in 'Ulysses'* (Oxford University Press, 2002), *James Joyce* (Reaktion, 2006), and *The Strong Spirit: History, Politics and Aesthetics in the Writings of James Joyce 1898–1915* (Oxford University Press, 2012). He is General Editor of the forthcoming Penguin editions of Joyce's works.

MARJORIE HOWES is Associate Professor of English at Boston College. She is the author of *Yeats's Nations: Gender, Class, and Irishness* (Cambridge University Press, 1996) and *Colonial Crossings: Figures in Irish Literary History* (Field Day, 2006), and co-editor of a number of volumes, including *Semicolonial Joyce* (Cambridge University Press, 2000), *The Cambridge Companion to W. B. Yeats* (Cambridge University Press, 2006), and *The Irish Revival: A Complex Vision* (Syracuse University Press, 2023).

CLARE HUTTON is Professor of Literature and Book History at Loughborough University. She is the author of *Serial Encounters: 'Ulysses' and the Little Review* (Oxford University Press, 2019) and was curator of *Women and the Making of 'Ulysses'*, a major exhibition hosted at the Harry Ransom Center, University of Texas at Austin in 2022. She is the author of many articles about Irish literature and book history and is now working on *The Textual Culture of the Irish Literary Revival* for Oxford University Press.

SEAN LATHAM is the Walter Professor of English at the University of Tulsa, where he served for twenty-one years as editor of the *James Joyce Quarterly*. He is the author or editor of ten books on modern literature and culture, including *Am I a Snob?* (Cornell University Press, 2003), *The Art of Scandal* (Oxford University Press, 2009), *The Little Review 'Ulysses'* (with Bob Scholes and Mark Gaipa, Yale University Press, 2015), and *The World of Bob Dylan* (Cambridge University Press, 2021).

VICKI MAHAFFEY is Professor Emerita at the University of Pennsylvania and the University of Illinois at Champaign-Urbana. A former Guggenheim Fellow, she has published widely on Joyce and modernism. Her most recent monograph is *The Joyce of Everyday Life* (Bucknell University Press, 2024).

KATHERINE MULLIN is Professor of Modern Literature and Culture at the University of Leeds. She is the author of *James Joyce, Sexuality and Social Purity* (Cambridge University Press, 2003) and *Working Girls: Fiction, Sexuality, and Modernity* (Oxford University Press, 2016). She is currently completing a third monograph, *Provocateurs: Censorship, Backlash, and the Invention of Modernism*.

LIST OF CONTRIBUTORS

JOHN NASH is Professor of Modern Literature at Durham University. His books include *James Joyce and the Act of Reception: Reading, Ireland, Modernism* (Cambridge University Press, 2006) and *James Joyce in the Nineteenth Century* (Cambridge University Press, 2013).

JEAN-MICHEL RABATÉ is Professor of English and Comparative Literature at the University of Pennsylvania, and Fellow of the American Academy of Arts and Sciences. He has published fifty books on modernism, psychoanalysis, philosophy, and literary theory, among which is *Joyce, Hérétique et Prodigue* (Stilus, 2022*)*.

JOHN PAUL RIQUELME (d. 2022) was Professor of English at Boston University. He was the author of *Teller and Tale in Joyce's Fiction: Oscillating Perspectives* (1983) and *Harmony of Dissonances: T. S. Eliot, Romanticism, and Imagination* (1991), and editor of Fritz Senn's *Joyce's Dislocutions: Essays on Reading as Translation* (1984), all published by Johns Hopkins University Press. He edited the Norton edition of *A Portrait of the Artist as a Young Man* (Norton, 2004).

DIRK VAN HULLE is Professor of Bibliography and Modern Book History at the University of Oxford and director of the Oxford Centre for Textual Editing and Theory (OCTET). He co-directs the *Beckett Digital Manuscript Project* (www.beckettarchive.org) and is co-editor of the *Journal of Beckett Studies*. His publications include *James Joyce's Work in Progress* (Routledge, 2016) and *Genetic Criticism* (Oxford University Press, 2022).

NOTE ON THE *CAMBRIDGE COMPANION TO JAMES JOYCE*, THIRD EDITION

The first edition of the *Cambridge Companion to James Joyce*, published in 1990, was one of the first ever Cambridge Companions. The second edition, in 2004, kept most of the original eleven essays and added several new and revised ones. Both were edited by Derek Attridge. This third edition is bigger again. It contains mostly new essays: eleven are entirely new, and the other four have all been revised. The third edition extends the work of the second edition by creating further space for Joyce's interests in gender, sex, and sexuality, and for renewed attention to his engagement with Irish history and writing. It also introduces additional essays on the everyday, the environment, serialization, and compositional and editorial matters. The traditional structure of the companion has been retained, with essays on the full range of Joyce's writing, within which there is now extra attention on *Ulysses*. Editorial matter has been extensively revised and updated.

CHRONOLOGY OF JOYCE'S LIFE

1882   James Augustine Joyce, born 2 February, Rathgar, Dublin.

1888   Joyce family moves to Bray, County Dublin. Attends as a boarder at Clongowes Wood College, run by the Jesuit order.

1891   Family financial difficulties leading to protracted series of house moves over the next decade. Consequently withdrawn from Clongowes and attends Christian Brothers school. Writes poem 'Et tu, Healy!' (now lost) on the death of Charles Stewart Parnell, whose political downfall the previous year was much mourned in the Joyce household.

1893   Attends Belvedere College, Jesuit school in central Dublin, as a scholarship day pupil and goes on to have considerable academic success there.

1898   Student at University College Dublin.

1899   Supports W. B. Yeats and the Irish Literary Theatre after attending riotous opening night of *The Countess Cathleen*. Refuses to join a student protest against the play.

1900   Joyce's enthusiasm for Ibsen evident in 'Ibsen's New Drama', published in the *Fortnightly Review* (for which Ibsen thanks him), and in 'Drama and Life', paper read to Literary and Historical Society at UCD. Some poetry and drama from this period lost.

1901   Private publication of 'The Day of the Rabblement', attacking populism of the Irish Literary Theatre.

1902   Graduates with degree in modern languages and leaves Dublin for Paris with idea of studying medicine.

1903   Compiles 'Epiphanies' while in Paris. Returns to Dublin on receiving telegram of mother's final illness. Mary Jane ('May') Joyce, née Murray, dies 13 August. Writes several reviews for Dublin-based *Daily Express* between December 1902 and November 1903.

CHRONOLOGY OF JOYCE'S LIFE

1904   Writes three stories for *The Irish Homestead*, which will later form part of *Dubliners*, and poems that will later form part of *Chamber Music*. Essay 'A Portrait of the Artist' rejected by John Eglinton at *Dana*, revised into autobiographical novel *Stephen Hero*.

         Short stint as schoolteacher in Dalkey. Resides briefly in Martello Tower, Sandycove, amid peripatetic existence.

         First date with Nora Barnacle (from an impoverished background in Galway) most likely on 16 June. Unmarried, they leave Ireland together on 8 October. Works as teacher of English at a Berlitz school in Pola, part of the Austrian Empire.

1905   Moves to Trieste, working at Berlitz school. Publisher Grant Richards (London) rejects *Dubliners* ('Two Gallants', 'A Little Cloud' and 'The Dead' not yet written) and *Chamber Music*. Son Giorgio born 27 July. Brother Stanislaus arrives to live with James and Nora, and provides financial support over the next decade.

1906   Brief, unhappy stint as bank clerk in Rome. Conceives but does not write short story 'Ulysses', about a Jewish Dubliner called Mr Hunter.

1907   Returns to Trieste to work privately teaching English. Daughter Lucia born 26 July. Writes 'The Dead'. *Chamber Music* published in London by Elkin Mathews. Gives series of three public lectures and begins association with news journal, *Il Piccolo della Serra*, for which he will write several articles between 1907 and 1912; these lectures and articles are largely concerned with Irish history, politics, and literature.

1907–1908   Writes three chapters of *A Portrait of the Artist as a Young Man*, creating the new novel from the discarded *Stephen Hero*.

1909   Two visits to Dublin. Signs contract with Maunsel & Co. to publish *Dubliners* and returns to open the Volta, Ireland's first cinema, on Mary Street, Dublin, with backing from Triestine acquaintances (withdrawing from the cinema in mid-1910).

1910   Sisters Eva and Eileen go to live with Joyce and Nora in Trieste.

1912   Joyce's last trip to Ireland, with Nora's family in Galway, and then Dublin. Protracted dispute with Maunsel leading to printer's destruction of printed sheets for fear of libel. In fury, on journey back to Trieste, Joyce writes 'Gas from a Burner' satirizing publishers and hypocrisy of English libel law. Privately distributed.

1913 Ezra Pound writes to Joyce to offer his help. Over the next decade Pound writes many enthusiastic published articles and private letters championing Joyce as a 'modern' writer.

1914 Perhaps the key year in Joyce's career. In January, the *Egoist* (ed. Dora Marsden) begins serialization of *A Portrait of the Artist as a Young Man*, instigated by Pound. Joyce re-approaches Grant Richards, who publishes *Dubliners* on 15 June, followed soon after by outbreak of WWI. Home Rule for Ireland now shelved in British parliament. Joyce and family face internment in Trieste. Begins work on *Ulysses*, which is paused by writing *Exiles*.

1915 *Exiles* completed. Joyce, Nora, and children granted permission to leave Trieste and move to neutral Zurich on pledge of neutrality. Stanislaus detained in Austrian internment camp. Joyce receives financial support from Royal Literary Fund.

1916 First book publication of *A Portrait* (New York: Huebsch). Joyce receives financial gifts from Harriet Shaw Weaver (Englishwoman, now editor at *Egoist*) with offer to publish *Portrait*. Easter Rising in Dublin: violent suppression of nationalist rebellion.

1917 First of many serious eye operations. Weaver begins long-term, initially anonymous, financial support. First UK edition of *A Portrait* (by the *Egoist*).

1918 *Exiles* published. *Little Review* in United States begins serialization of *Ulysses*. Irish War of Independence 1918–1921.

1919 Returns to Trieste post-war. *Egoist* publishes five episodes of *Ulysses*.

1920 Joyce and family move to Paris, living there (mostly) until 1940. Stanislaus remains in Trieste. September issue of *Little Review* containing 'Nausicaa' is seized by US customs: editors Jane Heap and Margaret Anderson charged with obscenity, ending serialization of *Ulysses* and prospect of book publication in United States and elsewhere. Joyce makes an outline of the episodes of *Ulysses* for Carlo Linati to help him interpret it ('the Linati schema').

1921 Agreement between Joyce and Sylvia Beach for Shakespeare & Company (the name of her Paris bookshop) to publish *Ulysses* in limited edition of 1,000 copies for subscribers. Joyce continues to revise, adding significantly to proofs. Joyce makes a different schema of episodes for Valéry Larbaud.

Treaty of Independence takes effect at end of 1921.

1922 *Ulysses* published by Shakespeare & Company on 2 February, Joyce's fortieth birthday, to generally negative, bemused, and offended reviews. Later in the year, significant reviews by Larbaud in France, Edmund Wilson in the United States, and T. S. Eliot in England. Further printings of *Ulysses* follow through the twenties.

  Civil War in Ireland ensues on the passing of the treaty. Nora and children caught in fighting during short visit to Ireland.

1923 Joyce's eye problems especially acute through the mid-twenties and continue the remainder of his life. In 1923, has teeth removed in mistaken belief it will assist ocular health. Series of operations in mid-twenties; often near-blind and in considerable pain. Able to work with magnifying glass, crayons, and much assistance.

1924 First instalment of 'Work in Progress' (which will become *Finnegans Wake*) published in *Transatlantic Review*. Negative reactions from Pound, Stanislaus, and others; Weaver cautious but continues financial support.

  Joyce turns down Yeats's formal invitation to visit Ireland.

1926–1927 Samuel Roth reproduces unauthorized instalments from *Ulysses* in his *Two Worlds Monthly* (printed and distributed in the United States). Joyce organises international condemnation of Roth and eventually wins a legal injunction.

1927 Second verse collection, *Pomes Penyeach*, published by Shakespeare & Co. First of many instalments from 'Work in Progress' to appear over the coming years in Parisian avant-garde literary journal *transition*.

1928 A section of Joyce's new work published as *Anna Livia Plurabelle* to secure copyright.

1929 Essays written by Samuel Beckett and *transition* writers among others, arranged by Joyce to explain his new work published as *Our Exagmination ... of 'Work in Progress'*. Together with *Anna Livia Plurabelle*, these publications help to generate some limited critical support for the new work. French translation, *Ulysse*.

1930 First book-length analysis of *Ulysses* appears: *James Joyce's 'Ulysses': A Study*, by Stuart Gilbert, friend of Joyce. Written with Joyce's assistance, the book points out many Homeric parallels.

1931 While staying in London, Joyce and Nora marry to enable legal rights for the family to inherit his estate. Father, John ('Jack') Joyce, dies.

1932	Birth of grandson Stephen Joyce (to Giorgio and Helen), who will go on to control the Joyce estate through late twentieth century. Lucia, whose behaviour has caused concern in recent years, suffers breakdown and is hospitalized.
1933	*Ulysses* obscenity trial. Judge Woolsey lifts the ban in *The United States v. One Book Named 'Ulysses'*. Random House publishes first US edition.
1934	*James Joyce and the Making of 'Ulysses'* by Frank Budgen (another friend) makes use of Joyce's revisions.
1936	First UK edition of *Ulysses* published by Bodley Head.
1939	*Finnegans Wake* published. The first biography, by Herbert Gorman, published. WWII begins.
1940	France falls to the Nazis in May–June. After a struggle, Joyce gains permission to leave Paris. He and Nora move to Zurich. Lucia remains in a French sanitarium.
1941	The first book to deal with all Joyce's major works – *James Joyce: A Critical Introduction* by Harry Levin – appears in series 'Makers of Modern Literature'. Joyce dies, aged 58, on 13 January following complications arising from an operation for a perforated duodenal ulcer. He is buried in Fluntern Cemetery, Zurich. Paul Léon donates Joyce papers to the National Library of Ireland, under fifty-year seal; thus beginning one of the world's most significant Joyce collections.
1950	Collection of Joyce papers begins at University of Buffalo; will include many papers from Sylvia Beach.
1951	Collection of Joyce papers begins at Yale University.
1951	Nora Barnacle Joyce dies in Zurich, buried in Fluntern Cemetery.
1957	Collection of Joyce papers begins at Cornell University, initially from widow of Stanislaus.
1959	Richard Ellmann's biography published.
1961	Death of Harriet Shaw Weaver; donation of Joyce papers to British Library under ten-year seal.

ABBREVIATIONS

D	*Dubliners* [1914], ed. Terence Brown. London: Penguin, 1992. Text ed. by Robert Scholes.
FW	*Finnegans Wake* [1939]. London: Faber & Faber, 1988. Cited by page and line number.
GJ	*Giacomo Joyce*, ed. Richard Ellmann. New York: Viking Press, 1968.
JJ	*James Joyce*, by Richard Ellmann. Revised and expanded edition. Oxford: Oxford University Press, 1982.
JJA	*James Joyce Archive*, ed. Michael Groden et al. New York: Garland, 1977–1979. 63 volumes. Cited by volume and page number.
Letters	*Letters of James Joyce*, 3 vols. Vol. 1 ed. Stuart Gilbert. New York: Viking Press, 1957. Vols. 2 and 3 ed. Richard Ellmann. New York: Viking Press, 1966. Cited by volume and page number.
OCPW	*Occasional, Critical, and Political Writing*, ed. Kevin Barry. Oxford: Oxford World's Classics, 2000.
P	*A Portrait of the Artist as a Young Man* [1916]. The definitive text, corrected from the Dublin holograph by Chester G. Anderson and edited by Richard Ellmann. New York: Viking Press, 1969.
PE	*Poems and Exiles*, ed. J. C. C. Mays. London: Penguin, 1992.
PSW	*Poems and Shorter Writings*, ed. Richard Ellmann, A. Walton Litz, and John Whittier-Ferguson. London: Faber & Faber, 1991.
SL	*Selected Letters of James Joyce*, ed. Richard Ellmann. London: Faber & Faber, 1975.
SH	*Stephen Hero* [1944], ed. Theodore Spencer, incorp. additional manuscript pages ed. John J. Slocum and Herbert Cahoon. New York: New Directions, 1963.
U	*Ulysses* [1922], ed. Hans Walter Gabler, with Wolfhard Steppe and Claus Melchior. New York: Random House and London: Bodley Head, 1986. Cited by episode and line number.

JOHN NASH

Introduction

Placing Joyce

James Joyce's writing career began with a short, naturalistic story in *The Irish Homestead* (1904) and ended with *Finnegans Wake* (1939), a book that even his supporters found unreadable.[1] The story of how Joyce moved from an apparently unassuming strain of naturalism in his early fiction to the kaleidoscopic deconstruction of language and form in his final work is one of the great arcs of world literature. Across this span of three-and-a-half decades, Joyce produced landmark publications that would disrupt and re-imagine the writing of fiction across the globe, all the while remaining centred on the social conditions of his upbringing in early twentieth-century Dublin. Although Joyce has just four 'major' works to his name, their achievement is staggering: he re-wrote the terms of engagement for modern short fiction, the *Bildungsroman*, and the novel; he made a critical intervention in the Irish Literary Revival and became a touchstone of what we have come to call modernism; he invented new modes of naturalism and narration, combining fastidious attention to material detail with the most intimate of revelation; he re-mapped classical and mythical influence on literary form; and finally, as if all that was not enough, he created his own riotous subversion of the English language.[2] Associated with the heyday of European modernism, rooted in Irish history and culture, engaging an anti-imperial politics with frank and challenging depictions of bodies and sex, Joyce's *oeuvre*, despite censorship and snubbing, has had colossal influence over the past century and more.

Despite the abstraction of Joyce as modernist and as globalized figure in a certain version of world literature, and notwithstanding the irony that drips from *A Portrait of the Artist as a Young Man*, there is a case for considering seriously, or at least somewhat seriously, Stephen Dedalus's over-reaching desire – expressed in his diary at the end of *Portrait* – to 'forge in the smithy of my soul the uncreated conscience of my race' (*P* 253).[3] To start to address that ambition, Joyce's use of the word 'race' appears to mean, broadly

I

speaking, Irish people. His most concerted elucidation of the topic comes in a 1907 lecture given in Trieste, 'Ireland, Island of Saints and Sages', although he does not address the ambiguities of that term beyond acknowledging the interlaced histories of various peoples in Ireland: 'Our civilisation is an immense woven fabric in which very different elements are mixed' (*OCPW* 118), nor does he look too deeply into who 'Our' refers to.[4] (The issue is also taken up in Chapters 2 and 9 by John Paul Riquelme and Marjorie Howes, respectively.) The terms in which Dedalus casts his lofty ambition are closely identified with his background: – 'soul' and 'conscience' gesture towards a shared intellectual inheritance for Joyce and his alter ego Stephen, both 'steeled in the school of old Aquinas' (*PE* 105). Dedalus's aim to formulate some expression that might potentially represent Irish people is, of course, couched in irony and ambiguity ('forge' meaning forgery?), although the fact that Joyce articulates Stephen's thought in this way and with such prominence implies a tentative attraction to the project – even if the project of articulating a national conscience (an as yet 'uncreated' one) will remain always illusory and private ('in my soul').[5]

Trying to 'place' Joyce in this way is no easy matter. Joyce's complex socio-political positioning goes hand-in-hand with often radical formal and linguistic expression, and it is surely this nexus of innovation, together with his multi-directional political signification, that intrigues and delights readers. He remains entranced by Aquinas, Homer, Shakespeare, and Irish mythology, while writing with evident relish about soap, cocoa, and meaty foods, about 'unfortunate' priests (*D* 123) and Dublin trams. In doing so he evinces a particularity in attention to detail – of the physical world, of Irish history, of all manner of allusions to literature, music, current events, and whatever he was reading; despite this 'particularism', there has been a long tradition of reading his work as 'universal', only incidentally Irish.[6]

Although he lived his adult life as an immigrant in continental Europe (and the holder of a British passport), Joyce may be regarded as the principal prose writer of Irish modernity, writing almost with obsession about the repressive limitations, the humour, the nods and winks of Catholic lower middle-class Dublin in the early twentieth century, on the cusp of Independence. (Chapters 7 and 8 by Seamus Deane and Jean-Michel Rabaté, respectively, address the Irish and European dimensions of his work and thought.) Many in Ireland, not least those who differed from Joyce by social and religious background, recognized the importance of this distinctive voice as intimately linked to 'the mind of Catholic Ireland' and 'Catholic democracy in Ireland'.[7] Even a cursory reading of any of Joyce's texts – much of *Dubliners* or the Christmas dinner scene in *Portrait*, for example – reveals a deep distrust of the institution of the Catholic Church, and, in particular, what Joyce saw as its unholy alliance with British political power and Irish populism in bringing down Charles Stewart Parnell (*OCPW* 191–6). Yet the world he knew and the critically interpretative approach he took to that world were steeped in Catholicism. The other side of the coin of oppression is British imperial rule, which, when it is not intruding directly into events, hovers as a backdrop, at times threatening, at other times offensive, like an unwelcome guest. The opening scene of *Ulysses*, featuring the ethnographical Englishman Haines in residence at the Martello Tower, brilliantly illustrates the apparently benign presence of soft (intellectual) power and the way in which corresponding expectations pattern behaviour.[8] Something not dissimilar is enacted through the hierarchy that structures the story 'Counterparts', where the intersection of social class and national background creates a series of oppressions to be passed down from boss to worker, English woman to Irish man, violent father to abused son. But Joyce is careful not to map straightforward allegories: in 'Counterparts', the hierarchy is implied by accent rather than stated outright.[9] Instead, characters, allusions, events all mesh within distanced, naturalistic depiction. And in *Ulysses*, Joyce's ire is directed more at Mulligan's false hospitality than at Haines's imposition. Hence British rule appears enmeshed amid intersectional contingencies (as noted by Marjorie Howes in Chapter 9).

One way to approach the trajectory of his career is through a longstanding topic in Joyce studies, concerning the extent to which Joyce remains attached to a naturalistic project that manifests signs of its undoing as early as *Dubliners*, while making possible new forms of representation. According to one critic, 'Joyce's insistence on presenting a stubbornly recalcitrant lived reality remains consistent from *Dubliners* through *Ulysses*' and is evidence that naturalism had a 'continuing appeal' for him.[10] In this view, the naturalism of *Dubliners* firmly roots Joyce's ongoing concern for the social life of Dublin, where private worlds ravaged by alcoholism, abuse, and repression are directly connected to the public worlds of Catholic Church surveillance and the long history of political oppression and resistance. (I discuss the naturalism of *Dubliners* in Chapter 1.) *Portrait* explicitly develops the process by rendering personal perception as an intermediary, a method that was signalled from the earliest pages of childhood perception, and which is most fully realized in *Ulysses*. In short, the groundbreaking interior monologues of *Ulysses* extend the principles of a naturalist account by appearing to show how a character thinks. Coupled with this, Joyce's naturalism is attested by his sympathetic understanding of the ordinariness of everyday life's enthralment to powerful social forces. From short stories that mask their momentousness amid unfinished sentences and the 'epiphanic' revelations in chance moments ('epiphanies' are one aspect addressed in Chapter 6 by Vicki Mahaffey) to the commodities and accumulated stuff of *Ulysses*, Joyce takes care to put readers into particular material environments, most obviously the streets of Dublin. The same critic is surely right that Joyce 'operated within a set of problematics that have defined naturalism' – which he identifies as how to derive meaning from materiality, how to convey others' lived experience, and how to 'totalize details' within a coherent framework without imposing an external 'totality' – but the extent to which Joyce also challenged and revised those 'problematics' is a continuing debate.[11]

In building his works from 'everyday' matter, Joyce embraced the ordinary functions of the body (as Sean Latham remarks in Chapter 12). Moments such as following Bloom into the outside lavatory extend Joyce's naturalism with humour and an empathetic understanding for the ways in which mundane details constrain and shape life.[12] As he reads a story from *Titbits* magazine while defecating, the two actions intermingle in Bloom's interior monologue: 'It did not move or touch him but it was something quick and neat' (*U* 4.511–12). If this suggests a judgement on the quality of the story he reads (Bloom also 'wiped himself with it' – *U* 4.537), it is made without the condescension towards popular culture once associated with modernism.[13] Instead, products and their advertisements become constituent parts of intimate lives (such as Plumtree's potted meat); popular cultural references sit side-by-side with the prestige of opera and Shakespeare.

Joyce is also one of the most frankly explicit writers about sex while at the same time debunking the hypocrisy of false prudishness (as discussed by Katherine Mullin in Chapter 11): in *Portrait*, for example, Stephen Dedalus's rebellion against Church and home is fired largely by sexual desire, to the extent that sex – like art – becomes one of the ways in which a new sense of individual independence gains traction. Less well-known works such as *Exiles* and *Giacomo Joyce* are primarily concerned with variations of illicit desire (as Vicki Mahaffey discusses in Chapter 6). In these three works, written around the same period, sex and desire occasion feelings of shame and guilt, and only fleetingly does anything like liberation emerge. As an example from the 'Wandering Rocks' episode of *Ulysses* illustrates, matters of sex are also wrapped up in a complex web of representation, voyeurism, and exchange.

In the central, tenth section, of 'Wandering Rocks', Bloom becomes the focal point: now in a nearby bookshop, he procures a gift for Molly at the same time as Boylan does so (in section five of the chapter). In one sense, both men are purchasing for themselves: Boylan's lascivious anticipation of vigour is objectified in the fruit that he buys, including 'fat pears', 'ripe shamefaced peaches' (*U* 10.305–6), setting the tone for Boylan's encounter with Molly, which she will graphically recall in 'Penelope'. Bloom has chosen a book for Molly, *Sweets of Sin*, which triggers his own gratification. Reading from *Sweets of Sin*, he unerringly eyes a racy passage (the phrase '*her heaving embonpoint*' particularly captures his imagination – see U 10.616, 10.622, and 16.1468). Bloom struggles in 'Mastering his troubled breath' (U 10.638), as the rhythm of the syntax mirrors his racing pulse ('Yes. This. Here. Try' – U 10.610). Bloom has alighted on a passage of particular resonance: 'the beautiful woman' of *Sweets of Sin* has spent 'all the dollarbills her husband gave her' on 'wondrous gowns and costliest frillies' designed to entice her lover, 'For him! For Raoul!' (U 10.608–9). That Bloom clearly relishes this scene, at the same time that he knows his own wife and her lover are preparing to meet, is one clue among several that he connives in Molly's affair, performs a voyeuristic role towards that affair, and even takes some vicarious partial fulfilment from it (as the 'Circe' episode makes painfully explicit). This fictional passage performs a seductive allure, an enticing otherness indicated by 'dollarbills', the name Raoul, the borrowed French terms *déshabillé* and *embonpoint*. One might even say that Bloom's act of reading this passage paves the way for its enactment between Molly and Boylan later that afternoon. Joyce's ambiguous gender politics are also at play here: pairing Boylan and Bloom, and absenting Molly, the juxtaposition of the two men becomes an exchange between them, where the gift is not fruit or a book but Molly herself.[14] (Marian Eide develops the point about Joyce's ambiguous gender politics in Chapter 10.) The physical absence of Molly through the middle of the book makes her eventual appearance, when she narrates 'Penelope', all the more provocative.

The tone of this scene from 'Wandering Rocks' is comic but not sentimental: undercutting any pathos or pretension is the humour of the material world. This detachment has been achieved partly through the episode's cinematic form: nineteen sub-sections, criss-crossed by 'interpolations' that create a montage of events occurring at the same time in other parts of the city.[15] Where perhaps, with a different writer, a sentimental attention may have fallen on Bloom's gift as one of love and sacrifice, making this a moment of pathos, instead the scene climaxes with the shopman spitting his 'puked phlegm', tapping *Sweets of Sin*, and intoning – one can't help but think that he does so in a creepy croak – 'That's a good one' (U 10.641). So this passage is not only one of generosity but also of selfishness, of loss and betrayal, of sex and voyeurism, of the book industry and commercialism. And at the heart of it all is another scene of reading (in addition to Bloom's experience on the toilet), of a sort that Joyce returns to over and again, a self-reflective distortion of the interpretive process, spinning the web from which the novel is constructed.

It is evident that the claim that Joyce's basis in naturalism underpins his work as a whole also fails to account for a great deal. For one thing, material and everyday environments are sometimes transformed into sites of symbolic or totemic importance in Joyce's writing, which typically mixes and substitutes the sacred and the ordinary. In such instances, Aristotle and Aquinas provide the basis of an aesthetics for the modern world.[16] Beyond the accommodation between naturalism and symbolism that we see in *Dubliners*, Joyce's evident fascination with objects leads them to attain other qualities, either through weight of accumulation (the lists of 'Ithaca') or in taking on lives of their own (as in 'Circe'). In these instances, the physical world overwhelms and undermines a naturalist approach. It is precisely the surfeit of things, and a corresponding overload of information, especially in *Ulysses*, that also threatens ultimately to displace the naturalist mode in Joyce's later work. Take 'Ithaca': as critics have remarked, the lists of detailed answers are sometimes far in excess of what is useful or intelligible to readers and lead us quickly towards irrelevance.[17] (This question of the book's form, as seen through early readers, is addressed by Scarlett Baron in Chapter 3.) The lists of books on Bloom's shelves, the items in his drawers, the household things on the kitchen dresser – where each item appears much like the next – proliferate to mask the potential significance of their contents. The books and drawer items finally tell us little that is meaningful about Bloom; whether or not he (or the reader) takes in the potential meaning of the empty pot of Plumtree's potted meat – a gift from Boylan, the flakes of which he will soon discover in his bed – we cannot be sure. The key here is the narrative voice of the 'Ithaca' episode, as it moves with apparent indifference while still interjecting a note of independent personality: see, for example, the forty-two-line homage to water that follows a question about 'What in water did Bloom ... admire?' (*U* 17.185–228). The answer is fulsome in its compilation of data, yet also streaked with an un-Bloomian tone that takes a humorous delight in its own encyclopaedic range ('its vast circumterrestrial ahorizontal curve' – *U* 17.208). In this way, naturalism overflows, and potential symbolism is drowned. As Hugh Kenner has observed, *Ulysses* 'parodies the naturalistic novel with genial ferocity'.[18]

It has been argued that the mid-point of *Ulysses* is where Joyce's writing develops from its basis in naturalism, albeit an oddly performative naturalism, and now becomes something arrestingly new.[19] What follows, from 'Wandering Rocks' on, is perhaps the single most daring and brilliant manoeuvre in English-language fiction, a gearshift in the history of literature: from now on, each episode or chapter will be told in a new and different voice, a pastiche of styles that parodies Joyce's sources and imitates his characters, as a succession of different styles takes over the book. (That does

Introduction: Placing Joyce

not mean that the historical and political rootedness of these styles and episodes should be disregarded, as Andrew Gibson argues in Chapter 4.) These styles include, among others, an exaggerated imitation of patriotic revivalism, a dramatic script, a question-and-answer catechism, and Molly's concluding monologue. Given this transition from the 'initial style' (*SL* 242) of the opening episodes, we witness what Karen Lawrence has described as the 'breakdown of the novel as form and the creation of an encyclopaedia of narrative choices', which creates a 'shift of attention from the dramatic action of the plot to the drama of the writing'.[20] In doing so, the apparent arbitrariness of 'style' is questioned, and Joyce's earlier episodes in the first half of *Ulysses* similarly fall under suspicion. This is all the more remarkable given the achievement of *Dubliners* and *Portrait*, in which a form of naturalism – built upon material realities, social forces, expression of character, and the slipperiness of language – had been successfully created. The stylistic explosion in *Ulysses* would become one of the great achievements of modernism.

Seventeen years later, Joyce followed *Ulysses* with *Finnegans Wake*, a book whose language is its narrative and its point (in Chapter 5, Finn Fordham argues for approaching the *Wake* as a form of narrative). This is a text that seems forever to be describing itself: 'It is told in sounds in utter that, in signs so adds to, in universal, in polyguttural, in each auxiliary neutral idiom, sordomutics, florilingua, sheltafocal, flayflutter, a con's cubane, a pro's tutute, strassarab, ereperse and anythongue athall' (*FW* 117.12–15). Famously, in the *Wake*, Joyce draws on dozens of languages, of which he knew about half-a-dozen well, as well as on names of flowers and fauna (florilingua), the world's rivers, and so on. (The environmental aspect of Joyce's work is addressed by Jim Fairhall in Chapter 13.) The creation of this Wakean language, which so dismayed his supporters, was a way of writing the universal into the particular. Joyce's friend Stuart Gilbert, who published an important study of *Ulysses* in 1932, thought that this was actually a narrowing or retrenchment on Joyce's part: global allusions and multilingual puns were the work of 'The provincial Dubliner. Foreign is funny.'[21] At the same time, Irish history and myth, its politics, learning, and literature, are heavily represented in the *Wake* – in St Patrick, the early Church, the *Book of Kells*, and so forth, right up to the 1922 Treaty, signed just before the publication of *Ulysses*. Indeed, the *Wake*'s genesis was in notes Joyce took on the reception of both *Ulysses* and the Treaty and ensuing Civil War.[22] And if the *Wake* is 'about' anything, it seems to be about a letter, which is also the treaty – and De Valera's alternative, 'Document no. 2' – and *Ulysses*, whose reception was also divided amid confusion and contestation:

> While we in our wee free state, holding to that prestatute in our charter, may have our irremovable doubts as to the whole sense of the lot, the interpretation of any phrase in the whole, the meaning of every word of a phrase so far deciphered out of it, however unfettered our Irish daily independence, we must vaunt no idle dubiosity as to its genuine authorship and holusbolus authoritativeness. (FW 117.34–118.04)

Seen from this post-1922 perspective, the *Wake* is, then, an imaginative investigation of the conditions of these documents, told with Joyce's wry anticipation of all those 'prearranged disappointments' (*FW* 107.33–4) to which books, political settlements, and all kinds of independence might eventually lead.

Above all, *Finnegans Wake* gloriously embodies Joyce's delight in the comedy of language. From the '*simony*' of *Dubliners* that inflects Simon Dedalus, to the invective and tall tales of the newsmen and pub-goers of *Ulysses*, to the way Bloom's perusal of a tea display leads to recollection of the missing letter in his 'high grade ha' (*U* 5.24), language itself offers a comic, often deflationary, insight into characters' humanity. At the same time, this was also a matter of substance, and an important aspect of this new language is its un-Englishness. If *Ulysses* was a means to rejuvenate a tired European culture – the *Odyssey* rendered '*sub specie temporis nostri*' (*SL* 271) – then the *Wake* may be considered an attempt to 'wipe alley english spooker ... off the face of the erse' (*FW* 178.6–7) – where earth is also, appropriately enough, Ireland. If Joyce remained in Ireland by living abroad, it was because Ireland offered the models for a synopsis of world history. 'Yet is it but an old story, the tale of a Treestone with one Ysold' (*FW* 113.18–19).

Much of Joyce's work was published in serial form in modernist magazines, sometimes over a protracted period: *Portrait* in *The Egoist*, *Ulysses* in *The Little Review* (prior to the US customs seizure of 'Nausicaa') and elsewhere, and *Finnegans Wake* in *transition* and elsewhere. The publication histories of all Joyce's work illuminate the conditions he worked in, and the context of serialization in modernist magazines forms part of Joyce's rich cultural signification as it appeared alongside a huge variety of works, editorials, adverts, and so on.[23] This also meant that these texts were subject to different editorial practices and multiple stages of revision. (Clare Hutton discusses aspects of the serialization of *Ulysses* in Chapter 14.) The complexities of *Ulysses* and *Finnegans Wake*, in particular, mean that the various draft and publication stages are especially fruitful for scholarship, especially as more papers come to light. (Dirk van Hulle addresses these matters in Chapter 15's discussion of 'genetic' criticism.)

Introduction: Placing Joyce

The difficulties that Joyce encountered ranged from the material conditions of his family, to the oppressive social structures of early twentieth-century Dublin, to charges of obscenity and offensiveness. His writing tackles these matters directly and forms a career that, in doing so, consistently challenged modes of representation. The daring of 'Penelope', in purporting to represent a woman's thought without apparent mediation, and the exuberance of *Finnegans Wake* exemplify a certain literary 'singularity'. his work speaks to many peoples and places, while being deeply rooted in his own origins, and at the same time this is a writing that tests the limits of literature, as if Joyce were to say that the pen has no bounds. As Jacques Derrida reminds us, Joyce's apparently encyclopaedic ambition, his condensation of histories and languages and literary forms, is also 'indissociable from an *absolutely* singular event'.[24] Our roles as readers revolve around doing justice to that singularity.

Notes

1. In Ezra Pound's estimation of an early draft 'nothing short of divine vision or a new cure for the clapp can possibly be worth all the circumambient peripherization' (*JJ* 584). In *Finnegans Wake* Joyce referred to Pound's letter by offering as an alternative title for the book, 'A New Cure for an Old Clap' (*FW* 104.34–5).
2. The term 'major' is justly used by Derek Attridge in his introductory essay to previous editions of this companion: 'Reading Joyce' in *The Cambridge Companion to James Joyce*, ed. Derek Attridge (Cambridge: Cambridge University Press, 2004), p. 25 n2. However, it should not blind readers to the significance of his other work. For example, Suzette Henke describes *Exiles* as a turning point in Joyce's 'convoluted investigation of heterosexual and homoerotic desire'. Suzette Henke, *James Joyce and the Politics of Desire* (New York: Routledge, 1990), p. 85.
3. On Joyce's ironic distance from his autobiographical alter ego, see, for example, Hugh Kenner's analysis of the final chapter of *Portrait* in *Dublin's Joyce* (1955, repr. New York: Columbia University Press, 1987). The issue is touched on by John-Paul Riquelme in Chapter 2.
4. On Joyce and race, see Vincent J. Cheng, *Joyce, Race and Empire* (Cambridge: Cambridge University Press, 1995); Len Platt, *Joyce, Race and 'Finnegans Wake'* (Cambridge: Cambridge University Press, 2007); and Malcolm Sen, 'Joyce and Race in the Twenty-First Century' in *The New Joyce Studies*, ed. Catherine Flynn (Cambridge: Cambridge University Press, 2022). In common with the racial theory of his time, Joyce does still seem to think of 'race' as a distinctive and meaningful category, even if he uses it nebulously and does not question the concept in the same way that he questions nationality, which he says may be a 'useful fiction' (*OCPW* 118). For further remarks on Joyce's notion of race in the context of ethics, see Marian Eide, Chapter 10.

5. Stephen's line echoes an aim of the Irish Revival, but compare Joyce's irony with W. B. Yeats's more assured address to a possible national audience and national culture in poems such as 'To Ireland in the Coming Times' and 'The Fisherman'.
6. Most famously, from as early as the 1910s, Pound helped to formulate a Joyce who was 'universal' and not concerned with 'the promotion of Irish peasant industries'. Ezra Pound, '"Dubliners" and Mr James Joyce', *The Egoist*, 1.14 (July 15, 1914), 267. Available at the Modernist Journals Project: modjourn.org/issue/bdr521034/. A serious instance of particularism may be found in Andrew Gibson, *The Strong Spirit: History, Politics and Aesthetics in the Writings of James Joyce, 1898–1915* (Oxford: Oxford University Press, 2013).
7. John Eglinton, 'Irish Letter', The Dial, lxxxvi (May 1929); 417–20, repr. in Robert H. Deming, ed. *James Joyce: The Critical Heritage. Volume Two 1928–1941* (London: Routledge & Kegan Paul, 1970), p. 459. Joseph Hone, 'A Letter from Ireland', *London Mercury* v (January 1923): 306–8, repr. in Robert H. Deming, ed. *James Joyce: The Critical Heritage. Volume One 1907–1927* (London: Routledge & Kegan Paul, 1970), p. 298.
8. Still the best analysis of this angle is in Vincent J. Cheng, *Joyce, Race and Empire*. See his analysis of the opening Martello Tower scene, pp. 151–62.
9. See John Nash, '"Counterparts" before the Law: Mimicry and Exclusion' in *Re: Joyce*, ed. John Brannigan, Geoff Ward, and Julian Wolfreys (London: Palgrave Macmillan, 1998).
10. Simon Joyce, *Modernism and Naturalism in British and Irish Fiction, 1880–1930* (Cambridge: Cambridge University Press, 2015), p. 110.
11. Joyce, *Modernism and Naturalism*, p. 110.
12. 'Mr Joyce has a cloacal obsession. He would bring back into the general picture of life aspects which modern drainage and modern decorum have taken out of ordinary intercourse and conversation'. H. G. Wells, 'James Joyce', *Nation* (24 February 1917), 710, repr. in Deming, *James Joyce: The Critical Heritage, Vol. 1*, p. 86.
13. For explorations of this theme, see R. Brandon Kershner, ed. *James Joyce and Popular Culture* (Gainesville: University of Florida Press, 1996).
14. Among many explorations of gender and sexuality, see Henke, *James Joyce and the Politics of Desire* and Joseph Valente, ed. *Quare Joyce* (Ann Arbor: University of Michigan Press, 1988).
15. Clive Hart discusses the interpolations in 'Wandering Rocks' in *James Joyce's 'Ulysses': Critical Essays*, ed. David Hayman and Clive Hart (Berkeley: University of California Press, 1974), Appendix A, pp. 203–14.
16. From a long line of scholarship in this area, see Fran O'Rourke, *Joyce, Aristotle, and Aquinas* (Gainesville: University Press of Florida, 2022).
17. David Trotter, *The English Novel in History, 1895–1920* (London: Routledge, 1993), p. 299–302.
18. Hugh Kenner, 'Joyce and Ibsen's Naturalism', *The Sewanee Review* 59.1 (1951): 75–96, 76.
19. David Hayman, *'Ulysses': The Mechanics of Meaning* (Madison: University of Wisconsin Press, 1982, rev. ed.).
20. Karen Lawrence, *The Odyssey of Style in 'Ulysses'* (Princeton, NJ: Princeton University Press, 1981), p. 10, p. 12.

21. Stuart Gilbert, *Reflections on James Joyce: Stuart Gilbert's Paris Journal*, ed. Thomas F. Staley and Randolph Lewis (Austin: University of Texas Press, 1993), p. 21.
22. Vincent Deane, Introduction in *The 'Finnegans Wake' Notebooks at Buffalo, Notebook VI.B.10*, ed. Vincent Deane, Daniel Ferrer, and Geert Lernout (Turnhout: Brepols, 2001), p. 11. On the Treaty and Irish Civil War in *Finnegans Wake*, see John Garvin, *James Joyce's Disunited Kingdom* (Dublin: Gill & Macmillan, 1976); Dominic Manganiello, *Joyce's Politics* (London: Routledge, 1980), p. 174–89; and David Pierce, 'The Politics of *Finnegans Wake*', *Textual Practice* 2.3 (1988): 367–80.
23. A founding study in this area is Mark S. Morrison, *The Public Face of Modernism: Little Magazines, Audiences, and Reception, 1905–1920* (Madison: University of Wisconsin Press, 2001), and a key resource is the Modernist Journals Project at modjourn.org.
24. Jacques Derrida, '"This Strange Institution Called Literature": An Interview with Jacques Derrida' in *Acts of Literature*, ed. Derek Attridge (New York: Routledge, 1992), p. 43.

I

JOHN NASH

Dubliners

Narration, Church, and Revival

The *Dubliners* stories arose from a chance opportunity when George Russell, a prominent revivalist figure, invited Joyce to make a little money by submitting stories to *The Irish Homestead*. Russell didn't want the readers to be disconcerted – but that would precisely be the effect of Joyce's stories. Eventually published ten years later, having overcome threats of censorship and libel law, the expanded collection made a significant intervention in the Irish Literary Revival, pointing unerringly at some unpleasant truths, and established Joyce as a noted prose realist disrupting a movement more associated with poets and dramatists. These stories would later come to be seen also as key documents in the development of modernist fiction, their naturalism tempered by symbolism and a multi-layered interpretative openness that makes them among the most prized of modern short stories.

In July 1904, Russell had suggested that Joyce might contribute to the *Homestead* stories of 'simple, rural?, livemaking?, pathos?' although his warning 'not to shock the readers' (*Letters II* 43) did not deter Joyce from submitting stories that implied negligence, even abuse, in the Catholic Church ('The Sisters'), domestic violence and oppression ('Eveline'), and colonial servility and financial corruption ('After the Race').[1] That all three were published speaks to the stories' deceptively straightforward narration – the subtle indirectness and reservation of Joyce's style – and may perhaps owe something to the 'dearth of copy' available to the paper's editor.[2] As a collection, the short stories of *Dubliners* provide a cold portrait of the social realities of a specific time and place (Dublin around the turn of the twentieth century), written with a devastating implied judgement on the social causes of the delusions, repressions, and injustices of the citizens of 'old jog-along Dublin' (*D* 73). Joyce relished this opportunity to express his already established predilection for naturalism: for several years already he had been an advocate for Henrik Ibsen's dramatic realism, declaring to the Literary and

Historical Society at University College, 'Life we must accept as we see it before our eyes, men and women as we meet them in the real world' (*OCPW* 28). But this did not mean a meek acceptance of things, still less of the political powers as they were, for Ibsen or for Joyce, but rather a cold-eyed identification of how those powers – of Church and state – had produced 'life ... as we see it'. This was the problem of naturalism as Joyce confronted it: how to convey a critique in a faithful account of actual conditions.[3] In *Dubliners*, Joyce developed a style that would express obliquely his rage against those powers while principally describing 'men and women as we meet them'. Or, as Joyce put it in a 1906 letter to his brother Stanislaus, he wanted to write a 'moral history of my country':

> My intention was to write a chapter of the moral history of my country and I chose Dublin for the scene because that city seemed to me the centre of paralysis. I have tried to present it to the indifferent public under four of its aspects: childhood, adolescence, maturity and public life. The stories are arranged in this order. I have written it for the most part in a style of scrupulous meanness. (*SL* 83)

It is worth looking at how that 'moral history' is conveyed through 'scrupulous meanness'. The development of that style can be traced in part from the versions that appeared in the *Homestead* to the revised stories that appeared when the collection was eventually published in book form in 1914. Compare, for example, two versions of a single paragraph from 'Eveline', the first from the *Homestead* in 1904 and the latter as revised in 1905 and then published in *Dubliners*:

> Home! She looked round the room, passing in review all its familiar objects. How many times she had dusted it, once a week at least. It was the 'best' room, but it seemed to secrete dust everywhere. She had known the room for ten years – more – twelve years, and knew everything in it. Now she was going away. And yet during all those years she had never found out the name of the Australian priest whose yellowing photograph hung on the wall, just above the broken harmonium. ('Eveline', *The Irish Homestead*, 10 Sept. 1904)

> Home! She looked round the room, reviewing all its familiar objects which she had dusted once a week for so many years, wondering where on earth all the dust came from. Perhaps she would never see again those familiar objects from which she had never dreamed of being divided. And yet during all those years she had never found out the name of the Australian priest whose yellowing photograph hung on the wall above the broken harmonium beside the coloured print of the promises made to Blessed Margaret Mary Alacoque. (*D* 29–30)

In the revised version, Joyce focuses attention more on the perspective of Eveline, introducing her indecision as a state of mind. He does this in three ways. The longer second sentence now covers what had been three sentences of the earlier version, bringing readers closer to the character by associating with her thought processes ('reviewing', 'wondering'). There is a subtler use of free indirect narrative; 'where on earth' is a phrase belonging clearly to Eveline herself, one that adds an intricacy missing from the inverted commas around 'best'. Finally, the new emphasis on the conditional term 'Perhaps' brings an additional, better-fitting sense of vacillation.

Joyce's decision to repeat 'familiar objects' – the phrase now appears twice in the published text – reinforces the character's entrapment in her environment. It also directs attention towards those objects – the 'broken harmonium' and the (newly introduced) print of Blessed Margaret Mary Alacoque. As critics have pointed out, Joyce here carefully constructs a form of symbolism: the broken harmony of the household is suggested, and an allusion is made to the seventeenth-century French nun upon whose visions was founded the Catholic practice of venerating the Sacred Heart.[4] Readers can then link this familiar object to the 'open-hearted' Frank, an unlikely saviour, who, it may seem, 'would save' Eveline (D 32–3).[5]

Joyce thus uses an everyday object in a Catholic home in early twentieth-century Dublin to point towards the oppressions experienced by a worn-down young woman, helplessly transfixed between, on the one hand, her 'duty' to God and 'promise to keep the home together' and, on the other hand, the naïve 'impossible' romance of 'escape' (D 33–4). Yet all this is far from explicit: Joyce leads readers towards inferences but does so with restraint. The scene is carried off in a style that indicates 'a stubbornly recalcitrant lived reality' while also 'internalizing and psychologizing the forms by which it is observed'.[6] The conditionality of this writing – in which 'would', 'could', 'perhaps', and 'as if' are key terms through the stories – creates a double sense of the undecidable interpretive dilemmas of both transfixed characters and readers. This 'style of scrupulous meanness' is a free indirect narrative that carefully balances ironic superiority with identification, so characters are neither wholly undermined nor quite sympathetic. The symbolism that points at social commentary is grounded in the naturalism of 'familiar objects'.

Joyce's deployment of free indirect narrative creates a delicate balancing act. The technique was used by its great pioneer, Jane Austen, to create a largely, if not wholly, sympathetic identification with heroines such as Emma Woodhouse. In Joyce's hands the technique often enough reveals a character's misperceptions or ignorance, as with Austen, but Joyce does not produce a sympathetic near-identification. This free indirect narrative may be benign, as in the case of Maria in 'Clay' – who sees that the 'fire was nice and bright' (D 95) – or Lily in 'The Dead' – who 'was literally run off her feet' – or it may be more pointed, as in the comment about Gabriel's speech that 'The table burst into applause and laughter at this sally' (*D* 205), where the word 'sally' especially betrays his self-regarding pomposity. In 'A Little Cloud', the narrative again reveals the point of view of the protagonist, Little Chandler, even at times so closely following his train of thought, by use of 'you' to refer to himself – 'You could do nothing in Dublin' (*D* 68) – that it borders on interior monologue.[7]

The point, however, is not to condemn the individual character but to bring to the surface those obscured wider social forces acting upon individuals.[8] In 'After the Race', the narration is focalized through Jimmy Doyle, who is said to have an attitude of 'reasonable recklessness' (*D* 37) towards life, a phrase that simultaneously combines revelation of the character's self-deceptive point of view and locates readers in a position of superior knowledge. Jimmy's father gets even more direct treatment: he 'had begun life as an advanced Nationalist' but 'modified his views early', suggesting that this change of political tack went hand-in-hand with being 'fortunate enough to secure some of the police contracts' (*D* 36). Joyce's focus on the single term 'fortunate' to betray the forces at work is striking: the Doyle family fortune is masked as merely a stroke of luck, 'fortunate enough'. This 'scrupulous meanness' implies an ethical corruption at the root of social advancement. Jimmy's delusion is visible to readers but not to himself. His 'excess' (*D* 36) leads to short-term gambling losses and, most likely, a longer-term poor investment. The willing self-deception in Jimmy's voice can clearly be heard in the euphemism and periphrasis of the following sentence: 'Of course, the investment was a good one and Ségouin had managed to give the impression that it was by a favour of friendship the mite of Irish money was to be included in the capital of the concern' (*D* 37). The free indirect discourse thereby allows the characters' own language and perceptions to betray them, while maintaining an arm's length critical distance.

The naturalism of Joyce's 'style of scrupulous meanness' is a complex affair: moulding an internal viewpoint with an ironic detachment, it nevertheless tempers its depiction of actuality by creating space for some suggestive wordplay. In 'After the Race', the 'mite' of Irish money is a dim echo of the might it loses out to, and the 'capital' that obscures Jimmy's insecurity echoes the city, which 'wore the mask of a capital' (*D* 39). If this style is 'meanness' it is also peculiarly generative. Another example illustrates how Joyce's writing manages to convey a formal naturalism while at the same time drawing attention to its artifice. In the following excerpt from 'A Little Cloud', which describes Little Chandler's departure from work as he makes his way through the city, these different aspects of Joyce's style are all present:

> He emerged from under the feudal arch of King's Inns, a neat modest figure, and walked swiftly down Henrietta Street. The golden sunset was waning and the air had grown sharp. A horde of grimy children populated the street. They stood or ran in the roadway or crawled up the steps before the gaping doors or squatted like mice upon the thresholds. Little Chandler gave them no thought. He picked his way deftly through all that vermin-like life and under the shadow of the gaunt spectral mansions in which the old nobility had roistered. No memory of the past touched him, for his mind was full of present joy.   (D 66)

Specific, actual place names merge with simple sentence structure to form an account of the built environment and its population, conveying a form of naturalism. Yet the narrative voice is much more layered, moulding as it does Chandler's point of view in free indirect discourse that betrays his snobbery (the tenement children are a 'horde', 'grimy', 'like mice') with an allusiveness that undercuts him: Joyce carefully places Chandler in parts of the city with a particular political history that he misconstrues. In addition, Joyce still makes space for a characteristic wink at the reader, hinting at the potential for deception, as well as realism, in the narrative voice. The sentences 'Little Chander gave them no thought' and 'No memory of the past touched him' are obviously untrue: he does think about the children and the past, as the preceding sentences are very much free indirect narrative. It is as if the narrative catches Chandler in the act of repression: despite the denial, 'thought' and 'memory' (or imagined memory) are exactly what Joyce has just shown us. Moreover, this evasion of surroundings reveals that this would-be poet 'of the Celtic school' (D 68) is a slippery character, conveying a slipperiness that Joyce associates with the Irish Literary Revival more generally.

Joyce's revisions to the first story, 'The Sisters', originally published in *The Irish Homestead* in August 1904, echo this pattern. The later version emphasizes the boy narrator's perception and confusion and is better focused on his mysterious relationship with the priest. At the beginning of the story, the boy 'said softly' to himself 'night after night' the word *'paralysis'* (D 1), setting a tone for the stories that follow. The word 'paralysis' was absent from the first version of the story but was introduced as part of the extensive revisions Joyce made in summer 1906. As we have seen, Joyce also used the term in his letter to Stanislaus around the same time as he revised the story. With good reason, the word 'paralysis' has been a keyword for critical studies of *Dubliners*, whose characters all suffer crippling inertia and alienation, so that the city itself seems trapped.[9] In the revised version of 'The Sisters' the word is foregrounded in italics and the word itself has become a feature of curiosity: *'paralysis.* It had always sounded strangely in my ears …

It sounded to me like the name of some maleficent and sinful being. It filled me with fear, and yet I longed to be nearer to it and to look upon its deadly work' (D 1). Evidently, this is more than the announcement of a theme that will pervade the stories, although it is also that, since characters are routinely thwarted, inert, unable to act. But beyond this, the boy narrator signals the allure of language, playing with the strange sounds of 'gnomon' and 'simony' (D 1). This itself acts as an enticement, or warning, that the narration of these stories will be less straightforward than it appears. Further still, the boy takes a curious pleasure in the equivocal charm of language: the word brings fear as well as longing, and is the harbinger of death.

In these opening lines, Joyce not only introduces the social paralysis of the city – the oppression and stunted growth felt by many characters – but also creates a language of that condition through repetition. Note the boy narrator's compulsion to repeat the words 'every night', mouthing 'softly to myself' (D 1). Other stories echo this verbal repetition. Eveline cannot flee the domestic scene, fated by her 'promise to keep the home together as long as she could'. She will repeat the life of her dead mother, and again Joyce shows that life's repetitions are also linguistic: Eveline is haunted by her mother's 'constant' (D 40) echoing voice and is unable to evade the voice of Frank 'saying something ... over and over again' (D 40). Similarly, the boy narrator in 'An Encounter' longs for an adventure, such as those in the stories he reads, 'to happen to' him (note the passive tone), only to be confronted by a potentially predatory, sadistic 'old josser'. This man's speech, 'slowly circling round and round in the same orbit' is 'monotonous' and 'repeated over and over again' (D 26). The whole sorry and sordid episode is but 'an' encounter, as if this horrendous episode is a regular occurrence. Later, in 'A Painful Case', the alienated, cynical and ascetic Mr Duffy discovers the death of his would-be lover and 'heard in his ears the laborious drone of the engine reiterating the syllables of her name' (D 117). In 'Clay' Maria mistakenly repeats the same verse of the song she sings, *I Dreamt That I Dwelt*. In 'Counterparts' both the plot of the story and the job of Farrington, as scrivener or legal copyist, are structured around literal repetition. It turns out that paralysis is also a kind of circular language, an echo, a reiteration. In *Dubliners*, words are 'monotonous', 'reiterating' 'every night', 'over and over', 'round and round'; stories are retold, voices are imitated. Joyce's 'centre of paralysis' is not just a place, with its forcible repetition of actions: it's a way of being in language. We can even hear this language of paralysis in the melancholic refrain in the famous chiasmus that closes 'The Dead': 'falling softly ... softly falling ... falling faintly ... faintly falling' (D 225). Experience, then, is also a way of inhabiting language, or to put it another way, language is one of the factors that shape and limit experience.

As well as hinting at a discreet form of wordplay, the stories suggest that characters' relationships with speech and writing are a formative aspect of inertia. Characters have uncertain relationships with the language they use, which may alert readers that the naturalism of Joyce's style packs degrees of deception.[10] In 'The Sisters', ellipses dominate half-silent conversations, many spoken lines remaining unfinished. Mrs Mooney and her daughter in 'A Boarding House' don't need language to communicate since their 'persistent silence could not be misunderstood' (D 58). In 'An Encounter', the boy and his friends are bluntly told that the adventure stories they enjoy are 'rubbish'. In 'A Little Cloud', Chandler is stuck at one remove from the poetry he wants to write: 'He wondered whether he could write a poem to express his idea' (D 68) (note again the conditional tone). The most educated and articulate characters are likewise estranged from their words: Mr Duffy in 'A Painful Case' 'had an odd autobiographical habit which led him to compose in his mind from time to time a short sentence about himself containing a subject in the third person and a predicate in the past tense' (D 104). Gabriel Conroy in 'The Dead' frets over the dinner speech he is obliged to give, seeing himself as 'a nervous well-meaning sentimentalist, orating to vulgarians' (D 221). Although these cases differ, they share an alienation from the language that might otherwise have assisted the characters to understand their own condition. Instead, in these cases, forms of speech and writing act as mechanisms that subtly reinforce the status quo. Language, then, is one of those factors that must be encountered as part of the material conditions that Joyce's naturalism seeks to depict. In doing so, the stories' concomitant fascination with the pliability of language, as well as its silences and repetitions, suggests how Joyce's adaptation of naturalism is also an indication of his modernism: in representing the world in his 'nicely polished looking glass' (SL 90), he also invites readers to delve amid the interpretive uncertainties.

It is fitting that perhaps the overriding emotions in these stories are confusion and shame. To the extent that characters have a self-conscious awareness of their predicament, feelings of shame abound. 'Araby' concludes with the unnamed boy admitting that 'I saw myself as a creature driven and derided by vanity; and my eyes burned with anguish and anger' (D 28). At the end of 'A Little Cloud', Little Chandler has 'tears of remorse' and is 'suffused with shame' (D 81). Unmarried Maria in 'Clay' seems only dimly aware of her predicament; still, her recollection of the encounter with the man on the tram leaves her 'confused', and she 'coloured with shame and vexation and disappointment' (D 99–100). Gabriel Conroy feels a 'shameful consciousness of his own person' (D 221). At the same time, characters often suffer confusion and helplessness. As they fail to fully grasp the reality of their situation, which results in embarrassment, tears, and self-hatred, readers are compelled to piece together relationships between external forces and events and internal feelings and processes.

The external world that Joyce presents is focused on the social customs of lower-middle-class Catholic Dublin, and this is a key aspect of Joyce's initial significance as a young writer. Joyce's peripatetic upbringing gave him a lifelong fascination with the city: his father was in and out of work (more 'out' than 'in' as the years went on) and often in debt, and the family moved frequently, sometimes even under cover of darkness to avoid creditors. Making 'rapid downhill progress', they stayed in at least eleven properties over the ten years from 1892 until Joyce's first departure for the continent (*Letters II* lv).[11] Joyce became familiar with the built environment of the city: perhaps not so much Dublin's Georgian squares but the wide streets that made walking easier, and more especially its shops, churches, and pubs; its transport, trade, and housing; its people and the social groups and divisions they formed. *Dubliners* in turn is populated by shopkeepers and shop assistants, clerks, salesmen, and domestic workers, with occasional steps up and down the social ladder. Not for nothing does money change hands in these stories: the passing of a coin is an ordinary but important social rite, one that can also have devastating consequences, especially in 'Two Gallants' and 'The Dead'. Joyce was acutely aware that to live in Dublin at the turn of the twentieth century was to inhabit a very particular corner of modernity. 'When you remember that Dublin has been a capital for thousands of years, that it is the "second" city of the British Empire, that it is nearly three times as big as Venice', he wrote to his brother Stanislaus in 1905, 'it seems strange that no artist has given it to the world' (*Letters II* 111). Joyce would repeat that gift, in a different, more expansive way, with *Ulysses*. Both works – more so than Joyce's other writing – are studies of his home city and its citizens. Indeed, very many of the characters of these short stories not only have bit-parts in other stories but also appear in *Ulysses*, reinforcing the impression of a small, easily navigable city. If this suggests a certain claustrophobia, that feeling is compounded by the gossip – or fear of gossip – that so frequently underpins characters' actions. The Dublin of *Ulysses* is a more variegated place, and it is also a more public place. In the short stories of *Dubliners*, Joyce opens more doors into family life than in *Ulysses*. These are spaces in which familial oppression weighs heavily. Joyce presents a city stultified by the dual oppressions of Church and state, enacted at the local level through the collapsing patriarchal weight of barely functioning families. From the sisters of the opening story to the aunts of the final story, by way of several violently abusive husbands and fathers, absent parents, estranged siblings, failed romances, and sexual exploitation, the Dublin that Joyce gave to the world revealed a city in which the failures of the public sphere were re-enacted in the private sphere.

Those failures were the symptoms of colonial rule and modernity, within a specifically Catholic context. The overwhelming majority of Dubliners around the turn of the twentieth century, when the stories are set, were Catholic, and their opportunities were severely restricted by the English administration, physically located in Dublin Castle and operated through the law courts, policing, and an Anglo-Irish establishment. If in some ways Dublin in the early years of the twentieth century experienced the growth spurt of modern infrastructure in its tram network, its bridges, and its slum clearances, it was also very much economically deprived. Social conditions were appalling: Dublin had one of the highest infant mortality rates in the world, overcrowded tenements especially in the centre and just north of the river, and a barely existing sewage system that left the Liffey stinking.[12] A place 'caught between geography and history', its social unevenness, cultural mix, and charged political arena made it an especially rich example of the ways in which colonial conditions were also those of modernity.[13] Additionally, life operated for the most part under the rules and surveillance of the Catholic Church, which Joyce saw as complicit in the downfall of Charles Stewart Parnell, the political hero of his youth. Given the Church's reach into the home, well documented in *Dubliners*, so too personal factors expressed the alienation of Joyce's class: ethical corruption, sexual repression, sexual exploitation, alcoholism, physical violence towards women and children, self-hatred, and depression all feature as character traits in Joyce's stories. Several stories in the collection attest to one critic's observation of 'the narrowed options in Irish life since the Famine – the church, the marriageless state, and emigration'.[14] Indeed, the married state, as portrayed in *Dubliners*, is no improvement, given the way that domestic violence has established a cycle of oppression. 'How could I like the idea of home?' Joyce complained (*Letters II* 48).

The social power of the Church is illustrated by the ways in which individuals accord, however reluctantly, with Church lore and, in doing so, re-enact their own oppression. Religious doctrine, intersecting with customary behaviour, can be informally reinforced through widespread concern with what other people think: 'What would they say of her', wonders Eveline (*D* 30). The fact that 'Dublin is such a small city: everyone knows everyone else's business' (*D* 61) determines the course of events in 'The Boarding House'. Mr Doran attends confession to seek absolution of his sin in his affair with Polly, 'the Madam's daughter', aged nineteen (*D* 57).

Despite the painful experience ('the priest had drawn out every ridiculous detail'), he is 'almost thankful' to be given direction in pursuing the 'loophole of reparation' (D 60). As with Little Chandler, Mr Doran's timidity is no opposition to the convention of marriage. Against his instinct, 'a force pushed him' into line (D 63). Although priests feature as characters only in 'The Sisters' and 'Grace', many *Dubliners* stories allude to an oppressive context of conformity in which the Church exercises a heavy conservatism that weighs psychologically and socially. This can still be felt even when acknowledging that occasionally these stories also show individuals registering private reservations. For example, in 'The Dead' Aunt Kate describes the prohibition of women in church choirs, as decreed by Pope Pius X shortly after taking office, as 'not just' and 'not right' (D 195).

Joyce focuses most extensively on the relationship between social customs, religious observance, and Catholic faith in 'Grace'. The tale is often cited as an attack on priestly and congregational hypocrisy since it thematically echoes the emphasis on the word 'simony' in 'The Sisters' (D 1) to reveal how spiritual faith can be subjected to worldly, financial transactions. Mr Kernan – a convert to Catholicism on marriage, originally from 'Protestant stock', 'fond ... of giving side-thrusts at Catholicism' and now 'an incurable drunkard' (D 156) – is duped by his friends into participating in a Church retreat. The story features a running analogy between spiritual matters and business interests, including frequent references to 'the retreat business' (D 171). Father Purdon's character is well-known as 'a man of the world' (D 164), his physical presence 'crowned by a massive red face' (D 173) to emphasize that he is one of the boys 'like ourselves' (D 164), the 'crown' hinting at supplication to another power. Fr Purdon's simplistic interpretation of a difficult passage from scripture (Luke 16:8–9) as 'specially adapted for the guidance of ... business men and professional men' (D 173) and his self-description as a 'spiritual accountant' (D 174) make the theme of simony blatant enough: the Church sells piety to a congregation who willingly perform their attention and top up the collection boxes.

Joyce's personal alienation from the Catholic Church is well documented – including his rejection of doctrine and refusal to bend to custom – not least in his portrait of Stephen Dedalus (it was under the pseudonym 'Stephen Daedalus' that he published the *Irish Homestead* stories). Nonetheless, it is clear that the Church exerted a powerful pull on Joyce, and his indebtedness to a particularly Catholic tradition – both intellectually and socially – remains one of the significant hallmarks of his work. Although some critics have dismissed the idea that Joyce is a 'Catholic writer' because of his personal renunciation of belief, his historical grounding in specifically Catholic-cultural and Irish matters, his allusions to church history and doctrine, and his obsession with the relationship between faith and doubt mean that this aspect of his writing cannot be dismissed.[15] 'Grace' helps to illustrate why Joyce's treatment of Catholicism matters. The story depicts a detailed engagement with the ways in which social life in Joyce's Dublin was closely entwined with forms of religious practice, allowing for a wide spectrum of beliefs, understanding, and personal adjustments. The long-suffering Mrs Kernan (no first name given) appears to have assumed religious practice and faith insofar as it has been useful to her: 'Her beliefs were not extravagant. She believed steadily in the Sacred Heart as the most generally useful of all Catholic devotions and approved of the sacraments. Her faith was bounded by her kitchen but, if she was put to it, she could believe also in the banshee and in the Holy Ghost' (D 157). In doing so, Mrs Kernan appears to equate aspects of Catholic faith with traditional superstitious belief in the banshee or fairies – a tendency that the Church had been eager to dissuade people from through the nineteenth century, with limited success.

The story revolves around the casual, even cynical, treatment of questions of belief. Mr Kernan is a convert who misuses Church terms (the nave is a 'pit' – D 165) and is happy to go along with Catholic ritual for social reasons; Mr M'Coy struggles to differentiate Catholic and Protestant beliefs but supports the Jesuits for their prestige ('the boyos who have influence' – D 163); and both Mr Fogarty, 'a modest grocer' (D 166) and failed publican, and Mr Power, who secretly resents M'Coy, are subservient to the Castle official Mr Cunningham. Although Cunningham is the acknowledged authority of the group, he frequently misleads them in his disquisition on recent Church history. That these men make factual errors in their account of Church history and devise the plot of the retreat from social motives rather than from piety is often taken to represent Joyce's criticism of the Church's domination of an ignorant congregation. This is the case; however, the significance of the story also lies in the sociability of this group, their varying accommodations to Church lore, and the ways in which they concoct a shared religious identity. This community excludes Mr Harford, denigrated as 'an Irish Jew' (D 159) for his 'usurious' (D 158) business association with Mr Goldberg; it opines that 'our religion is *the* religion, the old, original faith' (D 165); it establishes a snobbish hierarchy of religious orders; and it colludes with the blunt popular nationalism of Fr Tom Burke.[16] Of course, this is a community that Joyce largely scorns, yet it is important that he represents it. The social formation of a lower middle-class Catholic culture that was closely attuned to commerce was essential for the growth of modern Ireland: these are people who struggle to operate in a capitalist system within which their opportunities are severely curtailed and who are both beholden to and cynical of the Church and tradition. For onlookers such as W. B. Yeats, this class was anathema and was represented by him in 'September 1913' as the fingers that 'fumble in a greasy till / And add the halfpence to the pence / And prayer to shivering prayer'.[17] One of the significant aspects of Joyce's depiction of this loose community is its representation of Catholicism as a social enterprise in which belief, piety, and understanding of the faith are largely accepted (although never absolutely), or mediated, alongside some cynicism, ignorance, alternative traditions, and humour. It is still nonetheless very much a Catholic community. By the same principle, it is difficult to state point blank that Joyce was not a Catholic writer because he did not believe or because he also sharply criticised the church. As he shows here, and elsewhere, one's identity as a Catholic is complex and inconsistent, as well as historically and politically situated.[18] In short, it matters that Joyce was Catholic and wrote with knowledge and insight about Catholic thought, culture, and experiences.

The two aspects that I have focused on so far – namely Joyce's adaptation of a form of realism to reveal an urban Ireland that had rarely been seen and his ability to write about middle-class Catholic Dublin from the inside – make *Dubliners* a significant intervention in the Irish Literary Revival, with which Joyce had an ambivalent relationship. Joyce's apparent intention to 'write a moral history of my country' may signal a partial alignment with the revivalist search for a national literature, as though he shared some of the aims of the revival but deployed a different means. As Clare Hutton states, the biographical evidence is not straightforward.[19] Joyce would initially have had some sympathy for the aims of the Irish Literary Theatre (he applauded Yeats on the controversial opening night of *The Countess Cathleen*), but within two years he was openly dissatisfied with its perceived surrender to populism (*OCPW* 50–2). Nonetheless, in the years during which he wrote the *Dubliners* stories and tried to arrange for their publication, Joyce did at times regard himself as 'one of the writers of this generation who are perhaps creating at last a conscience in the soul of this wretched race', as he put it (*Letters II* 311). This letter to Nora may have had a touch of bombast about it, but these lines (familiar to readers of *Portrait*) imply a context in which the stories contributed something distinctive to the wider literary revivalist movement. Joyce was then under the impression that his collection of stories would be published in Dublin by Maunsel, a noted revivalist publisher, but Maunsel prevaricated for three years (in which time they published J. M. Synge and other revivalist writers) until finally refusing – leaving Joyce at one of his lowest ebbs on his final departure from Ireland in 1912 and prompting the viciously funny broadside 'The Holy Office'. This snub marked a clear line in his relationship with revivalist literary culture and no doubt helped contribute to the ironic cast given to the *Portrait* of Stephen Dedalus that he was then writing.

Without doubt the textual evidence of *Dubliners* – especially in 'A Little Cloud', 'A Mother', and 'The Dead' – reveals a disparaging cynicism towards revivalist culture, although Joyce does not point the finger at specific literary figures or publications in the way that he does in *Ulysses*. As Joyce saw it, some aspects of revivalism lent themselves to exploitation and anti-intellectual populism. One example is the way that, in their different stories, both Mr Chandler and Mrs Kearney consider the advantage of a distinctively 'Irish-looking' name (*D* 69), especially one with revivalist overtones such as Kathleen (reminiscent of *Cathleen Ní Houlihan*).[20] In both cases, Joyce's implication is of a manufactured authenticity masquerading as something national and artistic. Chandler imagines that 'English critics, perhaps, would recognise him as one of the Celtic school' – if only he 'could write a poem' to express his melancholic temperament! (*D* 68). The suggestion is that the 'Celtic school' played to an English audience and that the intention to create a national literature based upon Ireland's 'ancient idealism' merely created a further unreal impression of the country that perpetuated its exploitation.[21]

'A Mother' implies that at least some of the success of the revival was due to a conniving entrepreneurialism detached from moral integrity. Crucially, Joyce situates this revivalist spirit as integral to the Catholic, urban bourgeois class. Hence the story is in many ways a synecdoche for Joyce's Dublin, as it depicts the entanglement of middle-class Catholicism with nationalist identity formation through the cultural and Gaelic revivals. Joyce points out that the revival is occurring within the narrow confines of a city in which hearsay dominates. 'When the Irish Revival began to be appreciable Mrs Kearney determined to take advantage of her daughter's name and brought an Irish teacher to the house'; 'a little crowd of people would assemble after mass ... musical friends or Nationalist friends; and when they had played every little counter of gossip, they ... said good-bye to one another in Irish' (*D* 135). Joyce expresses his scepticism of the Irish language movement by portraying it as simply another social lubricant, a product that would only mask the underlying causes of unjust social conditions. In making her daughter's name 'appreciable' – that is to say, turning it to profit – Mrs Kearney puts her at odds with the organizer of the concert at which she will perform, one Mr Holohan (whose name closely resembles Houlihan), who is himself in league with the 'bored' alcohol-fuelled journalists (*D* 143). In this scenario, money trumps all integrity, artistic or patriotic.

The language revival recurs in 'The Dead' at the end of the collection (as indeed does Kathleen Kearney). Here, in one of several awkward moments with women, Gabriel Conroy is teased by Molly Ivors for not 'keeping in touch' with his 'own language' (D 189): '– And haven't you your own land to visit, continued Miss Ivors, that you know nothing of, your own people, and your own country?' (D 190). Gabriel turns down her idea of holidaying to Aran.[22] This popular nationalist conflation of land, people, and language merges in the trope of 'the west', an idea as much as a defined locality.[23] Despite the many continuities between 'The Dead' and the preceding stories, the introduction here of the Irish nation beyond Dublin is one significant point of departure.[24] Composed over the summer of 1907, it was written rather later than the other stories and indeed would not have been part of *Dubliners* at all if Grant Richards had published the collection when he first intended. Often described as a novella, its length allows for greater development of character and scene, not least in the superb dialogue between Gabriel and Gretta Conroy – including her tale of love for the dead youth Michael Furey, in Oughterard, County Galway – and ending with Gabriel's lyrical meditation and apparent decision (or fated compulsion?) that 'The time had come for him to set out on his journey westward' (D 225).

If Gabriel's 'journey westward' is sincere, it may betoken the kind of epiphanic self-realization not granted to any other character in *Dubliners*. Many readers have taken this view: the 'shameful consciousness of his own person' that 'assailed' Gabriel (D 221) mutates under the moral weight of the past and the snow that falls 'all over Ireland' (D 225) into a generous emotional empathy. This may cast him among the universally humane ('all human beings ... fall into union' – *JJ* 252) or identify him with the nation and the people he had formerly scorned.[25] If seen in this way, the ending of 'The Dead' offers a new perspective on the entire volume, as if the foregoing stultification and aphasia could be transformed by the right level of human understanding. Surely, though, that would be too much at odds with the Dublin Joyce has presented: as if readers of the collection could really accept that one man's heroic liberal guilt can provide cultural redemption!

An alternative approach may be found in the analyses of the relationship between the political and the aesthetic by Seamus Deane and Margot Norris. For Deane, the closing lines of 'The Dead' signal a transformation in Joyce's writing, the start of a new phase in his career when he abandons broadly political critique in favour of 'aesthetics': the emphasis on repetition in the closing scene produces an 'echoic lyricism' in which 'everything dissolves into writing'.[26] Certainly, 'The Dead' does inaugurate something distinctive in Joyce's closures. All four of his prose books feature uncertain endings which may hint at a new liberation or alternately reinforce the confinement that preceded it. However, this ambiguity remains a disappointment to Deane, who argues that 'rather than say that this is an admirable and rich ambiguity we should perhaps recognize that this is what happens when critique is aestheticized into a form of writing that has the ambition to be entirely autonomous'.[27] Surely though, critique is not dispensed with altogether, and none of Joyce's work really seeks such autonomy from the social. As one small example, it is hard to read this passage without noticing how it continues the patronizingly superior tone of Gabriel's views of the women around him, referring to Gretta in free indirect narrative, even in the closing moments, as 'she who lay beside him' (D 224).

For Norris, the shift in Joyce's writing signals an awareness that art is also always already politicized, that art is, as it were, part of the problem:

> By eschewing using his art polemically to criticize social oppressiveness, Joyce is able to critique art's own oppressive practices. He has his text, on the one hand, maintain implicit faith ... that art is above politics. On the other, he disrupts it with incidents that show that art is the product of social forces.[28]

Ultimately, it is impossible to separate the heightened aestheticism of the ending from the political import of the story; indeed, this is a narrative that contextualizes Gabriel in his reading, viewing, and hearing of art, and pulls the rug from beneath his (typically unvoiced) wish 'to say that literature was above politics' (D 188).

Many readers have interpreted the final 'westward' turn as a form of national reconciliation, or at least an imaginative reconfiguration of nationhood.[29] Furthermore, the prominent song 'The Lass of Aughrim' carries additional, related connotations of colonial and sexual oppression. Bartell D'Arcy's rendition of the ballad is overheard by the assembled partygoers and notably moves Gretta, for whom it recalls Michael Furey, who had sung it for her. As Vincent Cheng and others have noted, Aughrim is well known in Ireland, and certainly it was to Joyce, as the site of the Battle of Aughrim (12 July 1691), at which Irish Jacobite forces were finally crushed by the English (and Dutch) army under William III – perhaps the most decisive military moment in the colonial conquest of Ireland, imposing Orange (Protestant) rule and bloodily subjugating Irish Catholic resistance.[30] An Irish and Scots traditional ballad (existing in several versions), 'The Lass of Aughrim' relates the tale of a young woman's exploitation, even rape, and abandonment by Lord Gregory, as told from her point of view when she calls on him with their dead child in her arms. As the principal speaker of the ballad, the Lass of Aughrim is further coerced into revealing the extent of this forcible seduction by the disbelieving master, not unlike the way in which Gabriel's cold, aloof queries elicit Gretta's alarming revelation of Furey's demise ('I think he died for me' – D 221). The song sets a broad context without spelling an allegory; indeed, the symbolism of art and song, snow, Calvary, and naming all lead in multiple directions and are framed within a self-consciously theatrical narration, but they have in common implications of death and rebirth – in short, revival. The spectral appearance of Michael Furey provides the most devastating example in a series of dead characters whose spirit is evoked to dominate a story and cast shadows over the living, including the priest in 'The Sisters', Mrs Sinico in 'A Painful Case', and Parnell in 'Ivy Day'. In this case, Furey's intense passion weighs heavily, hindering Gretta as well as Gabriel, whose 'effort of reason' (D 222) may quell the unexpected emotional turmoil only to extinguish itself too.

The notable line that appears potentially to reset Joyce's relationship with Ireland and the revival is the sentence, 'The time had come for him to set out on his journey westward' (D 225). Short and apparently simple, the line sits at the edge between external narration and the personal, interior voice that begins the following sentence, 'Yes, the newspapers were right' (D 225). Richard Ellmann refers to the former line – 'The time had come for him to set out on his journey westward' – as 'somewhat resigned': 'It suggests a concession, a relinquishment' (JJ 249). For Ellmann, this is an heroic act, not in its 'westward' orientation but in its noble sacrifice. The sentence does lack positive volition, but it is not altogether reluctant; indeed it is itself something of an echo, as if confirming what was already agreed ('The time had come .... Yes'), and in this sense it resembles that famous word 'Yes', which has such importance at the end of *Ulysses* and immediately follows here. Joyce once said that 'yes' was 'the least forceful word' in the language – it signals agreement rather than an independent initiation – and this closure too reads like a similarly ambivalent exploratory moment.[31] It is as if, through Gabriel, Joyce the exile signals his part in a dialogue that he knew to be irresolvable. Joyce is fully aware that as readers reach these final lines, a sort of chasm begins to open; these last words initiate a journey that will take us back to our beginnings.

Notes

1. *The Irish Homestead: The Organ of Irish Agricultural and Industrial Development* ran from 1895 to 1918. In 1904 the editor was not Russell but H. F. Norman. It was the weekly paper of the Irish Agricultural Organisation Society (IAOS), whose commitment to self-help and economic co-operatives, focusing on the dairy industry, suggested an economic rather than political solution to 'the Irish question'. The delicate political position of the IAOS might be read in the career of its leader, Horace Plunkett, an Anglo-Irish aristocrat, whose career moved from Unionist MP to supporter of Home Rule and member of Ireland's first Seanad (Senate) in 1922 before he retired to England after his home was burned in the civil war.

2. Hans Walter Gabler, 'Introduction' in James Joyce, *Dubliners*, ed. Margot Norris (New York: Norton, 2006), p. xv. Gabler provides a detailed account of the composition and publication history of the stories, xv–xxxi, and of the editorial questions raised, xxxi–xliii.
3. For an articulation of this issue see Catherine Flynn, '*Dubliners* and French Naturalism' in *The New Joyce Studies*, ed. Catherine Flynn (Cambridge: Cambridge University Press, 2022), pp. 50–63. On *Dubliners* in the context of Irish short fiction, see Heather Ingman, *A History of the Irish Short Story* (Cambridge: Cambridge University Press, 2009).
4. See Don Gifford, *Joyce Annotated: Notes for 'Dubliners' and 'A Portrait of the Artist as a Young Man'* (Berkeley: University of California Press, 1982, second ed.), p. 48.
5. For a consideration of this story in the context of emigration narratives as published by the *Irish Homestead*, see Katherine Mullin, 'Don't Cry for Me, Argentina: "Eveline" and the Seductions of Emigration Propaganda' in *Semicolonial Joyce*, ed. Derek Attridge and Marjorie Howes (Cambridge: Cambridge University Press, 2000), pp. 172–200.
6. Simon Joyce, *Modernism and Naturalism in British and Irish Fiction* (Cambridge: Cambridge University Press, 2015), p. 110.
7. Valéry Larbaud coined the term 'monologue intérieur' in his article 'James Joyce', *Nouvelle Revue Française* (April 1922), partially reproduced in *James Joyce: The Critical Heritage. Vol. I, 1907–1927*, ed. Robert H. Deming (London: Routledge & Kegan Paul, 1970), pp. 252–62, p. 262.
8. See also the discussion of free indirect narrative in Luke Gibbons, *Joyce's Ghosts: Ireland, Modernism and Memory* (Chicago: University of Chicago Press, 2015), ch. 3.
9. On revisions to 'The Sisters' and the significance of 'paralysis' for the collection, see Florence L. Walzl, 'Joyce's "The Sisters": A Development', *James Joyce Quarterly* 10.4 (1973): 375–421, repr. 50.1–2 (2012–2013): 73–117.
10. For an exemplary account of the ways in which these stories pose interpretive dilemmas and suggest unreliable narration, see Margot Norris, *Suspicious Readings of Joyce's 'Dubliners'* (Philadelphia: University of Pennsylvania Press, 2003).
11. Stanislaus recollects that, 'In Dublin the steps of our rapid downhill progress, amid the clamour of dunning creditors on the doorstep and threatening landlords, were marked by our numerous changes of address.' Stanislaus Joyce, *My Brother's Keeper: James Joyce's Early Years*, ed. Richard Ellmann (New York: Viking Press, 1958), p. 50.
12. See Mary Daly, *Dublin, The Deposed Capital: A Social and Economic History, 1860–1914* (Cork: Cork University Press, 1984); F. S. L. Lyons, 'James Joyce's Dublin', *20th Century Studies* 4 (1970): 6–25; and Luke Gibbons, *Transformations in Irish Culture*, Field Day Monographs (Cork: Cork University Press, 1996), pp. 165–70.
13. Seamus Deane, *Strange Country: Modernity and Nationhood in Irish Writing Since 1790* (Oxford: Clarendon Press, 1997), p. 95. In Declan Kiberd's analysis of the effects of colonialism, the characters of *Dubliners* are 'frozen in servitude' and can only perform 'copied and derived gestures'. Declan Kiberd, *Inventing Ireland* (London: Jonathan Cape, 1995), pp. 334, 330.

14. Donald T. Torchiana, *Backgrounds for Joyce's 'Dubliners'* (London: Allen & Unwin, 1986), p. 157.
15. Bizarrely, Geert Lernout states that it would be a 'great injustice to call him [Joyce] an Irish catholic writer' because he showed no support for the strong influence of the church in post-Independence Ireland. Geert Lernout, *Help My Unbelief: James Joyce and Religion* (London: Continuum, 2010), p. 207.
16. See the entry in the Dictionary of Irish Biography: www.dib.ie/biography/burke-thomas-nicholas-tom-a1183.
17. W. B. Yeats, 'September 1913' in *The Collected Poems of W. B. Yeats* (London: Macmillan, 1982), p. 120.
18. There have been various attempts to reclaim Joyce as Catholic, such as Kevin Sullivan, *Joyce among the Jesuits* (New York: Columbia University Press, 1958), and to situate his work within Catholic thought, such as Mary Lowe-Evans, *Catholic Nostalgia in Joyce and Company* (Gainesville: University Press of Florida, 2008).
19. A useful overview of Joyce and the revival is Clare Hutton, 'The Irish Revival' in *Joyce in Context*, ed. John McCourt (Cambridge: Cambridge University Press, 2009), pp. 195–204.
20. *Cathleen Ní Houlihan* (1902), an acclaimed play by W. B. Yeats and Lady Gregory. Cathleen (or Kathleen) Ní Houlihan, a traditional figure of Ireland, is a 'poor old woman' who seeks regeneration through the sacrifice of young men who die for her. Yeats's play *The Countess Cathleen* was the inaugural production of the Irish Literary Theatre in 1899. I discuss 'A Mother' in the context of *Cathleen Ní Houlihan* and other aspects of Joyce's relationship with the revival in John Nash, *James Joyce and the Act of Reception* (Cambridge: Cambridge University Press, 2006), ch. 1.
21. The manifesto of the Irish Literary Theatre had declared its intention to 'show that Ireland is not the home of buffoonery and easy sentiment, as it has been represented, but the home of an ancient idealism'. They appealed to a national audience to support 'a work that is outside all the political questions to divide us'. See Christopher Morash, *A History of Irish Theatre 1601–2000* (Cambridge: Cambridge University Press, 2002), p. 116.
22. J. M. Synge had taken Yeats's advice to live on Aran 'as if' he were 'one of the people', as recalled by the latter in W. B. Yeats, 'Preface to the First Edition of *The Well of the Saints*' in W. B. Yeats, *Essays and Introductions* [1937] (New York: Macmillan, 1968), p. 299.
23. On the ambiguity of 'the west' in 'The Dead' and *Portrait*, see Marjorie Howes, '"Goodbye Ireland I'm going to Gort": Geography, Scale, and Narrating the Nation' in *Semicolonial Joyce*, eds. Derek Attridge and Marjorie Howes (Cambridge: Cambridge University Press, 2000), pp. 58–77.
24. At one stage – July 1905 – Joyce planned a sequel to *Dubliners*, to be called *Provincials* (*Letters II* 92).
25. See Vincent J. Cheng, *Joyce, Race and Empire* (Cambridge: Cambridge University Press, 1995), pp. 145–7.
26. Seamus Deane, 'Dead Ends' in *Semicolonial Joyce*, ed. Attridge and Howes, pp. 34, 36.
27. Ibid., p. 34.
28. Norris, *Suspicious Readings*, p. 236.

29. For different versions of this reading in the context of the revival, see Ingman, *A History of the Irish Short Story*, pp. 108–12, Emer Nolan, *James Joyce and Nationalism* (London: Routledge, 1995), pp. 24–35, and Nash, *James Joyce and the Act of Reception*, pp. 46–61.
30. Cheng, *Joyce, Race and Empire*, p. 143.
31. As Joyce told Louis Gillet, the word 'yes' 'denotes acquiescence, self-abandonment, relaxation, the end of all resistance' (*JJ* 712).

2

JOHN PAUL RIQUELME

Stephen Hero and A Portrait of the Artist as a Young Man

Recursion, Time, Emergence, and the Nation

Early readers of *A Portrait of the Artist as a Young Man* aware of the recent history of Irish writing would have heard in Joyce's title an echo of Oscar Wilde's *The Picture of Dorian Gray*, concerning Basil Hallward's painting of young Dorian that reveals the artist himself. Disgraced by his conviction for acts characterized legally as 'gross indecency', Wilde is never mentioned in *A Portrait*, as he is in *Ulysses*, perhaps because Joyce was more at ease later about acknowledging his precursor's influence. Rather than aligning himself with Wilde, Stephen Dedalus protects himself in *A Portrait* by taking St Thomas Aquinas as a main source when he speculates on beauty. We are not told that Stephen is acting strategically, rather than simply drawing automatically on his Catholic education, but his auditor, Lynch, asks him, 'Are you laughing in your sleeve?' (*P* 209). Joyce may also have felt that the resemblance of the titles would evoke Wilde's book and life sufficiently as a backdrop for reading *A Portrait*. Early in *Dorian Gray*, Hallward calls his work 'a portrait of the artist'.[1] The Greek names of the central characters in both works reinforce the link, though the narratives differ markedly because Stephen's attempt to become an artist in Ireland contrasts with the English Dorian's self-destruction in England. Both Wilde's *Picture* and Joyce's *Portrait* belong to the *Bildungsroman* tradition – that is, to the novel of development – which their narratives challenge and transform by presenting the central character's growth to maturity as deviating from cultural expectations rather than fulfilling them.[2] Joyce's narrative, however, points towards a new nation's emergence. Wilde's does not.

Joyce's projection of non-linear emergence rather than merely linear development involves the style as well as the story. In that regard, *A Portrait* contrasts with the earlier more linear *Stephen Hero* (begun in 1904 but unpublished in his lifetime), and it is a significant step towards the even more experimental *Ulysses*. Joyce follows and extends Wilde by producing an intensely recursive narrative that includes various feedback loops, with the work and some of its elements folding back on themselves in open-ended, enigmatic, self-generating ways. Wilde's title, for example, refers both to Hallward's painting and to the book itself, and when Dorian stabs the painting, he also stabs himself. Joyce's blurring of boundaries proceeds differently and more pervasively by means of repetitions, free indirect discourse, and the ambiguity about whether his title suggests that the portrait is the actual writer's self-portrait or possibly the character's creation. The book's self-reflexive elements suggest at times self-generation, a process of emergence that includes the possible coming into being of an Irish nation, not just an Irish artist, though the shape of what could emerge is unclear.

Joyce's essay 'Oscar Wilde: The Poet of "Salomé"' confirms that he was thinking about Wilde and *Dorian Gray* while writing *A Portrait*. The essay's occasion was the 1909 performance in Trieste of Richard Strauss's opera *Salomé*, whose libretto Wilde's of the same name had inspired. As noted at the end of *A Portrait*, 1909 was the mid-point of the decade that it took Joyce to transform his manuscript of *Stephen Hero* into *A Portrait* (published serially beginning in 1914). The article indicates that Joyce knew Wilde's works well, recognized Wilde's deeply Irish qualities, and blamed the English for Wilde's downfall. He mentions the influential Victorian writer and art critic Walter Pater, who taught at Oxford when Wilde studied there. Pater's writings were central to English aestheticism, a movement whose attitudes were characterized as 'art for art's sake'. Although influenced by aestheticism, mediated primarily by Wilde and W. B. Yeats, Joyce and his young artist character encounter difficulties and project goals that require a different engagement with history and material reality than a Paterian worship of beauty enables.

After his imprisonment, Wilde, the most brilliant playwright of the English theatre in the 1890s, died in poverty in France in 1900 during Joyce's second year of university studies in Dublin. Joyce expresses his antipathy for the English treatment of Wilde by comparing him to his namesake, Oscar, the only son of Ossian in Celtic myth, 'tragically killed by the hand of his host while sitting at table' (*OCPW* 148). Taking exception to the idea that Wilde was 'a monster of perversion' who emerged inexplicably from 'the modern civilization of England', Joyce calls him 'the logical and inevitable product of the Anglo-Saxon college and university system, a system of seclusion and secrecy' (*OCPW* 150). In Joyce's view 'English authorities' punished him not for committing a crime but rather for provoking a 'scandal' (*OCPW* 150) by being exposed for acts that many others had committed. From that perspective, Wilde resembles the Irish parliamentary leader, Charles Stewart Parnell, mentioned prominently in *A Portrait*, the leading advocate for Irish Home Rule (a form of limited autonomy) in the late nineteenth century. Like Wilde,

Parnell was hounded by the English press, who made sensational news out of his adultery. Leaving out of *A Portrait*'s narrative the death of Stephen's sister, harrowingly described in *Stephen Hero*, and the death of his mother, important in *Ulysses*, Joyce highlights the impact of Parnell's downfall and death on Stephen and his family. That impact is not primarily personal, as are the deaths of his sister and mother, but political in ways that affect our response to the rest of Stephen's story. Instead of Wilde's demise, we are invited to consider the fate of a mythic figure, Icarus, who, like Wilde, misjudged the risk he faced. Unable to fulfil their promise, the political leader, the literary precursor, and the mythic youth combine to colour from the outset our sense that Stephen faces dangers.

Considering Wilde's fate, it is understandable that Stephen chooses, as did Joyce, the Continent rather than England in which to make a writing career. As critics have noted, Stephen's resentment towards the English is evident in the lengthy scene in part V in which he talks with the English priest who is the dean of studies at University College Dublin.[3] The scene's mixture of styles is significant. As an English convert to Roman Catholicism, the priest represents two foreign presences within Irish culture. Just before the encounter, Stephen asks himself if the College, as a Jesuit building, is 'extraterritorial', a place where he is 'walking among aliens' (P 184). Stephen and the priest are at odds over the English language, specifically the words *tundish* and *funnel*, both part of the English lexicon, though *tundish* is rarer. When Stephen thinks to himself 'How different are the words *home, Christ, ale, master* on his lips and on mine' (P 189), he has in view differences in pronunciation and in meaning. Especially because Parnell's Home Rule initiative for Ireland had not succeeded, the Irish as a nation did not think of *home* with the same sense of autonomy and security as could the English. Despite the fact that the priest is 'a countryman of Ben Jonson' (P 189), whose songs please Stephen (P 176), he misunderstands Stephen's figurative use of the word 'lamp' (P 188) during their conversation. The divergences are multiple.

In critically probing English attitudes, Joyce follows Wilde in *Dorian Gray* by echoing Pater's writings. The echoing occurs in the language and action involving the English priest. The intellectually flatfooted Englishman tries to teach Stephen 'an art', one of 'the useful arts', 'lighting a fire' (P 185). On the one hand, he is posing a challenge to Stephen's emphasis on fine, rather than practical, arts. In *Stephen Hero* it is evident that he does so out of resentment. On the other hand, the priest's action and speech recall mundanely and ironically one of Pater's best-known assertions, from the 'Conclusion' to *The Renaissance*, concerning art's ability to stimulate impressions with an intensity like fire: 'To burn always with this hard, gem-like flame ...'[4] Pater extols not the lighting of a literal fire but the kindling and maintaining of an internal flame. In his lengthy thoughts, Stephen responds critically to the priest in language reminiscent of Pater's rhetoric of beauty and his use of present particles. He thinks about the man's lack of 'beauty', despite a history of 'tending ... bearing ... waiting ... striking' (P 185). This Irish student turns an English writer's style against another Englishman, whose flame tending, presented in a realistic style, bathetically evokes the English writer. Stephen mimics in order to undermine.

Like Wilde in *Dorian Gray*, Joyce includes Paterian language without explicitly encouraging readers to accept or reject it. We are left to measure the irony, which in Wilde's case is arguably deep and directed with a vengeance against English attitudes that he links to Pater's aestheticism.[5] Joyce instead throughout *A Portrait* juxtaposes styles in a way that challenges the adequacy of both literalizing and aesthetic tendencies. Although still under Pater's influence late in *A Portrait*, Stephen is on the verge of the breaking away that *Ulysses* confirms. The stylistic mixture that begins developing in *A Portrait* renders memory in ways that engage readers in a process of looking back critically and also looking forward; it has a marked temporal aspect that at times evokes multiple moments at once rather than separating them into a linear sequence. It takes advantage of the diverse, contradictory Irish colonial situation that Stephen faces in order to displace more single-minded styles that could reinforce the status quo. The shift is from aestheticism, with roots in English aestheticism and an apparently apolitical emphasis on beauty, towards an aesthetic politics – that is, towards an art that recognizes its embodiment and its situation within history. *A Portrait* moves in the direction of the extravagantly diverse writing of *Ulysses*, towards a hybrid style that, through mimicry, amalgamation, and transformation, allows us to occupy multiple perspectives virtually simultaneously, with a resulting self-corrective tendency.

Conceptually and politically, the mixed style corresponds to the 'place of unknown instability' and 'fluctuating movement' that Frantz Fanon identified as the third stage in generating a national consciousness within a culture that has been dominated from the outside, as Ireland had been by England.[6] Joyce rejected Irish attitudes corresponding to Fanon's first two stages: assimilation to the dominant culture's values and customs, countered either immediately or later by aggressive repudiation of them through adopting indigenous practices. He was neither a 'West Briton' (D 188, SH 64), that is, a British sympathizer who behaved as though Ireland were a western province of England, nor a supporter of Irish nationalism as a nativist return to cultural roots.[7] Stephen shares Joyce's critical attitudes. His unaccepting stance towards the English priest is matched a few pages later by his determination not to accede to Irish pressures to conform. His Irish nationalist friend Davin asserts that 'a man's country comes first', taking priority over being 'a poet or mystic' and advises Stephen to 'Try to be one of us' (P 203). Stephen, however, says he will not serve. When Stephen implies that he is not 'a monster' but instead has been produced by 'This race and this country' (P 203), he echoes Joyce's position that Wilde was the product of cultural institutions, not a 'monster of perversion' (OCPW 150).

The threat to Stephen's freedom is not primarily England but Ireland, whom he calls 'the old sow that eats her farrow' (P 203). He identifies the 'nets flung at' the soul in Ireland 'to hold it back from flight', including 'nationality, language, and religion'. Rather than becoming 'one of us', he will 'try to fly by those nets' (P 203), suggesting a literal escape from Irish constraints. To 'fly by those nets' suggests avoiding but also flying by means of them, that is, turning them to strategic advantage. Stephen's Paterian rhetoric directed against the English priest is one example of taking advantage of a potentially entangling net, though not an Irish one, except in so far as Yeats had succeeded in importing his enthusiasm for Pater to Ireland. Joyce's mixture of distinctly Irish and Catholic elements of scene, behaviour, thinking, and speech in a composite style also turns nets, those that Stephen mentions, to other purposes, as does Stephen when he grounds his formulations about beauty on St Thomas Aquinas. By contrast with more single-minded, monological styles, Joyce's diverse style remembers rather than forgets as part of a dialogical process that revises and resists instead of accepting outright. A critical style of recollection that collects and transforms diverse elements is not, however, available to Joyce or Stephen from the start. Joyce earns it over time. Whether his artist character will do so is an open question, but his style of thinking moves in that direction.

We can measure the distance Stephen and his creator travel away from aestheticism by comparing the central character of *Stephen Hero*, called Stephen Daedalus, with Stephen Dedalus in *Ulysses*. Near the end of what has survived of *Stephen Hero*, Stephen claims that one function of writing is 'to record ... epiphanies', 'the most delicate and evanescent of moments' (SH 211). By epiphany he means 'a sudden spiritual manifestation, whether in the vulgarity of speech or of gesture or in a memorable phase of the mind itself' (SH 211). Stephen's interest in writing evocative prose vignettes, like ones Joyce himself produced, is aesthetic, but 'vulgarity' invites a realistic style. Joyce moved beyond aestheticism's influence by producing in *Dubliners* (written 1904–1907) a realistic style antithetical to Pater's lush, late-Romantic writing. Stephen has yet to take that step in *A Portrait*, where he thinks admiringly in part IV of 'a lucid supple periodic prose' (P 167) reflected in his diction of 'ecstasy' and 'trembling' (P 172).

Beyond *A Portrait*'s end, in episode six of *Ulysses*, he narrates a realistic vignette in a contrasting unadorned, grittier style (*U* 7.921–1075). One of the headlines in that portion of the episode is 'LIFE ON THE RAW' (*U* 9.938).

The evidence is mixed concerning Stephen's artistic potential, including his readiness to face and affect historical realities, and the problem of judging him is difficult for several reasons. Prior to *Ulysses*, we are arguably dealing with significantly different Stephens, about whom, despite the resemblances, contrasting judgements can be made because the narratives of *Stephen Hero* and *A Portrait* differ significantly beyond the spelling of the character's surname. In *Ulysses*, Stephen's narrative continues from *A Portrait* with a gap in time but no evidence of discontinuity in the character. Joyce complicates our response to the artist character(s) by assigning many details from his own life to Stephen. He used, for example, 'Stephen Daedalus' as a pseudonym when publishing three early versions of *Dubliners* stories (*JJ* 164). The intimate renderings of Stephen's thinking in *A Portrait* and *Ulysses* also blur the boundary between narrator and character, despite the third-person narration. Because Joyce is writing fiction, not autobiography, we cannot identify the author narrowly with the character; nevertheless, the texts frequently encourage us to consider the alignment.

In presenting Stephen before *Ulysses*, Joyce employs the two epiphanic modes of stark realism – 'the vulgarity of speech or of gesture' – and visionary fantasy – 'a memorable phase of the mind itself' – as delimiting extremes in his character. In both *Stephen Hero* and *A Portrait*, Stephen alternates between visionary and material, internal and external. Continuing to feel attracted by visionary possibilities until the end of *A Portrait*, he is influenced by them when he writes both his villanelle and his journal. But the evocations of Stephen's competing allegiances differ substantially in the two narratives. In *Stephen Hero* Stephen is both ruthlessly analytical and visionary. At a crucial moment, his encounter with the disturbing reality of his sister's death (*SH* 164ff) intensifies both his critical bent and his visionary yearnings. In *A Portrait*, by contrast, Joyce presents the two perspectives of realism and fantasy as aspects of style, not just as aspects of character. Having emerged as mutually modifying and mutually challenging attitudes, these styles of Stephen's thinking overlap and evoke each other. In *A Portrait* realistic and visionary are complexly intertwined elements in a style emphasizing memory. The double temporal orientation points towards the more allusive opening style in *Ulysses*.

Beyond being personal in *A Portrait* and *Ulysses*, memory is cultural and historical. Joyce's writings recognize equally the cultural memory of myth and the historical realities of contemporary life, as well as the process by which those present realities have come into being. One of Joyce's achievements that eludes Stephen even in *Ulysses* is the merging of these kinds of memory in styles that also acknowledge the personal and the aesthetic. In *Ulysses* Stephen says that he is 'trying to awake' from the nightmare that is history (U 3.377). Instead of treating history as a bad dream from which we might wake up and escape, Joyce engages with history, using a realistic style strategically in a stylistic mixture that interprets and transforms history and realistic detail by merging them with myth. When Joyce attributes mythic aspects to characters in styles that both recognize and challenge the ostensible limits of realism and history, he actualizes a potential that Stephen has yet to grasp. In his dialogue on art, 'The Critic as Artist' (1891), Wilde has Gilbert say, 'The one duty we owe to history is to rewrite it.'[8] Joyce accepts this duty but understands that when we make history we cannot do so just as we please. By calling his artist character *Dedalus*, a name both passed on from Stephen's Irish father and bestowed by the narrative's Irish author, Joyce realizes a cultural memory that invites a forward direction towards possessing what Stephen wishes for at the end of *A Portrait*, something that 'has not yet come into the world' (P 251). Dedalus is simultaneously the artist character's heritage and a name that he can live up to only by influencing the history of the future. In *A Portrait*, it is not obvious that Stephen is ready to take a step that neither repeats the past nor ignores history. The dates at the book's close, 1904 and 1914, however, point forward from the narrative's end to a future time when Stephen could be more able to take such a step. For readers who conclude that Stephen is the author of the third-person narration about his younger self, the dates can indicate that Stephen has already taken that step ten years after the narrative closes. Whether or not we accept that the book is informed by this structural feedback loop, as we shall see there are significant moments of recursion and non-linear emergence in the book's details. Absent in the surviving sections of *Stephen Hero*, these moments anticipate *Ulysses*.

In *Ulysses* Stephen remembers his former commitment to art that captures spiritual manifestations and eschews history. In the third episode, on the beach, Stephen (and readers) may remember his former allegiance to a spiritual, aesthetic notion of art because the surroundings remind him of the beach scene at the end of part IV of *A Portrait*. The situation has changed, however, because Stephen's mother has died during the unnarrated period following the end of *A Portrait*. Her death is the often unstated background for Stephen's thinking, including his re-evaluating of his situation and his trajectory, his past and his future. Stephen's recollection, in which he addresses himself, focuses on his epiphanies:

> I was young ... Books you were going to write with letters for titles. Have you read his F? O yes, but I prefer Q. Yes, but W is wonderful. O yes, W. Remember your epiphanies on green oval leaves, deeply deep, copies to be sent if you died to all the great libraries of the world, including Alexandria? Someone was to read them there after a few thousand years, a mahamanvantara. Pico della Mirandola like. Ay, very like a whale. When one reads these strange pages of one long gone one feels that one is at one with one who once ...   (U 3.136–46)

Stylistically Joyce has advanced beyond *A Portrait*. There is nothing quite like this allusive, parodic, internal dialogue in either *Stephen Hero* or *Dubliners*. The style of *A Portrait* comes closer to it, prepares the way for it, but does not fully reach it. The language reflects on and reinterprets the past. In this self-mocking moment, Stephen retrospectively places his epiphanies among his grandiose, youthful projects, as adolescent fantasies. He has framed mystical traditions in a newly self-critical perspective.

The exaggerated use of the impersonal pronoun 'one' and the evocation of art's timeless quality respond with irony to Pater's essays, in particular his 'Pico della Mirandola'.[9] As with Stephen's other withdrawals from his enthusiasms, this one is only partial because an effect remains. In *A Portrait*, he distances himself from the Catholic Church, but his religious upbringing, especially his Jesuit education, continues to inform his thinking. The mixture of intimate knowledge and scepticism in the Ulyssean Stephen's thoughts, his former attraction but current aversion to the aesthetic reverence that inspired the epiphanies, points to one of Joyce's major stylistic achievements. Joyce develops this double temporal perspective, the perspective of memory, before *Ulysses*, especially in *A Portrait* and 'The Dead.' By means of it we can experience simultaneously both scepticism and the deeply felt impact of thoughts and events in the central character's changing sensibility. Rather than being static, the style expresses repetition, reconsideration, and movement. Joyce's inherently double, or multiple, interiorized style renders the ambivalence and dissonance of Stephen's mental life through the interplay of self-scrutiny and recollection. As Joyce complexly presents them, ambivalence, dissonance, and critical interplay inform the mental process of creativity as a process of emergence. They also embody what Wilde called 'the truth of masks', that is 'a truth in art', an insight whose 'contradictory is also true'.[10] The ambivalent elements stand in dynamic relation.

Joyce's early fiction moves from *Stephen Hero*'s episodic fragments, through the stripped-down realism of most of the *Dubliners* stories, to the discontinuous narrative and flamboyant narration of *A Portrait*. It shifts from either fantasies or detailed realistic presentations, suggesting the epiphanies mentioned above, to recollections or other mental activity, structured like memories, that mingle the imaginative and the ostensibly objective. The mixture can involve judgement and movement forward of a dynamic kind for characters and readers. The mediation announces itself stylistically, often through obscure allusions and personal references that hinder as well as enhance our understanding; this style is opaque rather than transparent. It can also enable us to recognize and experience forms of recursion that generate questions and options for understanding as essential to choosing and acting. The passage from episode three presents by retrospection Stephen's move through and away from mystical aestheticism to self-irony and self-judgement. Similar self-critical moments occur briefly in *A Portrait*, as when Stephen mentions in his journal that his conversation with Emma involved his making a silly-looking gesture, 'like a fellow throwing a handful of peas up into the air'. He then goes on to remark on the incident's effect on him in an exaggerated style: '... it seems a new feeling to me. Then, in that case, all the rest, all that I thought I thought and all that I felt I felt, all the rest before now, in fact ...... O, give it up old chap! Sleep it off!' (*P* 252). He is making light not only of his action but of his process of re-evaluating what has gone before.

A self-adjusting dynamic is increasingly important in Stephen's thinking as Joyce renders it in arresting, revealing moments of style and narrative that concern multiple temporal perspectives and processes of emergence, whether they concern making art or the nation's future and how to affect it. A particularly resonant passage concerning dynamic self-awareness in time occurs in episode nine of *Ulysses*, when Stephen is presenting his reading of Shakespeare's plays in relation to Shakespeare's life to a few literary intellectuals gathered in the National Library. Although it is an extreme moment of Stephen's allusive, convoluted mental play and Joyce's style for depicting it after *A Portrait*, there are passages in the earlier work that already indicate Joyce's conceptual and stylistic direction. After evoking the way 'the artist' proceeds to 'weave and unweave his image' (*U* 377–8), generating a new identity on analogy with Penelope's remaking the tapestry she weaves in *The Odyssey*, Stephen refers to a passage, also mentioned in *A Portrait* (*P* 213), from Percy Shelley's *Defence of Poetry* that concerns artistic creation and links it to a recursive temporal perspective:

> In the intense instant of imagination, when the mind, Shelley says, is a fading coal that which I was is that which I am and that in possibility I may come to be. So in the future the sister of the past, I may see myself as I sit here now by the reflection from that which then I shall be. (*U* 9.381–5)

The statement pertains to a double temporal movement of re-evaluation that anticipates a future in which retrospection and re-evaluation occur, here tied to the remaking of the artist's image in the act of imaginative creation. The product of such an experience could be a narrative that reflects on the artist's past. As Heraclitus says, the way forward and the way back are one.[11]

Early in *A Portrait*, in the disastrous clash of views about Parnell during Stephen's first Christmas dinner at the adult table, we encounter a simpler, more linear, static statement concerning retrospection when Dante says that 'he'll remember all this when he grows up' (*P* 33). Later, during the visit to Cork with his father to liquidate the family property, Mr Dedalus presents a static kind of recollection in which Stephen must listen to 'stories he had heard before' (*P* 91) that recall the past in order to maintain its contours. His father enjoins him to repeat his own youthful behaviour by 'mix[ing] with gentlemen' (*P* 91). This is a version of the rote behaviour that the Jesuits insist on in another vein, as when Father Arnall at the retreat in part III enjoins the adolescents 'to repeat after me' (*P* 134). It is also central to the *Bildungsroman* before Wilde and Joyce transformed it by focusing on young characters who deviate from prescribed patterns. Stephen tries to conform to a rigid pattern of spiritual exercises in part IV, to insure that 'The past was the past' (*P* 146). He learns, however, that the past does not die, because he will never be free from the 'sin of his past life before absolution' (*P* 153). The past does not stand in a stable, linear, developmental relation to the present and the future. At this point of the narrative, Stephen's sense of temporality and his ability to express it reach a new level. In a passage that twice repeats the word 'instant', in advance of the language of episode nine of *Ulysses* above, Stephen's decision not to become a priest emerges as a temporal statement about the present in relation to the future, a statement that points towards that later episode:

> He would fall. He had not yet fallen but he would fall silently, in an instant. Not to fall was too hard, too hard, and he felt the silent lapse of his soul, as it would be at some instant to come, falling, falling but not yet fallen, still unfallen but about to fall. (*P* 162)

Readers cannot know that this passage anticipates the later one until we encounter episode nine, remember the earlier one, and reconsider its implications, in a process that mimics the one Stephen formulates in *Ulysses*. The temporally inflected moment of recognition and choice in part IV, expressed in an echoic style of repetitions, is followed a few paragraphs later by Stephen's joining with his poverty-stricken siblings in song when he realizes that they are expressing their own future without having yet experienced it in actuality: 'Even before they set out on life's journey they seemed weary already of the way .... and [he] heard in all the echoes an echo also of the recurring note of weariness and pain. All seemed weary of life even before entering on it' (P 164).

In the first four parts of *A Portrait*, Joyce exercises his conceptual and stylistic ambitions to present Stephen's developing sensibility as an artist and as Irish. Those ambitions and that sensibility are on more expansive display in part V, particularly in the writing of the villanelle and in the immediately following narrative segment concerning the birds. As we shall see, in part V Joyce associates Stephen's thoughts and judgements with a process of emergence in a stylistic mixture that attends to the nation as well as art.

Critics have disagreed about how ironically we can reasonably judge Stephen's accomplishments and his future as an artist.[12] Some see a strong alignment with Joyce and evidence of significant accomplishment and future promise for becoming a Daedalian master. Others find little evidence of maturity and identify Stephen with the doomed Icarus. On the one hand, the poem that Stephen produces in the second section of part V, an example of a complicated form, a villanelle, is derivative, one of many such poems written late in the nineteenth century. On the other, his attempt to write a formally complex poem is ambitious. There is less disagreement concerning the quality of the section in which Joyce narrates the poem's coming into being. It is a tour de force that includes in overlapping imbricated relation third-person description, intimate narration of thought, writing, and speaking. It includes as well Stephen's recollection of an attempt to write a poem ten years earlier with the same young woman in mind when she was a girl. Because of the repeated but quite different act of writing after a ten-year period, the production of the villanelle constitutes a prominent recursion in the narrative, one that can be linked to the future ten years reflected in the dates at the book's end, during which Joyce wrote *A Portrait*.

The pages that follow the villanelle are equally arresting as they present Stephen responding in heightened language first to the flight of birds, which he sees from the steps of the National Library, and then to Yeats's play *The Countess Cathleen* (1892), which resulted in a protest from fellow students. Stephen first describes the birds' 'dark darting quivering bodies flying clearly against the sky as against a limphung cloth of smoky tenuous blue' (P 224). He then thinks in sequence about his mother's reproaches, presumably concerning his abandoning the Catholic faith; 'the hawklike man whose name he bore'; the Egyptian 'god of writers', Thoth; and a similar word in Gaelic (P 224–5). And then the birds return 'with shrill cries', representing a form of weaving and unweaving, 'ever going and coming, building ever an unlasting home under the eaves of men's houses and ever leaving the homes they had built to wander'. He returns to the question he posed when he first saw them, 'What birds were they?' (P 224, 225), followed by another,

'Then he was to go away?' We can ask as well, what has Stephen been watching? When he thinks about his mother's reproaches, they are 'murmured' (P 224), tellingly so because the flight of the birds is a murmuration. Murmuration is a type of swarming, or collective action, among birds that is self-organizing, each individual bird behaving independently without centralized control to create an emergent result. Something new and unpredictable emerges from and as the fluctuating movement of an ungraspable instability. This is obviously not a linear process, and it is recursive.

The framing of Stephen's thoughts, including linking his mother to murmuring, in the context of his experience of a murmuration, suggests that his thinking and the style in which it is expressed, with its multiple colons, multiple open-ended questions, multiple allusions, and highly figurative and echoic language, is itself a kind of murmuration. His thoughts are flying in emergent process, an unpredictable one that is not linear and not narrowly defined by existing patterns, including the rules that he has been encouraged to obey during his upbringing. His motion towards this kind of thinking has been variously anticipated in small but revealing ways when retrospectively considered. For example, during a mathematics class in part III, Stephen draws on his exercise book in a manner that is non-Euclidean and emergent:

> The equation on the page of his scribbler began to spread out a widening tail, eyed and starred like a peacock's; and, when the eyes and stars of its indices had been eliminated, began slowly to fold itself together again. ... [T]he eyes opening and closing were stars being born and being quenched.   (P 102–3)

Because of Daedalus's creation of wings, birds and their feathers are significant elements in Stephen's story. Feathers are fractal in structure, made up of recursive elements of different scales that here are linked to the emergent phenomenon of star formation and subsequent destruction, a weaving and unweaving. Stephen's idle drawing points towards the later murmuration.

Before shifting away from the birds in murmuration, when Stephen thinks about departing Ireland, he remembers the farewell passage spoken by Cathleen in Yeats's *The Countess Cathleen*. His decision to depart has 'come forth' like a bird flying from a turret (P 226). The memory of the play mingles with the coming forth because a coming forth is a kind of opening, or emerging, and it was 'the night of the opening of the national theatre'. Structurally, *A Portrait* is organized around repeated stylistic juxtapositions, with highly stylized, fluent language of an aesthetic kind followed by contrasting realistic language concerning unpleasant realities.[13] The opposing elements of Stephen's experience are on display in such contrasts, which often occur at the junctures between narrative sections that are unbridged by transitional language. Here, however, his fluent meditation involving the birds and various mythic and literary references is not sharply separated by a narrative juncture from the scene on opening night. Instead, the shift occurs within Stephen's thoughts, mediated by his recollection of the play's language, which refers to a bird. The repeated word 'cries' (*P* 224, 226) links the birds' 'shrill' ones to the audience's 'mocking cries'. The passage shifts towards divergent conceptions of the nation, Yeats's cultural nationalistic vision of a community that could become a nation, and the antagonistic, pugnacious view represented by Stephen's 'fellowstudents', who engaged in ugly shouting on behalf of a narrow conception of Ireland. There is no indication that Stephen sides absolutely with Yeats about the nation, but he shows no sympathy whatsoever for the student response. His thinking about something national here and about the future of his 'race' (*P* 253) – by which he seems to mean the Irish as constituted by shared ancestry and history – at the book's end indicates a direction of travel that has not been clear earlier. We do not know whether Stephen's now substantially achieved murmurative thinking can be extended in a meaningful way to a national emergence, but the possibility has come into view.

In the narrative's remaining pages, Stephen continues to exhibit his difference from his fellow students, already extensively presented in the section of part V preceding the writing of the villanelle. Some of them, such as Davin, engage in nationalist activities that are a prelude to the 1916 Easter Rising, an irrevocable step towards the emergence of the modern Irish nation in the year *A Portrait* appeared as a book. Others have passed examinations that qualify them for civil service jobs, in which they will work on behalf of the English to administer Ireland or on behalf of the Empire to oversee other peoples ruled by the English. After the paragraphs concerning the birds and Yeats's play, however, the frequent passages of Stephen's thoughts are marked by questions, most of them open-ended in an extension of his murmurative thinking. Stephen's questions protect him from the single-minded answers that Davin and the future civil servants have found. They indicate a habit of mindfulness that tends to be self-critical and self-correcting, as when he asks, 'Could his mind then not trust itself?' (*P* 233). His questioning is dynamically open to weighing possibilities and adjusting.

His thinking also tends towards temporally recursive perspectives. In the dialogue there is a joking mention, in relation to Goggins's flatulence, of a descriptive grammatical term for a future passive tense, *paulo post futurum*, which refers to an event that will happen soon. It means 'a little after the future', pointing to what will be. The mention could be discounted as trivial except that Stephen soon after expresses the goal of his work in a question that involves a loop in time. As he looks at the bourgeoisie sitting comfortably in the drawing room of a hotel, he asks: 'How could he hit their conscience or how cast his shadow over the imagination of their daughters, before their squires begat upon them, that they might breed a race less ignoble than their own?' (P 238). The transforming effect would have to occur after the future birth of another generation, but the cause would come earlier, before its effect would be evident. The mention of conscience and race anticipates Stephen's statement near his journal's end. Before we reach that point in the journal, we hear that Stephen's father urges him again to fulfil conventional expectations, this time by studying law, the body of rules that make for continuous social stability from the past to the future. If Stephen were to enter the legal profession, he would become a servant of the state, and the narrative of his life would conform to the traditional *Bildungsroman* plot, with the achievement of socially recognized success. The diary entries following indicate that he thinks differently about temporal continuities, that is, about maintaining the status quo: 'The past is consumed in the present and the present is living only because it brings forth the future.' Then, mentioning one of Yeats's characters, Michael Robartes, who is an aesthetic priest of the dark imagination longing to revive past beauty, Stephen articulates a different goal: 'Not this. Not at all. I desire to press in my arms the loveliness which has not yet come into the world' (P 251). By implication, he wants to be the source of that yet-to-emerge beauty.

In order to achieve that goal, he will leave Ireland, not in an act of rejection but, as he reports telling Davin, because 'the shortest way to Tara was via Holyhead' (P 250), that is, the quickest path to the seat of the ancient kings of Ireland, twenty-seven miles from Dublin, is to take the ferry seventy-seven miles across the Irish Sea to the Welsh port, Holyhead. This is a spatial version of a temporal and conceptual paradox about discovering or inventing an authentic version of Ireland. Traveling away from the destination makes for a shorter trip; taking longer is the quickest way; the way forward is the way back. The goal of the spatial and temporal path is 'to forge ... the uncreated conscience of my race' (P 253). In the book's middle, the word *conscience*, meaning a sense of right and wrong behavior, occurs frequently during the retreat. Here and in Stephen's question about shaping a future generation's imagination, it means instead awareness or self-understanding, as it does in the title of Fanon's essay 'Mésaventures de la conscience nationale'.[14] Inherent in the goal is the prediction, the speaking before the fact, of a postcolonial national identity, prior to the nation's coming into being. The question remains whether Stephen can take advantage of his disparate conflicting perspectives and experiences to forge a hybrid, multi-perspectival, temporally recursive style of writing and thinking as an indissoluble enabling counterpart for an Irish emergence onto a global stage. Like Fanon's 'fluctuating movement' in a 'place of as yet uncharted instability', Stephen's portrait turns out to be the name of a question about the future and its relations to the past, about our need not to ignore history but to bring it into being by rewriting it and reinventing ourselves on new terms.

Notes

1. Oscar Wilde, *The Picture of Dorian Gray*, ed. Isobel Murray (Oxford: Oxford University Press, 1981), p. 5.
2. On Joyce and the *Bildungsroman*, see: Gregory Castle, 'Coming of Age in the Age of Empire: Joyce's Modernist *Bildungsroman*', *James Joyce Quarterly* 50.1–2 (2012–2013): 359–84, and his book *Reading the Modernist Bildungsroman* (Gainesville: University Press of Florida, 2006); Tobias Boes, '*A Portrait of the Artist as a Young Man* and the "Individuating Rhythm" of Modernity,' *ELH* 75 (Winter 2008): 767–85, and his book, *Formative Fictions: Nationalism, Cosmopolitanism and the Bildungsroman* (Ithaca: Cornell University Press, 2012); Jed Esty, *Unseasonable Youth: Modernism, Colonialism, and the Fiction of Development* (Oxford: Oxford University Press, 2012); Daniel Aureliano Newman, *Modernist Life Histories: Biological Theory and the Experimental Bildungsroman* (Edinburgh: Edinburgh University Press, 2019). Of note for her compelling discussion of gendered identity is Christine Froula, *Modernism's Body: Sex, Culture, and Joyce* (New York: Columbia University Press, 1996).
3. Hugh Kenner comments on 'the Dean's English [as] a conqueror's tongue' in *Dublin's Joyce* (London: Chatto & Windus, 1955), p. 116, and see Declan Kiberd, *Inventing Ireland: The Literature of the Modern Nation* (London: Jonathan Cape, 1995), pp. 273–4.
4. Walter Pater, *The Renaissance: Studies in Art and Poetry* [1893], ed. Adam Phillips (Oxford: Oxford World's Classics, 1986), p. 152.
5. I argue for Wilde's ironic relation to Pater in John Paul Riquelme, '*Oscar Wilde's Aesthetic Gothic: Walter Pater, Dark Enlightenment, and The Picture of Dorian Gray*', *Modern Fiction Studies* 46.3 (2000): 609–31.
6. Frantz Fanon, 'On National Culture' in *The Wretched of the Earth*, trans. Constance Farrington (New York: Grove Press, 1965), p. 227; trans. of *Les damnés de la terre* (1961; repr. Paris: Édition Gallimard, 1991), pp. 272–3. I have modified Farrington's translation of '*ce lieu* de déséquilibre *occulte*' because her 'zone of occult instability' does not try to translate the French *occulte* but instead repeats the similarly spelled English word, which is misleading. *Occulte* in Fanon's complicated statement does not mean occult in the sense of the supernatural. It could mean concealed, hidden from view, or covered over, with the implication of as yet ungrasped or not yet articulated. We do not know in advance what exactly it will be. I render it here as 'place of unknown instability' and later as 'place of as yet uncharted instability'. The temporal implication, warranted because of Fanon's future orientation, is in line with my reading of 'uncreated' as yet to be created in Stephen's statement about the conscience of the race.

7. Critical discussion of *Stephen Hero* and *A Portrait* focusing on Joyce's complicated relationship to nationalism includes Emer Nolan, *James Joyce and Nationalism* (London and New York: Routledge, 1995), pp. 36–47; Vincent J. Cheng, *Joyce, Race, and Empire* (Cambridge: Cambridge University Press, 1995), pp. 57–75; and Gregory Castle, *Modernism and the Celtic Revival* (Cambridge: Cambridge University Press, 2001), pp. 188–207.
8. Oscar Wilde, 'The Critic as Artist' in *The Artist as Critic: Critical Writings of Oscar Wilde*, ed. Richard Ellmann (Chicago: University of Chicago Press, 1982), p. 359.
9. Pater, *The Renaissance*, pp. 20–32.
10. Oscar Wilde, 'The Truth of Masks' in *The Artist as Critic*, p. 432.
11. Charles H. Kahn, *The Art and Thought of Heraclitus: An Edition of the Fragments with Translation and Commentary* (Cambridge: Cambridge University Press, 1979), Fragment 60.
12. Wayne Booth discusses the difficulty the reader faces in judging Stephen without explicit guidance from the narrator in a widely reprinted essay, 'The Problem of Distance in *A Portrait of the Artist as a Young Man*' in *The Rhetoric of Fiction* (Chicago: University of Chicago Press, 1961), 323–36. Robert Scholes also discusses the difficulty in 'Stephen Dedalus, Poet or Esthete?' *PMLA* 89 (1964): 484–9. Hugh Kenner, whose negative judgement of Stephen has been influential, discusses Stephen in 'The *Portrait* in Perspective' in *Dublin's Joyce*, pp. 109–33, which has also been widely reprinted. He extends his argument in a more convincing later essay, Hugh Kenner, 'The Cubist Portrait' in *Approaches to Joyce's 'Portrait': Ten Essays*, ed. Thomas F. Staley and Bernard Benstock (Pittsburgh: University of Pittsburgh Press, 1976), pp. 171–84. S. L. Goldberg provides a more sympathetic judgement of Stephen in his *James Joyce* (Edinburgh: Oliver and Boyd, 1962). I argue for a positive judgement of Stephen in John Paul Riquelme, *Teller and Tale in Joyce's Fiction: Oscillating Perspectives* (Baltimore: Johns Hopkins University Press, 1983).
13. Hugh Kenner was probably the first critic to identify this rising and falling pattern in 'The Portrait in Perspective', where he writes that each chapter 'works toward an equilibrium which is dashed ... in the next chapter'. Kenner, *Dublin's Joyce*, p. 122.
14. Fanon, 'The Pitfalls of National Consciousness' in Fanon, *The Wretched of the Earth*, pp. 148–205; *Les damnes*, pp. 187–248.

3

SCARLETT BARON

Ulysses

Form of Forms

What is the form of *Ulysses*? Like so many questions put to it in the singular, *Ulysses* answers in the plural. *Ulysses* is a book of forms, and this multiplicity is not only defining but explanatory of the text's position at the apogee of many a literary canon (however contingent such individual and collective judgements necessarily are).

Harry Levin called *Ulysses* 'a novel to end all novels'.[1] John Middleton Murry described it as 'unlike any other book that has been written'.[2] Hugh Kenner is one of myriad readers to have deemed *Ulysses* 'the decisive English-language book in the century'.[3] For Martin Amis, it is 'incontestably the central modernist masterpiece' – one so singularly original as to make it 'impossible to conceive of any future novel that might give the form such a violent evolutionary lurch'.[4] Such awed identifications abound across the book's hundred-year-old history. But whence, precisely, comes this widely hailed exceptionality? A 'book of many turns' that constantly 'changes its mind as it progresses' and flits between styles from episode to episode (and often within episodes as well), *Ulysses* puzzles readers by its stark departures from conventional forms – its refusal to merge smoothly into the 'horizon of expectations' that, according to Hans Robert Jauss, conditions the approach to any text.[5] This acute formal difference, more than any particular insight about human nature, caused the book to stand out – first between 1918 and 1920, during its serialization in *The Little Review*, and then again in 1922, when it appeared in bound form under the imprint of Shakespeare and Company. While this staggered 'shock of the new' seems commensurate with the extent of Joyce's deviation from early twentieth-century literary norms, it is telling that *Ulysses* should remain disorienting even to readers encountering the text in the twenty-first century.[6] Eric Bulson, writing in 2014, refers to it as a 'morphological nightmare'.[7] In the same year, Tom McCarthy dubbed it 'a kind of rapture of literature, an event that's both ecstatic and catastrophic, perhaps even apocalyptic'.[8] Framed and partially tamed though it has been by a century's worth of industrious annotation and interpretation (and there can be no question that today's first-time readers of *Ulysses* face a less drastically difficult challenge than their predecessors), *Ulysses* retains its capacity to confuse, affront, and fascinate.

Chapter 3 explores this capacity to confuse through the prism of form and through the history of readers' responses to the mystifying parade of forms in *Ulysses*. Its central contentions are that the apprehension of the book's form is inseparable from the apprehension of its formlessness and that this exquisitely calibrated balancing act explains its position at the apex of the literary field. Through its extensive intertextuality and practice of a range of generic forms, Joyce's shape-shifting book invites its own critical insertion not only into what his contemporary T. S. Eliot solemnly called 'the tradition' but also into a much wider field of non-canonical writing, encompassing such forms of mass culture (the newspaper, the magazine, advertisement pages) as shape the 'Aeolus' and 'Nausicaa' episodes.[9] Simultaneously, by flouting expectations of narrative centrality, chronological sequence, and stylistic unity – by making it impossible to simply follow a story – *Ulysses* resists absorption into any single critical system. Seemingly basic questions remain unanswerable. Is it a novel? Is it an epic? Is it 'a series of self-contained units'?[10] For Jeri Johnson, this undecidability reflects the fact that the book 'exist[s] in at least two distinct, and distinctly different, forms at one and the same time'. '[D]istilled essence of novel' on the one hand and 'extravagant, symbolically supersaturated anti-novel' on the other, it is, to use her term to capture this formal polyvalence, 'allotropic'.[11] All at once conjuring and reinventing familiar forms, *Ulysses* shimmers tantalizingly on the verge of categorizations (is it a novel or an epic, an encyclopaedia or a work of fiction, realistic or symbolic, neutral or parodic, Irish or European?) without ever allowing itself to be straightforwardly assimilated into any one of them.

First Impressions: A 'Formless', 'Gargantuan', 'Damned Monster-Novel'

Contemporary readers of *Ulysses* have advantages over those who encountered it when it first appeared. They know – or at least most will know – that the book is unusually demanding; that puzzlement about its form is a common, indeed near-universal, experience; and that such perplexity is intrinsic to its full appreciation. As Philip Kitcher remarks, 'Undergraduates flock to courses on Joyce, classes focused on *Ulysses*, often because they want to penetrate a novel widely viewed as baffling.'[12] The reception history of *Ulysses* is instructive as both a record of its perceived originality in its own time and as a counsel of perseverance and aesthetic open-mindedness in the face of its discombobulating formal makeup. And this history is important, too, because later responses are usually, at least to some degree, conditioned by earlier ones. As Derek Attridge and Daniel Ferrer point out, 'we always, and inevitably, read through and by means of previous readings', taking into account the 'strategies for ... assimilation' of those who preceded us in the collective 'enterprise of making Joyce's texts readable'.[13] Though this conditioning constitutes no guarantee of cumulative progress (not least because the very notion of critical progress is close to impossible to define), it does make the stages of a work's interpretation – with all its revisionary twists and about-turns – worth attending to.

When *Ulysses* appeared, 'The first impression the book gave', according to Kenner, 'was that it was formless.'[14] There were reasons why this sensation should be particularly stark in Joyce's early readers. The book's serialization in *The Little Review* – and its subsequent banning after the obscenity trial brought against the periodical in 1920 – added to the bewilderment experienced by its reviewers (see Clare Hutton's discussion in Chapter 14). As Richard Aldington complained in 1921 – when four of the book's episodes had yet to become available – 'The serial publication has lasted an abnormally long time, and ... there is some excuse for my impatience in speaking of *Ulysses* while it is still fragmentary.'[15] Compounding the frustrations induced by the book's protracted and halting dissemination was the fact of its 'monumental dimensions'.[16] Joyce himself anticipated readerly disquiet on this score, referring to 'the enormous bulk and the more than enormous complexity of [his] damned monster-novel' even before the opus was complete (*SL* 271). One early commentator was repelled by the book's lack of economy: 'The very format of the book is an affront. Bloom could have been drawn effectively in a quarter of the words.'[17] Murry noted that 'it is very big': 'Had it been half the size', he added, 'it might have been twice as big.'[18] Ezra Pound repeatedly hinted at his unease about the book's 'Gargantuan' size.[19] '*Ulysses* contains 732 double sized pages, that is to say about the size of four ordinary novels', he noted in May 1922.[20] Indeed, privately expressed misgivings ('Sirens ... is too long', he wrote to Joyce in 1919) lend an air of bad faith to his continued public insistence on the 'great unwieldy' tome's Flaubertian 'compression' and 'intensity'.[21] Such irritation remains a commonplace of the book's reception to this day: although the Irish novelist Roddy Doyle ruffled feathers in 2004 by stating that '*Ulysses* could have done with a good editor', his view is hardly unusual.[22]

'Chaos'

As well as registering discomfiture at the scale of Joyce's 'fat book', reviewers repeatedly commented on the impression of chaos it afforded.[23] Even so complexity-loving a reader as Pound – who first received Joyce's manuscripts as foreign editor for *The Little Review* – found himself disoriented by the absence of signposts: 'As there are no numbers or headings to the typescript of yr. chapter it is not always easy to keep an exact tab.'[24] The observation was echoed two years later by Holbrook Jackson, who was by then at least contending with the finished text of the first edition: 'Chapters have no apparent relation to one another', he noted, 'and neither numbers nor titles.'[25] Another reviewer, writing under the pseudonym 'Aramis', lamented that 'Two thirds of it are incoherent.'[26]

The book's failure to make sense as a unified whole, some suggested, was more than a design flaw: it was an assault on readerly decency. Where 'R. H. C.' praised 'a noble experiment', Aldington argued against experimentation if it came at the cost of 'clarity, sobriety, precision – the good manners of literature'.[27] 'The greatest affront of all', fumed Jackson, 'is the arrangement of the book.' '*Ulysses*', he went on, 'is chaos. All the conventions of organised prose which have grown with our race have been cast aside as so much dross.'[28] This idea of the book as an assault on accepted norms was echoed by Clive Bell, who in 1921 opined that Joyce 'rags the literary instrument', 'deliberately go[ing] to work to break up the traditional sentence, throwing overboard sequence, syntax, and, indeed, most of those conventions which men habitually employ for the exchange of precise ideas'.[29] Similarly, S. P. B. Mais bemoaned the fact that in Joyce's hands 'all standards go by the board'. It was essential, he asserted, in a paean to conservative aesthetics, to 'preserve the noble qualities of balance, rhythm, harmony, and reverence for simple majesty that have been for three centuries the glory of our written tongue'.[30] Murry, too, saw in Joyce a rebel wreaking havoc not just 'against the lucidity and comprehensibility of civilized art' but also 'against the social morality of civilization'.[31] '*Ulysses* has form, a subtle form', he conceded, 'but the form is not strong enough to resist overloading, not sufficient to prevent Mr. Joyce from being the victim of his own anarchy.'[32] This worry about the practical consequences of too 'subtle' a form illustrates the early twentieth-century tendency to draw a line connecting aesthetic and ideological revolution – to see formal ambiguity as a potential threat to social harmony, and, indeed, to civilization itself.[33]

As this sample of concerned and exasperated early responses illustrates, the perception of *Ulysses*'s formal intractability was immediate and acute. Though Henry James had stated in the nineteenth century that '[a]rt derives a considerable part of its beneficial exercise from flying in the face of presumptions', and Virginia Woolf, writing in 1919, enjoined the modern novelist to 'base his work upon his own feeling and not upon convention', the extreme originality of *Ulysses* seemed to try the goodwill of many critics to the limit.[34] Joyce, in many readers' eyes, went too far, the violence of the upheaval he staged placing him beyond the pale of comprehensibility. As Murry observed, 'He is so individual that very few people will know when the bomb has exploded ... in order to be a successful anarchist you must work within the comprehension of society.'[35] According to Attridge, originality does not consist in a complete break with what went before but depends instead on a 'close relation to the circumambient matrix'.[36] Joyce seems, with *Ulysses* – so his contemporaries' first responses suggest – to have approached the asymptotic limit where novelty, seemingly untethered from its immediate cultural context, teeters on the brink of nonsense.

The risk Joyce took by composing so formally anomalous a book was that his art would seem so outlandish as not to be deemed to fall within the province of literature at all. As Caroline Levine asks of Constantin Brancusi's *Bird in Space* – which in 1928 found itself at the centre of a trial precipitated by its disregard for 'familiar traditions of representation and national standards of taste' – so *Ulysses* seemed to pose the question: was it possible that the work could be *too* original? If it was completely unlike other art objects, it might represent such a radical break from the past that it would cease to count as art altogether. Institutionally speaking, an art object has to repeat the norms of art in some recognizable way in order to belong to the art world at all.[37] Just as art, if it is to be acknowledged as such, must be 'innovative but not too innovative, and free but not too free', so literary works need to be at least potentially relatable to other elements of 'the tradition' if their authors' 'individual talent' is to be perceptible as such.[38] As Kenner puts it in his study of *Ulysses*: 'Printed words on a page – any words, any page – are so ambiguously related to each other that we collect sense only with the aid of a tradition.'[39] Joyce, it seems, was aware of the danger that he might have gone too far and that his work might, without some intervention on his part, find itself dismissed to that 'unvisited limbo or infinite rubbish-ground' to which bad novels are exiled.[40]

A Meticulous Plan?

If Joyce's writing turned out to be too 'subtle' – that is, 'excessively removed from generic controls' – he would need to create his own critical framework.[41] As early as 1920 – '[p]iqued', as Forrest Read puts it, 'by charges that his work was formless and chaotic' – he set about issuing the authorial exegesis that would redeem *Ulysses*, link it to 'the tradition', and thereby reclaim its ostensible amorphousness as a 'triumph of form'.[42] As Kenner notes, '*Ulysses* is the first of the great modern works that in effect create for themselves an *ad hoc* genre ... and so entail an *ad hoc* critical tradition.'[43]

Famously, the guidance Joyce issued – the schemas shared with Stuart Gilbert and Carlo Linati – proved as generative of befuddlement as elucidation. With their discrepant listings of the book's hours, scenes, colours, persons, technics, sciences/arts, sense (meaning), organs, symbols, and correspondences, the schemas point the assiduous reader in manifold directions, offering analysis as much as synthesis, complexity as much as simplification, proliferation as much as reduction.

Though it afforded some disconcerted readers of *Ulysses* relief, Joyce's attempt to assert the presence of form in what had previously seemed formless has been at the root of considerable critical dismay. If '[i]t is the work of form to make order', Joyce's tables, though visually designed to marshal the profusion of a long, dense, diachronic reading experience into neat, spatialized, synchronic order, seem to perform that labour from the outside.[44] The form extrinsically imposed by these idiosyncratic, performative documents is, as James Blackwell Phelan remarks, 'strange' and 'multiplex': in their eighteen-part declensions of the key items of the book's episodic structure, Joyce's grids effect a 'riot of formal multiplication' amounting to a claim of 'spectacular overdetermination'.[45] What they convey, from the paratextual sidelines, is that everything in the book is controlled by many different constraining factors – that everything, in other words, forms part of a meticulous plan.

In 1972, A. Walton Litz referred to some of the claims advanced by the schemas as 'outrageous'.[46] A few years later, Kenner influentially dismissed the Homeric parallels as an elaborate confidence trick 'more apt to provide slogans than insights'.[47] In his view, the correspondences seem far-fetched even after they have been pointed out, retaining currency only because of the book's title. Phelan, writing in 2018, comments with wry humour on the 'satanic unhelpfulness' of the 'exponentially mixed metaphor' the schemas lay out; they are, in his assessment, a recipe for 'readerly derangement'. It is hard not to agree that Joyce's orthogonal rows and columns can seem like a 'comic extravagance', and, indeed, 'preposterous' in their pedantic elaboration.[48]

Whether they elicit fascination, amusement, or disbelief, Joyce's instructions functioned as illocutionary acts that effectively orchestrated a vast body of similarly focused critical responses. Indeed, for all their 'exorbitance', Joyce's elucidations were taken seriously by influential contemporaries. With a little help from devoted admirers, the book's chaos took on form along the lines of the design the author had himself drawn up and circulated. It did so not only in the sense that the schemas determined the principal themes of Joyce criticism for decades but also in the sense that the very act of authorial formalization appears to have had a retroactive impact on the internal constitution of the book (which Joyce had at the time yet to complete). As Michael Groden explores in *'Ulysses' in Progress*, Joyce's schemas inflected the shape of his still-evolving text, operating as a blueprint for modifications introduced in the final stages of its genesis.[49]

'A Book Which Has a Key'

One of the most influential converts to the Joycean cause was Valéry Larbaud, whose famous lecture on *Ulysses*, given on 7 December 1921 in Paris, shed light, with the author's help and blessing, on the structure of the book.[50] Though some initial readerly consternation was understandable, 'the cultivated reader' would, he maintained, find order in what might at first seem 'incoherent'.[51] By dint of diligent immersion, apparent formlessness would resolve into ingenious, complex form. Progressing through *Ulysses*, he explained,

> We begin to discover and to anticipate symbols, a design, a plan, on what appeared to us at first a brilliant but confused mass of notations, phrases, data, profound thoughts, fantasticalities, splendid images, absurdities, comic or dramatic situations, and we realize that we are before a much more complicated book than we supposed, that everything which appeared arbitrary and sometimes extravagant is really deliberate and premeditated; in short, we are before a book which has a key.[52]

That key, the proof of the book's overdetermination, was the 'summary – key – skeleton – schema' that Joyce himself had provided (*SL* 271).

Throughout, Larbaud emphasizes the cohesion of the text. Alien though they might seem, the book's 'digressions, or rather appendices, essays composed outside of the book and artificially interpolated into all of the "tales" ... belong to the book'.[53] It is not clear what Larbaud has in mind in mentioning 'digressions' and 'appendices'. Does he refer to the interpolations of the 'Cyclops' episode, in which parodies of nationalist mythologizing interrupt the first-person narrative? Or to the parodies of canonical English prose styles that structure the 'Oxen of the Sun' episode? Such descriptive fumblings in the dark are reminders of the formal disorientation the book produced in even highly motivated, appreciative early readers. Larbaud's insistence on the integration of the book's parts is all the more striking. As Joyce had informed Linati that 'each adventure' was both an independent bounded unit (an intersection of hour, scene, organ, art, etc.) and 'interconnected and interrelated in the somatic scheme of the whole' (*SL* 271), so Larbaud drives home the book's overarching unity.[54]

A Mosaic or a Web?

Larbaud's explanation of *Ulysses* showcases two common ways of thinking about form: the 'mechanical' and the 'organic'. Both feature in the definition given in the *Oxford Dictionary of Literary Terms*: 'Since the rise of Romanticism, critics have often contrasted the principle of organic form, which is said to evolve from within the developing work, with "mechanic form", which is imposed as a predetermined design.'[55]

Larbaud's emphasis on the book's 'lines of design' partakes of the mechanical approach. *Ulysses*, he explains, consists of '[e]ighteen panels' or 'compartments' and, as such, constitutes 'a genuine example of the art of mosaic'.[56] Yet even while he carries out this separation of the book into inorganic fragments, Larbaud also repeatedly stresses the interconnections that make of it 'a close web': 'Although each of these 18 parts differs from all the others in form and language, the whole forms none the less an organism, a book.' This mixing of metaphors – this emphasis on unity by seemingly contradictory analogical means – is typical in Joyce studies and in literary criticism more generally.[57]

Both of these characterizations emphasize integration, but each approach tells a different story about how the book's formal patterning came about. An organic account holds that form emerges spontaneously in the writing process, with the subject matter, in Joyce's words, 'not only condition[ing] but creat[ing] its own technique' (*SL* 271). A mechanical account gives chronological priority to the author's choice of certain forms. Each approach is necessarily partial and ultimately speculative. Even genetic critics can only go so far in the tracking and dating of particular authorial intentions (which may predate any surviving manuscript trace). The writing process, dynamic as it is, blurs the lines, as Groden's analysis of the evolution of *Ulysses* compellingly shows. Nonetheless, the ways in which authors and critics describe form are highly revealing because they tend to imply evaluative judgements. In the early years of Joyce's reception, for example, organic analogies typically betokened approval while mechanical analogies bespoke denigration of the book's perceived artificiality.

'The Significance of the Method Employed'

The responses of Joyce's influential contemporaries reflect this division. In '*Ulysses*, Order, and Myth' (1923), Eliot dismisses Aldington's identification of Joyce as 'a prophet of chaos'. Lauding him instead as a 'man of genius' acting on an impeccable 'method', he asserts that Joyce's use of myth in the book 'has the importance of a scientific discovery'. The Homeric framework, he avers, 'is simply a way of controlling, of ordering, of giving a shape and a significance to the immense panorama of futility and anarchy which is contemporary history'.[58] As these grave cadences convey, form, for Eliot, stands as no less than an antidote to the formlessness of the world and history. To twenty-first-century sensibilities, such a high-formalist claim seems almost astonishing for its faith in the capacity of literature to contain – and, indeed, rectify – the messiness of the world.

Eliot's emphasis on the salutary powers of form to curb and even remedy social anarchy underplays the ambiguities generated by Joyce's system of correspondences. In 1945, Joseph Frank brought these to the fore by suggesting that the 'unbelievably laborious fragmentation of narrative structure' involved in Joyce's use of 'spatial form' makes special demands of the reader. Indeed, engagement with the book's deployment of 'an infinite number of references and cross-references which relate to one another independently of the time-sequence of the narrative' requires a painstaking process of 'fitting fragments together and keeping allusions in mind'.[59] Joyce's division of the book into planes and episodes ensures that any serious reading of *Ulysses* must be plural: 'Joyce cannot be read – he can only be re-read. A knowledge of the whole is essential to an understanding of any part.'[60] Far from limiting and fixing interpretation through an act of 'ordering', then, Joyce's 'mythical method', seeding readerly sensations of formlessness as much as of form, instigates a dynamic hermeneutic process that generates proliferation as much as it does control.

'Mere Mechanics'

Not all early readers, however committed to rigorous form, were so positively impressed by Joyce's disregard for narrative continuity and unorthodox recalibrations of the relationship between form and content. Ezra Pound saw the paraphernalia of the schema as both an unduly mechanical apparatus and an unseemly display of the materials of the artist's workshop. While his letters to Joyce divulge private frustrations, even his public endorsements seem ambivalent at best. In his 'Paris Letter' of 1922, he confusingly declares that the schemas are a compositional oddity, 'chiefly [Joyce's] own affair, a scaffold, a means of construction', whilst also proclaiming that '[t]he result is a triumph in form, in balance, a main schema, with continuous inweaving and arabesque'.[61] Pound had articulated his understanding of form as a compromise between 'freedom and order' in *The Egoist* five years earlier: 'It is perfectly obvious that art hangs between chaos on one side and mechanics on the other. A pedantic insistence on detail tends to drive out "major form".'[62] For Pound, Joyce's orthogonal axes and detailed accompanying explanations registered as a manifestation of the kinds of mechanics that, taken to excess, risked jeopardizing the achievement of 'major form'. The colloquial diction of a much later review confirms the disapproval aroused by Joyce's conceit: 'The parallels with the *Odyssey* are mere mechanics, any blockhead can go back and trace them. Joyce had to have a shape on which to order his chaos. This was a convenience.'[63] Wyndham Lewis's critique of Joyce's mechanicity came later but was more lengthy, more forthright, and more categorical. In 'Analysis of the Mind of Mr James Joyce', an essay published in *Time and Western Man* in 1927, Lewis vituperates against *Ulysses*'s 'mechanical heaping up of detail'.[64] As Pound had warned in 1917 against 'insistence on detail' at the cost of 'major form', so, for Lewis, the book's maniacal overinvestment in minutiae and 'the latest technical devices' testifies to an absence of vision.[65] For both authors, the reference to mechanics goes hand in hand with the critique of a debased kind of form – one in which the author's intellect is 'sabotage[d]' through subjection to pre-existing forms.[66] For Lewis as for Pound, '[a]rt is ... a fight against mechanics.'[67]

Pound's distaste for Joyce's Homeric trappings extended to the ruptures in the sequential fabric of a book in which, as Sean Latham notes, '[i]nterruption itself [is] an integral part of [the] aesthetic'.[68] Pound prized *Ulysses*'s naturalism – much as he had the 'clear hard prose' of *Dubliners* and the 'hard, clear-cut' style of *A Portrait of the Artist as a Young Man* – as a sign of Joyce's affiliation to the French novelistic tradition.[69] Conversely, he disliked the backward chronological movement that presides over the fourth episode, wherein the novel's clock is wound back to eight a.m. so that Bloom's morning hours (spanning 'Calypso', 'Lotus-Eaters', and 'Hades') are given to us after Stephen's (covered in 'Telemachus', 'Nestor', and 'Proteus'): 'To the reader who is really reading *Ulysses* as a book and not as a design or a demonstration or a bit of archaeological research, this chop-off has no particular intrinsic merit.'[70] For Pound, what Eliot had so welcomed – Joyce's sidelining of the 'narrative method' and embrace of what Kenner dubs 'the synchronic' – smacked of 'mere mechanics'.[71]

A 'Combination of Styles'

What Lewis's attack on *Ulysses* brings into focus – as Larbaud's, Eliot's, and Pound's do not – is the starkness of the stylistic variations demarcating its episodes from each other, a fragmentation fully consistent with Joyce's decision to write the book 'by different means in different parts'.[72] One of Lewis's central lines of attack is that *Ulysses* is not, in fact, original – though he concedes that it may have a lesser claim to 'challenging novelty' – but represents instead the fruit of an 'orgy of "apeishness"'.[73] His reference to it as an 'encyclopedia of [E]nglish literary technique' is not intended as praise but as an expression of distaste for all within it that he deems imitative, derivative, second-hand.[74] Lewis repeatedly emphasises Joyce's 'technical itch' and talent as a 'craftsman'.[75] *Ulysses*, as he portrays it, is a pointless exercise that bespeaks only a silly dedication to the vacuous parading of a 'hundred or so styles': its 'very complex, overcharged façade' and 'stylistic complications' betray only the 'conventionality of mind' characteristic of a mere 'workman'.[76]

Though Pound publicly purported to appreciate the range of Joyce's satire and parodies, he made his disgruntlement at *Ulysses*'s constant stylistic changes privately known – exclaiming, for example, that 'even the assing girouette of a postfuturo Gertrudo Steino protetopublic don't demand a new style per chapter'.[77] Eliot, for his part, makes no mention of the book's accordion of styles in '*Ulysses*, Order, and Myth'.[78] But it is arguably in these 'formal pyrotechnics', even more than in the (so easily missable) Homeric correspondences, that the most original departure of *Ulysses* resides and from which its special exhilarations spring.[79]

Indeed, much of the interest and pleasure of *Ulysses* reside in its progression from style to style – in the journey on which it takes us from the manageable familiarity of Edwardian realism dominating 'Telemachus' and 'Nestor' to the dense abstraction of Stephen's ponderings in 'Proteus'; from the bourgeois realism of Leopold Bloom's putterings about his home and environs in 'Calypso', 'Lotus-Eaters', and 'Hades' to the abrupt adoption of imitative form in 'Aeolus', in which headline-like announcements break up the account of events unfolding in a newspaper office; from the relatively familiar Bloom-centred narrative of 'Lestrygonians' to the showy high-jinks and scholarly erudition of 'Scylla and Charybdis' – to name but a few of the formal deviations that punctuate the less overtly experimental first half of the book. After 'Wandering Rocks', often regarded as a mid-point between the book's more familiar and more radically defamiliarizing narrative tendencies, the second half, multiplying our exposure to an array of markedly distinct 'technics', continues to develop the reader's awareness of the mediating power of form. When we encounter the musical extravaganza of 'Sirens' ('Clapclap. Clipclap. Clappyclap.' – *U* 11.28); the 'gigantic' interpolations of 'Cyclops' ('In Inisfail the fair there lies a land' – *U* 12.68); the clichés of popular fiction and lady's magazines that throng the pages of 'Nausicaa' ('With all the heart of her she longs to be his only, his affianced bride' – *U* 13.215–16); or the saccharine Victorian section of 'Oxen of the Sun' ('And as her loving eyes behold her babe she wishes only one blessing more, to have her dear Doady here with her to share her joy' – *U* 14.1319–20), we may well half-recognize the forms that underlie them (as those of orchestral form, revivalist mythologizing, cheap romance, and Dickensian sentimentality).[80] And yet by this time we know – because *Ulysses* has taught us to know – something more important than the intertextuality of forms: we know that in this book forms are transitory, and that these forms will, like others before them, give way to other evocative stylistic pastiches, other provisional 'systems of consistency'.[81] This oscillation – between the emulation of identifiable forms and their regular supersession by others – is key to *Ulysses*'s overall formal suggestiveness. Through its ceaseless metamorphoses – pursued to the end via the hallucinatory drama of 'Circe', the '[r]elaxed prose' of 'Eumaeus', the '[c]atechism' of 'Ithaca', and the unpunctuated interior monologue of 'Penelope' – *Ulysses* 'chang[es] the ways in which the art of fiction is understood' by showing up every style as a 'system of limits'.[82] Conspiring 'against all attempts to locate some "style" of the Author', it 'passes across a range of fictions, of forms', inculcating in the reader the embrace of multiplicity.[83]

For Eliot, Joyce's use of the 'mythical method' sealed the end of the novel; in *Ulysses* he found writ large Joyce's 'dissatisfaction with the form' and his 'need of something stricter'.[84] Yet whatever 'strictness' Eliot projects onto Joyce's book does not account for its stylistic profusion – a feature that lends itself equally well to interpretation as novelistic or post-novelistic. *Ulysses*, for instance, accords well with Bakhtin's definition of the novel genre as a system of languages, a 'combination ... of styles', a 'style of styles'.[85] And yet in some ways Joyce's 'recasting of the novel' as a 'repertoire of fictions' stretches even so capacious a category as that of the novel to the limit, its radical departure from existing norms positioning it as an outlier, a defining exemplification, in fact, of the limitations of generic tabulations.[86] Indeed, Joyce's construction of the book as a fluid continuum of form and formlessness – evocative of holograms, kaleidoscopes, or Gestalt shifts – accounts for its resistance to incorporation within conventional generic grids. Its great success as a work of art is to have managed to, in Wordsworth's phrase, 'create the taste by which [it] is to be relished' – to have convinced the critical world of the virtue of its very uncategorizability.[87] Not only is *Ulysses* 'allotropic' – but its unrivalled formal heterogeneity has become synonymous with true originality, and thus with high art. It is by atomizing the book's parts from each other, by refusing to abide by traditional expectations of unity in art, and thus by disallowing singular readings, that *Ulysses* has achieved its 'stellar position in the modernist canon'.[88]

Ulysses: Form Of Forms

The consequences of Joyce's formal innovations are philosophical and ethical as well as aesthetic. As Fritz Senn observes, *Ulysses*'s 'abrupt turns' and 'changes of the stage' have the power to jolt us out of 'our customary inertia'.[89] For Kitcher, the lessons the book has to teach have to do with plurality: by giving the reader a different kind of access to interior minds (primarily through refinements of interior monologue and free indirect discourse) and by making his book an 'odyssey of style', Joyce 'brings home to readers a rich chorus of voices, a dazzling array of perspectives'.[90] 'Central to *Ulysses*', contends Kitcher, 'is the idea of attending to *different* voices, to understanding the world from alternative *human* points of view.'[91] This 'perspectivism ... disrupt[s] old prejudices and point[s] to new possibilities' – or, as Stephen Heath says, it works against a conversion of the world into 'a realm of essence'.[92] *Ulysses*, in other words, fosters a kind of enlightened relativism, an awareness of the stylistic and ideological constructions by which all views of the world are conditioned.

In 'Scylla and Charybdis', Stephen, thinking of his own evolving bodily and psychological constitution, strains intellectual sinew to make sense of the paradoxical compatibility of personal change with continuous identity. He is, as he reflects – repurposing an Aristotelian phrase for the soul – a 'form of forms', subsisting as itself 'by memory ... under ever-changing forms' (U 9.208–9).[93] By this point in the book, the expression has twice already retained his attention, in 'Nestor' and 'Proteus' respectively (U 2.75; 3.280). Amid the formal and semantic upheaval of *Ulysses*, and in the context of so thematically literary an episode as 'Scylla', the phrase's motivic prominence gestures beyond its applicability to Stephen's musings about the self in time, reading as an encapsulation of the conundrum of form in *Ulysses*. 'Form of forms': the aptness of this strikingly tautological locution as a description of the work as a whole is connected to *Ulysses*'s enduring generic unplaceability. The book triggers the reader's habit-formed urge to find unity – contour, wholeness, meaning, and essence – setting us on a potentially endless quest for the one 'controlling design' that would resolve formal multiplicity into coherent, formal singularity.[94] Yet its staging of repeated formal upheavals ultimately denies us such satisfaction. This longstanding resistance to the reader's desire for form is both the measure and the guarantor of the book's originality, for, as Attridge explains, if the 'process of accommodation' were complete – if the work were to be slotted into existing literary categories – it would, ceasing to obtrude against the 'horizon of expectations', disappear from view.[95] *Ulysses*, embarking on its second century, shows no sign of such evanescence.

Notes

1. Harry Levin, *James Joyce: A Critical Introduction*, rev. ed. (New York: New Directions, 1960), p. 171.
2. John M. Murry, review, *Nation and Athenæum* xxxi (22 April 1922): 124–5, repr. in *James Joyce: The Critical Heritage. Volume One 1907–1927*, ed. Robert H. Deming (London: Routledge & Kegan Paul, 1970), p. 195.
3. Hugh Kenner, *Joyce's Voices* [1978] (London: Dalkey Archive Press, 2007), xii.
4. Martin Amis, 'The War Against Cliché: *Ulysses*' (1986), in *The War Against Cliché: Essays and Reviews 1971–2000* (London: Vintage, 2002), pp. 441–6, 446.
5. Fritz Senn, 'Book of Many Turns', *James Joyce Quarterly* 10.1 (1972): 29–46. Karen Lawrence, *The Odyssey of Style in 'Ulysses'* (Princeton, NJ: Princeton University Press, 1981), p. 53. Hans Robert Jauss, 'Literary History as a Challenge to Literary Theory', trans. Timothy Bahti, repr. in *The Norton Anthology of Theory and Criticism*, 2nd ed., ed. Vincent B. Leitch (London: Norton, 2010), pp. 1406–20, 1410.
6. Robert Hughes, *The Shock of the New: Art and the Century of Change* (London: BBC Books, 1980).
7. Eric Bulson, '*Ulysses* by Numbers', *Representations* 127.1 (2014): 1–32, 12.
8. Tom McCarthy, '*Ulysses* and Its Wake', *London Review of Books*, 36.12 (19 June 2014): 39–41, 39.
9. T. S. Eliot, 'Tradition and the Individual Talent' [1919], in *Selected Essays*, 3rd ed. (London: Faber & Faber, 1963), pp. 13–22.
10. Fritz Senn, 'Book of Many Turns', p. 29.
11. Jeri Johnson, Introduction to Ulysses, ed. Jeri Johnson (Oxford: Oxford World's Classics, 1993), xvii.
12. Philip Kitcher, *Joyce's 'Ulysses': Philosophical Perspectives* (Oxford: Oxford University Press, 2020), p. 1.
13. Derek Attridge and Daniel Ferrer, 'Introduction: Highly Continental Evenements', in *Post-Structuralist Joyce: Essays from the French*, ed. Derek Attridge and Daniel Ferrer (Cambridge: Cambridge University Press, 1984), pp. 4, 6.
14. Kenner, *Joyce's Voices*, p. 87.
15. Richard Aldington, 'The Influence of James Joyce', *English Review*, xxxii (April 1921), 333–41, repr. in Deming, *Critical Heritage*, vol. 1, pp. 186–9, 186.
16. A. Walton Litz, 'Pound and Eliot on *Ulysses*: The Critical Tradition', *James Joyce Quarterly* 10.1 (1972): 5–18, 5.
17. Holbrook Jackson, 'Ulysses à la Joyce', *To-Day* ix (June 1922): 47–9, repr. in Deming, *Critical Heritage*, vol. 1, pp. 198–200, 199.
18. Murry, pp. 195, 197.
19. Ezra Pound, 'Past History', *The English Journal* XXII (5 May 1933), repr. in *Pound/Joyce: The Letters of Ezra Pound to James Joyce: With Pound's Essays on James Joyce*, ed. Forrest Read (London: Faber & Faber, 1968), p. 249. Hereafter *Pound/Joyce*.
20. Ezra Pound, 'Paris Letter', *The Dial* LXXII.6 (June 1922): 623–9, repr. in *Pound/Joyce*, pp. 194–200, 198.
21. Pound to Joyce, 10 June 1919, *Pound/Joyce*, 158. Pound, 'Past History', *Pound/Joyce*, p. 250. *Pound/Joyce*, p. 130 – these words, sent by Pound to the editors of *The Little Review* in December 1917, appeared in the periodical as part of its announcement of *Ulysses*'s forthcoming serialization in January 1918.

22. Angelique Chrisafis, 'Overlong, overrated and unmoving: Roddy Doyle's verdict on James Joyce's *Ulysses*', *Guardian* (10 February 2004), theguardian.com/uk/2004/feb/10/booksnews.ireland. *Ulysses* did, of course have an editor. Pound made changes to the early episodes when they appeared in *The Little Review* – much to Joyce's displeasure. See Paul Vanderham, 'Ezra Pound's Censorship of *Ulysses*', *James Joyce Quarterly* 32.3/4 (1995): 583–95.
23. Nabokov called it 'a fat book of more than two hundred and sixty thousand words'. Vladimir Nabokov, 'James Joyce: *Ulysses*' in *Lectures on Literature* [1980] (New York: Harcourt, 1982), p. 285.
24. Pound to Joyce, 2 June 1920, *Pound/Joyce*, p. 173. The letter was sent on receipt of the 'Nausicaa' and 'Oxen' episodes.
25. Jackson, in Deming, *Critical Heritage*, vol. 1, p. 199.
26. 'Aramis', 'The Scandal of *Ulysses*', *Sporting Times* 34 (1 April 1922): 4, repr. in Deming, *Critical Heritage* vol. 1, p. 192. Three years earlier, an exasperated Pound had appealed for 'a few signposts. perhaps twenty words coherent in bunches of 3 to 5'. Pound to Joyce, 10 June 1919 in *Pound/Joyce*, p. 157.
27. R. H. C., 'Readers and Writers', *New Age* (28 April 1921): 89, repr. in Deming, *Critical Heritage*, vol. 1, pp. 185–6, 186. Aldington, p. 189.
28. Jackson, p. 199.
29. Clive Bell, 'Plus the Jazz', *New Republic* xxviii (21 September 1921): 92–6, repr. in Deming, *Critical Heritage*, vol. 1, p. 183.
30. S. P. B. Mais, 'An Irish Revel: And Some Flappers', *Daily Express* (25 March 1922), n.p., repr. in Deming, *Critical Heritage*, vol. 1, p. 191.
31. Murry, p. 196.
32. Ibid., p. 197.
33. See Caroline Levine, *Forms: Whole, Rhythm, Hierarchy, Network* (Princeton, NJ: Princeton University Press, 2015), pp. 25–37.
34. Henry James, 'The Art of Fiction', *Longman's Magazine* 4 (September 1884), repr. in *Partial Portraits* (London: Macmillan, 1888), p. 395. Virginia Woolf, 'Modern Fiction' in *Selected Essays*, ed. David Bradshaw (Oxford: Oxford University Press, 2008), p. 9.
35. Murry, p. 196.
36. Derek Attridge, *The Singularity of Literature* (London: Routledge, 2004), p. 36.
37. Levine, pp. 69, 70–1. The trial was triggered by customs officials' refusal to allow that Brancusi's sculpture was a work of art – a decision that had consequences for the rate of taxation applied to its importation into the United States.
38. Ibid., p. 73. Eliot, 'Tradition and the Individual Talent'.
39. Hugh Kenner, *Ulysses* (Baltimore: Johns Hopkins University Press, 1987), p. 3.
40. James, 'The Art of Fiction', p. 383.
41. Kenner, *Ulysses*, p. 3.
42. *Pound/Joyce*, p. 190. Ezra Pound, 'Paris Letter', repr. in *Pound/Joyce*, pp. 194–200, 197.
43. Kenner, *Ulysses*, p. 3.
44. Levine, p. 3.
45. James Blackwell Phelan, '*Ulysses*, Annotation, and the Literature of Information Overload', *James Joyce Quarterly* 55.1–2 (2017–2018): 35–57, 43, 45.
46. Litz, 'Pound and Eliot on *Ulysses*', p. 17.
47. Kenner, *Joyce's Voices*, p. 105.

48. Phelan, pp. 36, 50.
49. Michael Groden, *'Ulysses' in Progress* (Princeton, NJ: Princeton University Press, 1977).
50. T. S. Eliot's journal, *The Criterion*, published an English translation of the lecture. Valéry Larbaud, 'The *Ulysses* of James Joyce', *Criterion* 1.1 (October 1922): 94–103.
51. Ibid., pp. 96, 94.
52. Ibid., p. 97.
53. Ibid., p. 97.
54. There is some irony in Larbaud's contention that the form he sedulously outlines in his lecture is intrinsic rather than extrinsic – textually embedded rather than paratextually derived – when he himself relied so much on the steer Joyce provided.
55. Chris Baldick, 'form', *Oxford Dictionary of Literary Terms*, 3rd ed. (Oxford: Oxford University Press, 2008), p. 134.
56. Larbaud, p. 100.
57. This mixing of metaphors might be viewed as a fair response to Joyce's own references to the book's 'scheme' and 'technique[s]', on the one hand, and to it as a 'somatic' whole representing the 'cycle of the human body', on the other (*SL* 270). See Scarlett Baron, 'Joyce's Art of Mosaic', *James Joyce Quarterly* 57.1–2 (2019–2020): 21–34.
58. T. S. Eliot, '*Ulysses*, Order, and Myth', *The Dial* LXXV.5 (November 1923): 480–3, 481, 482, 483.
59. Joseph Frank, 'Spatial Form in Modern Literature', *The Sewanee Review* 53.2 (1945): 221–40, 235, 232, 234.
60. Ibid., pp. 234–5.
61. Ezra Pound, 'Paris Letter', repr. in *Pound/Joyce*, pp. 194–200, 197.
62. Ezra Pound, 'Arnold Dolmetsch', *The Egoist* IV.7 (August 1917): 104–5, 104.
63. Pound, 'Past History', *Pound/Joyce*, p. 250.
64. Lewis, p. 91.
65. Pound, 'Arnold Dolmetsch', p. 104. Lewis, p. 109. Lewis almost certainly saw Pound's essay, as an extract (ch. VI) from his novel *Tarr*, which had been appearing in *The Egoist* since April 1916, began on the very next page. Wyndham Lewis, 'Tarr', *The Egoist* IV.7 (August 1917): 106–9.
66. Lewis, p. 112.
67. Pound, 'Arthur Dolmetsch', p. 105.
68. Sean Latham, 'Interruption: "Cyclops" and "Nausicaa"', *The Cambridge Companion to 'Ulysses'*, ed. Sean Latham (Cambridge: Cambridge University Press, 2014), p. 151.
69. Pound, '*Dubliners* and Mr James Joyce', in *Pound/Joyce*, pp. 27–8. Pound, 'James Joyce: At Last the Novel Appears', *The Egoist* IV.2 (February 1917): 21–2, repr. in *Pound/Joyce*, pp. 88–91, 90.
70. Pound, 'Past History', *Pound/Joyce*, p. 250.
71. Eliot, '*Ulysses*, Order, and Myth', p. 483. Kenner, *Joyce's Voices*, p. 49. Pound, 'Past History', *Pound/Joyce*, p. 250.
72. Lewis, p. 112. Joyce to Ezra Pound, 9 April 1917 in *Pound/Joyce*, p. 105.
73. Lewis, p. 99.

74. Ibid., p. 92. Joyce himself referred to *Ulysses* as 'a kind of encyclopaedia'. Joyce to Carlo Linati, 21 September 1920 (*SL* 271).
75. Lewis, pp. 92, 106.
76. Ibid., pp. 112, 112, 91, 112, 114.
77. Pound to Joyce, 10 June 1919, *Pound/Joyce*, p. 157. For some of Pound's comments on Joyce's styles, see for example Ibid., pp. 194, 196.
78. Seamus Heaney likens *Ulysses* to the opening of an accordion of language on 'Desert Island Discs', BBC Radio Four, 16 June 2012, bbc.co.uk/sounds/play/p009mdcy.
79. Barry McCrea, 'Family and Form in *Ulysses*', *Field Day Review* 5 (2009): 74–93, 78.
80. 'Gigantism' is the term used to describe the 'technic' of 'Cyclops' in the Gilbert schema.
81. Kenner, *Joyce's Voices*, p. 88.
82. 'Relaxed prose' and '[c]atechism' are terms used in the Linati and Gilbert schema respectively. Kitcher, p. 1.
83. Stephen Heath, 'Ambiviolences: Notes for Reading Joyce', in *Post-Structuralist Joyce*, ed. Attridge and Ferrer, pp. 31–68, 33, 38.
84. Eliot, '*Ulysses*, Order, and Myth' pp. 483, 482. 'If it is not a novel, that is simply because the novel is a form which will no longer serve', p. 482.
85. Mikhail Bakhtin, 'Discourse in the Novel' in *The Dialogic Imagination: Four Essays by M. M. Bakhtin*, ed. Michael Holquist, trans. Caryl Emerson and Michael Holquist (Austin: University of Texas Press, 1981), pp. 259–422, 262.
86. Kitcher, p. 5. Heath, p. 38.
87. William Wordsworth to Lady Beaumont, 21 May 1807, in *The Letters of William and Dorothy Wordsworth, Vol. 2: The Middle Years, Part I: 1806–1811*, ed. Ernest De Selincourt, 2nd ed., rev. Mary Moorman, 2 vols. (Oxford: Oxford University Press, 1969–1970), p. 150. Wordsworth attributes the insight to Coleridge.
88. Kitcher, p. 1.
89. Senn, 'Book of Many Turns', p. 41.
90. Karen Lawrence, *The Odyssey of Style in 'Ulysses'*. Kitcher, p. 10.
91. Kitcher, p. 19.
92. Ibid., p. 211. Heath, p. 39.
93. The phrase is a translation from Aristotle's *De Anima* (*On the Soul*), which Joyce read and took notes on during his time in Paris in 1902–3. See Fran O'Rourke, '*Allwisest Stagyrite*': *Joyce's Quotations from Aristotle* (Dublin: National Library of Ireland, 2005).
94. Kenner, *Joyce's Voices*, p. 83. The phrase is Litz's: 'Like most critics of Joyce, I had been lured by the multiple designs of his art into believing that somewhere there existed one controlling design which contained and clarified all the others.' A. Walton Litz, *The Art of James Joyce: Method and Design in 'Ulysses' and 'Finnegans Wake'* (Oxford: Oxford University Press, 1961), v.
95. Attridge, *Singularity of Literature*, p. 48. 'Works of art ... *depend* on their resistance to accommodation across time ... complete cultural accommodation would spell the end of the work's existence as art', p. 49.

4

ANDREW GIBSON

Reading *Ulysses* Historically

Modes and Methods

In a letter to Harriet Weaver in 1919, Joyce said of *Ulysses* that 'The word *scorching* has a peculiar significance ... not so much because of any quality or merit in the writing itself as for the fact that the progress of the book is in fact like the progress of some sandblast ... Each successive episode, dealing with some province of artistic culture, leaves behind it a burnt up field' (*Letters I* 129). In the same year, having completed 'Sirens', he told George Borach, 'I, the great friend of music, can no longer listen to it. I see through all the tricks and can't enjoy it any more' (*Letters II* 459). Taken together, the two statements suggest a project of Brecht-like rigour.[1] In the first statement, the imagery is important. A sandblast clears away often thickly sedimented, densely layered surface accumulations. Joyce's image, however, cunningly inverts the commonplace associations of such a process. Conventionally, the accumulations mar or obscure some aspect of a building, monument, or piece of statuary of official, political, or cultural distinction. But Joyce's attitude to monumental constructions of that kind was at best dispassionate. When he wrote of the progress of his sandblast, it seems extremely unlikely that he had a restorative work in mind, and nothing in *Ulysses* would bear that assertion out. He partly aims at something like the reverse, cleansing the historical surface of superstructures to get at the meaning of the scorched earth of Irish history: hence the historically resonant image of the 'burnt up field'.[2] But at the same time, what the progress of Joyce's sandblast uncovers, like a vast, unsuspected Byzantine mosaic, is the structure of a labyrinth. After the sandblast has been and gone, it is of the labyrinth we have to think.

This essay begins by aiming at saturation: that is, it submerges itself in detail, from the start and at length. Joyce criticism, however accomplished, has frequently tended to begin from a theoretical model or a mode of theorizing, abstraction or an abstract set of assumptions. This has effectively become a (if not the) dominant critical tradition. It has seemed all the stranger in that there is possibly no novel more concrete and crammed with historical specifics than *Ulysses*. Joyce himself did not work from a scheme in the first instance, whatever the privilege traditionally afforded the schemae in studies of the book. He began with stuff, historically material stuff. Accordingly, so does this essay. This may seem like a meek reversion to empiricism. But that is not how I see my practice because detail, in *Ulysses*, is, firstly, endlessly historical and, secondly, repeatedly *loaded*. It is not just neutral evidence awaiting empirical procedures. Joyce superlatively grasped implication in the seemingly mildest of shifts in discourses, states of mind, and social exchanges. He was a master of certain kinds of subtlety, almost *nonpareil*. Again and again, there is more in Joycean detail than meets the eye. The difficulty – an immense difficulty, not least because we grow more and more remote from Joyce's world – lies in pinning down that surplus of meaning. Finally, however, this essay works out from detail to a theoretical statement, which is how I place theory relative to Joyce. Theory remains important to thinking about his work – just not as a point of departure. The statement is precisely about the modes and methods of thinking Joyce historically. It is inseparable from the analysis of 'Sirens'. Here a particular mode of historical thought and the figure of the labyrinth come together: Chapter 4 aims to show how 'Sirens' opens up a labyrinth of historical paths as an example of the Ulyssean labyrinth *in toto*.

In his letter to Weaver, Joyce stated that 'Sirens' was constructed from 'all the eight regular parts of a *fuga per canonem*: and I did not know in what other way to describe the seductions of music beyond which Ulysses travels' (*LI* 129). This seems to point in the direction of an abstract concept, but it was also the kind of carrot Joyce had to dangle before the enthusiasts of the time, who would usually have had little if any interest in laborious explanations of the local context. Yet if such a project governs the episode, we must wonder how scholars have been able to come up with so many different versions of its musical structure: sonata, opera, polyphony, the leitmotif, Schönbergian atonalism, the musical.[3] What are we to make of the proliferation of mutually exclusive readings, as is so often the case in Joyce scholarship, founded on abstraction? Are they all present? Is no 'truth of the text', however largely, approximately, and provisionally defined, even on principle, conceivable? Surely, at the very least, we might opt for Karen Lawrence's view – 'The text of "Sirens" as a verbal composition supersedes the text as an imitation of a musical composition' – or that of Harry Levin, who questioned whether the episode has a musical structure at all; or we might even follow Anthony Burgess, who thought literature was definitively incapable of bridging the gap between itself and music.[4]

Iron scepticism may take us too far: it was possible for earlier Joyce scholars like Charles Peake to *sing* quite a sizeable part of the actual music present in 'Sirens' from memory, if in fragments. But singing 'Sirens' in snatches does not bear out the notion of any abstract scheme. Many readers have doubted whether there is much convincing evidence of either a *fuga per canonem* or fugue in the episode. It seems distinctly possible that Joyce was making elevated claims, quite probably in a deliberately and knowingly tongue-in-cheek manner. This would be particularly the case, if, as seems to be the case, he got his notes on the *fuga per canonem* from the well-heeled, patrician, upper-middle-class, public school-educated, Anglocentric, establishment English composer (though a good one), Ralph Vaughan Williams.[5] Joyce would have known what the borrowing meant. 'How's that for high?' (meaning 'high class'), as he said of 'Oxen of the Sun' (*LI* 140). If so, it would be a mischievously ironical crow of triumph.

As Lawrence states, 'Sirens' reproduces a lot of 'literal music'.[6] It is crammed with concrete scraps of historically material music with a historically immediate meaning in a historically material context. True, if one section of the episode requires us to import a mode of understanding, one unrelated to material history, it is the opening passage. The most common view of it is as an overture, and it certainly begins the episode and introduces various 'musical themes' to come, as musical overtures to operas or oratorios increasingly did during the nineteenth century. The various elements, however, if they recur later, do so in wayward fashion and by no means necessarily in the same form. At the same time, it's not a self-standing overture of the kind that Beethoven, Mendelssohn, Brahms, Tchaikovsky, and others wrote in the nineteenth century. The passage lacks the coherence of an overture and is scarcely accessible at all without reference forward, which is hardly characteristic of overtures. We might better think of it as a linguistic version of a musical cacophony. Music and language make each other material, interrupt and distort each other, and even make each other ugly. However, the cacophony has limits. It is determinate and regulated, not random. In that respect it – and to some extent the episode as a whole – seems closer to such modernist experiments in musical form as William Walton's *Facade*, also of 1922, and a work that, like 'Sirens', derives much from popular music rather than classical overtures. Importantly, like *Ulysses*, *Facade* appalled genteel, conservative-minded, backward-looking English hearers and reviewers. The *Manchester Guardian* precisely dubbed it a 'relentless cacophony'.[7] The sheer cultural shock of Joycean cacophony is what matters most in the opening passage, a cacophony that directly addresses a specific and determinate historical situation.

The overture is the first of what I'll call the episode's sequences. Here, at once, we encounter Joyce's 'scorched earth' strategy – the corruption, breaking up, or even annihilation of music declared and in play. The passage is a statement of principle, an announcement of a bottom line. Here we might link Joyce to Edith Sitwell, whose poems form the basis of *Facade*. But where *Facade* was undoubtedly partly an expression of Sitwell's horror at the Great War, 'Sirens' suggests that, again, Joyce had other purposes in mind. After the opening passage, we encounter the two barmaids, Lydia Douce and Mina Kennedy. They are listening to the horses in the viceregal cavalcade with which 'Wandering Rocks' ended. Various connecting tissues refer us back to the previous episode. The two determining powers that bracketed 'Wandering Rocks', Church and state, remain at stake in 'Sirens', if in a different manner. We are still concerned, that is, with the subjects of two empires. The temptation of the Sirens, however, is not the Homeric one. It is, rather, a temptation to which Joyce's Sirens actually *give way*, letting melody or sonority beguile them into a neglect of hard political truth. In the same way, old Parnellite and Fenian sympathizer Simon Dedalus will be apparently oblivious to the political subtext of 'M'appari', the central aria in an opera, *Martha*, which sturdily confirms established class relations in place even as it pretends to a more liberal, even levelling, vision and, as in the song itself, presents love as transcending such worldly concerns.

The progress of the Joycean sandblast, however, means being tied to the mast, not surrendering. Joyce rather asks us to be aware of the way fascination with the cavalcade – the young women are 'agog' (*U* 11.69), like the 'gratefully oppressed' (*D* 35) – lures Miss Kennedy and Miss Douce into a kind of obeisance to English wealth and power. This reveals itself in a language that is not their natural idiom, a kind of idly aspirational, displaced tribute that chafes incongruously against their vernacular.[8] Mina Kennedy's 'Exquisite contrast' (*U* 11.68), for example, comes straight out of contemporary English fashion magazines (which often included sections on court or high life). Both young women spruce up their tone, aping middle-class respectability or, as Declan Kiberd says, 'affect[ing] gentility'.[9] 'O wept! Aren't men frightful idiots?' (*U* 11.79), exclaims Miss Douce. The automatic elision of Jesus from the oath, its conventionally nice expression of horror – Joyce knows exactly what social tone the adjective 'frightful' summons up, as will be the case later with 'insolence' (*U* 11.99) – and its nice avoidance of Hiberno-English ('eejits'), all bear Kiberd out. The 'unmannerly' boots (*U* 11.94) is important, too, since his levelling manner with the young women repeatedly helps us place them and their uses of language more exactly.

This is not to suggest that Joyce is critical of the two barmaids 'as women'. The idea would be quite foreign to him. He is preoccupied with the acute historicity of idiom and what it tells us about power and influence and their mechanisms. His concern is cultural anatomy, revealing, in minute detail, what Gregory Castle calls the division or splitting of the colonial subject.[10] This division has its cruelty, its poignancy and pathos, but also its vitality. The almost Eumaean clumsiness of 'impertinent insolence' itself gives the game away. The young women can't actually sustain the manner. The point is starkly clear when Douce declares, 'If he [the boots] doesn't conduct himself [not quite right; dropping the adverb or adverbial phrase after 'conduct' is a slang usage] I'll wring his ear for him a yard long [exhilarating collapse of pretension into creative demotic]' (U 11.104–5). The same kind of incongruity is there in 'I'll complain to Mrs de Massey *on* you [my italics]'. Lydia Douce is surely aware of the august resonance to the name of the Ormond Hotel's proprietor.[11] It is Anglo-Norman, and in England goes back to the Norman invasion, in Limerick to Strongbow's.[12] The name was originally de Mascy, later simply Massey. It is not clear who has added the touch of class that, to an Irish (or English) ear of the time, came with a Frenchifying enhancement, but it may very well be Douce herself. At all events, the little bit of swank fits in exactly with the theme of class pretension and plays off nicely against Douce's relapse into a Hiberno-English idiom close to a lower-class English one ('I'll complain ... on you'; cf. 'I'll tell on you').[13]

We could trace such intricacies in Joyce's presentation of the barmaids at some length: in Douce's concern about getting sunburn (associated with the working classes until the 1920s, because so many of them worked outdoors) or her holiday in Rostrevor, in 1904 a very modestly fashionable retreat, presumably the absolute maximum she can afford, and to which she may be trying to add an extra hint of glamour in claiming it has a 'strand' (U 11.197–8), when it is actually five miles from the sea. This stands in contrast to her engaging willingness to join Marie Lloyd in saucy innuendo (U 11.148).[14] The ambivalence of Douce and Kennedy's relationship to a colonially derived or inflected class culture is also present in their relationship to Church-derived notions of respectability. But it's important, too, to note a different, recurrent feature of the episode: the stress on how far Dublin's has historically been a culture of migrants, whether Catholic, Protestant, or Jewish. Unsurprisingly, they emerge in relation to the progress of the novel's wandering Jew, Bloom: Huguenots, most obviously Prosper Loré (U 11.150), but also the Moulangs (U 11.86), originally the (du) Moulins; Italians, notably Nannetti's father Giuseppe, statuary manufacturer, Bloom's memory ('hawk[ing]', U 11.186) being fictional, but also Aurelio Bassi (U 11.151), another statuary manufacturer (and picture-frame-maker), 'from Italy' but 'resident in Dublin' and naturalized in

1915, according to the National Archives at Kew.[15] Pietro Ceppi, however, was apparently Swiss, arriving in Dublin in 1861.[16] Aaron Figatner (U 11.149) was Jewish. And so on.

Joyce's broad emphasis here is deliberate. But his insistent noting of the traces of foreign influx (particularly in the nineteenth century) along the waterfront cuts right across the confining binary of colonizer/colonized or the empires and their subjects. It opens up a new avenue, a fresh perspective, on Dublin, allows us to conceive of it differently. It doesn't cancel out the importance of the colonial theme but sets a limit to it and the orientation it encourages. The theme, however, can quickly return. Thus for example when Lenehan remembers his schooling – 'round o and crooked ess' (U 11.244) – he recalls a teacher's mnemotechnic for learning the alphabet: 'call o, round o, s, crooked s, t, the gentleman with the hat on'.[17] Kiberd acutely suggests that some of the sentences in 'Sirens' are like parodies of a school primer, reflecting a culture where the colonizer's language had been widespread in education only for a couple of generations.[18] Lenehan is certainly recalling his own colonial schooling. So too when he also recalls the deliberate enunciation involved in reading out loud in class: 'Ah fox met ah stork' (U 11.248): the reference is to *Aesop's Fables*, a classic much in evidence in Irish national schools from the 1831 Education Act onwards. The period saw a growing concern with the Anglicization of Irish schoolchildren and the need to have them learn English 'properly'. Lenehan is humorously displacing a detail from a colonial structure of power, perhaps consciously. But there is also a nuance, a touch of irony that turns the vector round and points us back in the direction we seem to have come from: for in humorously mimicking a (paternalistic and patronizing) structure, Lenehan also falls back into it, pointedly, in talking to a young woman.

The music that is materially and most vividly present in 'Sirens' is attached to words, and any music we hear in the episode will necessarily remain speculative unless partly verbal. The content of music turns out repeatedly to matter, as in song. More or less the first actual reference to a song we get (U 11.219), after the 'overture', is an allusion to Percy French's appropriately ambivalent 'The Mountains of Mourne' (1896), in which the speaker, an Irish labourer hoping to make his fortune in London, regretfully identifies with the 'gratefully oppressed' (D 35) who cheer the English king ('Still I cheered, God forgive me, I cheered with the rest').[19] Kennedy and Douce might almost say that, too, even if they do not literally cheer. But the sentimental Unionism of the song extends, diversifies, and inflects the theme of 'grateful oppression', asking us to add to our interpretation of Kennedy and Douce's colonial doubleness, whilst contributing to what is becoming a maze of historical and political meaning.

The dominant forms of music in 'Sirens' can be sorted into two main groups, the first consisting of imported music, which tends to mean English and colonial, but also European (and occasionally American) introduced through colonial channels, often with implications that make it coherent with the English imports, notably in the case of class. The second group comprises Irish music. Supporting materials buttress both groups. In neither group is a single, monolithic meaning or set of meanings in question. Meaning is nuanced, or split and fissured, pointing in complex directions, though this particularly emerges out of a 'deep reading' of so-called allusions, which assumes that Joyce knew both the songs and frequently their contexts well. The two groups can be organized around key texts – 'The Shade of the Palm', *Floradora*, 'M'appari', and *Martha* on the one hand, 'The Croppy Boy' on the other. This means that the episode has a roughly tripartite structure but with crossings-over between the three parts. Put very simply, these parts involve colonial domination, Irish resistance, and, finally, with Bloom's fart, radical displacement. This is one version of the 'stylistic competition' that Steven Connor suggests governs much of *Ulysses*.[20]

If there is a musical 'idea' at the centre of the episode, it lies in what Len Platt evokes as staple fodder for the modernizing, urban, aspirational English lower-middle classes of the time. Light opera or operetta and musical comedy formed part of a 'bourgeois and petit-bourgeois culture in ascendancy'.[21] Though we should in principle distinguish quite carefully between light opera and operetta and their audiences, there is not much evidence in 'Sirens' that Joyce did, and we can take them together.[22] The first point to make is that the works in question repeatedly reflect or promote 'dreamy dreams'.[23] As Platt tells us, they turn out to be 'retreatist', by which he means that they escape 'into romance and fantasy' and are in full flight from stark contemporary social realities, most obviously (in England) those produced by industrialization.[24] They do so crucially in the cases of race, gender, and, above all, class, which they repeatedly mystify. Thus, in *The Daughter of the Regiment*, the theme of stepping up in class is prominent. Marie, *vivandière* to a regiment of the French army, turns out to be the illegitimate daughter of the Marquise of Berkenfield. The plot of *Martha* has a maid of honour to the Queen of England, Harriet Durham, disguise herself as the servant girl Martha of the title and escape the tedium of the court, only to win the love of the farmer Lionel. Class seems to be an insurmountable barrier to their union, but all is fortunately resolved when Lionel turns out to be the (wrongly) banished earl of Derby. The composer Flotow was himself of aristocratic stock. Unsurprisingly, he shifts the most important location of the story from Greenwich (in the original ballet) to the posher and more prosperous Richmond. Joyce would have exactly understood all of this. He could not have taken such risible plot-lines seriously.

So, too, when Richie Goulding refers to Simon Dedalus singing, "'Twas rank and fame ... lives on' (*U* 11.779–80), we need to be aware not only that the reference is to Manuel the muleteer's aria in Act III of Balfe's *The Rose of Castile* but also that Elvira, Queen of Léon, has just been outraged by the discovery that the muleteer is not in fact the King of Castile's brother in disguise, as she'd thought. Her anger, however, is premature: he (Manuel) reproaches her with valuing rank, fame, and 'empire' over true love, shortly before revealing himself in fact to be the king. The aria is paradigmatic of the opera's pretended indifference to markers of social distinction that in fact are pervasively confirmed in place, as is repeatedly evident elsewhere in the episode. The same point applies to *La Sonnambula*, *The Bohemian Girl*, and other key pieces in 'Sirens', if sometimes with complications. It is inconceivable that Joyce was not aware of the mystification of class relations in all this or of musical comedies' appeal to the social fantasies of their audiences. Furthermore, in Ireland, such works were colonial imports. The fantasies not only involved alienation from social realities but were alien twice over. Joyce heard such alienation in and as music. This is partly why the episode can sound so Brecht-like.

The theme of the mystification of social relations is bolstered by allusions to other, related materials, from sentimental Victorian and Edwardian songs to traditional theatre. Note for instance the treatment of the class theme in Goldsmith's *She Stoops to Conquer*, alluded to at *U* 11.335. The materials include dancing, stock phrases, and even, at one point, *Don Giovanni*. But the implications of such materials are not uniform or homogeneous. *Floradora*, for instance, includes both retrograde and progressive meanings. It hinges on another sudden revelation of comparatively elevated social or economic status after love has happened 'naturally'. Dolores conveniently turns out to be heir to the Floradora fortune (made from perfume). *Floradora* is conservative in its sympathetic treatment of the decline of traditional landlordism (though it deftly makes the 'Celtic' element Welsh; it was not Welsh but Irish landowners who were in the news). But Dolores is also a Filippina. *Floradora* actually ridicules the Victorian pseudo-science that underwrote convictions of European racial superiority and is atypical of the genre in its indifference to questions of racial purity.[25] So, too, the ostensibly domestic, sentimental, and religious song 'The Lost Chord' (*U* 11.478) is actually partly about 'discordant' gender relations.[26] This isn't surprising, since the author of the original poem, Adelaide Anne Procter, an establishment figure who was also Queen Victoria's favourite poet, was an advocate of women's rights.

All this confirms that, as Platt emphasizes, English musical comedy was a deeply ambivalent phenomenon. It was escapist, and much of it was characterized by its 'devotion' to 'reproducing' or consolidating a supposed 'aristocratic glamour'.[27] It was frequently nationalistic, jingoistic, and xenophobic. It was much concerned with forms of racial othering (not least in the case of continental Europeans) that were crucial to the construction of a national sense of self. Yet it also bore many of the hallmarks of a burgeoning modernity, and could celebrate them. It 'commandeer[ed]' other cultures 'in the cause of a triumphant modernity in ways that clearly benefited "the politics of imperialism"'. But its modern concerns could also seem liberalizing, enabling, and in certain ways democratizing.[28] Such contradictions ramify still further when, as in 'Sirens', we see them at a greater distance or find them refracted through an Irish and colonial context. As elsewhere in *Ulysses* – Gerty and women's magazines would be an obvious example – the effect of new, emergent cultural forms aimed at newly emergent classes, particularly women, are not susceptible to any simple and reductive analysis.

This is very important to the anatomy of a (colonial) social and cultural formation. Joyce understands and not only makes fun of the cultural forms in question but also recognizes their positive significance. He grasps their ambivalence, but partly as conflict or division. However, he also supersedes them, by which I mean that he goes beyond both the mystifications involved in the episode's dominant forms of music and the contradictions that haunt them but, on further inspection, turn out to be repetitive, static, sterile, unproductive. Then again, the work of supersession, like following a fresh path, also runs up against limits or blockages, indicating that Joyce is once more negotiating an extremely complex *passage*. The supersession involves an Irish and even a nationalist identification, subject to the proviso that we recognize that the nationalism is specifically Joycean and appears relative to the specific materials of *Ulysses*. It doesn't refer to a set of terms imported from elsewhere. We might centre the movement around Bloom's 'Poop of a lovely ... Golden ship. Erin' (*U* 11.580–1). Briefly, ingenuously, and engagingly, he links the image of the (Celtic) harp to that of a ship making headway in lovely '[g]old glowering light' (*U* 11.580). Throughout the nineteenth and into the twentieth century, the national flag of Ireland, known as the Green Flag, always showed a gold harp on a green background, and the significance of the harp, here, is unmistakable. This is a particularized, little nationalist epiphany, tender and *sui generis*, if mixed with other materials. Hence Erin, the romantic name for Ireland, crosses Bloom's mind.

The theme of feeling for Ireland has already been fleetingly established here and there in the episode, in traces running from Percy French to Thomas

Moore. It has attracted analogies and more obliquely related materials. The source of Lenehan's 'See the conquering hero comes' (*U* 11.340) is Thomas Morell's libretto for Handel's oratorio *Judas Maccabaeus* (1747). The words had become a commonplace, often introduced, as Lenehan introduces it, light-heartedly. But this again indicates, however slightly, an ordinary, mundane failure of political consciousness. In the oratorio, the Jewish people have won a triumphant victory. In real life, the returning hero was the Duke of Cumberland, famous for his victory over the Jacobites at Culloden. In much of Britain he was Sweet William to his supporters, the loathed 'Butcher' Cumberland to his critics and foes, including a lot of rootedly heterodox, obscure, provincial British minds, as well as Joyce's father and his like, because of his policy of no quarter and the army's subsequent pacification – or devastation – of the Highlands. In 1747, Cumberland had recently returned from Scotland. Handel devised the oratorio as a compliment to him. It was well-known, regularly played at the opening of new railway lines and stations in Britain throughout the nineteenth century, its imperial (and Protestant) significance still clear and fit for purpose in the early twentieth century.[29] Its relevance in the context of 'Sirens' is multiple. It allows Lenehan to jibe at Boylan's expense. But it also supplements the episode's treatment of invasion and betrayal, whether military, political, or personal.

However, if this points us in one direction, the words 'my dancing days are done' (*U* 11.599), from the song 'Johnny I Hardly Knew Ye', point us in another, and Bloom's words 'The harp that once or twice' in still another. We again confront a labyrinth of paths. 'Johnny I Hardly Knew Ye', a song that recurs in *Finnegans Wake*, is about one aspect of the colonial horror: an Irishwoman sings of her lover, whose 'dancing days' are indeed over because he has returned from life as a soldier in the British colonial army in Ceylon with various parts of his body missing. Thomas Moore's 'The Harp That Once Through Tara's Halls' bleakly evokes the defeat of Irish 'pride' and 'glory' and subsequent Irish powerlessness, not least the loss of the Irish parliament under the Act of Union, with Bloom's mordant revision of the opening words making its own small contribution.[30] But whilst he almost offhandedly identifies with the poem's particular brand of nationalism, Bloom also subverts its melancholy and grandiosity. There is again a collision of perspectives, almost a superfluity of meaning, in this colonial context.

Then comes 'The Croppy Boy', the most important song in the episode, and towards which it has been leading, if in complex ways. It belongs to a long tradition of rebellious or seditious Irish ballads, its particular theme being the Rebellion of 1798. The young 'croppy' – the name had revolutionary overtones, referring to the close-cut hairstyle of French revolutionaries that the rebels adopted – stops off at church on the way to fight. He tells the priest that he has lost father and brothers in the rebellion and then confesses his venial sins and the patriotic imperative, which overrides his basic gentleness ('I bear no grudge against living thing'). The priest unmasks himself, revealing a ferocious and brutal 'yeoman captain' who delivers the boy to execution. The respective characters of the two men were partly what gave the song its particular Irish appeal. That Tom Kernan should refer to it as 'our native Doric' (*U* 11.991) confirms the sense of a lastingly tragic and brutal history.

Joyce's feeling for the song is undoubted. He performed it on 27 August 1904 – that is, shortly before his departure from Ireland – at the Antient Concert Rooms. Various phrases in the episode can serve as evidence: the tone of '[t]he voice of dark age, of unlove, earth's fatigue' (*U* 11.1007) is closer to that of Stephen than most of the rest of the episode. Compare *'diebus ac noctibus iniurias patiens ingemiscit'* (*U* 3.466), or

> He heard the choir of voices in the kitchen echoed and multiplied through an endless reverberation of the choirs of endless generations of children: and heard in all the echoes an echo also of the recurring note of weariness and pain. All seemed weary of life even before entering upon it.   (*P* 164)

Or compare 'griped', meaning 'clawed [out]', used of Father Cowley playing 'black deepsounding chords'. A gripe is also a clutching or pinching pain ('gripe' meaning complaint is later and American in origin). But the additional hint of the mediaeval 'gripe', meaning 'griffin' or 'vulture', not least in the figure of a gargoyle, has the effect of momentarily turning Cowley into a stony, uncanny, even harrowing figure. Indeed, the number and density of the echoes of 'The Croppy Boy', far exceeding those of any other song in 'Sirens', their sedimentation, is significant, suggesting a retelling of the tale and a homage and memorial to the figure himself. As Kiberd says, '[h]owever sentimental their appeal', Joyce knew that such songs 'helped restore a national sentiment that came to a climax in 1916'.[31] In his own way, he was contributing to the process. Most striking of all is the shortening of 'yeoman captain' to 'Yeoman cap' (*U* 11.1083). The yeomanry system was created in 1796 to raise infantry and cavalry among loyal tenants. During the rebellion the yeomen repeatedly showed themselves to be unruly, ill-disciplined, and at times exceptionally barbaric. In a way, they were the Black and Tans of the time and were shrouded in a similar mythology. It was chiefly they who applied to horrible effect the pitch caps – linen caps besmeared inside with hot pitch – to the heads of captured rebels. In 'Yeoman cap', Joyce worked a grim reference to the practice into the episode.

Yet identification with a suffering and ill-used people, even a revolutionary identification, is finally also a blocked route in this labyrinth. It takes us only to a certain point, and Joyce understands its limits. The block, the pointer in a new direction, is Bloom. The value of his modernity has been accumulating throughout 'Sirens', if intermittently. We can see the overlap of the two modes of thinking, Croppy Boy versus Bloom, in the relationship between 'Yeoman cap' and its context. 'They know it all by heart', Bloom thinks, after the reminder of harrowing violence, 'The thrill they itch for' (U 11.1082–3). This is modern in tone, distancing and dispassionate, without necessarily smothering the shock effect of the historical allusion. Bloom's fart then completes the transition from the nightmare of history to (comic) detachment. Though the presentation of 'The Croppy Boy' builds over several pages, the rendering of the fart brings revolutionary and romantic pretensions crashing down.[32] This is above all the case with Robert Emmet's famous Speech from the Dock. The centenary of 1798 had given the nineteenth-century cult of Emmet a new lease of life.[33] Joyce responded to it with the deliberately gross mockery of Emmet, and modernity seems finally to gain a decisive ascendancy in the episode.

'Sirens' might thus seem to end with modernity: modern scepticism about superstructures, modern materialism, the modern insistence on embodiment. But such is the complexity of the labyrinth that the modernity Bloom represents in contrast to dark, melancholic historical retrospection is even more multiple and diverse than those terms suggest. This is the case, for example, with his sardonic comment on the hypocrisy and doublethink of wealth and power, notably in the case of the Guinness family. Aristocrats, capitalists, and philanthropists, they are suppliers both of refuge and the reasons why people needed it: 'Ruin them. Wreck their lives. Then build them cubicles to end their days in' (U 11.1018–19). The Guinnesses' Iveagh Hostel was known as 'the last refuge of boozers'.[34] Bloom echoes straightforward, familiar, contemporary British and Irish socialist critiques of the operations of privilege. Here his modernity points at a different angle, in a more immediately significant political direction than the singing of 'The Croppy Boy'. But it isn't in the same direction as the fart.

***

In the preceding analysis, I have adopted a different mode of historical analysis to those long dominant in Joyce scholarship. However capable and at times impressive these have been, on the whole, they have also been inclined to a quite un-Joycean idealism, in the philosophical sense that Joyce intended when he asked Beckett, 'How could the idealist Hume write a history?' (*JJ* 648). I will supply examples of three kinds of such scholarship.

Firstly, the idealism of the intellectual project: in Robert Spoo's austerely clever *James Joyce and the Language of History: Dedalus's Nightmare*, Joyce becomes a 'metahistorical' warrior intensely preoccupied with the prison-house of late nineteenth- and early twentieth-century historiography, with history as theoretical construction.[35] Dedalus's nightmare is the Nietzschean malady of history: teleology, monocausality, the Hegelian realization of spirit. Spoo's Joyce, then, is a principled opponent of historical idealisms. Yet Spoo also never frees himself from an idealism of his own. For all that he recognizes and identifies with Joyce's critique of the idealist element in Romantic historiography, he cannot escape the idealism licensed by the very concept of modernism he himself espouses. Though his Joyce takes the weight of historical circumstance, it is secondary for him, subordinate to the work of constructing a Foucauldian counter-memory. This Joyce's natural battlefields are the European archive, the library, and (prospectively) the campus. The difficulty here has been many-sided and long-standing. Criticism almost automatically relates any question of Joyce's socialism, for instance, to his reading (Ferrero, Marx, et al.), rather than, as William Empson understood, to a popular political mindset extremely widespread in a historical Britain and Ireland but varied and subtle and practically requiring reconstruction by now.[36] This idealist mode of historicization conditions Spoo's readings throughout. The Stephen of the *Telemachiad*, for example, is hobbled not by a vivid and immediate historical anguish that forces itself upon him like a macabre compulsion but by an intuitionist mode of historical thought associated with Collingwood and Croce.

Secondly, there is the idealism latent in the privilege afforded to the theoretical category. Published in 1986, Cheryl Herr's *Joyce's Anatomy of Culture* was a pioneering, even daring, venture. She asserted the need for serious historical research and carried it out at a time when there were few or no precedents and no established terms for it. She was also unusually aware of the difficulties that her own historical and material position raised for the project. Nonetheless, in the case of the press, the theatre, especially pantomime, and the sermon, she set out to reconstruct aspects of a historical world. The problem here, however, lies in what I call the category as a form of thought: Herr's reliance on categories – institution, ideology, system, code – that were already there from the start. Furthermore, though Herr struggled with this, the category turned out to be both totalizing and homogenizing, even postulating an underlying 'unity of [historical and political] design'. This could easily prove reductive, as in the case of her political history of the *Freeman's Journal*. If Joyce said anything about Ireland, it was that its worlds were everywhere torn, split, and fissured. In a millennially defeated culture, dispute and difference were bound to be pervasive.

But Herr tended to think of the contemporary (chiefly Irish) press, for example, as a singular 'institution', when it was an often bitterly contested space into whose conflicts and divisions Joyce inserted himself in specific if complex ways.[37]

Like Spoo, then, Herr finally exemplified a powerful tradition of the modernist will to abstraction from history. This also reveals itself in an idealist criticism that runs the risk of replacing history or introducing a substitute for it. James Fairhall's historical accounts of *Dubliners* and *A Portrait* are arrestingly exact and particular: the reading of *Dubliners*, for example, as concerning a 'glorified market town' of imperfectly urbanized second- or third-generation rural migrants steeped in disastrous and frequently traumatic memories is illuminating and important.[38] The problem with Fairhall's work emerges, precisely, with *Ulysses*. Fairhall knows of course that there is more at stake in *Ulysses* than representation. He also thinks that the novel has no vital concern with its immediate Irish material, that it has no serious Irish *parti pris* however complex – a not uncommon belief, certainly, in mid- to late twentieth-century criticism. Taken together, this means that *Ulysses* can be about 'both Irish and world history' equally.[39] So, in chapter 5, Fairhall discovers a *Ulysses* that is at least as much concerned with the Great War and 'a period of intensified imperial and national rivalries, of technological innovation, of social change' as it is with Dublin and Ireland. Thus the image of the Fenian bombing of Clerkenwell in 1867, specifically in 'Nestor', for example, tends to recede before what Fairhall claims is Joyce's actual 'primary reference ... the unheard firepower loosed in 1914'.[40] But this involves an idealist practice in that it maintains that *Ulysses* is not really insistently or even, necessarily, very much about what it declares itself to be about. The novel's most immediate concerns may be substitutable, and duly disappear.

A similar idealism of the historical arises in Catherine Flynn's sophisticated, well-informed, recent book *James Joyce and the Matter of Paris*: it isn't really about 'the matter of' Joyce's works, which is obviously Irish and, secondarily, British; nor is it really about 'the matter of Paris' in the sense in which *Ulysses* is self-evidently about the matter of Dublin. Flynn's book is about how a number of very distinguished nineteenth-century French minds intellectually recast Paris, not least, in a 'poetic prose', and how Joyce transferred that enterprise to a material Dublin – as an aesthetic, a thought. So Flynn performs a double substitution (Paris for Dublin, a 'sentient thinking' or 'somatic aesthetics' for historical materiality). In doing so, she gives a further lease of life to the critical tradition that takes Joyce's real concerns to be generalities: modernity; 'urban modernity', the metropolitan life; 'modern man', which she is at pains to distinguish from 'moral, political and social man'; and 'the human being', now rethought in terms of bodily life ('human bodies'), which Joyce pits against an ahistorically conceived world of 'competitive consumption'.[41]

So an idealism of the intellectual project, of the theoretical category, and of the substitutability or replaceability of Joyce's world: in effect, Joycean modernism licenses a modern version of allegorical reading that would be unthinkable if Jane Austen's Home Counties or Tolstoy's Russia were in question. It is understandable why an idealist historicism has held such sway in Joyce scholarship. Nonetheless, it is possible to set a historically materialist perspective over against it. I mean an authentically Joycean historical materialism, determined in its particularity by Joyce and his works, and avoiding both the Scylla of a more established and orthodox Marxist historical materialist criticism, which is not without its own idealism, and the Charybdis of simple empiricism. Joyce's is a superlative and superlatively original form of historical materialism. He is that significant a figure. He educates us in the meaning of the term. My historical materialism has many affinities with work by other recent Irish and British scholars but is methodologically distinct from theirs. What follows is a compressed resumé of how historical materialism works in a few of its aspects, finally now cast in abstract terms that correspond to my account of 'Sirens' without encompassing the whole of it.

With its genetic concerns and its archival research, Michelle Witen's recent *James Joyce and Absolute Music* in many ways seems like state-of-the-art Joyce scholarship. Published in the *Historicizing Modernism* series, it is avowedly historicist in method. Its history, however, is solely the history of ideas; in other words, it is a new, twenty-first century book that, under the aegis of modernism, practises the old idealist substitution all over again. The Joyce of 'Sirens' has a guiding idea to which he is devoted: nineteenth-century 'absolute music', 'pure non-referential music, music that does not refer to anything outside itself, wherein the structure and the form are inseparable'.[42] That 'absolute music' is non-representational is crucial: Witen's book has little or no interest in the lived history, personal, political, or cultural, that is actually present in 'Sirens' and its music, and vitally concerns both its characters and Joyce looking back; nor in the social meanings of those materials in their historical context, whether readily available or discoverable by art. Witen's Joyce, again, is an international modernist with a radically abstract project. Thus she makes much of the fugue, associated with 'absolute music'.[43] Relative to the idea, the historical Dublin, Ireland, and Britain that Joyce everywhere knows and treats as such are ultimately inert materials for art, about which, it seems, Joyce could not conceivably have really *cared*.

In this account, the music we should be hearing in 'Sirens' is not the music manifest in it. Joyce addresses something other than what seems to be the case, and this requires its own kind of historical lore and learning. By contrast, my reading of 'Sirens' seeks to reverse the vector of abstraction evident in both Witen's book and the other historicisms I've described. I try to do this by resorting to a key feature of any Joycean historical materialism – saturation, maximum immersion in the immediate historical world of the work itself. Crucially, however, this is as much to do with the *representans* as the *representandum* – that is, not only the world represented but the place and treatment of historically relevant languages, idioms, and discourses. But what then separates a materialist criticism from a set of annotations, the encyclopaedic principle, as in the admirable *James Joyce Online Notes*? The fact that Joyce's is a material thought. That is what art was for Joyce. Art involves a work of arrangement: the artful – that is, meaningful – distribution of practically numberless historical details; their weighting, and the many different kinds and degrees of stress and emphasis such weighting involves; in other words, an art, like Dante's, of extraordinary nuance. Criticism has long known that nuance was cardinal to Joyce, but by and large has cast it as literary irony, a comparatively safe concept. There is a lot more at stake in Joycean nuance, as W. B. Yeats knew when he referred to Joyce's as a '[a] cruel playful mind like a great soft tiger cat' (JJ 531). Yeats understood the historical specificity of nuance in Joyce, if perhaps somewhat ruefully. His comment begins to look like a shrewd and profound assessment of the younger man.

Dublin and Irish society in 1904 were immensely nuanced. They were nuanced because they had been deeply affected by a millennial British history determined by class, wealth, and power, which was already itself very nuanced. The effects of that history were further multiplied and ramified by Ireland's colonial status and the complexity of Irish history. This is all ungainsayable. Then Joyce imposes additional layers of implication. Nuance in Joyce is a dreadful demon. It is present everywhere but is often extremely hard to pin down. As time goes by, more and more of it slips away from us. Joyce knew that it would: hence he also bets on his own modernism, rather as Dante bet on God for the *Divine Comedy*. A historically and geographically restricted focus, however finely, delicately inflected, will not be enough to ensure survival. But that doesn't mean we shouldn't try to excavate Joycean nuances where we still can; to reconstruct them using a maximum range of (sometimes imaginatively chosen) resources. Some will be unexpected: two details in my 'Sirens' analysis, for instance, owe debts to novels by John Buchan and Evelyn Waugh (parodied voices, tones). It's worth adding, here, that a historically materialist criticism does not in principle separate Ireland from Britain. They were not separate in Joyce's mind because they were not at the time, however deeply conflicted their relationship. In that respect, a Joycean historical materialism is not a 'postcolonial' criticism. It tries to avoid the suspicion of projecting an image of an autonomous Ireland onto a period when it was not so. This is not to strip Joyce of his (distinctive and independent) nationalism or his project of any of its extraordinary political power, but rather to do full justice to its awesome historical subtlety.

I have broached just a few of the issues involved in what I take to be a properly Joycean historical materialism. Other central ones would include the vital question of the relationship between nuance and context, as in my discussion of 'Sirens' and the light operas. Merely considering the quotations from the operas is clearly insufficient. They summon up a great deal beyond themselves. But how is it possible to know that? The quotations from Shakespeare in 'Eumaeus' have a very different weight to those in 'Scylla', in that they are present as commonplace, downmarket tags whereas, in 'Scylla', the original contexts of Shakespeare references may be crucial.[44] But what are the criteria for saying that with some degree of confidence? Similarly, in my analysis of 'Sirens', there are decisions on plausibility or likelihood. What is their basis? They may implicitly rule out certain modes of reading as anachronistic. How, and on what principles? Do I really think I have escaped what I called the category? Actually, the answer is no: the point is not to dispense with the category but to specify it as intricately as possible, to mitigate its importance, or delay the resort to it. The call in this essay is nonetheless for more particularism, not just as attention to the infinite graining of particulars in Joyce's works but also, in David Fitzpatrick's sense,[45] as the work of uncovering what is specifically Irish, or British–Irish, in a given historical formation or process. But how is particularism reconcilable with the inevitable persistence of the category?

Here I can only underline what I think my historical-materialist analysis has shown about an aspect of 'Sirens', and, beyond it, *Ulysses*. The analysis follows the structure of the labyrinth. It shows how the labyrinth extends. As Timothy Martin says, 'Sirens' is more than just 'a juxtaposition of vignettes'.[46] It's a sequence of sequences. The sequences are not clearly distinct. They overlap and mingle, interrupting each other. They are composed of disparate elements that point in still other directions. No sequence is final. Each of them meets with a check or halt, which means we look to another. In a labyrinth, one can quickly find oneself back in the same place, if from a different angle. Labyrinthine irony may seem to open up new avenues and fresh perspectives, but it may also turn vectors round and point us back in the direction we seem to have come from. The indications from which we struggle to get our bearings are repeatedly ambiguous and divided, and point in complex directions. Yet the labyrinth is not a figure for indeterminacy or undecidability. Like the outer walls or boundaries of a labyrinth, *Ulysses* as a whole *contains* multiplicity, setting certain limits to it. In these and other ways, the Joycean labyrinth is a figure for an extremely complex thought operating in terms of openings and closures, checks and balances, solidarities and critiques, trajectories and limits. It is in the labyrinth that historical materialism ends, via a slowly but resolutely growing awareness of Joyce's historical meditation as itself labyrinthine.

Notes

1. Compare Karen R. Lawrence on 'Sirens' as an episode that 'lays bare' its 'inner workings'. Karen R. Lawrence, *Who's Afraid of James Joyce?* (Gainesville: University Press of Florida, 2010), p. 35.
2. See, to take a single instance, the discussion of Ireland in Neil Murphy, 'Violence, Colonization and Henry VIII's Conquest of France 1544–1546', *Past and Present* 233 (Nov. 2016): 13–51, at 33, where Joyce's term appears.
3. See Michelle Witen, *James Joyce and Absolute Music* (London: Bloomsbury, 2019), p. 119.
4. Lawrence, *Who's Afraid*, p. 35; Harry Levin, *James Joyce: A Critical Introduction* (London: Faber & Faber, 1942), p. 74; and Anthony Burgess, *The Man and Music* (New York: McGraw-Hill, 1982), p. 141. See Witen, *James Joyce*, p. 124.
5. See Susan Brown, 'The Mystery of the Fuga per Canonem Solved', *Genetic Joyce Studies* 7 (Spring 2007), geneticjoycestudies.org/GJS7/GJS7brown.html.
6. Lawrence, *Who's Afraid*, p. 35.
7. 'Futuristic Music and Poetry', *Manchester Guardian* (13 June 1923), p. 3.
8. A point made in different terms by Hugh Kenner, *Ulysses* (Baltimore: Johns Hopkins University Press, 1987), p. 88.
9. Declan Kiberd, *'Ulysses' and Us: The Art of Everyday Living* (London: Faber & Faber, 2010), p. 169.
10. Gregory Castle, *Reading the Modernist Bildungsroman* (Gainesville: University Press of Florida, 2006), p. 162.
11. See James Joyce, *Ulysses*, ed. with introduction and annotations by Sam Slote (London: Alma, 2012), p. 189 n. 6.
12. See www.irishsurnames.com.
13. See Tom Dalzell and Terry Victor, *The Concise New Partridge Dictionary of Slang and Unconventional English* (London: Routledge, 2008), p. 644.
14. 'Other eye' is a quotation from the 1890s popular music hall song 'When You Wink the Other Eye', as performed by Marie Lloyd, famous for innuendo.
15. See *James Joyce Online Notes* at jjon.org/jioyce-s-people/nannetti and discovery.nationalarchives.gov.uk/details/r/C11957628.

16. At least according to rootschat.com: rootschat.com/forum/index.php?topic=702347.27.
17. Horace Mann, *The Common School Journal for 1842*, vol. IV (Boston: William B. Fowle and N. Capen, 1842), p. 28.
18. Kiberd, *'Ulysses' and Us*, p. 169.
19. For 'The Mountains of Mourne', see Percy French, *Songs*, ed. James N. Healy (Dublin: Mercier Press, 1993), p. 40.
20. Steven Connor, *James Joyce* (Plymouth: Northcote House, 1996), p. 61.
21. Len Platt, *Musical Comedy on the West End Stage 1890–1939* (London: Palgrave Macmillan, 2004), pp. 15–17.
22. Ibid., pp. 1–3.
23. From Joyce's poem 'The Holy Office' (1904): 'That they may dream their dreamy dreams / I carry off their filthy streams' *(PSW 68)*.
24. Platt, *Musical Comedy*, p. 27.
25. Ibid., pp. 55–6.
26. The word 'discordant' occurs in the last line of the fourth verse: 'It seemed the harmonious echo / From our discordant life'. See Don Gifford, *'Ulysses' Annotated* (Berkeley: University of California Press, 2008), p. 299.
27. Platt, *Musical Comedy*, p. 83.
28. Ibid., p. 70. For a full account see pp. 3–5 and passim.
29. See, for example, Caroline Keen's account of its use at Manipur as described in *An Imperial Crisis in British India: The Manipur Uprising of 1891* (London: I. B. Tauris, 2015), p. 162.
30. Thomas Moore, 'The Harp That Once Through Tara's Halls' in *The Poetical Works of Thomas Moore*, ed. A. D. Godley (Oxford: Oxford University Press, 1910), p. 182.
31. Kiberd, *'Ulysses' and Us*, p. 171.
32. Among many critics who have commented on 'The Croppy Boy', R. Brandon Kershner interestingly and plausibly suggests that the target is less political rhetoric than 'heroic resignation'. *The Culture of Joyce's 'Ulysses'* (Basingstoke: Palgrave Macmillan, 2016), p. 15.
33. See, for example, Patrick Maume, *The Long Gestation: Irish National Life, 1891–1918* (New York: St Martin's Press, 1999), passim; and, for a relevant context, Anne Fogarty, '"Where Wolfe Tone's Statue Was Not": Joyce, 1798 and the Politics of Memory', *Études Irlandaises* (special issue: 'Irlande: Fin de siècles'), 24.2 (1999): 20–32.
34. The trust was founded by Edward Cecil Guinness, first earl of Iveagh, in 1890. In 1903 it was amalgamated by an act of Parliament to form the Iveagh Trust and so provide affordable housing for low-income residents. The Iveagh Hostel officially opened in 1905, but Dollard clearly already occupies one of what were to be its 508 cubicle rooms. The former chandler has become a beneficiary of aristocratic charity.
35. Robert Spoo, *James Joyce and the Language of History: Dedalus's Nightmare* (Oxford: Oxford University Press, 1994), pp. 38–65.
36. See his 'Joyce's Intentions', William Empson, *Using Biography* (1970; London: Chatto & Windus, 1984), pp. 203–16.
37. Cheryl Herr, *Joyce's Anatomy of Culture* (Urbana: University of Illinois Press, 1986), pp. 36, 49, 61, 69.

38. James Fairhall, *James Joyce and the Question of History* (Cambridge: Cambridge University Press, 1993), p. 74. He is quoting Frank O'Connor, 'James Joyce', *American Scholar* 36 (1967): 466–90, 490.
39. Fairhall, *James Joyce and the Question of History*, p. 164.
40. Ibid., pp. 164, 165.
41. Catherine Flynn, *James Joyce and the Matter of Paris* (Cambridge: Cambridge University Press, 2019), pp. 10, 11, 13, 106, 113, 114, 119, 122.
42. Witen, *James Joyce and Absolute Music*, p. 2.
43. Ibid., pp. 133–57.
44. For a superb example, see Len Platt, *Joyce and the Anglo-Irish: A Study of Joyce and the Literary Revival* (Amsterdam: Rodopi, 1998), p. 78.
45. David Fitzpatrick, 'The Modernization of the Irish Female' in *Rural Ireland 1600–1900: Modernization and Change*, ed. Patrick O'Flanagan, Paul Ferguson, and Kevin Whelan (Cork: Cork University Press, 1987), pp. 162–80, esp. p. 162.
46. Timothy Martin, 'Introduction' in *Joyce on the Threshold*, ed. Timothy Martin and Anne Fogarty (Gainesville: University Press of Florida, 2005), p. 2.

5

FINN FORDHAM

De-Confusing Confession at *Finnegans Wake*

Joyce began his career in fiction by putting confession under a sign of suspicion: with furtive gossip about the late Father Flynn, who, according to his sister, had been found 'sitting up by himself in the dark in his confession-box ... laughing-like softly to himself' (*D* 10). Joyce closed that career, writing, according to Nora, late into the night in his room the dark fiction of *Finnegans Wake*, also laughing to himself.[1] The mysterious subject of both sets of laughter can only be guessed at. Is *Finnegans Wake*, as some have thought, a confession of sorts?[2] Is Joyce somehow suspect because, resembling his creation Flynn, he is unable to take confession and sin seriously? The enigma of what was so funny is part of what keeps the machinery of interpreting Joyce's works ticking over.

The varied settings, forms and processes of confession, from church to parlour, courtroom to consulting room, and the multifaceted issues that surround them – psychological, social, and historical – provide abundant ways into the maze of *Finnegans Wake*. Some routes through have been acknowledged, but it is still a relatively uninspected theme of the book.[3] Being a labyrinth, we wander in the *Wake* and mistake our path, but errors of reading are so inevitable that they are easily forgiven and not felt as errors as such. Nor are they guaranteed to be portals of discovery. Given such entangled multiplicity, thinking about confession is liable to slip into confusion. Joyce was well aware of this possibility, for while he eschewed confession in his life, he explored it throughout his work. He played with the association that the half-rhyme confession–confusion seems to endorse. On three occasions in *Finnegans Wake*, he fused the process of confession with a state of confusion: 'the pardonable confusion' (*FW* 119.33), 'general uttermosts confussion' (*FW* 353.25), and 'the confusional' (*FW* 520.12). As a way to introduce terms for this chapter I will begin by offering exegesis of the first two of these fused phrases. I will then provide eight observations about confession in *Finnegans Wake*, intended to de-confuse the issues, before concluding about the role of confession and identity.

The first of the above phrases – 'the pardonable confusion' – appears in chapter I.5, which describes 'The Letter', ALP's testimony that is supposed to prove HCE's innocence and save him from having to confess or testify. One section (*FW* 119.12–124.21) uses the language of Sir Edward Sullivan's 1914 introduction to the Book of Kells, a paradigm of and inspiration for *Finnegans Wake* itself. In Sullivan's description, there are traces of a condescending tone: 'the quaintness of its striking portraiture' and 'a number of droll and impish figures'.[4] Joyce augments this in his parody of Sullivan, which explains why the 'confusion' is patronizingly judged as 'pardonable': such verdicts are made to confer authority on the judge. While the incredible intricacies of the Book of Kells are supposed to illuminate, communicate, and reflect a profound wonder at God's word and creation, judging the incredible intricacies of ALP's letter and Joyce's text as a *confusion* invites a suspicion that the *Wake* is in error and has something to confess, even if that something proves to be 'pardonable'. Readers find some relief in such metonymic logic, where the book as a whole seems to be represented by descriptions of local states. At first glance, the book is clearly in a state of general confusion, and readers might well suspect that, lurking in its dark depths, there are things that need confessing, on behalf of its characters or even its author. Some crime, though covered up, is blatantly there. Like the hunchback that HCE endures, the misshapen form of the language admits to some crime's existence though it never reveals its exact content. Calling the confusion 'pardonable', judgement precedes evidence. In a move that is typical of the *Wake*, Joyce pre-empted criticism of himself and of his book by parodying judgemental perspectives on it. This defers the act of confession: why confess one's sins, when you can have your confessor do it for you, especially when they get it wrong and condemn themselves in the process, leaving you blameless? As this chapter shows, this is a common pattern in *Finnegans Wake*, which, far from being written in a confessional mode, is continually a subversion of it.

The second phrase that combines confession and confusion pops up immediately after what is, I would argue, the keystone of *Finnegans Wake*: Buckley shooting the Russian General. Once Buckley's rifle '*expolodotonates*', there follows a '*general uttermosts confussion*' (*FW* 353.23–5), which, brilliantly fusing 'fission' and 'fusion', sounds an anticipatory echo of a nuclear explosion, something that was being projected in weapons research during the 1930s. Though at one level it describes a specific moment of intense dispersal – people running for cover from a thunderstorm – it also proffers a broader description of the book's overall condition: the noise is an all-purpose and extreme confession, voiced *for* and *by* 'the general', that is, a military commander, but also (as per Hamlet's usage), the generality of mankind, or the people. All violence and suffering indirectly confesses a common human guilt. But the precise content of this 'confession' is also obscured through a maximal and extreme fusion or confusion of confessions that *utters most*, that speaks more sins than anyone else. This evokes, with sensational apocalypticism, a prayer for forgiveness going up amongst the clouds and sounds, as it were, of an atomic ('Adomic' – FW 615.06) explosion. The muddled layerings of international politics and domesticity make this explosion less globally tragic and frightening than that: it's hard to distinguish catastrophe in amongst the cacophonic contingencies of the *Wake's* 'confussions'. All this *'general uttermosts'* confusion undermines the shame of confession, for it is, moreover, hard to tell the brag from the agenbite, denial from avowal.

In order to disentangle and defuse the *Wake's* 'confussion', to *de-confuse* it, I intend to use the sequentiality of narrative, the *Wake's* syntagmatic and diachronic dimensions. There are a number of narratives that can be examined: those within the *Wake* (how one thing follows another), narratives of composition (how one thing after another was written and rewritten), how narratives of confession evolved across Joyce's work, and how histories of confession can be seen to intersect with the composition and the reception of *Finnegans Wake*.[5]

I have three reasons for using this lens of narrative. First: a confession is of course itself a narrative within a larger narrative, and, in fiction at its technical best, it has a double aspect: fictions recite moments of crisis, and the recitation is itself a crisis, with repercussions of resolution, incrimination, or further complication. Confessional stories are a dramatic way of providing originary narratives, which, as we see in *Finnegans Wake*, may be triggered by questions or commands: 'What … brought about … this municipal sin business?' (FW 5.13–14), 'Tell me all. Tell me now' (FW 196.05). The responses, as stories, may satisfy a desire for knowledge, bring together isolated fragments, and bring journeys to an end, lightening the load of doubt. The metaphor of 'unloading' as a purpose of communication is announced in *Finnegans Wake*, at the climax of one of HCE's speeches: 'Fall stuff' (FW 366.30). HCE has just unloaded his excess emotional baggage about his own 'fall', being a boastful libertine or a 'Falstaff', finally realizing and confessing his flawed nature, just as Falstaff had to do when Hal cruelly failed to acknowledge him. The fall of such stuff seeks from his audience forgiveness, reconciliation, and resolution, all conventions of narratives of confession. But none of them are given in *Finnegans Wake*, which subverts or at least defers them all.

De-Confusing Confession at *Finnegans Wake*

A second reason is to keep alive our sense of linear sequence in *Finnegans Wake* and explore the functions of sequentiality. Work on the *Wake*'s narrative has been relatively dormant since the 1980s while two other approaches to the text – the philological and creative responses – have come to dominate.[6] The latter promotes perceptions that narrative places a straitjacket on the text, a position that, paradoxically, actually limits our understanding of the text – as narrative.[7] When we imagine only an awkward silence in the relationship between narrative and *Finnegans Wake*, we exaggerate the difficulties between them. When Joyce said, 'there is no go-ahead plot', he was not saying there is no plot whatsoever (*Letters III* 146). That things follow on from other things, whether in the tales that are told or in the way the tales are told, can be quarried for significance. Even shaggy dog stories have sequence and, indeed, rely on a quantity of sequential events to ensure that effects of timing are successful. We should keep alive our analyses of narrative, not in spite of its being hard to identity but because of it.

Thirdly, the narratives that build around confession may be used to think about how confession works as a totem in accounts of human identity. Analyses of confession have been particularly important to existential explorations of the human and of 'the human' as an effect of institutions, or regimes of truth. Such explorations address questions about whether humans are essentially or just occasionally fallen or innocent or redeemable, whether they should seek to do penance or feel shame but transcend that shame, whether the representation of a sin or the reasons for sin can ever be accurate or sincere. Is confession a relief for the individual, as it appears to Leopold Bloom when he thinks 'Confession. Everyone wants to' (*U* 5.425)? Or have institutions used the ritual of confession in order to turn 'Western man' into 'a confessing animal', as Michel Foucault believed.[8] *Finnegans Wake* may be called on for its perceived power as a prophetic work, a text that is at once sacred and secular, to answer such questions. But should our interpretations of its 'confusional' riddles be edifying, to help usher in a new idea of the human? Or is it a detached, purely aesthetic and non-didactic account of an unchanging humanity? In any case, which model of the human is it working with?

Confession, broadly speaking, appears in two contexts in the *Wake*: the religious and the secular. The religious one in its Catholic form is of course primary for Joyce, something he experienced directly and intensely at school. The form it took had been laid down and ritualized with special care by Catholic theologians as the 'sacrament of penance', which established and enforced a sequence, one to which Stephen Dedalus was subjected in *A Portrait*.[9] This sequence begins, of course, with sin: sin should lead to the hatred of sin, which should then raise the question of whether the subject is baptized or not. If they are, then the subject can and should confess, that is, accuse themselves and give evidence of their sin. This constitutes the auricular confession that takes place where the auditor or confessor has the 'power of the keys'.[10] If they do, and the confession is sincere, then this leads to a judgement of the confessant by the confessor. This leads to penance, which consists of repentance, reparation, and contrition. And this, once complete, leads to the remission of sin or absolution. The sin is now gone. This highly developed and baroque narrative of abstract circumstances is built upon a foundation of concrete, everyday experience of contamination and purification: a stain appearing and being washed away. The washerwomen of I.8 underpin this metaphor: hence one of them looking at the 'gangres of sin' in the clothes she is washing (*FW* 196.18). ALP is positioned after I.7 in which the confessant Shaun attempts to get his scatological brother Shem to confess to his sins.

The second and secondary context is the legal one, where some kind of public admission, often during a defence, is made in a courtroom. Bloom in 'Circe' does this, as does HCE at a number of points in *Finnegans Wake*. Joyce, without active experience of confessing in this context, drew for his knowledge from careful reading of famous trials – real and fictional – in journalism, novels, plays, and biographies throughout his life.

Both these institutional contexts may be echoed in the experiences of everyday encounters where we are accused of some fault or other, where we are expected to acknowledge or to counter with denial or banter. One example of this in Joyce's fiction is the pathetic scene where Heron torments Stephen to get him to admit 'that Byron was no good' (*P* 82). Stephen, being a good martyr, proudly refuses to do so, but feels humiliation in any case. Joyce's fascination with the power of these processes, especially in its primary Catholic forms, and his will to counter that power, never left him or his art: one distinct quality of his art reflects a proud unwillingness to submit to any authority that believed it had the right to pass judgement on him.

With these sometimes rival contexts of confession in place, I will now turn to eight basic observations on confession in the *Wake*.

1. Where does confession unfold in *Finnegans Wake*? The structure of confession is especially prominent, though ultimately subverted, in I.7, 'Shem the Penman'. There is also a flurry of confessional jargon scattered within confessional narratives in the penultimate episode that Joyce wrote for the book: II.3, sections 4, 5, and 6 (which consists of 'How Buckley Shot the Russian General', as related on a television in the pub, and the landlord's response to the story). That Joyce wrote these towards the end of the composition process but embedded them in the dark middle of the book may be relevant and suggestive for readers who speculate that *Finnegans*

Wake is somehow a confession on Joyce's part. In one of these scenes HCE admits that he had dreamt of his 'deepseep daughter which was bourne up pridely out of medsdreams unclouthed' (*FW* 366.14–15). While confessions may be anticipated during trials, like that of Festy King in 1.4 (*FW* 85.20–93.21), or during inquiries, like that of Yawn in III.3, in neither do they materialize. And so, the resolution that might come with confession does not materialize either.

2. Public confession: *Finnegans Wake* has a considerable quantity of public confession, though an exact sense of this is often unclear, as the scenes are so nebulous that whether there is an audience at all or how large it is at any given moment is hard to spell out. On the other hand, there is a general sense that this is a world with little privacy. The narrators of III.4, for instance, floating in and out of the bedrooms of the Porter family, are very close to being voyeurs.

In theology, public confession has a technical term: exomologesis. Joyce seems to have known the term, as he notes it down in his late Index notebook (composed early 1938), under the heading <u>Confession</u>. It appears near the end of the following mini-directory of terms, probably compiled from a work of reference:

> plinnyflowers, columellas
> Baldoyle Turf general's
> confession, he forgets
> supernat. sorrow, purpose of
> amendment, penance, confess[on?]
> tomb of martyr shrine, moral &
> physical presence metanoia
> confess. contrit, absol. [*sic*] satisfaction
> retain, remit, **excomologosis**,
> murder, idolatry, adultery.   (*JJA* 40, 182; notebook VI.B.46-83)

Joyce's intimidating quasi-omniscience can be qualified here, as his transcription misspells the word as 'excomologosis', an error that was carried over when he transferred the word onto his drafts. Joyce would transfer and transform nearly all of these words onto a couple of proof pages preparing for the last instalment of *transition* in May 1938. He used two of them to make the phrase 'metanoic excomologosis', which he inserted, amongst others, into the following sentence (in bold):

> *The saintly scholarist's roastering guffalawd of* **nupersaturals holler at this metanoic excomologosis** *tells of the chestnut's ... absolutionally rompty-hompty sucessfulness.*
>
> (*FW* 341.29-32. See *JJA* 55, 200 and 209; II.3§4 draft level 6, 6+)

At this late stage of composition, there is usually some intentional entropy in Joyce's transmissions anyway, as can be seen when 'supernatural sorrow' is spoonerized to become 'nupersaturals holler'. We will return in point 4 to this sense of a language that freely exhibits – that is, confesses – its own failings.

Shem's confession after Shaun's exhaustive denunciation in I.7 seems public, though, again, quite how public is tricky to say. Shaun has addressed an audience at the start – 'How is that for low, laities and gentlenuns?' (*FW* 177.08) – as if this character assassination is being publicly performed, but we do not hear from them at any point in the chapter. It may just be us readers of course. I will return to Shem's confession in point 5 below.

Through metaphorical layering, the Russian General's act of excretion is signalled as a confession, just as the General also appears in the guise of a pope. This figure of authority opens up and, as it were, unloads, seeking to purge himself, he hopes, in private. But the sniper Buckley sees him, which makes it public. The drama as a whole, moreover, unfolds on television in a 'public' house. It is related in the third person by a narrator who, in concluding his description, condemns him. An elaborately structured confession is performed during the tale, the General/pope self-harming: his eyes ('oggles'), his nose ('nosoes'), his mouth ('mouther'), feet and hands ('manucupes' and 'pedarrests'), and finally his phallus ('tree of livings in the middenst'):

> *He blanks his oggles because he confesses to all his tellavicious nieces. He blocks his nosoes because that he confesses to everywheres he was always putting up his latest faengers. He wollops his mouther with a sword of tusk in as because that he confesses how opten he used be obening her howonton he used be undering her. He boundles alltogotter his manucupes with his pedarrests in asmuch as because that he confesses before all his handcomplishies and behind all his comfoderacies. And (hereis cant came back saying he codant steal no lunger, yessis, catz come buck beques he caudant stail awake) he touched upon this tree of livings in the middenst of the garerden for inasmuch as because that he confessed to it on Hillel and down Dalem and in the places which the lepers inhabit in the place of the stones and in pontofert jusfuggading amoret now he come to think of it jolly well ruttengenerously olyovyover the ole blucky shop. Pugger old Pumpey O'Dungaschiff!* (*FW* 349.27–350.07)

The will to an artful order here resembles the sumptuous uniform of the General, which intimidates Buckley. It calls into question the sincerity of the confessions. As a public performance, this confession is a bid to achieve a sanctimonious status.

Having listened to Butt's version of Buckley's story, HCE, now as the Innkeeper of the Mullingar Inn, mirrors the Russian General and also performs a public confession before his customers, though it is formally much messier. He admits to reading a rude book on the lavatory, he asks to be excused of his choice of words, then concludes that he is 'guilty but fellows culpows', that 'It was felt by me sindeade' (*FW* 363.20), and, as we have heard, that he dreamed of his 'deepseep daughter which was bourne up pridely out of medsdreams unclouthed' (*FW* 366.14–15). While reconciliation is sought or expected, none is granted. HCE's expectation of mercy is denied in the kangaroo court of the pub.

3. There is no auricular confession in *Finnegans Wake*. Surprisingly, at no point do we ever enter the confessional, and there is no private confession made straight into the ear of a qualified priest. This is a corollary to the dominance of public confession. Twice before Joyce had accompanied his characters vividly into the booth, first in *A Portrait*, with a degree of sensational trauma:

> His sins trickled from his lips, one by one, trickled in shameful drops from his soul festering and oozing like a sore, a squalid stream of vice ... Blinded by his tears and by the light of God's mercifulness he bent his head and heard the grave words of absolution spoken. (*P* 144–5)

And then, as a riposte, with a comic account in Molly's final stream in *Ulysses*:

> he touched me father and what harm if he did where and I said on the canal bank like a fool but whereabouts on your person my child on the leg behind high up was it yes rather high up was it where you sit down yes O Lord couldnt he say bottom right out and have done with it what has that got to do with it and did you whatever way he put it I forget no father and I always think of the real father what did he want to know for when I already confessed it to God. (*U* 18:107–13)

It is as if with these two very different instances, he has dealt with the central confessional point of Catholicism and moved on, leaving the baroque structure of the sacrament of penance behind him, tottering without its keystone.

4. The unintentional or inadvertant confession. These confessions are best known as Freudian in the sense of the Freudian slip, but Joyce, aware that the mechanism was understood by writers long before Freud, would not have described them in this way. To provide one such slip from many possible examples, I hope a public confession will be pardoned: for the April 2019 'Lucia' event in Dublin I had written a paper that began with a personal note. 'I was fascinated as a teenager by Joyce'. But what I actually said, in a mangling worthy of HCE, was the less bland, 'I was fascinated by a teenager...'. I was unable to return to my paper until the laughter had died

down. Part of the comic effect in such slips is due to the perception of an awkward tabooed truth breaking through and a parody of communication rituals. The unintended meaning appears to be the truer or stronger one: the intended communication is a mask that slips with the repressed truth rising up in revelatory and, we tend to say, 'Freudian' ways. There are larger truths: for linguistic slips reveal the extent to which language is a mask; the truth appears, paradoxically, in error: its appearance is signalled in laughter. In *Finnegans Wake* the stutter provides a paradigm for this. An unintended bodily reflex makes the mask of a declared innocence and respectability slip. HCE's stutter is a parody of unintentional revelation: as we hear, he was a 'tuttut toucher up of poetographies' (*FW* 242.18–19) or, as he announces in 'Here Comes Everybody', 'one of my life's ambitions ... from an early peepee period' (*FW* 533.25–6). The same effect is felt wherever HCE or Shaun boasts or offers excuses. With the latter, HCE embodies the Latin phrase: *excusatio non petita accusatio manifesta*, that is 'when you provide an excuse that noone has sought you only accuse yourself'.

The language of *Finnegans Wake* as a compendium of mangled forms or lapsus linguae contributes as a whole to the presence of inadvertent confession. At every turn it draws attention to its own idiosyncrasies as flaws, as fallen. But while the language confesses its faults, it does so unintentionally, as HCE does. In any case, reading may redeem these 'faults' – that is, the language invites us to treat what looks like a broken and nonsensical machine as an effective producer of meanings. So, while its misshapen monstrous appearance is a sign of fallenness and error, its excesses are also a source of its power.

5. *Finnegans Wake* and qualified confession. In a qualified confession, an individual may admit to a personal fault but manages to spread blame outwards, to disperse and dissolve it, through shared responsibilities and gestures of universalization. There are two intriguingly similar examples of this, already alluded to above: Shem in I.7 and HCE in II.3. Shem's response to Shaun begins, 'My fault, his fault, a kingship through a fault' (*FW* 193.31–2), an adaptation of Richard III's famous and desperate battle cry as conjured by Shakespeare: 'A horse, a horse, my kingdom for a horse', where he is willing to sell (that is betray) the kingdom he mistakenly thinks is still his to sell.[11] Joyce fuses this self-deceiving plea with the sincere admission of guilt in the Catholic prayer, *Confiteor Deo omnipotenti*: 'mea culpa, mea culpa, mea maxima culpa'.[12] A great deal (a kingdom) may be at stake even when a small mistake is discovered. Through concatenation, even a little error by one person leads to a great loss for everyone. One bite of an apple and paradise is gone for ever, and, as the folk proverb has it, 'for want of a battle the kingdom was lost, and all for the want of a horseshoe nail'.

Shem adapts Richard III's desperation and the *Confiteor*, and admits blame for the loss of a kingdom but also shrugs it off by sharing the blame around: whether Adam *and* Eve, or Shem *and* Shaun, we are all partners in crime. Shem's qualified confession in response to Shaun's full-frontal attack quells and disperses it, rather than affirming its contents. He doesn't indicate a period of penance. The relativity of Mercy trumps the absolute judgement of Justice. This qualified confession beats Shaun on his own ground: Shem takes on the confessor's power of judgement and of something Shaun seems incapable of, forgiveness. Following the linear sequence here makes such readings possible.

The second qualified confession occurs when HCE, as we've heard, having watched the story of Buckley shooting the Russian General, announces that he is 'Guilty, but fellows culpows' (*FW* 363.20), that is, he admits being at fault, but all the other 'fellows' are culpable too. Though guilty, the fall that follows is qualified as a happy fall – a felix culpa.

In both cases the blame is shared and spread: yes, I'm at fault, but so are you, so is everyone. There is an element of mystification in such gestures, but they can be ethically moving. Godbole in Forster's *A Passage to India* performs the same when he speaks to Fielding: 'When evil occurs, it expresses the whole of the universe. Similarly when good occurs.'[13] HCE's qualified confession, however, unlike Shem's, does not let him off the hook. Instead of a forgiving flow of maternal waters, HCE is subject to a douche of insults emptied all over him. This is penance in the form of a public shaming and echoes the conclusion of I.3 when HCE receives a stream of invective from a drunk battering at his gate, the contents of which HCE carefully notes down. This echoes Shaun's accusations of Shem and the critical insults thrown at Joyce, which Joyce carefully took down. All are subsets of the crimes that humans accuse other humans of doing.

6. *Finnegans Wake* and involuntary confession. There is no confession in *Finnegans Wake* that is produced under coercion, from threats of blackmail or torture. In III.3, the third watch of Shaun (or Yawn), there are attempts at acquiring knowledge of the crime by four old investigators (also presented in the text as the 'Four Masters', four gospellers, four judges, senators, psychoanalysts), whose cross-examination appears inquisitorial. Matthew, the most aggressive of them, with an Ulster accent that is described at times as full of 'Northern Ire' (*FW* 522.04), gets impatient in his search for the truth:

- Ef I chuse to put a bullet like yu through the grill for heckling what business is that of yours, yu bullock?   (*FW* 522.01–2)

Deploying the conventional comic trope of the livid judge, the over-assertive aggression makes their authority appear ridiculous, inarticulate, and impotent. Anger has muddled Matthew as he interrogates Yawn. He might intend to say, 'If I choose to put a bullet through you for heckling, then that's none of your business.' But the question, even in this amended form, is absurd since, of course, it is his business. In any case, he, moreover, unintentionally turns his witness from being a target into a weapon ('a bullet like you'). Matthew also means to use the cliché to 'put someone through the mill', to make them work hard, but he gets that wrong, as the word 'mill' twists into 'grill'. This reinstates an element of threat since 'to grill someone' implies the application of heat during an interrogation, a 'grill' also being an instrument of torture, on which saints-to-be (St Lawrence, famously) or heretics might be burned, or on which part of a 'bullock' might be turned into a steak. Putting someone through a grill also sounds particularly grim, like turning someone into mince. But this defective threat fails to extract a confession from the witness, who is too slippery, and so the line of enquiry disappears. We've come a long way from Stephen's humiliating martyrdom at the hands of Heron in *A Portrait*.

We might look for evidence of coercion elsewhere in *Finnegans Wake*, especially in II.3 and the Russian General, which was being drafted and redrafted while the Moscow Show Trials, which began in 1936, were taking place. The public confession given by 'The Victar' (i.e., Victor, the victor, the Vicar), quoted above, is so extreme a performance as to suggest some coercion prior to the televised courtroom being entered. With the show trials, of course, any evidence of backroom torture was always carefully expunged. In *Finnegans Wake* 'the Victar's' confession issues from nowhere – who knows what triggered it? But the absence of evidence is not evidence that evidence has been expunged. This makes intentional echoes with the show trials hard to prove. Unable to ground my suspicion, *Finnegans Wake* falls back into its generally rather benign condition, one that tries to be un-horrified by those darker narratives that hover around crime and punishment.

7. *Finnegans Wake* is not a classically confessional text. Joyce knew well the canon of confessional texts, whether St Augustine's, Jean-Jacques Rousseau's, James Hogg's, or Cardinal Newman's, and all of them are referenced in *Finnegans Wake*. But *Finnegans Wake* is far from any kind of first person memoir. In fact, Joyce, from his earliest days of writing, strategically avoided the first person memoir, writing that might now be deemed 'autofiction' with all its attendant ironizations. This is clear from 'A Portrait of the Artist', one of the first pieces of extended artistic prose he wrote. Joyceans consider this to be an embarrassing and over-wrought text, a Nietzschean extravaganza. But it is partly *about* embarrassment, as Joyce admits that 'he descended among the hells of Swedenborg' and 'in a moment

of frenzy he called for the elves' (*PSW* 214, 218). Its experiments in detachment between the writer and his highly proximate subject 'he' will become a constant in Joyce's method. Joyce had established himself, like Mr Duffy in 'A Painful Case', as an illeist, using the third person as a veil over the I, projecting and objectifying himself. The third person distances Joyce from Dedalus and from the direct confessional tradition. In this, the early 'Portrait' is more of a foundational text than we realize. It announces that this artist has discovered a simple law of creative expression: 'Mastery of art had been achieved in irony' (*PSW* 216). But it's not just the discovery of detachment: it's the discovery that irony will be able to deal with the drama of an intense emotional life, without extinguishing it. Selected secret sins can be made public but not in a confessional mode. Highly personal materials will be processed throughout his oeuvre. In *Finnegans Wake* there are plenty of details that correlate closely with events in Joyce's and his family's life, personal and potentially shameful, and which are revealed, if in a coded form, in the voice of another. One distancing technique was to find people accusing him of things in print, in reviews, say, and then appropriating them for the *Wake*'s portrait of the artist, Shem. As with the early 'Portrait' sketch, Joyce let off steam around his own conscience. But he also teased his readers with material that appears personally revelatory, making readers reflect on their own prurience.

The tradition of confessional texts, especially after Rousseau, is one that reflects Europe's sectarian split. This brings me to my eighth and final observation.

8. *Finnegans Wake* and how the church split over confession. Joyce was, unsurprisingly, acutely aware of this split, which began during the Reformation, and provided, on the second page of *Finnegans Wake*, the first in a series of exemplary antagonisms, exclaiming, 'What clashes here of wills gen wonts' (*FW* 4.01). In the phrase 'What bidimetoloves sinduced by what tegotetabsolvers' (*FW* 4.09–10), Protestantism is referenced through an allusion that echoes beneath it: 'Bid me to live and I a true Protestant will be', while Catholicism is there in the liturgical phrase 'ego te absolvo' – I absolve you. The Protestant/Catholic split maps crudely onto English/Irish relations, which combine in references to Cromwell's hostility to Irish Catholics, as shown in his policy of sealing up confession boxes in Ireland. One of the margin notes of II.2 witnesses this: '*Ungodly old Ardrey Cronwall beeswaxing the convulsion box*' (*FW* 261.L05–8). But *Finnegans Wake* leaves few expressions of sectarianism unqualified, and this margin note is full of complicating layers. 'Cromwell' here is also a High King ('Ard-Ri') of Ireland, though here that is of 'Cornwall'; instead of sealing the confession boxes, he is polishing them with beeswax, less a job

for an ungodly person than some lowly servant of the Church. 'Confession' has moreover become a 'convulsion', so that the special controlled quiet of the confessional, intense but discreet, has been replaced by an uncontrolled body pushing violently back at a structure that aims to contain it, like a padded cell.

Central to these eight observations is how the irony of Joyce's method moderated confession as a sign of individual autonomy. Irony is art's riposte to the requirement of sincerity, and its origins might be traced to institutional demands for true and authentic confessional statements. These observations also make it possible to see a trajectory following this theme through Joyce's work. Put simply, there is a movement away from the confession box as a dramatic setting. Joyce's oeuvre starts very close, by eavesdropping on the confession box in 'The Sisters'; then, as we've seen, in *A Portrait* we follow Stephen, compelled by the hell-fire sermon of the retreat, into a booth. When Stephen is later invited to join the priesthood, he is tempted to do so for the reason that, once on the other side of the grille, he will hear the secret confessions of others. He chooses art instead, where the sins of others can be communicated in a different way, as mimetic fiction, bypassing the priest's commitment to the seal of secrecy. As a priest of the imagination, he will be able to pardon reimagined sins. Hence 'The Holy Office' (1904), when Joyce appropriated the priest's inquisitorial function of cleansing and redeeming the sins of others who, in this case, are the writers of the Celtic twilight: 'I carry off their filthy streams' so 'that they may dream their dreamy dreams' (*PSW* 98). 'The Holy Office' was written just two months after the time at which he had set *Ulysses*, wherein exactly contradictory attitudes to confession are expressed: 'Confession. Everyone wants to', says Mr Bloom (*U* 5:425), while Mrs Bloom grumbles: 'I hate that confession' (*U* 18:106–7). Bloom's perfunctory attempt to find a universal diagnosis of the compulsion to share one's shame (an apology for confession that both the Catholic Church and psychoanalysis were using at the time) is countered by the particularity of his wife's empirical view. Joyce seeks no resolution to this contradiction, allowing instead a plurality of functions for confession to unfold and flourish in *Finnegans Wake*, as we have seen.

My method in compiling these observations is intended to illustrate the value of reading narrative in *Finnegans Wake*. Narrative and syntagmatic approaches should supplement and qualify (not replace) two very different but prevalent ways of engaging with Joyce's novel. The first of these I'll call 'paradigmatic', which focuses on the unit of the word. Annotations are dominated by this approach, as is a genetic criticism that traces the sources of Joyce's notes and almost always focuses on single words or short phrases. This is not all of genetic criticism by any means, since genetic criticism has much to say about how syntagmatic structures evolved (whether in plots or in the sequences or expansions of paragraphs). Nevertheless, the Brepols edition of the Buffalo notebooks has strengthened the paradigmatic mode of focus on smaller linguistic units.

The second popular approach comes from avant-garde interpretations or tributes that respond to an understanding of the complexity, the nonsensical, and the apparent randomness that can be sensed in the language of *Finnegans Wake*. This can be seen in several of the musical responses in Derek Pyle and others' *Waywords and Meansigns*, a remarkable project of homage, where an unabridged reading of the entire book, chapter by chapter, is accompanied by original music produced by different performers/composers for each chapter.[14] Not much attention is given to the sense of narrative, however, nor to voices that might communicate any flow of narrative. Performing *Finnegans Wake* is a huge challenge for even the most highly skilled and trained readers, and so it is not surprising that the recitations in this project lack variety in voicing and pacing that might otherwise seek to emphasize its potential for narrative or character-driven drama. The project is not too concerned about this since it sees the text as a form of music, open to unclassical free styles of performance, resembling in spirit the experimental music that the project elicited. The music can be intriguing and highly inventive in its own right, drawing on avant-garde genres of free-jazz or sampling and layering diverse sounds. Inevitably, the relation of the musical atmospheres and the text is often arbitrary. The project seems to flaunt and celebrate this arbitrary quality, not seeking any particular 'sense' of narrative flow in the text to communicate through the music but emphasizing the sense of disconnect and a degree of random improvisation. Syntactic coherence within the linguistic unit of the sentence, the paragraph, the chapter, the book itself, is sidestepped by these approaches.

These two modes both have clear strengths, but they may distract us from developing ways of reading any narrative sequence in *Finnegans Wake*. There are, unquestionably, bizarre arbitrary jumps between many paragraphs, chapters, and events; disparate imagery is fused in a single word or phrase; the reader is repeatedly thrown into the deep end, especially at the start of chapters, with inexplicably fuzzy-edged scenarios and at best dreamlike scene setting. Reasons for a setting or intentions behind actions are difficult even to hypothesize, but none of these are reasons to limit consideration of the effects of sequentiality. These uncertainties are vital not in spite of but *because* narrative flow is so frequently disrupted in *Finnegans Wake*. Joyce, in any case, also wrote and adapted what he entitled '*tales*' and micronarratives, and invariably had a linear temporal scheme, which he referred to as a 'trellis' and on which he might hang his capacious details. One such trellis appeared in the structure for Book II, drawn up in 1926, something intended to fill the blank space between what he had by then already written of Books I and III, nearly all the episodes of which Joyce had seen into 'pre-publication' format:

> Between the close of [Δ] at nightfall and [∧] a there are or four other episodes, the children's games, night studies, a scene in the 'public', and a 'lights out in the village'. (*Letters I* 241)

This structure, adapted somewhat, reappears in a notebook from 1931, where the episodes are attached to hours:

8–9	Children's hour
9–10	A little learning
10–11	hist. survey
11–12	open air debate.

(*Notebook* VI.B.31–269, *JJA* 36, 308).

As rudimentary titles, these are open containers and hardly constitute a plot as such. But the linearity of their chronology, resembling the schedule of *Ulysses* – whose episodes are divided into hourly boxes – could not be clearer. Together they indicate a temporal structure for Book II, which remained and structured the composition. This is just one example of sequential structure.

Analyzing narrative and sequence may use structuralist narratology to understand the flows and forms of temporality, may assess causation or judge the roles of chance, may posit motivations or extract implied morality, or provide models of tragic or comic justice. All of this can be done with any narrative, even with *Finnegans Wake*. But to focus solely on these conventional methods would miss something special to *Finnegans Wake*. For sequential arrangement is also formal, contributing to musical effects of rhythm and dynamics, of crescendo and of diminuendo. There are many instances of the imitation of such musical structures. Chapter III.3, as we follow the growth of a quietly mewling baby to a mayor's vast oration, is the most obvious example of a crescendo. Book IV and I.8 offer diminuendos. The drama of confession – whether whispered or hollered, fast or slow, harmonic or discordant – contributes, of course, to this musical form.

The second reason for the emphasis on Wakean narrative and its syntagmatic dimensions is that they should enable sceptical approaches to generalized criticisms of the human condition. Such approaches help to subvert those accounts that reduce and essentialize human discourse to a particularly prominent but narrow mode, such as confession. The centrality of confession in accounts of human identity can be seen in that powerful strand of

De-Confusing Confession at *Finnegans Wake*

critical humanism in the post-Holocaust, post-war, and post-collaborationist writing that flourished in France, much of which came to be grouped under the term 'theory'. Albert Camus's view that 'a work of art is a confession' has often been quoted approvingly.[15] This generalization was extended by Foucault when he proposed that, 'Western man has become a confessing animal', a warning confirmed by Derrida in his maudlin *Circumfession* when he quotes himself: 'One always asks for pardon when one writes.'[16] This dominance of confession as a key marker of the human has recently been qualified with the idea that, rather than being *confessional* subjects, we are in fact *testifying* subjects. As Susannah Radstone writes, 'Discourses of testimonial witness may now be superseding confession's dominance in literature and other media.'[17] In either case, humanity is still in a courtroom. But should the essence of the flows of human discourse really be so easy to identify? How can a condition of 'general confession' give way to a condition of 'general testimony'? Is intellectual life so constrained as to get stuck upon certain phases of a discursive cycle? The problem with both these views is that they perceive human activity moving uniformly through history along a single channel, occasionally changing direction and content. A pluralist account of the human condition sees multiple modes operating simultaneously. The world of *Finnegans Wake* offers such an account, so its confessions are just one mode of utterance among several. These utterances always form part of a shifting sequence, elements of a 'nacheinander', in which one thing inexorably follows another. The syntax of how confessional narratives unfold is always itself significant. Shem's qualified confession leads to redemption for both confessor and confessant. The Russian General's general confession leads to his assassination. HCE's confession leads to character assassination and then collapse into a drunken stupor as Roderick O'Conor (*FW* 382.26). The various commodious cycles of narrative in the *Wake* allow different visions of the human to have their day. In the *Wake*, the confessional, the testimonial, but also the accusatory, the judgemental, the heckling, and the forgiving – all have their moments, and the wheel keeps turning. The coexistence and plurality of these processes can be called on to qualify any easy and sensational generalizations of what it is to be human.

But *Finnegans Wake* is not descriptive of a human totality either, much as we might like it to be. Though it draws on a profound memory of wide reading, it produces a partial history of the world that excludes, in particular, some of its darker aspects, like physical torture. *Finnegans Wake* includes no involuntary confessions produced under duress. It is a comedy after all, where torture and forced confessions have no place. It is not a reliably total description of this world. But it may have accidentally forecast one of the historical shifts we have witnessed: where the tide of the Catholic culture of confession has receded from its high water mark in 1910, when Pius X stipulated that seven-year-olds ought to attend confession regularly, and a new tide of public confession, made inevitable by new media and communication technologies, has risen, as if to take its place. Could the comic tortureless world of *Finnegans Wake* forecast yet more, by constituting an ideal of sorts, a prescription for a world to share in its responsibilities, to be more tolerant and forgiving than this one? Perhaps. But it is, I confess, beyond me to know such a thing, let alone assert it as such.

Notes

1. Richard M. Kain, 'An Interview with Carola Giedion-Welcker and Maria Jolas', *James Joyce Quarterly* 11.2 (1974): 94–122, 96.
2. Atherton, James, *The Books at the Wake* (Carbondale: Southern Illinois University Press, 1959), p. 13.
3. See Kimberley Devlin, *Wandering and Return in 'Finnegans Wake'* (Princeton, NJ: Princeton University Press, 1991); Damon Franke, 'In the 'nummifeed confusionary': Reading the Negative Confession of *Finnegans Wake*', *Journal of Narrative Theory* 30.1 (2000): 55–95; Wolfgang Streit, *Joyce/Foucault: Sexual Confessions* (Ann Arbor: University of Michigan Press, 2004); Chrissie Van Mierlo, *James Joyce and Catholicism: The Apostate's Wake* (London: Bloomsbury Press, 2014).
4. *The Book of Kells*, introduction by Sir Edward Sullivan (London: The Studio, 1920), pp. 1, 36.
5. For a useful overview of the twentieth-century 'decline of confession', see Bill Cosgrave, 'The Decline of Confessions: Disaster or Return to Normal?' *The Furrow* 34.3 (1994), 158–62.
6. On the *Wake* as narrative, see John Gordon, *'Finnegans Wake': A Plot Summary* (Dublin: Gill & Macmillan, 1986), and Danis Rose and John O'Hanlon, *Understanding 'Finnegans Wake': A Guide to the Narrative of James Joyce's Masterpiece* (New York: Garland, 1982).
7. For example, John Cage's *Writing for the Second Time through 'Finnegans Wake'* and Derek Pyle's *Waywords and Meansigns* both celebrate Joyce's text through adaptation, but their choices communicate little if anything about any narrative logic the text may have. See waywordsandmeansigns.com.
8. Michel Foucault, *The History of Sexuality*, vol.1, trans. Robert Hurley (Harmondsworth: Penguin, 1988), pp. 58–9.
9. See 'Penance' in Volume 11 of the *Catholic Encyclopedia* (1913), en.wikisource.org/wiki/Catholic_Encyclopedia_(1913)/Penance.
10. Ibid.
11. William Shakespeare, *Richard III*, Act 5 Scene 4, l.7.
12. www.preces-latinae.org/thesaurus/Basics/Confiteor.html.
13. E. M. Forster, *A Passage to India* [1924] (Harmondsworth: Penguin, 1979), part II, ch.19, p. 169.
14. See waywordsandmeansigns.com.

15. Albert Camus, *Carnets: 1935–1942*, trans. Philip Thody (London: Hamish Hamilton, 1963), p. 1.
16. Jacques Derrida, *Circumfession*, trans. Geoff Bennington (Chicago: University of Chicago Press, 1993), p. 46.
17. Susannah Radstone, 'Cultures of Confession/Cultures of Testimony: Turning the Subject Inside Out' in *Modern Confessional Writing*, ed. Jo Gill (London: Routledge, 2006), p. 167.

6

VICKI MAHAFFEY

Joyce's Shorter Works

At first glance, Joyce's shorter works – his poems and epiphanies, *Giacomo Joyce*, and *Exiles* – seem to bear a tenuous relationship to the books for which Joyce has become famous. It is questionable whether the epiphanies and *Giacomo Joyce* should even be called 'works': Joyce published neither in its original form, choosing instead to loot both for the more ambitious undertakings that followed.[1] Only forty of at least seventy-one epiphanies are extant, and their relationship to one another had to be reconstructed from manuscript evidence: the sketches that comprise *Giacomo Joyce* were similarly composed, arranged, and abandoned, but not destroyed. *Chamber Music*, although published in 1907, was orphaned when Joyce delegated the final arrangement of the poems to his brother Stanislaus. *Pomes Penyeach*, as the title suggests, is a modest offering of twelve and a tilly poetic 'fruits'. Only *Exiles* continued to hold Joyce's interest as an autonomous composition not destined for immediate verbal recycling.

The shorter works stand apart from the big books in other ways as well. They are humourless; what humour may be discerned in them is bitter or ironic, inspired by pained defiance (as in 'Gas from a Burner') or jaded cynicism (*'In my time the dunghill was so high'* from *Exiles* [PE 157]). They are spare, denuded of the variable styles and elaborate contexts that make *Ulysses* and *Finnegans Wake* seem inexhaustible. Finally, they are more closely interwoven with Joyce's personal experience.

Although the brevity and earnestness of the minor pieces distinguish them from the major ones, the distance begins to close when they are viewed structurally and thematically. *Chamber Music*, the epiphanies, and *Giacomo Joyce* are all composed of isolated, artistically rendered moments arranged into a loose progression; the three acts of *Exiles* divide thirteen unmarked scenes, each an intimate dialogue between two characters, stitched together by the conventions – both social and theatrical – of entrances and exits. The strategy of producing a longer and more complicated text by stringing together a series of 'beads' – seemingly self-contained scenes or episodes – is essential not only to the design of *Dubliners*, where the structural building blocks are short stories, but also to the increasingly complex episodic structures of *Portrait*, *Ulysses*, and *Finnegans Wake*. The minor works make it much more apparent that Joyce's narrative technique – even in the longer texts – is comparable to what imagist poets were doing when they created long sequences out of short poetic vignettes.[2]

If the shorter texts share the structure of Joyce's other works, they also provide the simplest statement of Joyce's most characteristic themes, which are treated polyphonically in his longer compositions: loss, betrayal, and the interplay of psychological and social experience. Strikingly, all of the shorter works record the experience of a loss: the arrangement of the epiphanies traces a loss of innocence; *Chamber Music* plays out the loss of youthful love, a theme picked up and translated into predominantly visual terms in *Giacomo Joyce*. Many of the poems in *Pomes Penyeach* echo the theme of lost youth, but the collection also includes more anguished treatments of different kinds of loss: in 'Tilly', a figurative loss of limb makes the dead speak; it is the illusion of beauty that is lost in 'A Memory of the Players in a Mirror at Midnight'. The list can be expanded to include loss of sight in 'Banhofstrasse', loss of life in 'She Weeps over Rahoon', loss of faith in 'Nightpiece', and loss of peace and security in the nightmarish 'I Hear an Army'; in the words of another 'pome', '*Tutto è sciolto*' (all is lost). *Exiles* is the most complicated of Joyce's briefer treatments of attrition, since it probes the loss of spontaneity and trust in life and love, which the action of the play suggests is irreparable.

As heroism is increasingly displaced by humour in Joyce's later works, his treatment of the relationship between subjective fantasy and objective drama, desire and reality, also grows more complex. *Giacomo Joyce* and *Exiles*, as lyrical and dramatic treatments of problems that would later inform *Ulysses*, at first seem to constitute a two-phase attempt to represent the pain of betrayal from a subjective and objective point of view, respectively: that of the artist's mind and that of a more detached spectator. *Giacomo Joyce*, from such a perspective, resembles the narrative epiphanies in its depiction of the sensitive artist as dreamer, whereas *Exiles*, like the dramatic epiphanies, presents the artist as a character who suffers from the dearth of honesty and integrity in those around him.

Connecting *Giacomo Joyce* and *Exiles* with the two kinds of epiphanies works only up to a point, however, since the oppositions between dream and drama, wish-fulfillment and satire, subject and object are gradually broken down. *Giacomo Joyce* cannot sustain its status as pure fantasy; outer circumstances begin to impinge on its dream world when the object of Giacomo's gaze enigmatically announces her preference for a man

Giacomo considers inferior, Barabbas over Jesus: '*Non hunc sed Barabbam!*' – and the speaker's imaginative superiority twists into self-criticism and despair: 'It will never be. You know that well. What then? Write it, damn you, write it! What else are you good for?' (*GJ* 16).³

Just as the lyrical, subjective cast of *Giacomo Joyce* dissipates in the strong light of fact, the objective, naturalistic, even clinical mood of *Exiles* yields to self-pity and hallucination. The upsurge of irrational forces begins when Richard Rowan suddenly sees his high-toned opposition to any intimacy between his friend Robert and the mother of his child as hypocritical. He confesses that a hidden desire prompted him to watch and passively abet their growing mutual attraction, as the play relentlessly pursues the self-interest buried in the accusation of betrayal. Richard confesses to Robert,

> [I]n the very core of my ignoble heart I longed to be betrayed by you and by her – in the dark, in the night – secretly, meanly, craftily. By you, my best friend, and by her. I longed for that passionately and ignobly, to be dishonoured for ever in love and in lust, to be ... To be for ever a shameful creature and to build up my soul again out of the ruins of its shame. (*PE* 200)

Richard admits that his furtive desire to be betrayed was motivated, paradoxically, by pride, a desire to occupy the 'wronged' position for a change. Bertha has consistently used her faithfulness to shame him: 'She has spoken always of her innocence, as I have spoken always of my guilt, humbling me' (*PE* 200). Richard's drive to know the truth propels him into a nightmarish world of imagination, the world of *Giacomo Joyce*. Returning from a walk along Dublin Bay in the third act, he tells Beatrice (channeling Caliban in *The Tempest*):

> There are demons ... out there. I heard them jabbering since dawn ... The isle is full of voices. Yours also. *Otherwise I could not see you*, it said.⁴ And her voice ... But, I assure you they are all demons. I made the sign of the cross upside down and that silenced them. (*PE* 244)

Once we see that *Giacomo Joyce* and *Exiles* not only represent an opposition between inner and outer reality but also offer complementary accounts of how that opposition breaks down, it is easier to appreciate how the two dovetail into the 'Circe' episode of *Ulysses*, which is simultaneously drama and fantasy, an extravagant celebration of the actor/viewer's superhuman dreams *and* subhuman instincts, his generous pride and shameful prejudices, and finally into *Finnegans Wake*.

Joyce reinterprets – and re-uses – his shorter works as readily as he uses any other material. The dependence of Joyce's longer experiments on the shorter ones raises a problem of relation: how can we account for the disjunction between what the shorter works lack (humour, complexity, and a self-consciousness that is acutely philosophical rather than painfully self-dramatizing) and what they share with Joyce's other writings (seriatim structure, concern with betrayal, hunger for experience, and the appropriation of other writers' voices)? One solution is to consider them as partially realized versions of Joyce's longer works, or as transitional pieces that illuminate the progression of his thought. Like the manuscripts, the shorter works provide information indispensable for reconstructing the 'continuous manuscript' of Joyce's writing career, an achievement that is at once fluid and discontinuous, fragmented and whole.[5] Unlike the manuscripts, though, which give insight into the arrangement of a published text by tracing the genesis of that arrangement and the false starts that help to define the finished shape, the shorter works preserve contextual as well as textual trials and errors: we see Joyce testing not only phrases but variant interpretations of problems like fidelity, combining the perspectives of different authors to create complex backdrops for his own treatments.

The most influential critical treatments of the shorter works show how easy it is to upset the fragile balance between a text's individuality and its applicability to larger contexts. In the case of the epiphanies, the prose bits to which Joyce gave that name are not always clearly separated from the concept of 'epiphany' as revelation. In contrast, the critical focus on the poems, *Giacomo Joyce*, and *Exiles* has tended to be too narrowly biographical or literary. Whether the perspective is telescopic or microscopic, the attitude inclusive or dismissive, what is lost is the depth and flexibility that come from a less consistent, and more Joycean, sense of the continuity and discontinuity of relation.

Epiphanies

The main difficulty presented by the epiphanies lies in the broad application of the word itself. In Greek mythology, *epiphany* referred to the unexpected manifestation of the divine, and in Greek drama it was used to describe the sudden appearance of a god on stage. Christianity appropriated the term for liturgical purposes to commemorate the day (celebrated on January 6) that the Magi brought gifts to the Christ child (which represents the first manifestation of divinity to foreign travellers).

In the manuscript of *Stephen Hero*, Joyce used 'epiphany' both to describe recorded moments that blend the trivial with the significant and to designate the revelatory climax of aesthetic apprehension. He introduces the 'local' instance of epiphany by describing Stephen's reaction to a fragment of overheard conversation:

> A young lady was standing on the steps of one of those brown brick houses which seem the very incarnation of Irish paralysis. A young gentleman was leaning on the rusty railings of the area. Stephen as he passed on his quest heard the following fragment of colloquy out of which he received an impression keen enough to afflict his sensitiveness very severely.
>
> The Young Lady – (drawling discreetly) ... O, yes ... I was ... at the ... cha ... pel ...
> The Young Gentleman – (inaudibly) ... I ... (again inaudibly) ... I ...
> The Young Lady – (softly) ... O ... but you're ... ve ... ry ... wick ... ed ...
>
> This triviality made him think of collecting many such moments together in a book of epiphanies. By an epiphany he meant a sudden spiritual manifestation, whether in the vulgarity of speech or of gesture or in a memorable phase of the mind itself. He believed that it was for the man of letters to record these epiphanies with extreme care, seeing that they themselves are the most delicate and evanescent of moments. (SH 211)

The collection of epiphanies receives further mention in *Ulysses*, where Stephen thinks to himself, 'Remember your epiphanies written on green oval leaves, deeply deep, copies to be sent if you died to all the great libraries of the world, including Alexandria? Someone was to read them there after a few thousand years, a mahamanvantara' (*U* 3.141–4). Several of Joyce's own epiphanies turned up among his papers and those of his brother Stanislaus, which Scholes and Kain arranged into a sequence based on manuscript evidence.[6]

In *Stephen Hero*, after the narrator relates an epiphany and reveals Stephen's determination to record a series of them, Stephen goes on to explain the idea of epiphany in theoretical terms to his friend Cranly. Epiphany, he argues, is the moment when the spiritual eye is able 'to adjust its vision to an exact focus' so as to apprehend 'the third, the supreme quality of beauty' in an object, its 'soul' or 'whatness', which the mind synthesizes from an appreciation of the first two qualities of beauty in the object, its integrity and symmetry:

> After the analysis which discovers the second quality the mind makes the only logically possible synthesis and discovers the third quality. This is the moment which I call epiphany. First we recognize that the object is *one* integral thing, then we recognize that it is an organized composite structure, a *thing* in fact: finally, when the relation of the parts is exquisite, when the parts are adjusted to the special point, we recognize that it is *that* thing which it is. Its soul, its whatness, leaps to us from the vestment of its appearance. The soul of the commonest object, the structure of which is so adjusted, seems to us radiant. The object achieves its epiphany. (SH 213)

When Joyce reworked this portion of Stephen's aesthetic theories for *Portrait*, he expunged any reference to epiphany, instead describing the moment of aesthetic apprehension as an experience of 'luminous silent stasis' (P 213).[7] In *Stephen Hero*, epiphany signaled an idealistic, even platonic belief in the superiority of the spirit, its ability to transcend chthonic materiality. As Stephen explains to Lynch in *Portrait*, for a long time he thought Aquinas's third stage of apprehension signified 'symbolism or idealism, the supreme quality of beauty being a light from some other world, the idea of which the matter is but the shadow, the reality of which is but the symbol', so that the goal of apprehension was 'the artistic discovery and representation of the divine purpose in anything' (P 213). Stephen's theory in *Portrait* is slightly but significantly different; the goal of aesthetic apprehension is no longer presented as a semi-religious celebration of the spirit's triumphant ability to manifest itself through matter but as a rare *balance* of spirit and matter, imagination and observation, an evenness of apprehension illustrated by the commingling of light and darkness in Shelley's image of the mind in creation as a 'fading coal' (P 213).[8]

Joyce used epiphany in another way as well, as Joyce's brother Stanislaus pointed out: to stage a psychological revelation of repressed or unconscious truth through slips or errors. In his papers, arranged and edited by Richard Ellmann under the title *My Brother's Keeper,* Stanislaus writes:

> Another experimental form which [Joyce's] literary urge took ... consisted in the noting of what he called 'epiphanies'; – manifestations or revelations. Jim always had a contempt for secrecy, and these notes were in the beginning ironical observations of slips, and little errors and gestures – mere straws in the wind – by which people betrayed the very things they were most careful to conceal ... The revelation and importance of the subconscious had caught interest.[9]

In Stanislaus's account, the epiphanies began as satiric attempts to expose the pretensions of others (or, more precisely, to record moments of inadvertent self-exposure), and they grew to include brief realizations of unconscious knowledge unexpectedly unlocked by language or dream.

Criticism has tended to favour the concept of epiphany over the prose sketches that bear the same name. Lacking context themselves, the epiphanies in their denuded manuscript state tempted early critics to deck them out in the heavy robes of myth, religion, and aesthetics.[10] However, most critics have agreed that the importance of the manuscript epiphanies may be traced to a few of their most marked features: the absence of authorial commentary that also characterizes Joyce's other work (except the abandoned *Stephen Hero*); the division of the epiphanies into two types; their structure, a sequential ordering of fragments that lacks development or 'plot'; the interplay of conscious and subconscious awareness; and their reappearance in the richer contexts of Joyce's subsequent works.[11]

The epiphanies evoke the desire and fear of discovery, but their exposures are all designed to assert the power and authority of the self over the external world. *Chamber Music,* as we shall see, transposes the theme of disclosure into a new key, taking it out of the psychological and mythic realm and into a private chamber, where attitudes of eroticism and morbidity are paramount.

The Poetry

The nature of Joyce's poetic accomplishment may be momentarily pinned down only by a pointed definition of what exactly is meant by 'poetry' in the context of his career. If by poetry we mean a composition in verse that manages, paradoxically, to combine richness of applicability with verbal compactness, bridging public and private experience; if we are talking about poems on the order of W. B. Yeats's 'The Tower' or 'Among School Children', Joyce wrote no such poetry, although it could be argued that he realized comparably 'poetic' aims in prose. However, Joyce did not restrict himself to prose; his earliest efforts were primarily in verse, and by the end of his career he had written over one hundred poems, parodies, and poetic fragments. What distinguishes Joyce's verse is not comprehensiveness or complexity; he seldom strives to integrate different levels of meaning in a single metrical stroke. Instead, Joyce uses conventional poetic forms and meters as a way of *simplifying* emotional experience, whether in the form of a musical lyric, a satirical limerick, or an angry broadside. Versification allowed him to pare away complexity in favor of a simpler emotional and verbal expressiveness (which may help to explain why several of the poems express feelings towards members of his family, such as 'A Flower Given to My Daughter' and 'Ecce Homo').

It is appropriate for a writer as contradictory as Joyce that his greatest poetry never assumes poetic form. Nevertheless, Joyce did write – and publish – two collections of verse, *Chamber Music* (1907) and *Pomes Penyeach* (1927), in addition to two earlier collections that he destroyed, and of which only fragments remain, *Moods* and *Shine and Dark.* In addition, he wrote numerous occasional poems, which tend to be comic or satirical – two broadsides, several limericks, regular quatrain poems, and quite a few poems designed to be sung to music.[12] His verses represent a wide variety of moods, from anguished nihilism or stung pride to lyrical wooing, but the range of emotion is not matched by a comparable versatility in poetic technique. Joyce's verses are deliberately constructed, like everything he wrote, and they do manage to create some unusual local effects, many of which gather around Joyce's use of one particular word to magnetize the meaning of an entire poem, but his poems are comparatively simple. Most of his poems are, more accurately, songs.

What differentiates Joyce's poetry most markedly from his own most successful prose is its paucity of voices and its 'enclosed' quality. *Chamber Music* might not be an inappropriate title for the majority of Joyce's metrical compositions; even the volume that bears that name is fairly representative of what Joyce achieved – and failed to achieve – in verse.[13] First of all, there is only one voice in *Chamber Music*, that of an alternately idealistic and sensual young lover. That voice serenades a conventionally golden-haired young woman who first appears playing the piano in her chamber (II). The burden of the lover's song is his desire to enter that chamber, which is a room, her heart, and, metaphorically, of course, her womb. At first, the enclosed spaces that he longs to enter are depicted as warm and inviting, but after the poem that Joyce identified as the 'climax' of the sequence (XIV), those spaces cool and grow shadowy, increasingly representing the darker allure of sleep and, ultimately, death.

At the outset of the sequence, the lover's desire for his beloved to 'unclose' herself to his love (see the seductive suggestion in poem IV that the woman unclose her gate to him) emerges by means of the analogies he sets up between his love songs and the music of the night wind, and between his beloved's hidden fire and the dawn. Gradually, however, the poems move towards enclosure and isolation within a chamber – which is not only a room but a portion of the human heart – rather than expressive freedom. In the final poem in the sequence proper (Joyce wrote to G. Molyneux Palmer that XXXV and XXXVI are tailpieces [*Letters I* 67]), voices begin to proliferate, as the voice within the lover's heart clashes with the voice of the winter outside his chamber, one crying 'Sleep now', the other forbidding further sleep. Appropriately, the music of the water has been displaced by 'noise' in XXXV, anticipating Joyce's punning treatment of a nightmare in *Ulysses* and in *FW* 583.8–9: horses (mares?) come out of the sea – *mer* – at night, ridden by disdainful charioteers in black armour. The Love of the first poem has been supplanted by war, 'An army charging upon the land', the idealized figure of garlanded peace ('Dark leaves on his hair') replaced with a multitude of embattled, shouting phantoms shaking in triumph their long, green hair.

The most influential early treatments of *Chamber Music* arranged themselves around the linchpin of the title. William York Tindall reflects back on *Chamber Music* from the perspective of *Ulysses*, where Bloom thinks of chamber music as the music Molly makes when she urinates in a chamberpot

(U 11.979–84). He connects this with stories about how the title was chosen (by Herbert Gorman and Oliver St John Gogarty), both of which involve chamberpots as receptacles for micturition.[14] Tindall identified urination as one among many dimensions of the title's meaning, suggesting that it was also a sequence about wantonness – Elizabethan 'chambering'.

Chamber Music sparsely records a seduction and its chilly aftermath, but the main implication of its title is that like a chamber music ensemble it explores the musical possibilities of a small enclosed space. Joyce emphasized the musical nature of *Chamber Music* not only through the title but also by setting one of the poems to music himself (XI) and by encouraging Geoffrey Molyneux Palmer to set others: 'I hope you may set all of *Chamber Music* in time. This was indeed partly my idea in writing it. The book is in fact a suite of songs and if I were a musician I suppose I should have set them to music myself' (*Letters I* 67). Technically, the stability and smallness of the poems' structure, together with the fact that they are all sung by the same voice, allow Joyce to explore not the landscapes of Dublin but a miniaturized interior chamber, which almost imperceptibly transforms itself into an image of the grave ('We were grave lovers', XXX). The external landscapes of the poem are all psychological and sexualized extensions of other inner chambers, a technique that Joyce learned from Yeats's *The Wind among the Reeds*.

Poetry seems to have remained a slight vessel for Joyce, a vehicle for expressing emotions of isolation or for preserving unique moments. As the title suggests, *Pomes Penyeach* are not worth much individually; they are inexpensive offerings of private moments, one protective and delicate ('A Flower Given to My Daughter'), another arming the speaker against nostalgia for the simplicity and trust of childhood ('Simples'), but most agonized or despairing. As Herbert Howarth once suggested, Joyce's poems are the productions of a Henry Flower (although 'A Memory of the Players in a Mirror at Midnight' could have been written by Virag); they are musical, nostalgic, and markedly sentimental – siren songs, such as the ones Bloom listens to and ultimately rejects in the 'Sirens' episode of *Ulysses*.[15] Joyce betrays an awareness of the danger of such songs in 'Simples', where the speaker prays for an Odyssean sailor's 'waxen ear / To shield me from her childish croon': the deficiency of his poems is their power to evoke a 'Flood' of nostalgia. Joyce never underestimated the power of a simple song to seduce the senses and shipwreck the desire for life, which explains why, perhaps, a song from *Pomes Penyeach*, 'Nightpiece', became the core of the 'Tristan and Isolde' episode of *Finnegans Wake*.[16] An early draft of the episode began as ironic marginalia that surrounds and eventually subsumes its sentimental centre: the romantic, despairing poem of youth.

Giacomo Joyce

Like *Chamber Music, Giacomo Joyce* is a seduction piece. But if the 'Sirens' episode provides a context against which the power and danger of *Chamber Music* can be read, *Giacomo Joyce* is best examined against 'Nausicaa', which takes painting rather than music as its technic. And if the danger of the music that seduces is a function of its univocality and its simplicity, *Giacomo Joyce* – against the background of 'Nausicaa' – shows that the danger of voyeurism is comparable to the seductive lure of the lyric. If *Chamber Music* lacks more than one voice, *Giacomo Joyce* lacks a view from more than one perspective: it is an example of what Joyce would later see as the distortion that results from failing to account for parallax.

Giacomo Joyce is a series of prose sketches formally akin to the narrative epiphanies. A fair-copy manuscript of sixteen pages transcribed onto eight oversized sheets of heavy paper, most probably in the summer of 1914, it is the only one of Joyce's writings to be set in Trieste, which is also where Joyce left it when he moved on to Zurich in 1915 (*GJ* xv, xi). The story – told through disjointed images rather than successive songs – loosely follows the lines of the one in *Chamber Music*, with emphasis falling once again on the waxing and waning of love, a waning that in this case is connected with the appearance of a rival. Unlike *Chamber Music*, however, *Giacomo Joyce* does not contain any suggestion that the love affair it chronicles – Joyce's relationship with a composite of pupils to whom he taught English in Trieste –was ever anything more than an 'affair of the eye'.[17] Unlike 'Nausicaa', in which Bloom's encounter with Gerty spends itself in a comically enlarged display of onanistic fireworks, *Giacomo Joyce* ends more bitterly when the object of the artist's gaze announces her preference for another man, for Barabbas (who is probably Popper's fiancé Michele Risolo) over Christ (Joyce).

What is most notably missing in *Giacomo Joyce* is the perspective of the woman, a perspective that is so strategically provided in *Ulysses*. Our first view of her is prefaced by a question – 'Who?' – and she emerges as a montage created by images of a pale face, furs, and quizzing glasses (*GJ* 1). Typical of the speaker's furtive mode of observing her is the sketch where he looks 'upward from night and mud', watching her 'dressing to go to the play' (*GJ* 6). His voyeurism grows more intimate as he pictures himself hooking her black gown, seeing through the opening 'her lithe body sheathed in an orange shift'. The shift 'slips its ribbons of moorings at her shoulders' and reveals her silver fishlike body 'shimmering with silvery scales' (*GJ* 7). She anticipates Gerty MacDowell when, 'virgin most prudent', her 'sudden moving knee' catches her skirt back and the viewer sees 'a white lace edging of an underskirt lifted unduly' (*GJ* 9).

The beholder appreciates the piscine or floral delicacy of her body but lacks access to her thoughts, her anxieties, her dreams. This is true even in the most bizarre sketch of the sequence, the interpolated dream scene that depicts her as a snake attacking him with a cold, aggressive lust:

> —I am not convinced that such activities of the mind or body can be called unhealthy —
> She speaks. A weak voice from beyond the cold stars. Voice of wisdom. Say on! O, say again, making me wise! This voice I never heard.
> She coils towards me along the crumpled lounge. I cannot move or speak. Coiling approach of starborn flesh. Adultery of wisdom. No. I will go. I will.—Jim, love! —
> —Soft sucking lips kiss my left armpit: a coiling kiss on myriad veins. I burn! I crumple like a burning leaf! From my right armpit a fang of flame leaps out. A starry snake has kissed me: a cold nightsnake. I am lost!
> —Nora! —   (GJ 15)

Paradoxically, her coldness inflames and terrifies Joyce; she is portrayed as a 'starry snake' (like Satan, who was once Lucifer, the lightbringer in the night sky) whose temptation he cannot resist, and he falls. It seems to be a dream punctuated by Nora calling to Joyce and Joyce calling back.[18]

Unlike *Chamber Music*, *Giacomo Joyce* seems to have been composed with no other listener (or viewer) in mind than 'Giacomo' himself. Such intense self-referentiality makes it difficult to trace the course of the imagined affair without the aid of biographical information to flesh out the details, and the disjointed patches of narrative are partially connected through literary allusions. Many early accounts of *Giacomo Joyce* therefore focus on biography or allusion, and the socio-political implications of Joyce's project in *Giacomo Joyce* remain less fully explored. It is less clear, for example, how Joyce's disturbingly ambivalent treatment of the young Jewish woman in *Giacomo Joyce* accords with his later presentations of women and Jews in *Ulysses*. The German graphic artist Paul Wunderlich has interpreted Joyce's interest in his student as erotic desire mingled with prophetic compassion for what would later be done to the Jews in Nazi-controlled Europe.[19] *Giacomo Joyce* plays on the incommensurability of artistic and social power, as well as that of sexual and racial privilege, but it does so in a way that protects Joyce's own privilege as a man, a gentile, and a writer. In *Exiles*, as well as in his later works, Joyce is quick to recognize such imbalances of power, devising a variety of strategies for drawing attention to them, but in *Giacomo Joyce*, as in the epiphanies and *Chamber Music*, such privileges are protected by the fear of their reversal.

Exiles

Exiles is the hinge between *Portrait* and *Ulysses*. Some would call it a rusty hinge, because critics and directors alike have had trouble figuring out what to make of it. What is it actually *about*? In the first published version of this essay, I argued that it was about 'the lack of compassion that precludes relationship', but I would now broaden this claim: *Exiles* is primarily about *estrangement*, especially estrangement at home, both interpersonal and political.[20] This play focuses on a homecoming that turns out to be what Freud called *Unheimlich*. Instead of uncanniness, however, the unhomelike Ireland to which the Rowan family returns produces torment. The agony is caused by a fundamental dishonesty: individuals presume to know the meaning of both freedom and individual identity, but that 'knowledge' emerges as self-deception. When their (conventional) expectations of allegiance are violated, they experience the other as a traitor. The possibility of love, or connection, remains shadowy because love is only possible when the possessive expectations that strive to shape it are confronted and dissolved.[21] Joyce writes that Richard's jealousy 'must reveal itself as the very immolation of the pleasure of possession on the altar of love' (*E* 114). None of the characters in *Exiles* is free, either sexually or politically; all are imprisoned and estranged from one another by unexamined expectations, misconceptions, and self-deceptions. As Stephen Dedalus will proclaim in *Ulysses*, pointing to his head, 'In here it is that I must kill the priest and the king' (*U* 15.4436–7). *Exiles* is a turning point in Joyce's lifelong affair with the beauty and difficulty of the strange because it dramatizes Richard Rowan's difficult struggle to accept the fact that strangeness is *internal* and domestic. The feeling of being an exile can be strongest at home, where it clashes with the fiction that everyone is or should be similar. The prospect of adultery produces a comparable kind of alienation in which the reality and unpredictability of human desire and need are brought into contact with the fiction that the feeling of absolute fidelity to a beloved is the only desire one will ever feel.

Exiles, then, is a play about the nets that draw one down, the nets that Stephen idealistically vowed to fly by, as if such flight were easy and the nets themselves readily apparent. The history of the play's composition shows that Joyce included and then excised references to the political situation in Ireland in 1912, when the play is set.[22] In an earlier version Roberto Prezioso, one of the models for Robert Hand, referred to Nora as 'Little Ireland'; the play once contained four references to Ireland, three of which were subsequently deleted.[23] Joyce also excised a reference to Home Rule that expressed uncertainty about whether it would ever come, and the play refers to two statues that John MacNicholas argues are those of William

Smith O'Brien and Charles Stewart Parnell. Richard even once claimed ('bitterly') that the language of God is Irish.[24] Andrew Gibson provides additional context for the political background in the play from the summer of 1912 (when the action takes place) to 1915, when Joyce finished writing it. The prospect that a Home Rule bill would finally pass, with Prime Minister Asquith's support, was tearing the country apart. Ironically, the Irish nationalists and the Liberal English government were on one side, with the Irish Unionists and English Conservatives on the other.[25] Gibson, then, reads *Exiles* as relying upon a subtle and complex allegorical structure in which Bertha is Ireland being fought over by a Protestant (Robert) and a Catholic (Richard). He argues that *Exiles* owes its desolation to that period of Irish history, in which 'closeness and interdependency coexisted with ... intense ... mutual alienation'.[26]

If the political situation in Ireland was producing alienation, and Joyce's play is about *Unheimlich* estrangement, it seems odd that Joyce would decide to downplay the play's embeddedness in its specific historical context, unless he was trying to broaden his focus to highlight the difficulty and painfulness of freeing oneself from inherited and learned beliefs and allegiances. The issue that seems to concern Joyce the most has to do not with the passage of a Home Rule bill or even women's suffrage; it is neither a Protestant nor a Catholic issue. It does not rely upon a binary logic at all, whether that is played out as women/men, Catholic/Protestant, or Irish/English. The real issue is a conceptual one; how can adults strip away the structure that has been given to their thinking and their choices by their social and historical environments? Can radical innocence (which Joyce calls 'virginity of the soul' and associates with genuine freedom) be regained, and, if so, how?[27]

In *Exiles,* Richard abdicates rule over his home, because he sees such dominion, with its possessiveness, politics, and intrigue, as incompatible with the freedom he associates with innocence, honesty, and the painful generosity of allowing the other to make her own choices. Such freedom is not uniformly or faithfully partisan – it cannot be. That may be what Joyce was doing by retaining the allusion to the Irishman Archibald Hamilton Rowan (1751–1854) while having Richard deny any kinship to him: Rowan was a controversial figure because he valued freedom of conscience over allegiance. Joyce may have envisioned Rowan as someone who escaped not only capture (by throwing his hat on the haha at Clongowes Wood) but also partisan brain-washing altogether. And he did so by being in two places at once, over the haha where his hat remained, and hiding behind a secret door in the castle; he was more than one person, capable of adopting more than one set of clothes or more than one side in an argument. Born in London, he was prevented from visiting Ireland until he was twenty-five. Although he joined the United Irishmen and became friends of Napper Tandy and Wolfe Tone, he later witnessed the Reign of Terror while in exile in France and then (presumably because of what he had seen in France) declined to help Tone free Ireland. He supported Catholic Emancipation *and* the Act of Union; because his allegiances seemed unpredictable, Peel called him a traitor in 1825.[28] Rowan, as someone sent to Newgate Prison for a crime he didn't commit and who escaped to other countries (France, America, and finally back to Ireland), may be the closest we can get to someone who lived by political and spiritual principles akin to those of Joyce himself. His loyalty seems to have been to his conscience rather than to one party or another, and that loyalty seems to have been strengthened when he found himself with a front-row seat to the French Revolution.

Exiles, then, may have an allegorical dimension, but it is not an allegory, and certainly not a political one. It is a drama about the difficulty of freeing oneself from inherited beliefs and from partisanship of all kinds, from political partisanship to fidelity to a spouse. This is why I think Harold Pinter's production of *Exiles* in 1970–1 may have been the only effective one because when he instructed the actors to speak in a monotone it conveyed the suggestion that their ideas and opinions were not their own; there is something robotic, something fundamentally unfree and anti-spiritual, about the faithful.[29]

This gets us to Richard's 'wound of doubt.' He calls it 'restless' and 'living' (*PE* 265) – it is a wound but its effects are painfully liberating. Although the language he uses to describe his doubt is melodramatic, it nonetheless insists that freedom should not be idealized. It cannot be gained through a coup or through the passage of a law alone; it is a practice, and that practice is painful. Doubt, then, is not what readers and critics often assume it to be: it is not a misgiving, not a passive uncertainty, but an active ethical principle. Alessandro Francesco Bruni once said that Joyce 'doesn't even believe the bread he is eating', but that does not mean he is nihilistic or incapable of commitment; it means he understands that the disabling lies of culture are readily internalized, and his wary, principled skepticism is a necessary safeguard for keeping conscience alive and flexible.[30] Richard Rowan says at one point, 'You are trying to put that idea into my head but I warn you I don't take my ideas from other people' (*PE* 176). Rowan, like Joyce, is trying not to join a team or restrict the honesty and growth of the people around him through an overly simplistic form of allegiance. His commitment is to honesty, especially honesty with one's self. This is a position we see Stephen adopting in a different context in 'Scylla and Charybdis'; when asked if he believes his own theory, Stephen says, 'No' (*U* 9.1067). But that doesn't mean he disbelieves it either; it means only that he sees categorical forms of belief as dangerous; his beliefs are experimental, heuristic, and provisional rather than limiting to the freedom of those around him.

The recipe for exile is dishonesty (especially to oneself) combined with partisanship and an insistence on the uniqueness, discreteness, and superiority of the self. As their names imply, Robert has been conditioned to be a robber and Richard is the rich man on whom he would prey, but Richard and Robert also care deeply for one another. It is their fidelity to situational positions that puts them at odds and strangles their friendship. Richard worries that he and Bertha are struggling with a similar impasse. So he places his faith in their son Archie, the future, who might be able to elude such predictable polarizations. Archie, like the patriot whose name he shares, seems still to be free.

There is a lot of work still to be done on *Exiles*. It is not a rusty hinge, but a lynchpin; understanding what Joyce was trying to work out (and why he needed to do it through drama rather than narrative) is essential to any effort to put together the arc of his career. It raises urgent questions about the nature of actual freedom and what must be discarded in order for acculturated adults to regain the freedom we can still see in children. The play implies that exile (with its attendant loneliness, humiliation, and deadness of spirit) is a sentence that society has imposed on most adults. As Joyce writes in his notes for the play, Richard's object is to produce 'a difficult good' (*PE* 343). Richard's abandonment of Bertha is designed to put her in the position of Jesus in the garden of olives: 'It is the soul of woman left naked and alone that it may come to an understanding of its own nature' (*PE* 344). Her temperament will be reborn, suffused with 'the wonder of her soul at its own solitude and at her beauty, formed and dissolving itself eternally amid the clouds of mortality' (*PE* 344). One could argue that the main import of the play, according to Joyce's notes, is not political or religious but spiritual. It is based on the parable of the Prodigal Son, in which Robert is the elder brother. 'The father took the side of the prodigal. This is probably not the way of the world – certainly not in Ireland: but Jesus' Kingdom was not of this world nor was or is his wisdom' (*PE* 344). The way of Ireland, then, is the way of the world, which is something Joyce himself seemed to be working very hard to escape.

Notes

1. For an argument that *Giacomo Joyce* should be approached as a work in its own right, see Louis Armand and Clare Wallace, eds., *Giacomo Joyce: Envoys of the Other* (Prague: Litteraria Pragensia, 2006), especially the introduction by Louis Armand.

2. See Michel Delville, 'Epiphanies and Prose Lyrics: James Joyce and the Poetics of the Fragment', in *Giacomo Joyce: Envoys of the Other*, ed. Armand and Wallace, pp. 101–30.
3. For more on the biographical circumstances behind *Giacomo Joyce*, see Vicki Mahaffey, '*Giacomo Joyce*' in *A Companion to Joyce Studies*, ed. Zack Bowen and James C. Carens (Westport, CT: Greenwood Press, 1984). See also Mahaffey, 'Fascism and Silence: The Coded History of Amalia Popper', *James Joyce Quarterly* 32.3/4 (1995): 501–22. Several essays in *Giacomo Joyce: Envoys of the Other* suggest additional women who may have contributed to the female figure in *Giacomo Joyce* as does John McCourt, *The Years of Bloom: James Joyce in Trieste 1904–1920* (Dublin: The Lilliput Press, 2000). See also Erik Schneider's recent video on Bice Ricchetti Randegger, https://www.youtube.com/watch?v=XbtVU5mmh7U.
4. This phrase is also used by the unnamed woman of *Giacomo Joyce*.
5. 'Continuous manuscript' is Hans Walter Gabler's term for the successive autograph notations that he uses as the copytext for his edition of *Ulysses*. Hans Walter Gabler, *Ulysses: A Critical and Synoptic Edition* (New York: Garland, 1984), vol. 3, p. 1895.
6. Robert Scholes and Richard M. Kain, eds. *The Workshop of Daedalus: James Joyce and the Raw Materials for 'A Portrait of the Artist as a Young Man'* (Evanston, IL: Northwestern University Press, 1965). Facsimiles of all the epiphanies were later published in *JJA* vol. 7, '*A Portrait of the Artist as a Young Man*': *A Facsimile of Epiphanies, Notes, Manuscripts and Typescripts*, ed. Hans Walter Gabler. The epiphanies were collected with the poems, the 1904 'Portrait' essay, and *Giacomo Joyce* in *PSW*. A new edition of the epiphanies appeared in 2024: *Collected Epiphanies of James Joyce: A Critical Edition*, eds. Sangam McDuff, Angus MacFadzean, and Morris Beja (Gainesville: University Press of Florida, 2024).
7. Both Hugh Kenner and S. L. Goldberg argued that Joyce's omission represents a deliberate attempt on Joyce's part to weaken Stephen's aesthetic theories. See Hugh Kenner, *Dublin's Joyce* (Bloomington: University of Indiana Press, 1966), ch. 9, and S. L. Goldberg, *The Classical Temper* (New York: Barnes and Noble, 1961), chs. 2 and 3, which prompted Robert Scholes to contest the meaningfulness of the term epiphany in a controversial article, 'Joyce and the Epiphany: The Key to the Labyrinth?', *Sewanee Review* 72.1 (1964): 65–77.
8. Morris Beja attempts to get around the difficulty posed by the 'spiritual' nature of epiphany by redefining spirituality; see *Epiphany in the Modern Novel* (London: Peter Owen, 1971), p. 74.
9. Stanislaus Joyce, *My Brother's Keeper*, ed. Richard Ellmann (London: Faber, 1958), pp. 134–5.
10. See, for example, Florence Walzl, 'The Liturgy of the Epiphany Season and the Epiphanies of Joyce', *PMLA* 80 (1965): 436–50. Even Robert Scholes asserts that 'the Epiphanies themselves for the most part bear out Stephen's condemnation of them. They are trivial and supercilious or florid and lugubrious, in the main. Their chief significance is in the use Joyce often made of them in his later works' ('Joyce and the Epiphany', p. 73).
11. Morris Beja has found at least thirteen of the extant epiphanies in *Stephen Hero*, twelve in *Portrait*, four in *Ulysses*, and one in *Finnegans Wake*. See Morris Beja,

'Epiphany and the Epiphanies', in *A Companion to Joyce* Studies, ed. Bowen and Carens, pp. 710–3.
12. Several of Joyce's poems are literally songs, among the most interesting of which is 'Post ulixem scriptum' (to be sung to the tune of 'Molly Brannigan'). Most of the extant poems and poetic fragments are available in facsimile in *JJA* I, ed. A. Walton Litz, and many are listed in Paul Doyle's bibliographical register of 'Joyce's Miscellaneous Verse', *James Joyce Quarterly* 2 (1965): 90–6 and his 'Addenda', *James Joyce Quarterly* 4 (1967): 71. One of the most influential arguments about the musical nature of *Chamber Music* is that of Herbert Howarth, '*Chamber Music* and Its Place in the Joyce Canon', in *James Joyce Today*, ed. Thomas F. Staley (Bloomington: Indiana University Press, 1966), pp. 11–27. On the similarity between *Chamber Music* and Elizabethan songs and airs, see Myra Russel, 'The Elizabethan Connection: The Missing Score of James Joyce's *Chamber Music*', *James Joyce Quarterly* 18 (1981): 133–45. There is an extensive history of musical adaptations and performances of *Chamber Music*, including Fire Records' 2008 two-disc musical setting of all the poems by various artists (discogs.com/James-Joyce-Various-Chamber-Music-1907-1-36/release/1652180) and *Goldenhair*, released by Node Records in 2017, featuring twenty-one of the poems set to music by Brian Byrne and performed by different singers (noderecords.com/release/goldenhair/).
13. *Chamber Music* does however pose uncharacteristic problems of attribution, since Stanislaus Joyce told W. Y. Tindall that both the title and the final arrangement of the poems were his. See *JJA* vol. 1 'Chamber Music', 'Pomes Penyeach' and Occasional Verse: A Facsimile of Manuscripts, Typescripts and Proofs, ed. A. Walton Litz.
14. James Joyce, *Chamber Music*, ed. William York Tindall (New York: Columbia University Press, 1954), pp. 70–80.
15. For Howarth's article, see note 12.
16. See David Hayman, ed. *A First Draft Version of 'Finnegans Wake'* (Austin: University of Texas Press, 1963), pp. 210–11.
17. Critics have suggested that Amalia Popper may be the primary but not the only source for the woman in *Giacomo Joyce*. An interesting addition to that composite is another one of Joyce's pupils, Anna Maria Schleimer. See Renzo Crivelli, 'A Portrait of the Artist as an Imaginary Casanova', in *Giacomo Joyce: Envoys of the Other*, ed. Armand and Wallace, pp. 295 ff. Crivelli says that 'she had no Jewish connections', (p. 297), but Brenda Maddox identifies her as 'part-Jewish' in *Nora: A Biography of Nora Joyce* (New York: Fawcett Columbine, 1988), p. 117. John McCourt would add Emma Cuzzi to this list, but he goes on to argue that it isn't important to identify the woman. 'Epiphanies of Language, Longing, Liminality in Giacomo Joyce', in *Giacomo Joyce: Envoys of the Other*, ed. Armand and Wallace, pp. 232–3. More recently, Erik Schneider has added Bice Ricchetti Randegger to the list: see www.youtube.com/watch?v=XbtVU5mmh7U.
18. One of the most illuminating recent discussions of *Giacomo Joyce* is by Ruben Borg, 'Love in Joyce: A Philosophical Apprenticeship', *Joyce Studies Annual* (2014): 42–62. Borg argues that *Giacomo Joyce* marks a shift in Joyce's view of love from a scholastic-theological definition to an understanding of love as intertwined with pity and desire, a view that Borg compares with Dante's.

19. *Giacomo Joyce*, with an introduction by Hermann Lenz (Dielsdorf: Matthieu AG, 1976). The edition of ten lithographs was limited to 125 copies. In Vicki Mahaffey, 'Wunderlich on Joyce: The Case against Art', *Critical Inquiry* 17 (Summer 1991): 171–91, I analyze the relation between Wunderlich's illustrations and *Giacomo Joyce*.
20. Vicki Mahaffey, 'Joyce's Shorter Works', in *The Cambridge Companion to James Joyce*, ed. Derek Attridge (Cambridge: Cambridge University Press, 1990), p. 200.
21. A. Nicholas Fargnoli and Michael Patrick Gillespie approach the problem of love from a different but equally compelling angle: they argue that 'estrangement [which produces the same effect as literal exile] ... results ... from the failure of unrestrained freedom to sustain friendship and love'. They suggest that Richard gives Bertha too much freedom, which causes her to suffer from 'mental paralysis' (Joyce's phrase), and they compare the paralysis that results from unlimited freedom with that produced by 'claustrophobia and constriction', as in *Dubliners*. See A. Nicholas Fargnoli and Michael Patrick Gillespie, *Exiles: A Critical Edition* (Gainesville: University Press of Florida, 2016), p. 11.
22. See John MacNicholas, *James Joyce's 'Exiles': A Textual Companion* (New York: Garland, 1979), especially the 'Historical Essay', pp. 5–50.
23. Ibid., pp. 10, 39.
24. Ibid., p. 39.
25. Andrew Gibson, *The Strong Spirit* (Oxford: Oxford University Press, 2013), pp. 213–32.
26. Gibson, p. 222. Gibson notes that the other main theme in the newspapers in 1912 was women's suffrage, linked to the nationalist movement by shared demands for self-governance and self-reliance (p. 230).
27. See Joyce's notes to *Exiles* (PE 343) and Richard's comment at PE 196.
28. MacNicholas, pp. 197–9.
29. Performed at London's Mermaid Theatre in 1970 and again by the Royal Shakespeare Company at the Aldwych Theatre the following year. Both productions stressed the quiet, threateningly conventional seriousness of the play. Bernard Benstock described the effect: 'All the lines were read with precise politeness at a slow tempo, with little emotion ever allowed to violate the proprieties; an undertone of quiet menace pervaded throughout, giving a certain shape even to the most "innocent" lines; and no suggestion of Joycean irony was permitted in the interpretation. It was magnificent, but it was not quite Joyce.' Bernard Benstock, '*Exiles*' in *A Companion to Joyce Studies*, ed. Bowen and Carens, pp. 361–2. See also John MacNicholas, 'The Stage History of *Exiles*', *James Joyce Quarterly* 19.1 (1981): 9–26. In a forthcoming book on theatricality in Joyce, Valérie Bénéjam treats *Exiles* as a theatrical failure, arguing that its disappointing reception prompted Joyce to infuse theatricality into his fiction. She also has an intriguing chapter on the epiphanies (Gainesville: University Press of Florida, scheduled for April 2026).
30. Alessandro Francini Bruni, 'Joyce Stripped Naked in the Piazza', *James Joyce Quarterly* 14.2 (1977): 127–59, 154.

7

SEAMUS DEANE

Joyce the Irishman

Joyce's repudiation of Catholic Ireland and his countering declaration of artistic independence are well-known and integral features of his life-long dedication to writing. The most important of Joyce's Irish predecessors was the poet James Clarence Mangan (1803–49), whose tragic life was represented by Joyce as an emblem of the fate of the Irish artist, betrayed through identification of himself with his country. Joyce's obsession with betrayal manifests itself in the lectures he delivered on Mangan, in Dublin in 1902 and in Trieste in 1907. Wherever he looked, in Irish political or literary history, he found betrayal. The great political crisis that dominated his early life – the fall of Charles Stewart Parnell – governed this reading of his country's past and helped him define the nature of the embattled relationship between him and his Irish audience. Parnell was, in Joyce's view, a heroic spirit brought low by his own people, who listened to Parnell's plea that they should not throw him to the English wolves. 'They did not throw him to the English wolves: they tore him apart themselves' (*OCPW* 196).

Betrayal was a Joycean obsession.[1] But betrayal implies a preceding solidarity, a communion between the victim and his treacherous compatriots. The most appealing form of solidarity was offered by Irish nationalism, in its variant forms, from the United Irishmen of 1798 to the Young Ireland movement of the 1840s and the more recent Fenian and Home Rule movements. Mangan's art, in Joyce's view, was caught in the toils of an implacable political crisis. So 'the most distinguished poet of the modern Celtic world' (*OCPW* 131) suffered oblivion in his own land because he was, on the one hand, not national enough and, on the other, too national ever to be appreciated for his own remarkable qualities as a poet. This paradox leads to Joyce's declaration that if Mangan is to achieve the posthumous recognition he deserves, it will be without the help of his countrymen; and if he is ever accepted by the Irish as their national poet it will only be when the conflicts between Ireland and the foreign powers ('the Anglo-Saxon and the

Roman Catholic') are settled. The history of Mangan, so construed, was a cautionary tale for the Irish artist.

Other aspects of Mangan's career have a direct bearing on Joyce. Mangan is a characteristic nineteenth-century Irish author in his fascination with translation as an act of repossession. He 'betrays' other languages into English, but his ultimate 'betrayal' is that of his own authorship. He is an intermediate, not an original author and yet, because of that, a central figure in the new cultural nationalism led by Sir Samuel Ferguson, Thomas Davis, and others.[2]

Joyce's own career is dominated by similar linguistic anxieties. He could write the spiritual history of his own country only when he found that mode of English appropriate to Irish experience, through which the Irish could repossess their experience in an English that was unmistakably an Irish English. In that light, Mangan was as important to him as was William Carleton to W. B. Yeats.[3] Although he shared the general view that Mangan was a nationalist poet, he also recognized that the poetry would not be seen for what it truly was as long as the blight of the two imperialisms, British and Roman Catholic, prevailed. Nor did he believe that nationalism was anything other than an extension of those imperialisms, despite its antagonism to them.[4] Thus, in Ireland, the problem of being a writer was linguistic and political. Joyce looked with scepticism on the possibility of maintaining one's integrity as an artist while being involved with a communal enterprise. Yet he also seems to claim that such integrity could only be achieved when communal and not merely personal possibility was realized in art. In that respect, his project went beyond what Mangan came to represent for him.

If Mangan served as the primary Irish example in Irish conditions of the essential loneliness of the artist, Oscar Wilde was the most notorious Irish example in English conditions. Joyce chooses to read the life and work of Wilde in a religious, specifically Catholic, light. Wilde died a Roman Catholic. For Joyce, there is a peculiar fitness in this last act of Wilde's life, in that it could also be felt as the last, convergent act of his art. It was in accord with 'the vital centre of Wilde's art: sin. He deceived himself by thinking that he was the harbinger of the good news of neo-paganism to the suffering people' (*OCPW* 151). Once more, we see Joyce translating an author into his own image or into the image of his own protagonist, Stephen Dedalus. Wilde is a type of the heroic artist brought down, like Parnell, by the mob. But his life, like Mangan's, contains within itself a spiritual truth that has been obscured by the public version of his career. In Wilde's case, that truth was best represented in his novel *Dorian Gray*. Wilde, as an artist, is no more the preacher of the new paganism to an enslaved people than was

Mangan the preacher of freedom to an oppressed community. In each case, the truth is to be found in the apartness of the artist, known only because it is preceded by a repudiation of fake solidarity. Wilde's peculiar blend of socialism and dandyism and his assiduous attempts to create a myth of himself have their affinities with Mangan's careful creation of an adversarial and tragic version of his own life. Mangan's re-siting of his poetry within the frame of the 'Orient', is analogous to Wilde's presentation of his own art as the 'new paganism' confronting bourgeois society. Like Mangan, Wilde assimilates natures foreign to his own, producing the fiction of a new and revolutionary community both as an alternative to existing social and political forms and as an antidote to and assertion of separateness. Again, we are involved in an act of translation. An original state of belonging is exchanged for a secondary state of separateness, which then, through its assimilation of 'foreign' materials, tries to reconstitute a more genuine communality.

For Joyce too, this is a central problem. He returns to it in the opening chapter of *Ulysses*, in which Buck Mulligan mouths the doctrine of Wilde's 'new paganism' (*U* 1.176). Mulligan, Wilde's 'Irish imitator' (*Letters II* 150), is a betrayer, the 'Usurper' (*U* 1.744), who refers to Caliban's rage at not seeing his face in a mirror and exclaims to Stephen, 'If only Wilde were alive to see you', which evokes Stephen's bitter retort that the mirror is a symbol of Irish art, 'the cracked looking-glass of a servant' (*U* 1.143–7). The mirror that is held up to nature is cracked, and it belongs to a servile race, a race of imitators, a people that cannot bear to see its own sorry reflection in the glass, nor bear to see that its authentic nature is not reflected in the glass. If it has any representational power at all, it offers only distortion, caricature.

Joyce thus claims that the issue of representation is critical, not to be deflected by Mangan's nationalism, by Wilde's 'new paganism', or by the imitative servility of a Buck Mulligan. Joyce sees his own role as that of the artist who will not, like Mangan, be distorted in the glass of communal desire. He will be the true artist. He will escape false representation and, in doing so, come to terms with the medium in which this representation has been made – the vexed medium of a language that carries within itself the idea of the re-presentation in one form of a culture that initially existed in another, earlier form. In an article of 1907, 'Ireland at the Bar', Joyce protested at the misrepresentation of Ireland to the world and chose, as an illustration of his theme, the story of a namesake, Myles Joyce, who was executed for a murder he did not commit. Tried in an English-speaking court, he knew no English. His language was Irish. For James Joyce, he is a symbol, one he will revert to again in *Finnegans Wake*. 'The figure of this bewildered old man, left over from a culture which is not ours, a deaf-mute before his judge, is a symbol of the Irish nation at the bar of public opinion'

(*OCPW*146). Representation is a language problem, but it is also a problem to decide what is to be represented when we have only a distortion of some putative original.

In *The Decay of Lying* (1891), one of Wilde's personae had confronted the inversion of the belief that art imitates life:

> I can quite understand your objection to art being treated as a mirror. You think it would reduce genius to the position of a cracked looking glass. But you don't mean to say that you seriously believe that Life imitates Art, that Life in fact is the mirror, and Art the reality?[5]

In looking in the cracked mirror that Mulligan has taken from the maid's room of his aunt's house, Stephen sees himself as others see him. What looks back at him from the servant's mirror is 'Life'; the consciousness that surveys this reflection is 'Art'. The mirror is offered him by the fake artist who steals from the servile the emblem of representation. This is of a piece with Joyce's objection to the Irish Literary Revival, expounded with force and bitterness in his pamphlet of 1901, 'The Day of the Rabblement'.

The artist who 'courts the favour of the multitude' (*OCPW* 51) becomes a slave to it. Joyce says that such an artist's 'true servitude is that he inherits a will broken by doubt and a soul that yields up all its hate to a caress; and the most seeming-independent are those who are the first to reassume their bonds' (*OCPW* 52). Enslavement to the 'rabblement' is the governing condition of representation. This truth had made itself evident in Mangan and had been seen by Wilde; the art of both had been cruelly punished by it. Now, in 1901, it was manifesting itself again in the work of the Irish National Theatre and its concession to folk-art, a sorry collapse after a promising beginning. Joyce was opposed to the folkish elements of the Irish Revival, which to him seemed to be dangerously close to committing itself to a version of pseudo-Irishness, once the preserve of the stage-Irish figure of nineteenth-century England and, by the last decade of the century, becoming the preserve of the newly 'Celtic' Irish. Yet Joyce had much in common with the Revival writers. In their work, Ireland, or an idea of Ireland, embodied vitality and the possibility of a new kind of community, radically different from that of the industrialized democracies. The distinction was enhanced by the transformation of Irish rural society, as in the famous instance of J. M. Synge's *The Playboy of the Western World*, where Mayo, the home of the Land League and the Agrarian War of the 1880s, became the site of the self-realization through language of the 'stuttering lout', Christy Mahon.[6] Joyce, like Wilde and George Bernard Shaw, was a Dublin writer. For him, as for them, Ireland was a negative idea, a place that threatened the artist's freedom and integrity. All three came from families that had been broken by various forms of fecklessness and alcoholism. They too transformed a bitter reality. Wilde became a dandy, Shaw became GBS, and Joyce became the professional exile from a home he never, imaginatively speaking, left. These three cosmopolitan writers, like the cultural nationalists of the revival, produced work of a self-conscious linguistic virtuosity in which English was manipulated to the point at which mastery in it began to sound like the mastery that can be achieved over a foreign language in which one had previously known incompetence. Like Mangan, Joyce and his contemporaries achieved representation of the idea of Ireland as an exercise in translation into a new language, hyphenated with English, but not English.

Joyce made it clear that, in his opinion, the revival was conceding to public pressure by allowing a caricatured, but popular, version of Ireland to become the abiding image of the Abbey Theatre. This was wrong on a number of grounds. It deprived the artist of his independence; it nurtured provincialism, and it did so in the guise of a return to the 'natural'. Exile safeguarded independence; cosmopolitanism helped to avoid provincialism; and the return to the natural was to be achieved not by a romanticizing of rural and peasant life, or of the idea of the Celt and his lost language, but by an unflinching realism that, like Ibsen's, stripped the mask from the pharisaic middle-class society of urban Europe and exposed its spiritual hypocrisy and impoverishment. In that respect, Ireland was indeed a special country. It lived under the political domination of England and the religious domination of Rome while it espoused a rhetoric of freedom, uniqueness, especial privilege. Ireland was, in fact, especially underprivileged and was, on that account, more susceptible to and more in need of an exemplary art than any other European country. It was in Joyce's art that the interior history of his country could, for the first time, be written. Joyce set himself up as the anatomist of Irish illusions, but this did not in any sense inhibit him from believing that, under the 'lancet of my art', 'the cold steel pen' (U 1.152–3), the soul of the country would be revealed. He medicalized the condition of his culture and subjected it to a surgical analysis. But the surgeon in Joyce attended upon the corpse of a dead or moribund country; the priest in Joyce attended upon the soul that was released from its terminal condition. If Ireland was to be seen, it would be in the full light of an Ibsenite dawn, not in the glimmer of a Celtic twilight. The revival was, from its inception, an anachronism. It was a bogus attempt to revive the old Gaelic culture that lay beyond the pale of the modern consciousness.

Joyce's civilization was not, therefore, that of Myles Joyce, of Yeats and Lady Gregory or the Abbey Theatre, or of Mangan. Equally, it was not that of the dramatists Richard Brinsley Sheridan, Oliver Goldsmith, Wilde, and

Shaw, all of whom performed the role of 'court jester to the English' (*OCPW* 149). It was the civilization of Catholic Dublin, related to but distinct from that of Catholic Ireland. Joyce tried to persuade the publisher, Grant Richards, that his collection of stories, *Dubliners*, was about a city that still had not been presented, or represented, to the world. It is an historical but not yet an imaginative reality. Although Dublin, Joyce claims, has been a capital for 'thousands of years' and is said to be the second city of the British Empire, no writer has yet 'presented Dublin to the world'. Furthermore, 'the expression "Dubliner" seems to me to have some meaning and I doubt that the same can be said for such words as "Londoner" and "Parisian"' (*Letters II* 122). In the following year, 1906, the publisher received from Joyce a sequence of famous letters, defending his text from charges of indecency and suggestions for changes, and declaring the importance of this 'chapter of moral history' as 'the first step towards the spiritual liberation of my country'. Richards is asked to 'Reflect for a moment on the history of the literature of Ireland as it stands at present written in the English language before you condemn this genial illusion of mine ...' (*Letters I* 63). 'It is not my fault', he writes a month later, 'that the odour of ashpits and old weeds and offal hangs round my stories. I seriously believe that you will retard the course of civilization in Ireland by preventing the Irish people from having one good look at themselves in my nicely polished looking-glass' (*Letters I* 63–4). This uncracked mirror, owned by a radically independent artist, was going to reflect a reality no-one had presented before. Dublin would find it an unwelcome sight, but Dublin and Ireland would be liberated by it. Joyce is an author without native predecessors; he is an artist who intends to have the effect of a missionary.

First, provincialism had to be exposed and explained as a disease, a paralysis of the will. In one sense, the clinical and 'scrupulous meanness' (*Letters II* 134) of the style of *Dubliners* is perfectly competent 'to betray the soul of that hemiplegia or paralysis which many consider a city' (*Letters I* 55). But Joyce's enterprise was founded on a paradox. Dublin was an absence, a nowhere, a place that was not really a city or a civilization at all. Joyce wanted to dismantle its provincialism and its pretensions; yet he also sought to envision it as the archetypal modern city, as the unique place in which all human history was rehearsed. It had to be both nowhere and everywhere, absence and presence. Somehow, he had to find the language that would register the city in both aspects. He had to scorn it for its peripherality and praise it for its centrality. Between these two possibilities, his strange language vacilates and develops.

Like the other Irish writers of the turn of the century, Joyce learned the advantages of incorporating into his writing the various dialects or versions of English spoken in Ireland. The chief features of the linguistic situation included a still-living oral tradition that had begun to influence the writing of fiction in Ireland more than sixty years before Joyce was born, in the work of several novelists, William Carleton above all. The English spoken by the mass of the Irish people and partly recorded in the works of these writers was oral-formulaic in its compositional principle and closely related to Irish. Much misunderstanding of this language and its supposed misconstructions was created by the application to it of the conventions of a literate print-culture. The inevitable collisions and confusions were often taken to be characteristic of a particularly 'Irish' cast of mind. This could lead, especially in times of political crisis, to a malign stereotyping of the Irish; it often led also to a benign view of Irish 'eloquence', quick-wittedness, and linguistic self-consciousness.[7]

Dublin was a strange mix of the oral and the literate cultures. It prided itself on its reputation for wit, good conversation, malicious gossip, oratory, drama, and journalism. Joyce's work reflects this aspect of the city's culture. It is a mosaic of set pieces – sermons, speeches, stories, witticisms, rhetorical extravaganzas, and mimicries. The culture of print is also reproduced and parodied. The 'Nausicaa' and 'Oxen of the Sun' episodes in *Ulysses* are among the best-known examples. Pulp-literature and 'high' literature are equally subject to this form of mimicry; language is always being proffered as a species of performance. In fact, the histrionic nature of Joyce's achievement aids and abets his peculiar combination of pedantry and humour. The weighty and arcane learning of a Stephen Dedalus has to be worn lightly if he is to keep his local reputation on the Dublin stage as 'the loveliest mummer of them all' (*U* 1.97–8). Moreover, it is one of the most important of all the Joycean performances that a character should take possession of the language of others, the public language, and render it as his inimitable own. This is one of the several functions of quotation in Joyce's work. The ability to incorporate the words of others into one's own particular language-system is a sign of a 'character', a presence on the Dublin scene. In the first few pages of *Ulysses*, Buck Mulligan quotes Latin, Greek, Wilde, Algernon Charles Swinburne, and Yeats, besides singing a song and blending all of this into his 'hyperborean' (*U* 1.92) conversational assault on Stephen. Quotation is one of the structural principles of *A Portrait of the Artist as a Young Man*: Stephen collects words and quotations with increasing eagerness until the novel finally becomes a quotation from Stephen's own writings. We are to presume that the world that gave itself to him in words has now become junior to his own word-world. To make the world conform to words is a characteristic aspiration of a culture that has found it for so long impossible to make its words conform to the world. The speaker of

Irish-English in the world of increasingly Standard English finds it too difficult to conform to the imperial way. He takes as his motto the advice: 'When in Rome, do as the Greeks do.' It is a linguistic way of subverting a political conquest.

Subversion is part of the Joycean enterprise. However, the bitterness attendant upon it is accompanied by the joy of renovation. There is nothing of political or social significance that Joyce does not undermine and restructure. Dublin and Ireland are dissected and yet both are revitalized; the English language is dismembered and yet reinvigorated; Catholic hegemony is both destroyed and reinstated; the narrowness of Irish nationalism is satirized, and yet its basic impulse is ratified. Even the most deadening features of his culture yield priority to its enlivening, creative aspects. He is one of the few authors who legitimizes the modern world, seeing its apparent randomness and alienation as instances of an underlying diversity and communion. If Dublin offered him nothing else, it at least provided him with the experience of a modern city that was also a knowable community. That sense of community, city-wide and country-wide, was possibly more alive and more widespread in his generation than in any since.

One of Joyce's undergraduate friends, Constantine Curran, has described how effectively Joyce suppressed in his fiction the intellectually vital aspects of life at University College Dublin and how carefully nurtured was the fable of his refusal to sign the student protest against Yeats's play *The Countess Cathleen* in 1899.[8] Similarly, it has been demonstrated how Joyce concentrated on the more derelict areas of Dublin in his effort to portray the city as the centre of paralysis and squalor.[9] In fact, Dublin was experiencing a revival of energies that outmatched anything known since the Act of Union in 1800. He was not unaware of this. In various articles he wrote on Irish political matters, Joyce shows himself to be a supporter of the Sinn Féin movement, which had been founded by Arthur Griffith, and as a rather uncritical admirer of Fenianism and its formidable influence. The most notable of these are the 1907 essays 'Fenianism', 'Home Rule Comes of Age', and 'Ireland at the Bar'; the 1910 article, 'The Home Rule Comet'; and the 1912 piece, 'The Shade of Parnell'. The collaboration between old Fenianism and the new Sinn Féin had, he believed, 'once again remoulded the character of the Irish' (*OCPW* 140). But the Irish parliamentary party at Westminster, which had overthrown its great leader Parnell in 1890, seemed incapable of recognizing that this remodelling had happened at home; instead they naively believed that the transformation of Ireland's fortunes would come from legislative changes in the English system – like the breaking of the veto of the House of Lords. The Irish national character had indeed altered, but the English were their old, unreconstructed selves and would never willingly yield to any separatist doctrine preached in Ireland. Yet the Irish themselves had their own, irredeemably fatal flaw. They could not be faithful to anything. Ireland's willingness to make common cause with British democracy, Joyce claims, should neither surprise nor persuade anyone: 'For seven centuries it has never been a faithful subject of England. Nor, on the other hand, has it been faithful to itself' (*OCPW* 159). Ireland has entered into the British domain but has never really been part of it; the conqueror's language has been adopted but his culture never assimilated; the Irish 'spiritual creators' have been exiled, only then to be boasted about back home. The governing motif of betrayal and the association between Ireland's treatment of its political and artistic heroes is perhaps less important than the implied reason for Ireland's traditional unfaithfulness. Having exiled her spiritual creators, she has no 'soul', no mode of existence in which faithfulness is a meaningful category. Instead of her true soul, she has surrendered all to the authority of the Church, a foreign institution that operates as a political system disguised as a spiritual one. Ireland has remained faithful to that faithless master only because she has been incapable of remaining faithful to her true self. That self, created by the artist, has no existence. Now it must be invented. Its invention demands that a certain view of Dublin, of University College, of Joyce's parents, of Mangan, Wilde, Yeats, and all the others must be accepted as an authentic version of the inner spiritual void in which the Irish artist – James Joyce – must function, creating out of nothing, fascinated by stories that recount the intricacies of betrayal, of the self and of others, as well as opposing stories of fidelity and solidarity. Treachery and fidelity are the terms that determine the development of Joyce's fiction, as they determine his reading of Ireland's past and present. The remodelling of the national character, undertaken by groups like Sinn Féin and the Irish Revival, is indeed a heroic enterprise, but it is a futile one unless it accepts that the remodelling has to begin with the problem of fidelity to Rome rather than with the problem of fidelity or infidelity towards the British system. It is Rome, not London, that rules the Irish mind. London will readily use Rome for its purposes. But the Roman imperium is the more subtle and pervasive because it encroaches on the territory that should be ruled by the artist.

If proof were needed, the developments in Irish political history seemed to provide it. Once Ireland had shaken off the shackles of British rule, Church rule became ever more dominant. 'The Church has made inroads everywhere, so that we are in fact becoming a bourgeois nation, with the Church supplying our aristocracy ... and I do not see much hope for us intellectually.'[10] Yet Joyce's views on the spiritual thraldom of Catholicism are a good deal less interesting than the methods he employed in his fiction to dramatize the profound conflicts that the pressure of Catholicism could generate in those brought up in its all-encompassing ambience. The hostility of the Church towards almost all movements for Irish liberation, from the United Irishmen to the Fenians, Parnell and beyond, is only the most superficial manifestation of these conflicts. At a deeper level, the challenge of Catholicism is to individual liberation, and Joyce, well-trained by the Jesuits and compelled by an attraction for the faith he wished to repudiate, envisaged that particular struggle in terms of the revolt of the artist heretic against official doctrine. Sometimes he modified this into a struggle between an aesthete-heretic against a provincial and philistine Church that had taken possession of the mob mind. But, at root, the conflict was even more painful. It was a conflict between a son and his parents – cultural, religious, biological – and a desperate attempt to go beyond the terms set by such a conflict by producing a theory of the self as its own parent, or, less desperately, a desire of the self for alternative, surrogate parents who would permit the imagination to live its necessarily vicarious existence. This is the plight of Stephen Dedalus in *Ulysses*.

There are two forms of Catholicism in Joyce's work. One is European, the other Irish. European Catholicism, as he has Stephen speak of it in *Ulysses*, is based on the doctrine of the Trinity; Irish Catholicism, influenced in this respect by the Italians, is a more sentimental faith, based on the idea of the Holy Family, the vulgar version of the Trinity. For all his undergraduate extravagance, Stephen is enacting a central Joycean dilemma. Catholicism provides him with two versions of parenthood and of community, Trinity and Holy Family. Literature provides, in the life of Shakespeare, matching versions. The Trinitarian version is that whereby Shakespeare is the author of the play *Hamlet*, which contains Hamlet the Father and Hamlet the Son; it also contains Gertrude, who is the mark in the play of Ann Hathaway's infidelity to Shakespeare. With Claudius and young Hamlet, she helps to create a grotesque version of the Holy Family. Equally, Trinity and Family can be replaced by Greek and Jew, and the relation between these can veer from much nodding in the direction of the Wildean attempt to preach a new Hellenistic paganism to Judaic-Biblical England, to the prurience of Bloom, staring at a Greek statue in the National Museum, observed and described by the pseudo-Greek, fake Wildean Buck Mulligan, who turns to Stephen and says, 'He knows you ... O, I fear me, he is Greeker than the Greeks' (*U* 9.613–15). In this ninth episode, the obsession with betrayal merges with the anxiety to find a basis within oneself for origin. The association between homosexuality and cuckoldry, clearly indicated in this and subsequent passages, includes the association between Greeks and Jews (via Wilde and Swinburne as modern Greeks, and Bloom as modern St Joseph). Further,

'Greek' homosexuality is the 'Love that dare not speak its name' (U 9.659), while 'Jewish' love is linked to the Holy Family, itself a betrayal of the doctrine of the Trinity and carrying within it the inevitable heterosexual betrayal that leaves Joseph a cuckold. In the true beginning, of which Christ's birth is the duplication, was 'the Word'. All through the 'Scylla and Charybdis' episode, the motif of naming, of losing or hiding the name of the father or of the origin, recurs as Stephen weaves his extraordinary theories. Yet for all the Greek and Jewish references, the ultimate reference is to Stephen himself and to Ireland, to Wilde and to Mangan (one of whose best-known poems is 'The Nameless One'), and even, by insinuation (in U 9.660–1), to Thomas Moore, who notoriously 'loved a lord' in the sense that he loved English society and wrote a song, 'O Breathe Not His Name', about Robert Emmet, the rebel, who pleaded that his epitaph not be written until his country took her place among the nations of the earth (see U 11.1274–94). All these sexual references finally achieve their full political dimension as Bloom enters Barney Kiernan's pub to confront the Citizen in episode 12, 'Cyclops'.

The notion of self-authorship, creation of the self by becoming one's own father, is entertained by Stephen in a series of reflections that begin with the invocation of a parent – God the Father, Shakespeare – and move to the notion of the father betrayed – King Hamlet, Saint Joseph – to the repudiation of the betraying woman, thence to the idea of homosexual, all-male love, and finally to the 'economy of heaven' where, as Stephen says, with a flourish, 'there are no more marriages, glorified man, an androgynous angel, being a wife unto himself' (U 9.1051–2). The four participants in this conversation, Mulligan, Best, Eglinton, and Stephen, are all bachelors. When Bloom leaves, passing between Mulligan and Stephen, Mulligan whispers: 'Did you see his eye? He looked upon you to lust after you' (U 9.1209–10). The role of Wilde (and Swinburne) has a clear function in the series of homosexual and literary allusions that punctuate the discussion. Homosexual love, of which he and Swinburne and the Shakespeare of the sonnets are representatives, is here presented as the Greek alternative to the heterosexual love, celebrated in marriage, to which – Stephen claims – Jews are more given than any others. 'Jews ... are of all races the most given to intermarriage' (U 9.783–4). As the conversation breaks up, it is the shadow of the cuckold, Bloom, that passes between the two young bachelors. If betrayal is to be avoided, parenthood, origin, must be removed from others to oneself. It is an impossible position, but then Stephen is, as Mulligan says, 'an impossible person' (U 1.223).

Every heretic mentioned in the text (Sabellius, Photius, Arius, Valentine), every author, every contrasting opposition, signals parenthood, priority, origin. The point is that Stephen is caught in a dream of origin that can never be realized. There is no ultimate beginning; there is only the desire for it, for a total independence from all and everyone else. This desire is itself generated by a fear of betrayal that, in turn, is associated with sexual infidelity. Ireland has betrayed itself over and over again, most recently and memorably in the sexual scandal of the Parnell affair; the Catholic Church betrayed its founding mystery, the Trinity, by substituting for it the story of the Holy Family, in which Joseph is betrayed into the position of the merely nominal father of God. Stephen and Bloom are both involved in parental and marital betrayals that are, in their turn, closely associated with religious affiliation, Christian and Jewish, while the 'Greek' Mulligan is the ultimate betrayer who cannot even recognize his own treachery towards Stephen. Just as he reads the Irish political tradition in the light of this theme, Joyce, through Stephen, reads Shakespeare and the English literary tradition in the same way. Church, state, and culture are the betrayed remnants of an originary purity towards which Stephen, as artist, dedicates himself. In such a situation, only art is beyond betrayal. It is the only activity to which Stephen can give his fidelity because it is a form of production in which his own authorship is secure. The problem is, of course, that Stephen is always about to be an artist. He has his theory complete, but it does not fit with the circumstances of flawed paternity that surround Bloom.

Ulysses is as concerned as *Dubliners* is with failure. The form of the failure is more brilliant because it is the result of sophisticated, exotic, ingenious readings of the past and of the present that are finally disabling for the readers – Stephen and Bloom in particular. The semiotic systems of Dublin, Irish history, literature, are all read under the sign of a betrayal that, while it exposes, does not reveal. That is to say, failure is exposed, but the way to success is not revealed. Stephen, remembering his meeting in Paris with the exiled Fenian Kevin Egan, and the stories of the Fenian escapades and associated Irish political enterprises, thinks of them all as phantasmal, failed and fading attempts: 'Of lost leaders, the betrayed, wild escapes. Disguises, clutched at, gone, not here' (*U* 3.243–4). In his 1907 lecture, 'Ireland, Island of Saints and Sages', Joyce declared, 'It is high time Ireland finished once and for all with failures' (*OCPW* 125). Yet much of his own work is precisely on this theme. He analyzes the psychology of subjection in his people by showing the paralysis that has overtaken them in their endless, futile quest for an origin that will provide them with an identity securely their own. Such an origin is always beyond history, since history, as we have seen, is for him a sequence of betrayals, the effect of which is to leave the Irish people leaderless, subjected to an authoritarian Church, bereft of the spiritual life that only the artist, in his quest for origin, can provide.

Characteristically, when Joyce does find the originary story, it involves a betrayal. The legend of the Fall of Man is an extra-historical narrative, which is repeated in endlessly diverse forms throughout human history. At the centre of this is Irish historical experience. It has the fall of man deeply inscribed upon it, from the story of the fall of the High King Rory O'Connor to the execution of the radical Republican Rory O'Connor in 1923. It moves from the era of Saints and Scholars to the Devil Era of the great modern leader, De Valera. Repetition is the law of this universe; in every event, the originary event reappears. Origin is always with us. Yet the origin is visible only when the story is told in the language that contains all languages, in the Ur-speech that is the language of the dreaming or subconscious mind of HCE, Everyman, who Haveth Childers Everywhere. *Finnegans Wake* is Joyce's Irish answer to an Irish problem. It is written in a ghost language about phantasmal figures; history is haunted by them and embodies them over and over again in specific people, places and tongues. If Ireland could not be herself, then, by way of compensation, the world would become Ireland. Thus is the problem of identity solved. Irish history is world history *in parvo*. The mutilated sequences of war, failure, disaster, lost language, broken culture are brought under the governance of a single, mastering story that renders everything thought to be unique as typical.

Yet just as *Ulysses* had made real order out of apparent chaos, *Finnegans Wake* sustains individuality within the frame of the archetypal. Individual items gain significance when seen as part of an overall pattern. Therefore, if the pattern is sufficiently hospitable, everything can be represented within a system. Nevertheless, the governing pattern has, in itself, an originary meaning that is replicated throughout all subsequent variations. Betrayal linked all the aspects of Irish experience; it is ordained in origin, confirmed in retrospect. The linking theme of transgression and betrayal is legitimized by the nature of language itself. Repetition, puns, homonyms, resemblances, echoes, carefully arranged, reveal a cousinship between the events that these sounds describe. Alliance word-sounds reveal an alliance between those things that the word-sounds represent. Joyce involves himself and us in a stupendous act of retrospective translation, whereby the distinctions and differences between words and languages are collapsed into a basic, originary speech native to the subconscious, not the conscious, mind. This is his version of the lost language of Ireland; it is also the lost language of the Irish soul, that entity not articulated into existence before Joyce. In effect, what this lost language tells is the story of the transgression that led to its loss, the story of the life of the soul lost to the life of the conscious mind, the narrative of an Edenic Ireland that, through sin, became postlapsarian and British.

Here we have the Mangan position transfigured. Where he made all his texts 'secondary' by positing a real or imaginary 'original' from which they derived, Joyce makes all other texts secondary by actually producing the original language of which they are the later derivations. Thus the divine thunder that inaugurates civilization, according to the theory of Vico, who plays a role in *Finnegans Wake* similar to that of Homer in *Ulysses*, can be translated, so to say, into the gunfire of an ambush in the Irish War of Independence or the boom of the guns at the Battle of Waterloo. The reader must go forward to the individual instance and back to the originating example. This is, after all, a dream that we are interpreting, and the language of dreams must, as Freud had shown, go through a series of readings before it can yield a meaning we can recognize, even though the meaning was already there in the original 'language'. This is what Joyce himself had done in reading the careers of Mangan, Parnell, Wilde, the Fenians. The Irish had dreamt in their own language and then betrayed the dream into the English language in such a manner that the original meaning had been lost, misread; as a consequence, for this transgression, they had been punished. English did not translate the dream because the Irish did not possess, had refused to accept, the culture that English represented. So Joyce, following in the steps of all of those who had been busily translating Irish material – especially legendary material – into English, went very much further than the second-hand Carlylese of Standish O'Grady; the Kiltartan dialect of Lady Gregory; or the peasant speech of Synge, who takes a drubbing, chiefly from Mulligan, in the 'Scylla and Charybdis' episode.

Joyce translated in the other direction. He brought English and as many other languages as he could manage – including Irish – back to the literary equivalent of the Indo-European from which they had all sprung. In doing this, he confronted the problem of parenthood, as well as the problem of translation and betrayal, on the level of language itself, not only on the level of language-as-narrative.

Given this, Joyce can indulge as freely as he likes in detail. The minutiae of Dublin life, ever-present throughout *Ulysses*, now undergo a second transformation. The geography of the city and the history of the country were readable there in specific, if generous, contexts. Dublin could be the Mediterranean, and Irish history could be a version of episodes from the Greek legends or from Biblical history. But in *Finnegans Wake*, Dublin's Phoenix Park can be anything from the Garden of Eden to the field of Waterloo. The strangest effect of this titanic effort of translation is that the text is never revealed; rather, it is produced by the reader. There is no question any longer of a skeleton key that will turn all the locks. This translation does not translate. The thousands of proper names in the text are so interwoven that even the minutest knowledge of Irish affairs does not legitimize, say, a reading of the text as a version of Irish history in a Babylonian dialect. Names specify, but these are names that also typify. The treachery that obsessed Joyce is fundamental to his practice of writing. For he leaves us to wonder if the text that he offers is one that has been so fully articulated that it can go no further, or if it is a text that is so encrypted as to invite endless articulation. 'Dublin' had never been represented in literature before. Perhaps he was the first to represent it, or perhaps he was the first to show that 'it' was not ultimately representable.

For all that, a remodelling of the idea of Ireland was under way. The country and culture Joyce repudiated was also the country and culture he re-imagined. The absence could become a presence. Time and again in his writing Joyce characteristically salutes and bids farewell to the Ireland he had left and to the Ireland he created in his absence from it and its absence from him.

Notes

1. See James Alexander Fraser, *Joyce & Betrayal* (London: Palgrave Macmillan, 2016).
2. See Frank O'Connor, *The Backward Look: A Survey of Irish Literature* (London: Macmillan, 1967), pp. 150ff.; Seamus Deane, *A Short History of Irish Literature* (London: Hutchinson, 1986); J. H. Andrews, *A Paper Landscape: The Ordnance Survey in Nineteenth Century Ireland* (London: Oxford University Press, 1975). See also Brian Friel's *Translations* (London: Faber, 1982) for a dramatic treatment of this theme.
3. William Carleton (1794–1869) published his *Traits and Stories of the Irish Peasantry* between 1830 and 1833. He is renowned as the first writer in English to provide an authentic account of the life and speech of the Irish peasantry. W. B. Yeats wrote an introduction to his own selection, *Stories from Carleton* (London: W. Scott, 1889). See also Emer Nolan, *Catholic Emancipations: Irish Fiction from Thomas Moore to James Joyce* (Syracuse, NY: Syracuse University Press, 2007), pp. 96–102.
4. See David Lloyd, *Nationalism and Minor Literature: James Clarence Mangan and the Emergence of Irish Cultural Nationalism* (Berkeley: University of California Press, 1987), p. 209. The classic study is Emer Nolan, *James Joyce and Nationalism* (London: Routledge, 1995); see also Michael G. Cronin, *Impure Thoughts: Sexuality, Catholicism and Literature in Twentieth-Century Ireland* (Manchester: Manchester University Press, 2012).
5. Oscar Wilde, 'The Decay of Lying' (1889) in *The Decay of Lying and Other Essays* (London: Penguin, 2010), p. 22.
6. J. M. Synge, *The Playboy of the Western World* (1907) in *Collected Works*, Vol. IV: Plays Book II, ed. Ann Saddlemyer (London: Oxford University Press, 1968), p. 121.

7. See Alan Bliss, *Spoken English in Ireland, 1600–1740* (Dublin: Dolmen Press, 1979).
8. C. P. Curran, *Under the Receding Wave* (Dublin: Gill & Macmillan, 1970), pp. 96–110. See also his *James Joyce Remembered* (London: Oxford University Press, 1968).
9. J. C. C. Mays, 'Some Comments on the Dublin of *Ulysses*', in *Ulysses: Cinquante ans après*, ed. Louis Bonnerot (Paris: Didier, 1974), pp. 83–98.
10. Arthur Power, *Conversations with James Joyce* (London: Millington, 1974), p. 65.

8

JEAN-MICHEL RABATÉ

Joyce the European

'Some day we shall have to choose between England and Europe.'
(Robert in *Exiles*, PE 158)

'*Soltanto, i nostri superuomini sanno scrivere la storia del futuro.*'
(OCPW 258)

Today, Dublin is a European capital, which was not the case in Joyce's time, even if Ireland's history, more than its geography, had tied it to the rest of Europe since the early Middle Ages; moreover it is the capital of the only English-speaking nation in the European Economic Community (EEC). Europe has become a contested and conflicted political entity, in large part because of fears that its identity is threatened. As a backlash against a drift towards a supranational union, the spectre of massive immigration has been agitated, which has caused a reflux of which the 'Brexit' crisis in Great Britain is one symptom. Many wonder what the term 'European' means, whether it refers to a common culture, a shared Romanity, a grounding in Christian tradition, or simply the convenience of having streamlined the rules for exchange in a powerful economic market. Can the adjective be applied to Joyce, and if it is, will he have anything to say about the state of Europe? In his excellent recent novel *The Capital*, Robert Menasse satirizes the continent's cultural and political divisions by highlighting the conflicting rhetorical strategies of its jealous technocrats. Menasse presents a group of Brussels-based 'Eurocrats' who end up proposing that a new capital of Europe be built on the grounds of Auschwitz: the past catastrophe would be the only uniting factor capable of bridging the gaps of a divided or 'paralyzed' union.[1] For Joyce, who died in 1941, and hence was spared the knowledge of what Auschwitz names, the term 'union' would have rung differently: it would have called up the long struggle for 'Home Rule' and the independence of a free Ireland against the 'Unionists' from Ulster and all those who were still attached to the British crown.

My epigraphs move from Robert Hand's statement in *Exiles* that a clash between Europe and Britain is looming to Joyce's Italian sentence, a refusal to believe in prophetic powers granted to literature or philosophy.² Joyce's analysis of Ireland's fate is said to come from an 'amateur sociologist', who remains sceptical facing Nietzscheans like W. B. Yeats and Oliver St John Gogarty, at a time when both wanted to see Ireland reoccupy its lost position as 'the Hellas of the North' (*OCPW* 124). Joyce's rejection of a Nietzschean jump into the future does not preclude an awareness of what both Friedrich von Schlegel and Walter Benjamin intuited, namely that 'The historian is a prophet who looks backwards.'³ When we struggle to make sense of past epochs, the dream of a universal history provides a neat heuristic fiction that can help us look for a different future. This idea is adumbrated by *Finnegans Wake*, a book that appears committed to the promotion of a linguistic version of Europeanism. Joyce writes tellingly, 'If there is a future in every past that is present...' (*FW* 496.35–6). His present from the 1930s held in reserve difficult choices for any writer. For him, at any rate, the first decision was between Britain, an imperialist power whose language he spoke and wrote, and an as yet unborn 'Union' of Europe.

Joyce's concept would have been buttressed on Giambattista Vico's theory of a universal history that took Rome as a point of departure for an understanding of how 'men make history' but do not 'make' nature. Vico's model of history finds its true anchor when he shows that, unlike other capitals in different civilizations, Rome was able to give humanity a political foundation by ushering in a universalist definition of the citizen predicated on openness and hospitality to all the slaves and refugees who came looking for protection and who were later assimilated, emancipated, and freed.⁴ Vico's insight provides a key to any approach to Joyce's conception of Europe. For Vico, Europe was not a stable concept but a dialectical image that had to be inscribed in the broader idea of cycles. By 'dialectical', I mean Vico's notion that class struggle shaped the formation of the Roman republic. Joyce can be called dialectical too in the sense that he always measured the city of his birth with other places and contexts from which it derived more meaning. If Joyce carried the picture of Dublin with him all his life, whether he was in Trieste, Rome, Pola, Zurich, or Paris, we can probe further the kind of dialectical European he was and remained.

A Globalatinized Europe

To be dialectical means that one can find the essence of a term by dwelling on its opposite, as Hölderlin discovered when he traveled south from Germany, reached the city of Bordeaux, and believed he saw Greece on the banks of the Garonne. After him, Nietzsche was in the habit of alluding to 'Hyperboreans' when referring to the 'Greeks' of the North who lived in Germany or beyond, in Scandinavia. As we can see from Joyce's Italian articles for the *Piccolo della Sera* in Trieste, he was knowledgeable about all these legends of former migrations in and out of Europe. A modern admirer of Joyce can put us on the right track: Jorge Luis Borges compares the situation of the Argentinian writer working at some distance from the core of Europe with the situation of Irish writers and contends that both have better access to the essence of Europe from their decentred positions: 'I believe that our tradition is the whole of Western culture, and I also believe that we have a right to this tradition, a greater right than that which the inhabitants of one Western nation or another may have.'[5] Quoting Thorstein Veblen, who had analyzed how Jews had exerted an intellectual pre-eminence in most European countries just because they could act freely in these cultures without feeling bound to their stereotypes, Borges extends the idea to two countries: Ireland and Argentina. Like the Irish writers who have renewed British literature (he names George Bernard Shaw, George Berkeley, and Jonathan Swift) because they felt different enough, Argentine writers can 'take on all European subjects'.[6]

Borges, who also felt both Jewish and English, thus complicates the predicament of 'minority' cultures like those of Argentina or Ireland. If he was later to reject Joyce's historicist and linguistic hubris in *Finnegans Wake*, his admiration for *Ulysses* never abated . The tradition of Europe is hence defined both by history, geography, and languages, especially one dominant language that transmitted its values and formed the common root of romance languages: Latin. A similar thesis was developed by another admirer of *Ulysses*, Ernst Robert Curtius. In a synthesis that presents Joyce as the apex of a European mindset, Curtius explains that the thirteen centuries separating Virgil from Dante were relayed by the five centuries separating Dante from Johann Wolfgang von Goethe. For centuries, Latin connected philosophers and writers like René Descartes, Gottfried Wilhelm Leibnitz, Baruch Spinoza, Vico, and Issac Newton, allowing them to correspond with the most diverse authors. Joyce indeed felt that his Jesuit education linked him with this lineage. We see echoes of this in *Ulysses*, with Stephen feeling limited by his knowledge of Latin, whereas Buck Mulligan wants to teach him Greek. The latter's Hellenism smacks of Oscar Wilde's theories, the turn-of-the-century delusion that a return to paganism will give back the wholeness of life corrupted by Christianity, an illusion shared by several German and British artists and intellectuals.

Quite differently, for Curtius, it is Latin that holds the key to Europe. He states clearly, 'One is a European when one has become a *civis*

Romanus.'⁷ He details the meanings of 'Romania' and defines the English language as a Germanic dialect transformed by Romance and Latin.⁸ *Finnegans Wake* is quoted twice and presented as a modern 'macaronic epic'.⁹ The Latin tradition adheres to the contours of the old Roman empire in its widest expansion, but Curtius does not forget the Irish, even if they were outside the pale: 'But in Ireland, which was never a part of the Empire, there arises an original monastic culture, which under Columban (d. 615) reaches out to the mainland. Bobbio and St. Gall are Irish foundations.'¹⁰

Here is the ground that Joyce covers enthusiastically in his 1909 Italian lecture, 'Ireland: Island of Saints and Sages', written for the *Piccolo della Sera* in Trieste. He surveys the works and lives of Sedulius, Fridolinus Viator, fiery Columbanus, St Gallus, and many others. Joyce's pride in listing all the Irish 'saints and sages' is nevertheless not devoid of critique. The critique is levelled both at the British, who invaded the island and laid it waste under Cromwell, and at the endless internecine warfare marked by constant betrayals, a liability that prevented any national solution, offering almost no resistance to foreign oppression.

Moreover, Joyce, unlike Yeats, did not believe in the myth of a national identity. For him, there was no identitarian and transhistorical essence of the 'Celts', a position that had been defended earlier by Ernest Renan, an author he nevertheless liked. Joyce rejected wholly the idea of racial purity: 'Our civilization is an immense texture in which the most various elements are mixed, in which Nordic rapacity, Roman law, new Bourgeois conventions and the rest of a Siriac religion are reconciled' (*OCPW* 118, translation modified). Nordic rapacity refers to invading Danes and Vikings, while the 'Siriac religion' alludes dismissively to Christianity, tellingly hinted at through the Aramaic language spoken by Jesus and his disciples. That idiom would be taken as a point of departure by Marcel Jousse for his understanding of an 'oral style' that he recreated in the Aramaic sermons of Rabbi Jeshua, sermons that impressed Joyce when he was finishing *Finnegans Wake* in the 1930s. Already in 1909, Joyce goes on relentlessly: 'In such a texture, it is useless to search for a thread that has remained pure, virgin and uninfluenced by other threads nearby. What race or language, if we except those that a humorous will seems to have preserved in ice such as the Icelanders, can nowadays claim to be pure? No race has less right to make such a boast than the one presently inhabiting Ireland' (*OCPW* 118, translation modified).

If Joyce kept alluding to 'races', which entailed that he saw the 'Celts' as being different, such an innate difference would not be founded upon blood lines or ethnic lineages but upon an ancient knotting of languages and cultures. The Danes, the Firbolgs, the Milesians or Spaniards, the Norman invaders, the Anglo-Saxon colonists, and the Huguenots have all been blended in a new entity. In a similar manner, Curtius insists upon the fact that the Germans were able to assimilate the Latin culture of their neighbours, whereas the Arab invaders refused to do so; this is why in his view the Germans could become European, while the Arabs could not. Curtius broaches the topic later developed by Jacques Derrida under the coinage 'globalatinization.' This neologism describes less the way a Roman concept of religion has spread to all parts of the globe than it does the connection between the overtones of 'religion', Latin, and English, when the latter two are considered as languages aiming at a certain universalism. As Derrida writes, 'For everything that touches religion in particular, for everything that speaks "religion", for whoever speaks religiously or about religion, Anglo-American remains Latin.'[11]

Curtius does not bypass religion in his survey of the Latin Middle Ages but never takes it as a dominant paradigm. In a book that feels at times pompous and erudite, there is room for pagan laughter. Curtius explains that laughter posed a problem to the Catholic Church. An excursus on 'jest in hagiography' announces the work of Mikhail Bakhtin, while offering a framework for a reading of *Finnegans Wake* – with its farting nuns and joking martyrs being cooked alive – and an acknowledgement that for the medieval mind, the erotic had to be classified under the heading of comedy.[12]

Indeed, an outsider like Bakhtin was the best commentator to provide a context for Joyce's Europeanism. His monumental book on Rabelais describes countless features developed in *Finnegans Wake,* a book exemplifying Bakhtin's thesis about the resilience of popular culture throughout Europe. This Europe included not only the most extended map of the Roman Empire but its neighbouring Slavic countries as well. In Bakhtin's view, popular culture offers forms in which there is no 'static image of their unity but instead the uninterrupted continuity of their becoming and growth, of the unfinished metamorphosis of death and renewal. For all these images have a dual body; everywhere the genital element is emphasized: pregnancy, giving birth, the procreative force.' Rather than stressing a cyclical time founded on the rhythms of nature, he insists that a certain future is contained in these forms:

> Popular-festive forms look into the future. They present the victory of this future, of the golden age, over the past. This is the victory of all the people's material abundance, freedom, equality, brotherhood. The victory of the future is ensured by the people's immortality. The birth of the new, of the greater and the better, is as indispensable and as inevitable as the death of the old. The one is transferred to the other, the better turns the worse into ridicule and kills it.[13]

Joyce the European

The European spirit deployed by Joyce always combines the high and the low, Curtius and Bakhtin, Virgil and Petronius, Dante and Rabelais, Swift and Laurence Sterne, in an explosive mixture that was perpetuated by Samuel Beckett.

'Paralyse Europe'

Joyce was aware of the stakes implied by appearing more European than Irish, as we see in the dilemma experienced by Gabriel Conroy in 'The Dead'. When Gabriel blurts out to the nationalist Miss Ivors that he plans to be taking his vacation in France, Belgium, or Germany, she is furious. He makes things worse by stating that he has no desire to know his own country or learn its language, Irish. Of course, Joyce is not Gabriel Conroy, but he defended a similar position facing the Irish renaissance in 1901–4 when he criticized Yeats's adherence to Celtic mythology. If in 'The Day of the Rabblement' he would praise *The Wind among the Reeds* as 'poetry of the highest order' (*OCPW* 51) and state that only the best Russian writers could have written 'The Adoration of the Magi', this was in order to show how modern Yeats could sound if only he would break 'with the half gods' (*OCPW* 51). There could be no truce with Celtic folklore. The true mentor was Henrik Ibsen, the 'old master' dying in Christiana; his modern successor was a German playwright, Gerhard Hauptmann.

In *Ulysses* we hear of the journalist Ignatius Gallagher, who has previously been presented as a blustery reminder that one should not be stuck in Dublin in 'A Little Cloud'. In London and Paris, he has explored the hot spots, exhibiting a cosmopolitan savoir-faire that crushes his timid friend, Little Chandler, under the weight of salacious anecdotes. When he reappears in *Ulysses*, it is as the author of the immortal sentence 'We'll paralyse Europe' (*U* 7.628). While it's not exactly clear what he means by this, since the sentence implies either creating a huge shock with exciting news or on the contrary blocking channels of distribution, it seems obvious that there has been a shift since *Dubliners*: the short stories denouncing Irish paralysis have turned into a huge encyclopaedic novel capable not only of containing Europe itself but also of subjecting it to the same treatment, which implies a new critical awareness. Paralysis is not only Irish but fully European.

Joyce began defining his political position as a critical European when he moved from Trieste to Rome, a city in which he attended various political meetings on the left. There he saw Guglielmo Ferrero, one of Italy's most promising public intellectuals and a writer who was a hero for him. This was in September 1906, when Joyce was twenty-four, barely making a living as a bank clerk in Rome and trying to complete *Dubliners*. He found Ferrero unprepossessing, writing, 'You would think he was a terrified Y.M.C.A. man with an inaudible voice' (*SL* 103). Ferrero, eleven years older than Joyce, nevertheless fascinated the Irish exile, who would ask that the historian's essays should be kept for him as they appeared in Triestine newspapers. Ferrero displayed a rare moral courage when castigating contemporary militarism and masculinist codes in *L'Europa giovane* (1898), a book about 'young Europe', which Joyce absorbed with relish.

Ferrero's fame rose during a North American tour when he was invited to the White House by President Roosevelt. This was after he wrote the six volumes of *Greatness and Decline of Rome* between 1903 and 1908. Ferrero gave the Lowell lectures at Harvard, in which he eviscerated famous characters of Roman history, including Caesar and Nero. Joyce began reading the Roman history cycle, which explains his rather cynical view of the capital as 'a man who lives by exhibiting his grandmother's corpse' (*SL* 108). For Ferrero, more important was that the grandfather's corpse would not die: Caesar always reappeared as resurgent Caesarism. *Greatness and Decline of Rome* finds its overarching theme in the struggle between the republic and the empire. Imperialism, kept in check by the early Roman Republic, was smuggled back by Caesar. European politics was split by a double 'genius', the spirit of democracy and the spirit of imperialism. Caesar was a corrupted mobster caught up in ugly scandals and finding redemption by becoming a successful general and dictator, which approximates Joyce's picture of both Shaun and Earwicker in *Finnegans Wake*. In this demystification, Ferrero attacked the German school of historiography, including authors like Theodor Mommsen, who presented Caesar as a providential man, a tactical genius who had been obliged to seize power to save Rome. Joyce disagreed with Ferrero on this point, preferring to believe that the German historians were right (*OCPW* 109).

The protracted tragedy of Caesarism required as its counterpart the deployment of a militarist ideology. Ferrero was a staunch pro-Dreyfusard and socialist, as was his famous father-in-law, Cesare Lombroso. No doubt, Ferrero saw his work as journalism or a variety of sociological fiction. What mattered for him was to be able to change the way people were thinking. Unhappily for him, the rise to power of Mussolini after WWI, and the links between Fascism, militarism, and imperialism, proved that while his theses had been correct, they could not make a dent in public opinion. Joyce was reading *L'Europa giovane* when he was toying with the idea of beginning a new story for *Dubliners* he intended to call 'Ulysses':

> In his book *Young Europe* which I have just read he says there are three great classes of emigrants: the (I forget the word: it means conquering, imposing their own language, &c), the English; the adhesive (forming a little group with national traditions and sympathies) the Chinese and the Irish ! ! ! ! : the diffusive (entering into a new society and forming part of it) the Germans. He has a fine chapter on Antisemitism. By the way, Brandes is a Jew. He says that Karl Marx has the apocalyptic imagination and makes Armageddon a war between capital and labour. (SL 128)

Readers of *Ulysses* can place these ideas in the context of Bloom's Jewishness and his political sympathies for Arthur Griffith and socialism. Joyce forgot the word *plasmativa* by which Ferrero described groups shaping their environment in their own image. Joyce is excited to see the Irish mentioned next to the Chinese, people who refuse to lose their identity but do not bully others, whereas the Jews in this scheme risk being discriminated against precisely because they apparently blend too much. The main idea that launched *Ulysses* as a novel was linked with a vision of European history that included all its migrations. Ferrero struggled with the messianic horizon of Karl Marx's theory. These insights would ferment and mature, leading Joyce to the idea of composing a double epic in which the Jews and the Irish follow parallel courses by retracing a Greek *periplum*. They circumnavigate the treacherous Mediterranean waters mapped by Semitic Phoenician explorers, as Victor Bérard showed, or walk up and down the streets of Dublin. Ferrero taught Joyce that Georg Brandes – the Danish critic he read about Shakespeare, Ibsen, and Friedrich Nietzsche – was Jewish, which has its importance for Stephen's disquisition in 'Scylla and Charybdis', when he attempts to 'prove' (*U* 9.764) that Shakespeare was a Jew.

Ferrero, who was not a Marxist, saw Marx as a typical Jew, blending a critique of society with an apocalyptic imagination. Joyce took much from *Young Europe*, especially its detailed treatment of anti-Semitism. Ferrero, who visited all of Europe and knew London, Berlin, and Moscow well, understood that phenomenon to have arisen in Germany. He compares Max Nordau, the notorious author of *Degeneration*, and Karl Marx, who emigrated to London, with Heinrich Heine, who lived in Paris. Ferrero defined the characteristics of the Jewish spirit as a tendency to adopt an ethical point of view by rejecting lies and prejudices.[14] Marx's *Manifesto of the Communist Party* should have been the gospel of the modern world. But such ethical priority was also founded upon a pessimistic world view, like that of the Book of Job, a Biblical allegory foregrounding 'the instability of fortune, which is common to all' – a thought that haunts Bloom's consciousness.[15] The defect is Jewish pride, an exaggerated confidence in one's intellect. He claims that every Jew believes that he can be the Messiah, a cliché echoed in the conversation of the anti-Semites in the pub of 'Cyclops'.[16] For Ferrero, the southern countries of Europe, including Italy and Greece, should acknowledge an innate difference corresponding to a more sensual and aesthetic sense of life, as opposed to countries of the North, which adhere to militarism and industrialization. Fundamentally, Ferrero's philosophy was close to anarchism, and he quotes Peter Kropotkin and Max Stirner. This influenced Joyce's attitude at the time, as we see when Stephen's position clashes with that of the Dublin intellectuals of the day.

Stephen against Irish Modernism

The library scene in *Ulysses* shows that while an Irish renaissance is under way, Stephen feels excluded. He has not been invited to parties celebrating new publications, reviews, and collections. I have previously shown that Joyce's alter ego was struggling not only against Yeats's passé and mythologizing view of Ireland but also against a more cosmopolitan version of Irish modernism represented by William Kirkpatrick Magee.[17] Magee, known as John Eglinton (under which name he appears in *Ulysses*), was a renowned essayist and influential figure in the Irish literary revival, who launched and co-edited a new review, *Dana*, which survived only one year, from May 1904. When *Dana* rejected Joyce's first *Portrait of the Artist*, it was as much because Magee felt that the novel was unreadable as that it was too sexually explicit. Magee's general position was that of a well-read European, and he too rejected Yeats's sentimental appropriation of Celtic mythologies.

Dana, in a spirit of modernist openness, offered balanced critical evaluations by presenting two versions of 'modernism': the controversy in the Catholic church opposing Abbé Loisy and the cardinals' rejection of Darwinism, and Nietzsche's philosophy of the future 'superman' founded upon the idea of the 'death of God'. In the first issue of *Dana*, the modernist debate in Catholicism was discussed by Edouard Dujardin, whose novel *The Bays are Sere*, written entirely as an interior monologue, Joyce had discovered during his first trip to Paris. (Joyce had been prodded by George Moore, another Irish cosmopolitan well acquainted with Parisian literary circles.) Dujardin concluded that the Church had made a huge mistake when it decided that Aristotle should trump Darwin.

Magee himself examined the philosophy of Nietzsche in the sixth issue. Magee discussed what shocked Catholics most, the proclamation of 'God is dead', making fun of philistines eager to have their God always available: 'The ordinary citizen does not like the doctrine of God to be challenged: he likes to think of God being there, as he likes to think of a limitless supply of coal in the bowels of Great Britain.'[18] For Magee, Nietzsche's thought was contradictory, and the origin of his flaws was his belief in the doctrine of the Superman, a hyperbolic offshoot of the Romantic cult of the genius. Magee wanted to deflate Yeats's neo-Nietzschean posturing and promote a classical modernism reluctant to cut all ties with religion or tradition. A similarly syncretic modernism would reappear in Eugène Jolas's neo-Romantic 'revolution of the word' in the late twenties. When Jolas campaigned for an international modernism that came to fruition in *transition* (active 1927–38), he also went back to the German Romantics, linking them, as André Breton had done, with twentieth-century avant-garde movements interested in exploring the language of the 'Night' and the unconscious.

In the fictional time of June 1904, Stephen Dedalus evinces different affiliations, as he rejects both Catholic modernism and the Nietzschean affirmation of power. His opts for a 'perverted' religiosity blending Berkeley, William Blake, Aristotle, and anarchist individualism. Stephen tells Bloom later that 'Ireland must be important because it belongs to me' (*U* 16.1164–5), which links him with the philosophy of the left Hegelian Max Stirner, who refused to be 'owned' by any common program, whether it was God, the Spirit, the Nation, the State, or even love. This attitude, closer to that of Leopold Bloom, with his endorsement of an Austro-Hungarian model that had impressed Griffith, was fraught with contradictions that Joyce explored in *Exiles*.

Joyce saw the need for a modernization of Irish culture and could no more agree with Yeats's mythological turn as a key to an Irish renaissance than with Stephen's youthful anarchism: Leopold Bloom would offer a temporary solution, and his nuanced position then found an 'eternal' countersign, one transformed into a hymn to nature in Molly's monologue. She embodies the 'revolutions' of the earth turning upon itself in its orbit, while Bloom and Stephen part ways, both caught up in the infinite expansion of the cosmos – an idea that had already struck Giordano Bruno as a new revelation. It is in such a broadening cosmic framework that one can then inscribe the early essays, the stories of *Dubliners* in which Irish nationalism clashes with cosmopolitanism, and also *Exiles*, all of which should be read as new strategies aimed at rethinking Europe. Joyce's immersion in the varied culture and cosmopolitan world of the only Habsburg sea harbour connected him with a different sense of Europe. His friendship with Ettore Schmitt brought a whiff of *Mitteleuropa*, which reminds us that Joyce and Franz Kafka lived and produced original work in the same country for a long time. Milan Kundera has insisted on a common attitude facing the 'minor' languages that he and Kafka saw emerging around them, Yiddish for Kafka and a more dominant Czech in his country after the end of the war, just as Irish became an official language of Ireland after independence.[19]

Kundera argued that Prague should be considered the geographical centre of Europe, which could have struck a chord in Joyce, who lived in Trieste, considering that both cities are almost aligned on the same meridian. Nevertheless, Kundera added that it would be a mistake to call Kafka a 'Czech' author: If Kafka had written his works in the Czech language, he would never have had such an impact on world literature. The same would obtain with Joyce, had he been able to write in Irish. For Kundera, one should distinguish the 'small context' of an author's nation and the 'large context' of a supranational history of culture, often considered today as the wide angle of 'world literature.' For Kundera, Europeanism is opposed to provincialism, which consists in refusing to see a specific literary production in the larger context. This discussion frames Joyce's position as a European author. We see the issue staged in *Exiles,* a play that has been well analyzed by Andrew Gibson in the context of the Irish politics of 1912.[20] It is helpful to repeat and reframe the anguished questions posed by its main characters in their echo of the looming clash between the nationalists, who saw Home Rule almost at hand, and the Unionists in Ulster, who were getting ready for a civil war.

Exiles dramatizes also the links between Dublin and Europe. In view of Tom Stoppard's spoof in *Travesties,* one may question Joyce's concept of 'exile', a term that should be problematized: it implied less a rejection of his nation's limitations than a program aiming at the modernization of a specific culture. This program entailed transforming Dublin into a European city against its immediate declared wishes, thus bypassing as well the problematics of British colonialism, imperialism, and the disappointing postcolonial moment marked by nationalism and bigotry. *Exiles* is a play that allows one to measure the depth of Joyce's suspicion facing his country. Richard, tempted by the writer's sublime but ineffective isolation, tries to rise above entanglements and betrayals. Joyce called his play 'three cat and mouse acts' (*PE* 351) so as to refer to the bill passed in 1913 that allowed the British police to free hunger-striking suffragettes and then bring them back to jail almost immediately after release.

The political discussions that abound in the play point to a new Ireland, free and independent: 'Exiles – also because at the end either Robert or Richard must go into exile – perhaps the new Ireland cannot contain both. Robert will go. But her thoughts will they follow him into exile as those of her sister-in-love Isolde follow Tristan?' (*PE* 351). Indeed, at the end, the exile Richard decides to stay in Dublin, temporarily perhaps, whereas the local journalist Robert chooses to move to England. If, as Gibson argues, the solution lies with Bertha and a new role for women in Ireland, such a chiasmatic exchange of two exiles forces us to probe the meanings of being European for the Irish.[21] At one stage, Robert, lighting a Virginia cigar, the kind one would find in the Austro-Hungarian empire, tells Richard that he is glad to feel European: 'These cigars Europeanise me. If Ireland is to become a new Ireland she must become European. And that is what you are here for, Richard. Some day we shall have to choose between England and Europe. I am a descendent of the dark foreigners. That is why I like it here' (PE 158). We have a double paradox: Robert likes to be in Dublin because he can smoke Richard's cigars and drink black coffee. Such dark cigars are most likely the 'Regie Virginier' cigars that Joyce would find in Trieste. These Austrian cigars are long, thin, and dark, with a straw one has to remove before lighting one. Robert senses that this gives him the air of being a 'bandit' ('a bandit cigar like this' [PE 158]). Indeed, he is a bandit, for he is ready to steal his best friend's partner before his eyes. Moreover, he sounds 'childish' when he claims that Ireland is ready to become sophisticated: 'The man who drinks black coffee is going to conquer Ireland' (PE 158). This was certainly not true of De Valera's free Ireland, though perhaps it is truer today. The play does not resolve all the tensions and ambiguities left in store when at the end Richard decides to stay. Joyce may have been hopeful in 1912, but history soon taught him that this would have been a mistake, a mistake that Joyce avoided making. His solution was different; it implied being fully European but in a minor key.

Europe Minor

Joyce refused to belong to an Ireland founded on national values and the Irish language, a Gaelic that he never mastered although it plays an important part in *Finnegans Wake*. Joyce's exile was first an economic exile, then an ideological one: he did not feel at home in the Irish renaissance or in De Valera's Ireland. Joyce, who retained a British passport all his adult life, chose to live in Paris, where the family would still use the Triestine dialect in their daily interactions. *Finnegans Wake* embodies a utopian yet forceful European inscription of Ireland, which leads to a two-pronged strategy: the creation of a hybrid language in which English provides only a syntactical basis. It is a capacious form capable of absorbing all other semantemes. Here is the linguistic pattern needed to rethink universal history – a universalism that had always been associated with the idea of Europe since the Enlightenment. Thus if *Ulysses* was a 'novel to end all novels', much as WWI had been thought to be a 'war to end all wars', *Finnegans Wake* was meant to rethink the idea of Europe. What were the roots of a distinct

European 'spirit' that would be different from an 'American' modernity? Paris would be the only place in which, with the help of Eugene Jolas's cultural cosmopolitanism, Joyce could rethink civilization after all the destruction and devastation as a *transition* to a more peaceful future.

Joyce could not have written *Finnegans Wake* in any city other than Paris, which was then the undisputed 'capital of letters' full of temporary exiles, of artists who for different personal reasons had shaken loose the links with their native countries to experience the excitement of uninhibited creativity, allied with cheap local currency that rendered extended stays possible. Not only Americans and British artists were flocking to the two poles of Parisian nightlife – Montparnasse and Montmartre – but also Spaniards, Russians, Canadians, Australians, Germans. It seemed that after WWI, Paris and Berlin were the only places to choose from to experience the fun and excitement of the new. For a while at least Paris was preferred by literary types, who felt that they were all destined to come to *la ville lumière* to learn about style and writing. Joyce found the city to be a convenience, having been first helped by Ezra Pound and Valery Larbaud, Sylvia Beach and Adrienne Monnier, then extending his bases. The adulation expressed by Eugène and Maria Jolas led to permanent support and publications, the whole effort relayed by newcomers like Beckett in the years 1928 to 1930. However, Joyce was ready to leave Paris for London at the time of his marriage, and he completed his earlier loop when he chose to spend the war years in Zurich.[22]

When Joyce took the ballad of Finnegan as a basis for his later work, he adapted an archaic ritual with pre-Christian Celtic features, jumping across centuries and mixing styles in a paean to postcolonial hybridity. His polyphonic text is made up of conflicting voices, whose din destroys authoritative discourse. By placing literature in the context of a history of popular culture capable of resisting political hegemony and orthodoxy, Bakhtin helps us read Joyce as an heir to Rabelais, who resorts to an anarchic laughter stemming from the lower parts, which includes the scatological and the obscene. The carnivalesque inversion of higher values leads to an irresistible affirmation from the low. We are invited to an Irish wake, a festive nightlife teetering upon the brink of excess; merriment subsists through testimonies of bereavement, whereas sadness and discordant strife interfere in the midst of a family gathering. *Finnegans Wake* is both funny and sad, releasing a mixture of moods ranging from the jovial to the sepulchral. Bruno's motto, '*In tristitia hilaris, in hilarite tristis*', remained valid for Joyce, with whom Harriett Weaver had agreed to 'play' by 'ordering' certain texts. One of them became the first page of *Finnegans Wake*, which contains a reference to 'the scraggy isthmus of Europe minor' (FW 3.05–6). Joyce's game aimed at realizing the dream of a new European language in which English would provide a grammar regulating the inclusion of vocabularies from more than thirty idioms. 'European' is turned into 'ear open' by a recurrent pun: 'In that earopean end meets Ind' (FW 598.15–16). Europe is linked with the Indian subcontinent by shared etymons called 'Indo-European'. Joyce believed in the theory of a common root for the 445 languages that are supposed to be cousins stemming from a single origin and are spoken by half the population of the globe.

In the Wake, allusions to Europe are mixed with puns on Semitic languages or Jewish peoples: '... semi-semitic serendipitist, you (thanks, I think that describes you) Europasianised Afferyank!' (FW 191.02–4). Or again: 'Then he caught the europicolas and went into the society of jewses' (FW 423.35–6). We recognize an allusion to the Piccolo della Sera, in which Joyce published his articles on Irish issues, and erysipelas, a skin disease hiding something like a heresy that might be 'caught' by contagion, plus the French slang word *'picoler'*, meaning to drink too much. Both sentences are spoken by Shaun to make fun of Shem and entail a view of Europe as negative or diminished.

In the Wake, therefore, Europe is not seen as a source of high culture, a stable root of identity, but is always presented in a dialectical manner via its opposites and caught up in endless wars and struggles for domination. Here is how Finnegans Wake begins its second paragraph: 'Sir Tristram, violer d'amores, fr'over the short sea, had passencore rearrived from North Armorica on this side the scraggy isthmus of Europe Minor to wielderfight his penisolate war' (FW 3.04–6). Salvatore Pappalardo has explored the links between this sentence and Ferrero's philosophy of history based upon the violence done to women by militaristic conquerors.[23] For Ferrero, Europe had been raped by a Zeus who might also be a British invader. When Joyce glossed the first stage of the sentence in a letter to Weaver from 15 November 1926, he foregrounded the legend of Tristan and Isolde and the geography of Dublin, adding a map in which we see Howth Head, the Liffey, the old Dublin plain, and Phoenix Park (SL 315–17). In the following letter dated 24 November, this is modified: 'Sir Tristram, violer d'amores, fr'over the short sea, had passencore rearrived fra North Armorica on the scraggy isthmus of Europe Minor' (SL 317), which confirms that there is no incompatibility between the site as Dublin and as Europe. Joyce superimposes both maps, going back to the ancient myth of the rape of Europa, who came from a Phoenician family. Europa was the daughter of Agenor, the Phoenician King of Tyre, one of the bravest of the Trojans, as the Iliad XIV,

l. 321–2 shows. King Minos, the inventor of the Cretan labyrinth, referred to by Ovid in the epigraph of *A Portrait of the Artist as a Young Man*, was one of her sons. Surprisingly, the roots of Europe would be in Asia Minor, which leads Joyce to conflate it with 'Europe Minor'.

I want to end by focusing on this image of a 'Europe Minor' that contains a message about a politics of the future going beyond the *Wake*'s publication in 1939. It is as if Joyce had done exactly the reverse of what Gilles Deleuze and Félix Guattari assume to be Kafka's position facing language. Whereas the French philosophers mistakenly assume that Kafka was writing a 'minor literature' because he was writing German in Prague, the contrary happened, as we saw Kundera suggest.[24] In the same way as Kafka, Joyce tackled the whole of Europe, the Europe of his times, not to gather it in a monumental tower of Babel but to make it 'minor'.[25] His is the new Europe of minorities who speak in all their idioms, each in a minor key. Hence Joyce's political views would not be conveyed by a strong voice delivering strong opinions, as committed authors would request at the time. Joyce was writing in a minor mode; he was playing with language, inventing a new game for all. His language issued from a 'magic flute', whose reedy sound contrasted with Pound's 'big brass band', as he wrote in December 1928 (*Letters I 277*).

Joyce had no difficulty in letting 'Dublin and environs' allegorize Europe itself. No doubt, this was a Europe that had shrunk or, in Paul Valéry's phrase, a Europe that appeared, as it did on the map, as a little 'cape' of the Asian continent. Nevertheless, it contained the seeds of renewal, at least thanks to the image of the phoenix still inscribed in Phoenix Park on the outskirts of Dublin. After WWI, Europeans discovered that 'civilizations were mortal', as Valéry wrote when he analyzed the 'crisis of the spirit'.[26] The famed European spirit had lost its absolutism; instead of being G.W. F. Hegel's absolute spirit, it metamorphosed into ghosts, the innumerable ghosts created by a world war. If Europe was the tip of a 'peninsula', a mere 'cape', a tiny excrescence emerging from a continent whose lines were redrawn by Russia's and Asia's awakenings, it nevertheless kept some potential given its varied languages, a common past, and the resources of multiple talents. Joyce's gambit would be to return to this site and redouble it, show it caught up between America and Asia in order to 'rearrive' there and wage a different war. It would not be a sexualized war of conquest, whose object is the 'rape' of a feminine island or a woman like Europe, but a linguistic war against all nationalist ideologies, thus keeping alive the dream of an old and new Europe, the site of openness and hospitality to the others it should be for a democracy still to come.

Notes

1. Robert Menasse, *Die Hauptstadt* (Berlin: Suhrkamp, 2017). See Chiara Bottici and Benoît Challand, *Imagining Europe: Myth, Memory and Identity* (Cambridge: Cambridge University Press, 2013), pp. 61–3 and 70–3 for the role played by the memory of the holocaust in the constitution of Europe.
2. The sentence is rendered as, 'Only our supermen can write the history of the future' (*OCPW* 125). A literal translation from Joyce's Italian would be, 'Only, our supermen know how to write the history of the future.' The placement of the comma slightly changes the meaning.
3. Friedrich von Schlegel, 'Athenaeum Fragments' [1798] in *Philosophical Fragments*, trans. Peter Firchow (Minneapolis: University of Minnesota Press, 1991), p. 27, n. 80. The famous sentence can be translated as 'a prophet in reverse' or 'a turned-back prophet'.
4. Giambattista Vico, *New Science*, trans. David Marsh (London: Penguin, 2001), pp. 236–47. See also Rémi Brague, *Europe, la voie Romaine* (Paris: Critérion, Idées, 1992). Brague agrees with Joyce's principle of 'Jewgreek is greekjew' (*U* 15.2097–8), while adding Rome as the foundational site and mediator between Athens and Jerusalem.
5. Jorge Luis Borges, 'The Argentine Writer and Tradition', trans. Ester Allen, in *Selected Non-Fictions*, ed. Eliot Weinberger (New York: Penguin, 1999), p. 426.
6. Ibid., p. 426.
7. Ernst Robert Curtius, *European Literature and the Latin Middle Ages*, trans. Willard R. Trask (London: Routledge and Kegan Paul, 1953), p. 12.
8. Ibid., p. 35
9. Ibid., p. 243.
10. Ibid., p. 23.
11. Jacques Derrida, *Acts of Religion*, ed. Gil Anidjar (New York: Routledge, 2002), p. 66.
12. Curtius, *European Literature*, p. 435.
13. Mikhail Bakhtin, *Rabelais and His World*, trans. Helene Iswolsky (Bloomington: Indiana University Press, 1984), p. 256.
14. Guglielmo Ferrero, *L'Europa giovane: Studi e viaggi nei paesi del Nord* (Milano: Treves, 1898), p. 335.
15. Ibid., p. 339. My translation.
16. Ibid., p. 342.
17. Jean-Michel Rabaté, 'Intellectual and Aesthetic Influences' in *The Cambridge Companion to Irish Modernism*, ed. Joe Cleary (Cambridge: Cambridge University Press), pp. 21–34.
18. John Eglinton, 'A Way of Understanding Nietzsche', *Dana* 1.6 (October 1904): 182–8, 183. See Modernist Journals Project at modjourn.org/issue/bdr429911/.
19. Milan Kundera, 'Die Weltliteratur: How We Read One Another', *The New Yorker*, 8 January 2007. www.newyorker.com›magazine›2007/01/08›die-weltliteratur.
20. Andrew Gibson, *The Strong Spirit* (Oxford: Oxford University Press, 2013), pp. 209–34.
21. Ibid., pp. 230–34.

22. On the significance of London, see Eleni Loukopoulou, *Up to Maughty London: Joyce's Cultural Capital in the Imperial Metropolis* (Gainesville: University Press of Florida, 2017).
23. Salvatore Pappalardo, 'Waking Europa: Joyce, Ferrero and the Metamorphosis of Irish History', *Journal of Modern Literature* 34.2 (2011): 154–77.
24. Gilles Deleuze and Félix Guattari, *Kafka: Toward a Minor Literature*, trans. Dana Polan (Minneapolis: University of Minnesota, 1986).
25. See John Nash, '"There being more languages to start with than were absolutely necessary": James Joyce's *Ulysses* and English as a World Language' in *Modernism and Non-Translation*, ed. Jason Harding and John Nash (Oxford: Oxford University Press, 2019).
26. Paul Valéry, 'La Crise de l'esprit', *Oeuvres*, vol. I (Paris: Pléiade, 1965), pp. 988–1000.

9

MARJORIE HOWES

Joyce, Colonialism, and Nationalism

Joyce's life spans a period in history when material conditions, political structures, and intellectual life throughout the world were profoundly shaped by the growth and decline of European empires and the flourishing of various nationalisms, both imperialist and anti-imperialist. When Joyce was born in 1882 the 'scramble for Africa' and the era that one influential historian has called the 'age of empire', had just begun.[1] When he died in 1941 the world was engulfed in WWII, a conflict that would fundamentally alter the balance of global power, and the age of decolonization was under way. Beginning (for the most part) in the 1990s, a good deal of influential Joyce scholarship has explored Joyce's relation to this historical trajectory.[2] Much of it has been informed by postcolonial studies, the academic field most explicitly committed to examining the complex set of issues and questions we can group under the general headings of 'colonialism' and 'nationalism'.[3]

Ireland's double status as both centre and periphery, agent and victim of colonialism, is important to any investigation of how Joyce's works engage with such issues and questions. Before the establishment of the Irish Free State in 1922, Ireland was arguably both a region of an imperial power and England's oldest colony. The Ireland Joyce was born into was in several respects a British settler colony. Ireland was dominated by the Protestant Ascendancy, which was both a political system that disadvantaged Catholics and a sociological group of often powerful and wealthy Anglo-Irish Protestants. By Joyce's time, their power was beginning to crumble, but Protestants still controlled much of Ireland's political and economic life, maintained some institutionalized discrimination against Catholics, and owned most of the land. They were descended from sixteenth- and seventeenth-century settlers and were separated from the majority of Ireland's population by religion, culture, and, to some extent, language. Unlike the populations of India or Africa, however, the native Irish were white, Christian, and anglicized in substantial ways. They were the victims of British imperialism in Ireland – but they were also the agents of the British colonial enterprise elsewhere. Irish emigrants helped populate the white settler colonies overseas, and many colonial soldiers and civil servants in places like India came from Ireland; many, but by no means all, were Protestants.[4] Even Irish nationalists who criticized and resisted British dominance of Ireland were perfectly capable of wanting to share in its imperial advantages and the wealth they generated elsewhere. Ireland, then, was both a colonized territory and part of a colonizing nation. This proposition does not represent a contradiction, nor does it make Ireland unique.[5]

Joyce found both ways of thinking congenial. He sometimes cast Dublin as an ancient and important imperial city, writing to his brother Stanislaus in 1905, 'When you remember that Dublin has been a capital for thousands of years, that it is the "second" city of the British Empire, that it is nearly three times as big as Venice it seems strange that no artist has given it to the world' (*JJ* 208). Other times he characterized Ireland as a colonized territory, and the Irish as a colonized people. In *A Portrait of the Artist as a Young Man*, Stephen talks to the English Dean of Studies and thinks, 'The language in which we are speaking is his before it is mine ... His language, so familiar and so foreign, will always be for me an acquired speech' (*P* 189). This quote describes a classic colonial condition, in which the British Empire tries to force its language and culture on the colonized, creating a divided subject for whom English is both familiar and foreign. As Vincent Cheng has demonstrated, Irish people in Joyce's works suffer the Orientalizing gaze of the English, which imagines them variously as violent, primitive, feminine, or exotic. At the same time, Joyce also shows that the Irish often turn the same kind of Orientalizing gaze upon people in other parts of the world, such as the Middle East or Asia.[6]

Dubliners is permeated by the sense that Dublin is too close to England and also too far from it, a city damaged by colonial power and by its distance from the metropolitan centres of that power. 'After the Race', for example, allegorizes the dilemmas of a particular kind of colonial subject, one who is willingly co-opted by the colonial power but is still prevented from realizing the success and status that co-optation seemed to promise. Like the Irish spectators at the race, Jimmy Doyle is 'gratefully oppressed' (*D* 30) by several interlocking forces: economic exploitation, British cultural hegemony, and his own social aspirations. These forces are masked as economic opportunity, egalitarian cosmopolitanism, and upward mobility, false appearances that help ensure Jimmy's enthusiastic participation in his own ruin. The story is preoccupied with such masking, and Joyce emphasizes that the other men skilfully manipulate appearances: 'Ségouin had managed to give the impression that it was by a favour of friendship the mite of Irish money was to be included in the capital of the concern' (D 32). Joyce uses 'capital' to tie Jimmy's aspirations to the predicament of colonized Ireland. Dublin had not been the effective capital of Ireland since the Act of Union in 1800. Jimmy's excitement over his inclusion in the group allows Dublin to appear to be a capital, even though it is not: 'That night the city wore the mask of a capital' (D 39). Similarly, Jimmy can only wear the mask of a cultured Cambridge gentleman with capital to invest.

Finnegans Wake also satirizes, and laments, the idea of a prosperous Irish capital city. The 'question and answer' section of Book I exposes this idea as a combination of grandiose pretensions and actual poverty: 'What Irish capitol city (a dea o dea!) of two syllables and six letters, with a deltic origin and a numinous end, (ah dust oh dust!) can boost of having *a*) the most extensive public park in the world, *b*) the most expensive brewing industry in the world, *c*) the most expansive peopling thoroughfare in the world, *d*) the most phillohippuc theobibbous paùpulation in the world' (FW 140.8–13). Here the city with Celtic origins declines to a ruinous end, as the 'extensive' gives way to the merely 'expensive', the strength of the brewing industry results in excessive love, even worship, of drinking (in 'phillohippuc theobibbous'), and the population of Dublin (the apparently correct answer to the riddle) is also a collection of paupers (in 'paùpulation').

In 'After the Race', Jimmy's family history includes a commitment to Irish nationalism, but his father 'had modified his views early' (D 36) in order to pursue material prosperity. When the 'buried zeal of his father' surfaces in Jimmy and he gets into an argument with the Englishman Routh, Ségouin diffuses the conflict by appealing to a universal rather than a national concept: he proposes a toast 'to Humanity' (D 39). The 'continentals'' exploitation of Jimmy is concealed by an empty cosmopolitan ideology that denies the differences in power and wealth among the participants, masking the group as a fellowship of equals: 'They drank Ireland, England, France, Hungary, the United States of America' (D 40). The outcome of the card game, which may have been set up specifically to fleece Jimmy, reinforces the inequality of the Irish and English members of the party; Jimmy loses the money he had planned to invest in Ségouin's business, and Routh is the big winner. Given his many critiques of Irish nationalism, it may seem perverse for Joyce to suggest here that Jimmy would have done better had he retained a livelier sense of nationalist grievance and Irish distinctiveness. But in this story Joyce shows that cosmopolitanism and universalism can function as covert British nationalisms and can help sustain imperialism rather than dismantle it, a point to which this chapter will return.

The play on a single word – 'capital' – in the story illustrates the fact that for Joyce language itself – the medium of his art – was inescapably structured by colonialism and nationalism. Other individual words repay even more extensive tracking: 'ivory' is a good example. In *Portrait*, young Stephen thinks of ivory in the context of sectarian animosities between Catholics and Protestants in Ireland: 'Eileen was a protestant and ... protestants used to make fun of the litany of the Blessed Virgin. *Tower of Ivory*, they used to say, *House of Gold!*' (P 35). Next, in a passage set at Clongowes Wood College (the Jesuit-run school), the novel introduces ivory's source in British colonies:

> Boyle had said that an elephant had two tuskers instead of two tusks and that was why he was called Tusker Boyle but some fellows called him Lady Boyle because he was always at his nails, paring them.
> Eileen had long thin cool white hands too because she was a girl. They were like ivory; only soft. (P 42)

Later, when Stephen walks to university his thoughts return to ivory: 'The word now shone in his brain, clearer and brighter than any ivory sawn from the mottled tusks of elephants. *Ivory, ivoire, avorio, ebur.* One of the first examples that he had learnt in Latin had run: *India mittit ebur*' (P 179).

Joyce uses the apparently idiosyncratic twists and turns of Stephen's mind to make a series of points. Following the associative logic of *Portrait*, the first two references to ivory establish a link between Protestant Ascendancy in Ireland and imperialism elsewhere, suggesting that the origins of Irish sectarianism and the oppression of Catholics lie within a larger British colonial project. On the other hand, with the addition of Tusker Boyle, who has been caught engaging in homosexual 'smugging' (P 42), Joyce suggests that Irish Catholics are also participants in an imperialist project. He repeatedly drew parallels between two empires that he thought dominated Ireland: the Catholic Church and the British Empire. Elsewhere in *Portrait* he emphasized that the co-founder of the Jesuit order, St Francis Xavier, was an imperialist. Xavier was a sixteenth-century Spanish missionary who travelled to India and Southeast Asia, and the rector describes him in explicitly militaristic terms as 'a great soldier of God' and 'a true conqueror' (P 108). Other elements in Stephen's Jesuit education work to erase the violence of colonialism, such as the phrase '*India mittit ebur*', which means 'India sends ivory', suggesting that the 'crown jewel' of the British Empire provides ivory voluntarily rather than being forced to do so. Imperial ideology often assumed or claimed that colonialism was benign because it brought Western civilization, Christianity, and/or a modern economic system to the colonies.

In the 'Wandering Rocks' episode of *Ulysses*, Father Conmee's 'ivory bookmark' (*U* 10.190) establishes further links between Jesuit missionary work and British imperialism, as Conmee thinks of 'the souls of black and brown and yellow men and of his sermon on saint Peter Claver S. J. and the African mission and of the propagation of the faith' (*U* 10.143–5). Conmee's perspective does not go unchallenged, however. Earlier in the novel, Leopold Bloom thinks about the same sermon, but in terms that reject the idea, shared by the British state and the Catholic Church, that imperialism benefits the colonies. He wonders wryly 'how they explain it to the heathen Chinee' and speculates that the Chinese would 'Prefer an ounce of opium' to Christianity (*U* 5.326–7). Taken together these references to ivory begin to suggest the complexity of Joyce's approach to colonialism, which encompasses both local and global perspectives and incorporates conflicting ways of characterizing, and judging, colonial projects.

This does not mean, however, that Joyce's writings register the complexities of colonialism and nationalism in ways that add up to what he 'believed' about them. For the most part, it would be a fruitless exercise to search through his works in the hopes of extracting a steady, coherent set of views on these subjects. Joyce made polemical statements that are clear in themselves, but once we begin to combine them they are often contradictory. As Emer Nolan has argued, 'His essays ... give an ambivalent, confused and even contradictory account of Irish nationalism.'[7] For example, in 1907 Joyce gave a public lecture in Trieste entitled 'Ireland, Island of Saints and Sages'. The lecture begins with ancient Irish history, when Ireland was 'a true centre of intellectualism and sanctity' (*OCPW* 108), and argues that when the 'foreign occupation' began, Ireland 'ceased to be an intellectual force in Europe' (*OCPW* 114). Joyce castigates the English for their brutality and materialism, something he did quite consistently, and speaks sympathetically of Irish nationalism: 'If a victorious country tyrannizes over another, it cannot logically take it amiss if the latter reacts. Men are made that way; and no one ... can still believe that a colonizing country is prompted by purely Christian motives' (*OCPW* 116). For Joyce, colonialism was above all a matter of economic exploitation, and the essay blames British rule for the catastrophe of the Great Famine, which began in 1845, and for the impoverished state of Ireland generally, asserting that 'Ireland is poor because English laws ruined the industries of the country, notably the woollen one; because, in the years in which the potato crop failed, the negligence of the English government left the flower of the people to die of hunger' (*OCPW* 119).

However, elsewhere in the lecture Joyce asserts that it is pointless to criticize the English: 'I find it a bit naïve to heap insults on the Englishman for his misdeeds in Ireland. A conqueror cannot be amateurish, and what England did in Ireland over the centuries is no different from what the Belgians are doing today in the Congo Free State, and what the Nipponese dwarfs will be doing tomorrow in other lands' (*OCPW* 119). And, having characterized British rule as tyranny, he then offers this further thought: 'I confess that I do not see what good it does to fulminate against English tyranny while the tyranny of Rome still holds the dwelling place of the soul' (*OCPW* 125). Although the essay began by outlining the rich accomplishments of ancient Ireland, Joyce concludes by rejecting the notion that contemporary Ireland could make claims to cultural superiority and political independence based on those accomplishments: 'If it were valid to appeal to the past in this fashion, the fellahins of Cairo would have every right in the world proudly to refuse to act as porters for English tourists. Just as ancient Egypt is dead, so is ancient Ireland' (*OCPW* 125). This last remark locates Ireland as part of a global colonial project, like Egypt, but it also suggests that the Egyptians do not, in fact, have the right to disdain serving English tourists. Joyce would live to see them claim that right; the British replaced an unpopular system of direct rule in Egypt with a more indirect system in 1922, and Egypt gained its independence in 1936. Nolan sums up the complexities of the essay, and Joyce's works in general, by concluding that, paradoxically, Joyce's 'writings about Ireland may not provide a coherent critique of either colonized or colonialist; but their very ambiguities and hesitations testify to the uncertain, divided consciousness of the colonial subject'.[8]

In the 'Cyclops' episode of *Ulysses*, the aggressively nationalist Citizen echoes some of Joyce's pro-nationalist comments in the Trieste lecture. In contrast, Bloom and some other 'moderate' voices offer the kind of universalizing formulation that prompted Joyce to label critiques of British imperialism 'naïve' in the lecture. For decades scholars assumed that the Citizen was a 'mad fool'[9] whose narrow-minded views the novel rejects and that Bloom represented a more enlightened or dialogical perspective. But during the 1990s several important interventions by scholars working with postcolonial approaches challenged this reading decisively. Enda Duffy's *The Subaltern 'Ulysses'* argues that the Citizen's single-minded nationalism and Bloom's tolerant cosmopolitanism are 'two stereotyped subaltern modes of subjectivity' imposed by the colonizer. For Duffy, 'The politics of the episode is not a matter of an inevitable confrontation between vicious chauvinist nationalism and rationalist liberalism ... Rather, what emerges as the crux of political agency is the extraordinary difficulty of overcoming ... the vision of colonial subjectivity preimposed by the colonial regime.' He concludes, 'The final staged fight between Bloom and the Citizen becomes the text's desperate effort to pitch the two versions of the colonial stereotype against each other in order to envision some form of postcolonial subjectivity to come'.[10]

Nolan's revision of the dominant reading takes a somewhat different approach, arguing that 'traditional accounts of "Cyclops" are in general rendered incoherent by their refusal to attach any positive qualities to the citizen or the kind of language that he speaks, in spite of the fact that his voice is one of the most "interesting" in literary terms, and probably the funniest in the book'.[11] Nolan points out that in the course of their argument Bloom actually defends capital punishment and the British Empire and suggests that 'in some respects the views of Joyce and of the citizen may actually *coincide*'.[12] The Citizen castigates the English for the devastation of the Famine and for ruining the Irish economy and impoverishing the country, rather than for imposing a foreign religion, language, or culture on them; his nationalist argument primarily targets economic injustice. As Joyce wrote to Stanislaus in 1906, 'If the Irish question exists, it exists for the Irish proletariat chiefly' (*JJ* 237). The Citizen extends his critique of imperialism as economic exploitation to African places like the Belgian Congo: 'Raping the women and girls and flogging the natives on the belly to squeeze all the red rubber they can out of them' (*U* 12.1546–7). As Nolan argues, 'These individuals identify themselves with the black subjects of British imperialism ... and also display considerable sympathy for both the people whom they see as the powerless lackeys of imperial might – the whipped sailors of the British Navy – and also its labourers, the British working-class.'[13] The Citizen astutely recognizes that British imperialism abroad helped quell working class unrest over economic injustice at home: 'That's the great empire they boast about of drudges and whipped surfs ... – And the tragedy of it is, ... they believe it. The unfortunate yahoos believe it' (*U* 12.1349–53). Thus the Citizen's nationalism is allied with forms of anti-imperial thought that were not varieties of nationalism, such as international socialism.

The economic basis of colonialism is evident elsewhere in *Ulysses* as well. In 'Nestor', when the imperialist Mr. Deasy prompts Stephen to guess 'the proudest word you will ever hear from an Englishman's mouth', Stephen's first answer, that 'on his empire ... the sun never sets', is a clichéd claim to the perpetual visibility of an enormous territorial empire. But this answer is wrong. According to Deasy, the real answer is '*I paid my way ... I owe nothing*' (*U* 2.253–4). By refusing to define colonialism as the military conquest of foreign territories and by defining it instead as an economic project, Deasy points to the economic exploitation that was central to Joyce's view of colonialism. He also engages in a particular kind of imperialist fantasy: the fantasy of economic independence. England extracts wealth from the colonies but does not acknowledge its dependence on them, thus rendering them invisible. As a result, the Englishman imagines he paid his way himself and owes nothing to anyone. Stephen has no access to this kind of fantasy; in response he thinks of everything he owes to other people; 'Mulligan, nine pounds, three pairs of socks, one pair brogues, ties, Curren, ten guineas. McCann, one guinea. Fred Ryan, two shillings. Temple, two lunches. Russell, one guinea, Cousins, ten shillings. Bob Reynolds, half a guinea, Koehler, three guineas, Mrs. MacKernan, five weeks' board' (U 2.255–9). Fredric Jameson has suggested that, under colonialism, a significant portion of the metropolitan economy is located elsewhere, in the very different world of the colonies. As a result, it is no longer possible for individuals in the imperial centre, as they go about their daily lives, to grasp how the system functions as a whole: there will always be a piece missing. He argues that the formal qualities of modernist literature – its fragmentations, hesitations, disjunctions – spring from this condition of incomplete knowing or partial invisibility.[14] Deasy embodies a version of this imperial ignorance while Stephen models an awareness of indebtedness; the colonized cannot escape the knowledge of their own exploitation.

Rather than ask whether or not Joyce endorsed Irish nationalism, it is more useful to suggest that he embraced certain forms or elements of nationalism, such as those that pursued economic justice and imagined alliances with oppressed people outside Ireland, and rejected others. He was particularly critical of nationalist discourses that elided the violence inherent in physical force nationalism by sentimentalizing the deaths of nationalist 'martyrs' or characterizing bloodshed and loss of life as inevitable. In 'Sirens' Bloom and others listen to 'The Croppy Boy', a nationalist ballad that ends by soliciting 'a prayer and a tear'[15] for the young man's death. This sentimental 'thoughts and prayers' response allows the listeners to avoid any responsibility for preventing violence or acknowledging its true ugliness: 'The chords consented. Very sad thing. But had to be' (U 11.1121). (See Andrew Gibson's discussion in Chapter 4 for more on this song in 'Sirens'.) The nameless narrator of 'Cyclops', on the other hand, criticizes in graphic terms the physical violence of racism in an American case of lynching: 'A lot of Deadwood Dicks in slouch hats and they firing at a Sambo strung up in a tree with his tongue out and a bonfire under him. Gob, they ought to drown him in the sea after and electrocute and crucify him to make sure of their job' (U 12.1324–8). The narrator uses a racial slur to describe the victim, but his horrifying and grimly humorous list of still other ways the mob could kill him – beyond the hanging, burning, and shooting depicted in the photograph – highlights the extremity of the violence rather than sentimentalizing death as necessary or heroic.

Similarly, the Citizen's critique of disciplinary flogging in the British navy highlights the helplessness of the victim and the harshness of his punishment, describing 'a young lad brought out, howling for his ma' whose superior then 'flogs the bloody backside off of the poor lad till he yells meila murder' (U 12.1335–7, 1344–5). Nolan uses this scene to further revise previous scholarship's sense that Bloom takes political stances in 'Cyclops' that Joyce admired and endorsed. In response to the Citizen's sympathy for the sailor who gets flogged, Bloom invokes a principle of universalism: 'Isn't discipline the same everywhere? I mean wouldn't it be the same here if you put force against force?' (U 12.1360–1). An important principle in postcolonial studies is the idea that Enlightenment concepts like reason, humanity, and justice were supposed to be universal but were in fact based on various exclusions: at different times women, slaves, proscribed religions, and non-European peoples were not part of their 'universality', so these concepts often functioned as supports to colonialism rather than challenges to it.[16] In a famous moment, Bloom counters the Citizen's emphasis on 'Force, hatred, history, all that' (U 12.1481) by insisting that 'love' is what 'is really life' for human beings (U 12.1483). Scholars have debated what we should make of this. Joyce did repeatedly invoke the importance of love. In *Portrait*, Stephen's friend Cranly tells him, 'Whatever else is unsure in this stinking dunghill of a world a mother's love is not' (P 263). And in *Ulysses* Stephen thinks of 'love' as the 'Word known to all men' (U 9.429–30). But several elements of the scene in 'Cyclops' also suggest that the text encourages readers to treat Bloom's pronouncement with scepticism, including an illustration that, like other universal concepts, 'Universal love' (U 12.1489) can be a mask for exclusion, injustice, and violence. The Citizen remarks: 'We know those canters, ... preaching and picking your pocket. What about sanctimonious Cromwell and his ironsides that put the women and children of Drogheda to the sword with the bible text *God is love* pasted round the mouth of his cannon?' (U 12.1506–9).

Joyce's work is full of such insights. In 'Nestor', Deasy asserts that the English 'are a generous people but we must also be just' to the Irish, and Stephen replies, 'I fear those big words, ... which make us so unhappy' (U 2.263–4). Stephen thinks about justice again in 'Proteus', this time in conjunction with the state-sponsored injustice of wrongful conviction: 'Yes, used to carry punched tickets to prove an alibi if they arrested you for murder somewhere. Justice. On the night of the seventeenth of February 1904 the prisoner was seen by two witnesses' (U 3.179–82). Bloom also raises the possibility that 'justice' may not be what it appears when he thinks about a chant that closes the second Seder at Passover: 'Justice it means but it's everybody eating everybody else' (U 7.13–4). By the time Bloom counters the Citizen's nationalist hostility with 'love' and with the assertion that he too belongs to a persecuted race – 'I'm talking about injustice' (U 12.1474) – the attentive reader will have conflicting impulses: one to admire Bloom for his advocacy of love and justice and his benevolent universalism, and another to understand that this universalism's 'big words' have an historical, troubling, and often hidden relationship to violence and colonialism. *Finnegans Wake* pursues this theme as well. In one version of the conflict between Shem and Shaun, Shaun, as 'Justius', prosecutes Shem 'with the empirative of my vendettative' in order to prove that he is mad (*FW* 187.31). 'Empiratives' – supposedly impartial imperatives or principles that actually enable the piracies and exploitations of empire – are precisely what Joyce traces through his investigations of big words and universal concepts.

For Joyce, both the Enlightenment concepts and the nationalist formulations the Irish could appropriate to articulate their political aspirations were marked by important debts to colonialism, as was the Catholic educational system that could help them to knowledge and prosperity. When Stephen turns from these to the English literary tradition, Joyce reveals that it too is marked by such debts. In 'Scylla and Charybdis', for example, in the midst of his discussion of Shakespeare, long considered one of the greatest writers in the English tradition, Stephen comments on Shakespeare's participation in the ideology of imperialism: 'His pageants, the histories, sail fullbellied on a tide of Mafeking enthusiasm' (U 9.754–4). Mafeking was a small town in South Africa that was half-heartedly besieged by the Boers during the Boer War (1899–1902). When it was liberated (without having been in much danger), celebrations in London were quite excessive in comparison with the actual military significance of the event. As Don Gifford observes, thereafter, 'Mafeking' became 'a term for extravagant (and essentially unwarranted) display of enthusiasm for the British Empire and expansionist policy'.[17] Stephen also contemplates the imperialist tendencies of a more contemporary literary giant, Matthew Arnold, whose influential *Culture and Anarchy* proposed culture as a means of educating, and therefore controlling, the elements that threatened society with anarchy, particularly the working classes. Arnold was also a committed liberal imperialist and published a series of lectures promoting the mutual benefits of Ireland's absorption into the British Empire.[18] Stephen envisions the students and their abusive hazing rituals at a British institution like Oxford, as though he were a Native American viewing white European invaders. He calls them 'Palefaces' (U 1.166), a term he also applies to some English tourists later (U 10.341), and then imagines 'A deaf gardener, aproned, masked with Matthew Arnold's face' (U 1.173–4). Stephen willfully embraces the position of the barbarous, anarchic 'native' and reduces Arnold's civilizing culture to the inconsequential pursuits of the gardener, weeding the hedges and mowing the lawns of Empire, unable or unwilling to hear the voices of the colonized.

Yet another 'big word' that bears directly on Joyce's engagement with colonialism and nationalism is 'history'. Buck Mulligan's English friend Haines expresses sympathy for the Irish but invokes the concept of history to deny England's responsibility for their plight: 'We feel in England that we have treated you rather unfairly. It seems history is to blame' (U 1.648–9). The idea that English oppression of Ireland is inevitable because it is dictated by 'history' is echoed by Deasy, who tells Stephen, 'All human history moves towards one great goal, the manifestation of God' (U 2.380–1). Such models of history are typically written by the rich and powerful, by people whose interests are served by asserting that what is – the existing state of affairs – is just. Such narratives work to further the dispossession of the colonized and displace their own interpretations of their subjugation. Stephen recognizes this while teaching a history lesson to his Irish students: 'For them too history was a tale like any other too often heard, their land a pawnshop' (U 2.46–7). The text also associates Haines with the wider British colonial project elsewhere in the world. Haines had a dream about 'shooting a black panther' (U 1.61–2); his dream invokes the violence of colonialism and the leisured sporting life of the Indian Raj. Stephen scornfully casts him as a 'panthersahib' and Mulligan as his 'pointer' (U 3.277). Haines's wealthy father was also involved in colonialism and the economic exploitation it involves; he 'made his tin by selling jalap to Zulus or some bloody swindle or other' (U 1.156–7).

Haines is not just a British imperialist; he is also an enthusiast of the Irish Literary Revival and helps to illustrate the complexities of Joyce's relationship to that movement. The revival was a form of cultural nationalism. Its proponents sought to identify, create, and disseminate an Irish national literature distinct from English literature. A separate national culture and literature, they reasoned, could function as an argument for, and help pave the way towards, political separation. They also hoped that recognizing and creating a separate Irish national culture would overcome the sectarian divide and foster national community. As we have seen, Joyce was often critical of British rule in Ireland, though he was also critical of some forms or aspects of Irish nationalism. Similarly, he heaped scorn on many of the revival's major texts and ideas, but he also had much in common with its writers and shared their goal of re-imagining Irish collectivity. That Haines is both an imperialist and a revivalist indicates Joyce's conviction that many revivalist tropes and texts were derived from English traditions and were produced for condescending English audiences. Haines goes to the National

Library to do folkloric research, buys Douglas Hyde's revivalist classic *Lovesongs of Connacht*, and appears to be working on a book about Irish folkways (U 1.365). In a scene that Vincent Cheng has read persuasively as a parody of 'an ethnographic encounter with a tribal culture', he expects the old milkwoman to embody Irish national culture and speaks Irish to her, but she confesses she does not understand the language.[19] This satirizes the language movement, which was an important project for some revivalists. Like other elements of the Irish Revival, the language movement was promoted mostly by middle and upper class intellectuals rather than by the Irish 'peasantry', who were thought to be the exemplars of Irishness. More broadly, it parodies the tendency of anthropology and colonialism to view the colonized as primitive, insular, and static rather than seeing them as having exchanges with the modern, cosmopolitan world. As Cheng concludes, the scene is 'Joyce's ironic comment on an Ireland that has been constructed and essentialized as a dying, Gaelic, primitive otherness, when in reality Ireland herself no longer fits this Orientalized stereotype'.[20]

But Joyce's engagement with the idea of national culture is more complex than a straightforward idea of satire would suggest. He does not so much reject the revival's efforts to renovate Irish culture and community as appropriate and transform them. Throughout chapter 5 of *Portrait*, Stephen inhabits many of the intellectual structures of the revival, even as he rejects that movement and wants to fly by the 'nets' of 'nationality, language, religion' (P 171). Cultural nationalism tended to define the Irish nation through concepts of Irishness, an essence that was judged to appear to a greater or lesser degree in various regions, populations, and cultural artifacts. Rural dwellers and the West of Ireland, for example, were often thought of as the most Irish and least anglicized. Stephen, too, is fascinated by the idea that there is a distinctive Irish 'race' with a secret essence that could be embodied by particular individuals. He scorns his friend Davin's interest in the Irish language and Irish myth, but he also characterizes Davin as a 'peasant' and thinks Davin might give him access to the 'hidden ways of Irish life' (P 152). He casts the countrywoman in the story Davin tells him as 'a type of her race and his own' (P 154) and wonders if a female acquaintance harbours the 'secret of her race' behind her 'dark eyes' (P 185–6). And at the end of *Portrait*, Stephen sets out to 'forge in the smithy of my soul the uncreated conscience of my race' (P 213). Like the thinkers of the revival, Stephen embraces notions of representative Irish individuals and collective essences. Characteristically, in the double meaning of 'forge', Joyce leaves open the possibility that such things are illusions that are faked. That Stephen should accede to some of the fundamental assumptions of the Irish Literary Revival while vociferously rejecting the cultural nationalism it promotes should not surprise us. It fits one of the major patterns through which Joyce charts the vagaries of Stephen's intellectual life. In a related example, his friend Cranly tells him 'your mind is supersaturated with the religion in which you say you disbelieve' (P 202). We can say the same thing of Stephen's relation to the revival – his mind is supersaturated with the cultural nationalism he claims to reject.

Joyce treats Stephen with a good deal of irony, but the same observation holds true for Joyce himself. Critiques of the revival do appear in a number of his works. In 'A Little Cloud' Little Chandler's childish poetic aspirations organize themselves around the idea of becoming a poet of the Celtic Twilight. Little Chandler is 'not sure what idea he wishes to express' (D 55), and, rather than trying to think of an idea, he concentrates on imagining reviews from English critics and on crafting a more Irish-looking pen name. This encapsulates Joyce's view of the revival as a movement that often lacked real intellectual content and manufactured clichéd versions of Irishness for condescending English audiences. In 'A Mother' Mrs. Kearney sees her daughter's participation in the Irish Revival as a way to advance her daughter socially and professionally rather than as an opportunity to pursue the goals of Irish nationalism. In 'The Dead' Miss Ivors encourages Gabriel to visit the West of Ireland and learn the Irish language, and Gabriel retorts, 'I'm sick of my own country, sick of it!' (D 235). On the other hand, like Stephen, Joyce was fascinated by the idea of national traits (JJ 382, 395, 515). And his works frequently raised questions about the meanings, mechanisms, and scope of Irish communities. He did not simply respond to the models of nationalism offered by the revival by parodying them; he also responded by imagining alternative collective visions of the Irish.

Ulysses offers various ways of conceptualizing national community. Bloom's definition of a nation in 'Cyclops' is both slightly nonsensical and also quite profound: 'A nation is the same people living in the same place ... or also living in different places' (U 12.1422–3, 1428). It can be read as a model of the nation that includes the Irish diaspora; it also indicates that the boundaries of the Irish nation are not reducible to the geographical boundaries of the island. As Nolan argues, gossip, rumour, and the oral tradition provide another model of national community.[21] Stories are told and re-told, bits of gossip circulate, coincidences and chance encounters abound, and characters display intimate knowledge of each other's lives. These forms of speech embody a traditional model of community based on the face-to-face interactions of its members. Other models of Irish collectivity are more anonymous. Benedict Anderson has suggested that the novel form itself, which often depicts members of the same community going about their lives simultaneously but without necessarily being aware of one another as individuals is ideally suited to the 'community in anonymity' of the modern nation.²² This is precisely the structure of 'Wandering Rocks', which depicts the denizens of Dublin individually but ties them all together through temporal coincidence; the separate vignettes of the episode all happen at the same time. The episode's final section imagines a diverse national community in which Dubliners are brought together by their shared subjection to British rule as the viceregal cavalcade passes through town. Here again, members of the community are also distinguished from one another because each individual responds differently to that display of imperial state power.

Unlike the Irish Literary Revival, Joyce generally did not construct versions of Irish community defined through a shared Irish culture. He rejected the idea of cultural insularity or purity, and examined how Irish culture was internally differentiated and existed in exchange with other cultures. Postcolonial scholars often explore such cultural mixing or hybridity. Joyce was fascinated by the popular culture of his day and collected scraps of it assiduously. Some of it was nationalist, like 'The Croppy Boy', but a good deal of Irish popular culture came from Great Britain and was saturated with references to colonialism. This fact often bothered revivalists, but it did not faze Joyce. Advertising, for example, persistently constructed images of the ideal domestic home by invoking the civilizing mission of empire. An 1899 ad for Pears' Soap ran: 'The first step towards lightening THE WHITE MAN'S BURDEN is through teaching the virtues of cleanliness. PEARS' SOAP is a potent factor in brightening the dark corners of the earth as civilization advances, while amongst the cultured of all nations it holds the highest place – it is the ideal toilet soap'.²³ Bloom, the ad canvasser, is both sceptical of advertising's blandishments and committed to their efficacy. He is both an architect and a critic of the processes that commodify the memory of nationalist heroes like Robert Emmet, the 'gallant pictured hero' in Lionel Marks's window (U 11.1274), or enable a cake of soap to generate consumer demand by appropriating the ideology of colonialism. He rejects Father Conmee's missionary project to 'brighten the dark corners of the earth' in 'Lotus Eaters' but uses the racialist language of that project to defend himself in 'Circe': 'I did all a white man could' (U 15.797). Perhaps Joyce had seen the Pears' Soap ad; when Bloom's animated soap implicates him further in the colonial project, Joyce echoes the ad's language further: 'He brightens the earth. I polish the sky' (U 15.339).

Joyce's engagement with colonialism and nationalism took many shifting and potentially confusing forms. His works consider various elements or conceptions of colonialism: economic exploitation, the civilizing mission, orientalism, and cultural hegemony. They reveal that institutions such as the Catholic Church and intellectual traditions like Enlightenment ideals and universals are complicit with colonialism, and that Ireland is best thought of as both a colonized and a colonizing nation. His works also canvass various kinds of nationalism: cultural, constitutional, parliamentary, and physical force. Joyce criticized some nationalisms, such as those that sentimentalized or elided violence, demanded cultural purity, or traded in stereotyped versions of Irishness. But he also proposed alliances between Irish nationalism and other political causes, such as socialism and anti-racism. And his works repeatedly took up the challenges of defining Irish nationality and imagining various forms of collectivity and community for the Irish. These complexities appear in Joyce's works on a number of levels, from single words and individual psyches, to Irish communities and institutions, to global networks and the sweep of large historical forces that helped define the age of Joyce as the age of empire.

Notes

1. Eric Hobsbawm, *The Age of Empire 1875–1914* (New York: Vintage Books, 1987).
2. See Derek Attridge and Marjorie Howes, eds., *Semicolonial Joyce* (Cambridge: Cambridge University Press, 2000); Vincent Cheng, *Joyce, Race, and Empire* (Cambridge: Cambridge University Press, 1995); Enda Duffy, *The Subaltern 'Ulysses'* (Minneapolis: University of Minnesota Press, 1994); Ellen Carol Jones, ed., *Joyce: Feminism / Post / Colonialism*, European Joyce Studies 8 (Amsterdam: Rodopi, 1998); Declan Kiberd, 'James Joyce and Mythic Realism' in *Inventing Ireland* (Cambridge, MA: Harvard University Press, 1996); David Lloyd, 'Adulteration and the Nation' in *Anomalous States: Irish Writing and the Post-Colonial Moment* (Durham: Duke University Press, 1993); Emer Nolan, *James Joyce and Nationalism* (London: Routledge, 1995); Joseph Valente, *James Joyce and the Problem of Justice: Negotiating Sexual and Colonial Difference* (Cambridge: Cambridge University Press, 1995); Andrew Gibson, *Joyce's Revenge: History, Politics, and Aesthetics in 'Ulysses'* (Oxford: Oxford University Press, 2002).
3. Because I am concerned with the broad spectrum of arrangements and projects, formal and informal, through which states pursued their empires, I will use 'colonialism' and 'imperialism' more or less interchangeably.
4. See Scott B. Cook, 'The Irish Raj: Social Origins and Careers of Irishmen in the Indian Civil Service, 1855–1914', *Journal of Social History* 20.3 (Spring 1987): 507–29, 520.
5. For an extended discussion of Irish participation in the Empire refuting the notion that this involves a contradiction, see Kevin Kenny, 'The Irish in the Empire' in *Ireland and the British Empire*, ed. Kevin Kenny (Oxford: Oxford University Press, 2005).
6. See Cheng, *Joyce, Race, and Empire*, pp. 151–84.
7. Nolan, *James Joyce and Nationalism*, p. 121.

8. Ibid., p. 130.
9. Hugh Kenner, *Ulysses* (Baltimore: John Hopkins University Press, 1987), p. 93.
10. Duffy, *The Subaltern 'Ulysses'*, p. 98, p. 121.
11. Nolan, *James Joyce and Nationalism*, p. 96.
12. Ibid., p. 100.
13. Ibid., p. 102.
14. Frederic Jameson, 'Modernism and Imperialism' in *Nationalism, Colonialism, and Literature*, ed. Terry Eagleton, Fredric Jameson, and Edward Said, introduction by Seamus Deane (Minneapolis: University of Minnesota Press, 1990), pp. 43–68.
15. Don Gifford, *'Ulysses' Annotated* (Berkeley: University of California Press, 1988), p. 293.
16. For a good treatment of decolonization and the critique of Eurocentrism, see Robert Young, *White Mythologies: Writing History and the West* (London: Routledge, 1990).
17. Gifford, *'Ulysses' Annotated*, p. 235.
18. Published as Matthew Arnold, *On the Study of Celtic Literature* (London: Smith, Elder & Co., 1867).
19. Cheng, *Joyce, Race, and Empire*, p. 156.
20. Ibid., p. 157.
21. Nolan, *James Joyce and Nationalism*, pp. 85–96.
22. Benedict Anderson, *Imagined Communities: Reflections on the Origin and Spread of Nationalism* (London: Verso, 1983; rev. ed. 1991), p. 36.
23. Quoted in Anne McClintock, *Imperial Leather: Race, Gender and Sexuality in the Colonial Contest* (New York: Routledge, 1995), p. 32.

10

MARIAN EIDE

Gender Politics

James Joyce's ideas about gender keep changing, and changing in unpredictable ways. In his lifetime, he said some crazy things about women and alienated any number of men.[1] But in the years since his death, he has gotten considerably wiser, and we, his readers, have very credibly seen our own most innovative concepts about gender reflected in his words. We have experienced that uncanny effect of Joyce already having arrived *avant la carte* where we are still struggling to navigate. For every generation, his books have proven the apt point from which to depart on a journey of understanding distinctions between and among the sexes. One of the reasons this writer remains so perpetually relevant is his sense that gender is formed in the political realm and is crucial to understanding human community, the polis, and thus the political. If gender is political, as my title asserts, it is so because it affects our attempts to live collectively and on shared terms. In the pages that follow, I focus on Joyce's last two works, and particularly on his dramatic episodes, 'Circe' in *Ulysses* and *Finnegans Wake* II.1. My objective is, in part, to support a rather literal exploration of gender as performance and, in part, to engage with passages in which identity is most mutable, providing the greatest challenge to our understanding of gender difference as stable. Embedded in the speech acts through which gender is performed is the consciousness of that performance; the gesture of gender is oriented to the material world and one's experience of it such that gender is as much a matter of phenomenology as of linguistic activity.

***

About a third of the way into the 'Circe' episode of *Ulysses*, Leopold Bloom magically transforms into the 'new womanly man' (*U* 15.1798–9), a gender status not to be made much clearer in the pages to follow. There are as many ways to understand this shift as there are progeny of his transition: he gives birth to only eight children in 'Circe' (*U* 15.1821) but imagines himself capable of fathering thousands in 'Lotus-Eaters' (*U* 5.571). Given his procreative capacities, his transformation can be read in essentialist terms in which Bloom's gender is reduced to his biology. If Bella/o the brothel Madame can plunge his or her arm *'elbowdeep in Bloom's vulva'* (*U* 15.3089), and if Bloom gives birth to eight children, then Bloom must be a woman, and biology is a fact that precedes and determines gender identity in the simplest terms – for not only is Bloom endowed with a woman's body but with her 'natural' desires and behaviours: 'O, I so want to be a mother', she says, speaking her biological destiny to reproduce in a manner acculturated as feminine. In that simple 'O' readers can hear the raised vocal pitch and see the swaying hips and even a limp wrist or two. This version of gender is in keeping with other essentialist ideas reported in conjunction with Bloom's miraculous virgin births. In preceding lines within the episode, men of African heritage are described in the most racist language possible, acting in minstrel shows.[2] Bloom himself, dressed in generically 'oriental' garb and speaking in a stereotypical patois, warbles a song to jeers from his audience (*U* 15.957–61). On this reading, Joyce is a man of his time: painstakingly revising the episode in Paris in 1920, he articulates the prejudices of his moment in which the Orient is inscrutably and exotically feminine, people of African heritage are valued primarily for their ability to entertain, and women are confined to the domestic, as Molly, in the pages of *Ulysses*, is confined to her bedroom. 'Delineating Molly mainly as a sexual being, Joyce confines her character to a conventional mold', Elaine Unkeless observed in 1982. 'Since Molly is confined to her house, or even to her bed, her perspective remains narrow.'[3] Echoing Unkeless's observation, Laura Doyle, in 1994, noted 'the 'blocked' spatial rendering of Molly', as she 'never leaves her house – nor, virtually, her bed – because the text depends on, all of its previous intersections accumulate toward, her fixed presence there'.[4] For feminisms of many generations the reduction of a woman's gender to corporeality mimicked too neatly a lengthy philosophical tradition that reduced women to the materiality of nature, to natural roles predicated primarily on the reproductive function.[5]

This essentialist strain can be seen in the episode's 'appeals to a pure or original femininity, a female essence, outside the boundaries of the social and thereby untainted (though perhaps repressed) by a patriarchal order'. It can also be read in the accounts of 'universal female oppression, the assumption of a totalizing symbolic system which subjugates all women everywhere, throughout history and across cultures'.[6] Far from joining in that patriarchal oppression then, Bloom's transformation testifies to it, remarking on the ways women's bodies are read as productive of particular behavioural patterns. Bloom, for example, calls on 'Dr Malachi Mulligan, sex specialist, to give medical testimony on my behalf' (*U* 15.1772–3). When other doctors join in the examination, Dr Dixon in particular observes Bloom's womanly 'moral nature', which is 'simple and lovable', and observes that Bloom has written 'a really beautiful letter, a poem in itself' (*U* 15. 1799, 1801–2). This latter observation supports an ideal not just of feminine virtue but also of a feminine language: 'Essentialism underwrites claims for the autonomy of a female voice and the potentiality of a feminine language (notions which find their most sophisticated expression in the much discussed concept of *écriture feminine*).'[7] The flows of Molly's body and the fluid associativity of her thought were among Hélène Cixous' primary examples of the affirmative poetics of *écriture feminine*.[8]

Transformed into a woman, the loquacious Bloom, whose thoughts have pervaded the text for a few hundred pages, is, at this point, reduced for much of the remaining episode to near silence, while subjected also to Bello's domination. Another way of looking at the scene is to see Bloom as feminized by public scrutiny and abuse. To be subject in that brutal way is to experience what it is like to be a woman or to be constructed as a woman. As Marilyn French wrote in 1976, 'For Bloom, being female means experiencing sex as surrender and violation, being treated as a maidservant, slave, mere body – a nonperson like the whores – and beast, layer of eggs and giver of milk.'[9] Observing the loss of power Bloom suffers as a woman is consistent with Joyce's sensitivity to women's plight throughout his writings. He understood entrapment by domestic responsibility when he wrote Eveline's story in *Dubliners*. He saw Gerty MacDowell's identity formed through the feminized sentimentalism of cheap fiction and women's periodicals. Yet perceiving these conditions, as Carolyn G. Heilbrun once noted, is not the same as militating against them, thus, 'He averted his gaze from what he himself called the greatest revolution of our time: "the revolt of women against the idea that they are the mere instruments of men".' In reducing Bloom to a coquettish, delicate flower who desires only to fulfill the biological destiny of reproducing, Joyce, as Heilbrun also observed, cannot 'imagine a woman whom convention did not offer him'.[10]

Perhaps 'convention' is the key term here. It is not biology that determines Bloom's destiny but convention. With Heilbrun's critique in mind, one can observe the extent to which Bloom's gender is constructed by his circumstances. It is not because he is a woman that he loses power and voice; it is when he loses power that he becomes a woman. For the transformation does not happen spontaneously but in a particular context: it follows his trial and the myriad unjust charges filed against him by his community and is sustained by Bello's sexual domination. Bloom's gender appears to be a social construction, the 'effect of complicated discursive practices'; the natural state does not precede the social context but is perceived through it.[11] It is culture that produces gender differences as power differentials. Joyce's contemporary, Virginia Woolf, also viewed gender as a construction based in part on political access. In *Three Guineas*, she wrote about the ways that political and social deprivations become the gendered virtues she lists as 'poverty, chastity, derision, and freedom from unreal loyalties'.[12] To repeat her famous line in other terms, unequal pay, sexual double standards, and exclusion from the inner circles of power render women less susceptible to the allures of money, to committing sexual exploitation, and to domination, more generally. As such Woolf's principles remind her readers that gender is a social construct created by its circumstances, but those circumstance may become crucial social virtues as well.

Under the medical surveillance that would seem biologically based, beyond the distortions of such social constructs, Bloom's gender is envisioned intersectionally, to borrow from Kimberlé Crenshaw.[13] Understood by his community to be Jewish, in spite of his multiple conversions to Christianity, he is perceived then to *smell* Jewish–'*fetor judaicus* is most perceptible' (*U* 15.1797), Dr Punch Costello observes. His effeminacy is produced in part by this perception in which his sex is inflected by his 'race', his masculinity compromised by his foreignness; he is seen as less manly than his Irish friends, who employ the brothel's services, announcing their masculinity through their compulsory heterosexuality. While the medical students are compelled to verify their perception by examining Bloom's body to ascertain the biological source of his putative femininity, what they see is mediated by the principles of their medical education and the prejudices of their political world.

Read in this light, one might observe that it is when Bloom returns to his voice and power in conversation with the nymph that his gender changes. Several decades after Joyce imagined this transformation, Simone de Beauvoir memorably observed that 'one is not born, but rather becomes, a woman', thus echoing Woolf's claim for gender construction.[14] With the ambiguous '*devient*' of the original, which can be translated both as 'being' and as 'cultivating or making', she presents the possibility of the 'second sex' as a choice made within systemic social constructs and constraints. Her words register the inequities into which women are born, the conventions that constrain them. However, '*devient*' also suggests that gender is a project in which men and women actively take part, a construct that, to adopt Judith Butler's gloss on Beauvoir's philosophy, we *perform*.[15]

Joyce also designates gender as a performance by literalizing Bloom's gender transformation as an act in a play, the genre of the 'Circe' episode.

If gender is primarily a social construct, then one might don gender as a man dons a dress when performing in drag, taking up womanly gestures along with feminine clothes. Bloom is seen with *'an elbow resting in a hand, a forefinger against his cheek'* (U 15.2337). Now there is nothing innately feminine about his language of gesture here, but culturally speaking, it comes across as effeminate. A reader may only interpret this gesture in such gendered terms because of a preexisting presumption that Bloom, usually a man, would ordinarily perform a different, putatively masculine set of gestures. If such is the case, however, then gender can be performed in a repertory of gestures that need not adhere to the biology of the body, and Bloom's more stereotypically masculine gestures throughout the book are as much a performance of his gender as the affectation recorded here when Bloom is treated as a woman. Bloom's transformations in Nighttown result from the accretion of gendered practices over time in which what seems to be a natural fact of sex is produced by a series of social assumptions and culturally inscribed fictions. What we have seen as behavioural expressions of bodily sex are actually more a vocabulary of styles that, over time and with a certain amount of simplification and rigidification, become a coherent script of gender that seems to arise from the natural source of the body rather than producing a framework through which the body is understood. Or as Judith Butler explains, 'Gender is an identity tenuously constituted in time, instituted in an exterior space through a *stylized repetition of acts.*'[16]

Butler's particular discovery in her break-out book *Gender Trouble* was that drag performance in queer spaces over many years elucidated the degree to which all gender performance is a kind of drag. '*In imitating gender, drag implicitly reveals the imitative structure of gender itself – as well as its contingency.*' 'Gender', she argued, emerges from 'a set of repeated acts within a highly rigid regulatory frame that congeal over time to produce the appearance of substance, of a natural sort of being.'[17] Gender, then, is an iterative, citational performance rather than a social manifestation of material difference. Donning identity like a costume or performing gender in a drag show with a set of stylized postures and movements points to the artificialities of the construct more generally. Gender is not so much an internal reality as a set of effects produced and reproduced continually to consolidate an impression of stable identity. When Bloom rests his forefinger coquettishly on his cheek he produces an effect of femininity, particularly one that echoes a series of such gestures understood to be feminine and subsequently enforced as norms in social structures that attempt to keep individuals driving in their particular lanes. In other words, while Bloom's gesture is performative in Butler's sense, it is not without consequence to his status, power, or agency in the world.

Is Bloom utterly powerless in the face of these political assumptions? Is he merely subject to the social world of gender difference? To the contrary, as Butler argues, 'The reconceptualization of identity as an *effect*, that is, as *produced* or *generated*, opens up possibilities of "agency" that are insidiously foreclosed by positions that take identity categories as foundational or fixed.'[18] While this insight might support an empowered view of gender as a series of choices, it is important to note that Bloom's gesture is performed from within a limited, and possibly limiting, repertoire of such gestures, and it is only within that repertoire that these moves can be understood. Identity, then, is citational, and while there is some agency within the social constructions that form this script, that agency is limited by the script itself. In this vast gestural vocabulary, there are nuanced terms between the sex binary that Joyce explored, beginning with his earliest writings; in *Stephen Hero*, for example, a priest gathers his 'soutane for the ascent with a slow hermaphroditic gesture' (*SH* 98). While we might no longer use the term 'hermaphrodite' nor stereotype the practical gathering of a long garment before climbing stairs, Joyce's early observation still opens a window into both Stephen's gender perceptions and the priest's gender performance.

Given the power of the script both the priest and the student follow, one might argue that biological sex does not exist prior to discourse. However, such a position raises questions about what the doctors in Nighttown found when they looked under Bloom's skirts. Under the medical students' examination, Bloom's sex is actually far more ambiguous than their individual observations allow. His bodily configuration seems to their novice eyes to be so unusual as to warrant display in a medical (or 'teratological') museum. They collaborate on a 'pervaginal examination' and also observe 'hypospadias', an arrangement in which the urethra opens on the underside of the penis instead of at the tip, which implies that Bloom must have a penis as well as the vagina that Bello invades. Mulligan describes the patient as 'bisexually abnormal', while Dixon hails him as the 'new womanly man' (*U* 15.1784–99). Given the medical testimony that follows, the term 'bisexual' does not seem to refer to his desires or sexual practices, as the term is currently used, but to his physical form. Perhaps if the chapter were written today the medical students would class Bloom as intersex and be no less excited by the rarity of their find. Perhaps like John Money, they would advise surgery to assign a single sex and prescribe a course of cognitive, behavioural therapy to induce gender conformity.[19] Referring to Money, I do not intend to filter Joyce's words through presentist assumptions. As Joyce was embarking on his writing career, sexologists (and most prominently Sigmund Freud in his *Three Essays* of 1905) were asserting that not all bodies have determined sex. Enduring since Freud's publication is the surveillance of these gender non-conforming bodies and the prurient need to find some biological truth to their physiology, to delineate physical contours and assign them unambiguous meaning. Toby Beauchamp observes, 'The category of transgender is produced through surveillance practices that both draw and dissolve its parameters, not only through spectacular or formal actions undertaken by state actors but also in the most mundane condition of our gendered lives.'[20] These are exactly the surveillance practices to which Bloom's ambiguous body is subjected.

But what is Bloom's experience of his own body, the feeling of his genitals under the eyes of the medical students, the touch of his finger on his cheek, his elbow resting in his own hand? Gayle Salamon observes that this realm of perception, the experience of the body, 'my sense of its extension and efficacy, the ways that I endeavor to make a habitable thing of it, and the use I make of it', these are for phenomenology the perceptions that 'retain pride of place as a means of determining truth'.[21] On this account, it is not that Bloom's time in Nighttown is haunted by hallucination but that the surreal style of the episode fittingly mimes Bloom's understanding of his body in these encounters, that he experiences himself in relation to the brothel madame as highly feminized, that under the gazes of the medical students disporting themselves with sex workers, he feels as though a specimen observed, prodded, and exposed.[22] The perpetual alterations in his gender over the course of these pages echo the felt sense of the body in relation to others.

The sex workers also understand their bodies through their sensory perceptions and those of their clients. Funny and flirtatious, they are also deeply degraded by their circumstances, which are hardly economically enviable: it is after his prize money runs out in *A Portrait of the Artist as a Young Man* that Stephen begins visiting streetwalkers. The fact that he can afford to employ one, without any visible means of income, indicates the low fees they could charge, the low worth they were accorded. In this context Stephen's experience of their kiss as an exchange of words 'the vehicle of a vague speech' (P 101), while still betraying a transactional and instrumentalist treatment of a woman, shows some sense of the human, communicative worth of this female stranger. Like the brothel's professionals, the pink-gowned streetwalker in *Portrait* experiences her gender through the desires and uses of her clients. Yet, the narrator of *Portrait* also admits to 'noting the proud conscious movements of her perfumed head' (P 100). This young woman's gender is produced in part by her felt sense of her body, a kind of proprioception; movement and placement in space, the perception of the body and awareness of its materiality – this physical knowledge informs one's gender identity, which is not the same as saying that biology defines gender. It is rather to argue that the experience of the body within the intricacies of consciousness produces gender.

***

Recently, gender studies has taken a phenomenological turn or, some might say, a return, a circuit back to the beginning of the twentieth century, to the principles from which Simone de Beauvoir derived her conclusions about the 'second sex' and the philosophical moment in its primacy in France when Joyce was residing in Paris in the 1920s and 1930s. Marcel Proust's experiment with the *madeleine* is said to have brought phenomenology from Edmund Husserl's Germany to France's literary culture, and Maurice Merleau-Ponty cemented its philosophical import in his teaching during the 1930s and leading up to his publication of *Phenomenology of Perception* in 1945. Though Joyce delighted in claiming he had not carefully read Proust, he was steeped in the literary world produced as much by the phenomenological imaginings of *A la recherce de temps perdu* as he was by the surrealist stylings that are a more obvious influence on the pages of 'Circe'.

The phenomenological context of bodily experience as subjected to gender surveillance is at the heart of the ninth chapter of *Finnegans Wake*, during which the twin sons, Shem and Shaun, and their younger sister, Issy, rehearse a play, and the boys seek the truth of their sister's gender by attempting to look under her skirt. That attempt is staged within a larger performance of a guessing game played with the spectrum of rainbow girls, the boys guessing the colors of the girls' undergarments and also speculating about what cannot be seen beneath those drawers. The guesses are always wrong, and the presumptive truth of the bodies remains unknown because the twilight game ends when HCE calls the children in for dinner. The episode is sandwiched between two chapters similarly devoted to gender surveillance. In the preceding chapter, two women trade stories about Anna Livia Plurabelle's sexual activities, subjecting her to the scrutiny of gossip. In the following chapter, 'Nightlessons', the children look under the skirts of their eternal geomater, ALP, to find a geometrical diagram rather than a biological fact. Of course, Joyce's plot is significantly more complex than this simple précis allows, and within this structure there are many digressions and micronarratives. I would like to focus on two issues the games raise: the age-old questions about how the circulation of power produces knowledge and the language of Issy's non-conforming gender.

The conflation of education and sexual experience compressed in the term 'carnal knowledge' guides one of the subplots in this chapter. Like her brothers guessing about the colour of her undergarments, Issy's tutor attempts to turn up her skirt and finger the fruits of her body. In a brief description of Issy's private education under the direction of this unnamed tutor, Joyce registers a pedagogical approach reminiscent of a far more famous educator of girls who is invoked throughout the *Wake*: Jonathan Swift, who met Esther Johnson when she was only eight years old, became her tutor, and maintained their relationship for the rest of her life. His letters to her were collected after his death and published under his pet name for her as *A Journal to Stella*. Some of Swift's biographers suggest there may have been a romantic or sexual relation between the writer and his very young student, a variation on a theme that Joyce pursues throughout his last book.[23] Issy endures sexual abuse in exchange for knowledge:

> A bimbamb bum! They vain would convert the to be hers in the word. Gush, they wooed! Gash, they're fair ripecherry!
> As for she could shake him. An oaf, no more. Still he'd be good tutor two in his big armschair lerningstoel and she be waxen in his hands. Turning up and fingering over the most dantellising peaches in the lingerous longerous book of the dark. Look at this passage about Galilleotto! I know it is difficult but when your goche I go dead. Turn now to this patch upon Smacchiavelluti! Soot allours, he's sure to spot it! (*FW* 251.18–27)

Issy's classical education spans the works of Dante, Galileo, and Machiavelli, grouped here not only for their contributions to knowledge but because they are all entombed in the Basilica of San Francesco in Ravenna, Italy, along with Michelangelo, who, given his place in the histories of gender and sexuality, is noticeably absent from the passage. While the narrator claims Issy can shake this oaf of a man, she actually seems trapped by his touch. It is disturbing to witness this teacher, who is so much older than his student, talking about her ripe cherry and soft peaches. He invites her to sit on his lap or in his armschair, making her as pliable as wax in his hands. Issy's tutor is also a 'toucher' (*FW* 251.29) who turns up her skirts the way he turns down the pages of the book of the dark from which he is teaching her. He finds her cherry ripe for the picking and crudely refers to her vulva as a gash. He fingers her tantalizing peaches – a lovely and also deeply creepy description of a prepubescent girl's genitals – while casting longing and languourous/dangerous glances at her.

It is difficult to assess the tone of this passage, which, while registering disturbing images of child sexual assault, does so with apparent joviality. Yet Joyce clearly understood the damage done by this kind of exploitation. In *Dubliners*, he indicates his concerns about child sexual abuse by the painful undertones describing the ruined priest and his ambivalent boy student in 'The Sisters' and by the queer old josser in 'An Encounter'. Should the writer not find this harm to girls an outrage rather than an amusement? And should he not see in the lengthy literary history of older men sexually assaulting girls a tragic strain?

One of Joyce's most eminent interpreters, William York Tindall, seemed to find the whole idea of deflowering maidens quite droll also. In 1969, Tindall deemed it appropriate to quote a Bond girl as an expert on gender and to find her tragic account of women's sexual precarity amusing. 'A virgin, says Pussy Galore, is a girl who can run faster than her brother, father or uncle.'[24] The Bawd in 'Circe' makes an alarmingly similar claim: 'Ten shillings a maidenhead. Fresh thing was never touched. Fifteen. There's no-one in it only her old father that's dead drunk' (U 15.359–60). There are several ways to understand the Bawd's words. Perhaps there is no one inside the house but the maiden's father, who apparently approves of the sale of his daughter's young body, but it is equally possible no one has had sex with this child except her father. If the antecedent of 'it' is 'maidenhead', perhaps the Bawd does not count the father's assault because, like Pussy Galore, she believes it is quite common for family men to rape their female kin. While Tindall appears complicit in the subjugation of women with his tawdry humour, it is also notable that fully one-third of the citations at the end of his volume are to the works of women scholars.

Setting the tone for that scholarship, Joyce may be making light of the tutor's manipulation of his student, but he may equally be imagining the child's resistance. There is some evidence of Issy's defiance in the lines that follow the description of assault:

> 'Twas ever so in monitorology since Headmaster Adam became Eva Harte's toucher, *in omnibus moribus et temporibus*, with man's mischief in his mind whilst her pupils swimmed too heavenlies, let his be exasperated, letters be blowed!'[25]   (FW 251.27–31)

Acknowledging the age-old history of men's power as educators, *in omnibus moribus et temporibus*, or a moral of the times so lengthy it would require an omnibus to describe, Issy sees the mischief that preoccupies men's minds. She responds to the sexual intrusion with sarcasm, rolling her eyes upwards. She blocks the tutor's intrusion along with his instruction: let him be exasperated, lessons be damned. Women, she comments, have had to put up with mansplaining since Adam and Eve. Of course, my politics and my love of Joyce make me read this passage as a mirror of my own moral investments because those eyes may equally be swimming upwards in pleasure from the sexual act commonly referred to with the verb 'blow'.

In this chapter, Issy comes into her gender through the perception of others, through their surveillance and their touch. The brothers look under her skirts for the body they anticipate will confirm her sex as female, a sight incestuously tantalizing to their burgeoning desires. Like one of the goblins at Christina Rossetti's market, the tutor or toucher feels ripe cherries and tantalizing peaches. The experimental language of Joyce's last book liberates Issy neither from the discipline of gender conformity nor from the social conventions that undergird the abuse of her body. Tragically, like so many girls before and after her, Issy is to come into her sense of her gender through the abuse of her body. Yet the men who ogle and grope her may be wrong about what they see and feel, for Issy's body is mediated by Joyce's prose in ambiguous terms, while her sense of her body is as resolute as it is fluid.

Issy administers her own lesson about grammatical gender and its binary system of noun classification: 'I is a femaline person. O, of provocative gender. U unisingular case' (*FW* 251.31–2). With these instructions, Issy refuses the version of herself that men and boys construct and asserts her felt sense of her living body, this proprioception, as mutable and queer. She describes herself as 'femaline', a word recently defined in urban dictionaries as a 'masculine person with feminine energies or traits.' But Joyce got there first; neither masculine nor feminine grammatically, Issy's gender is provocative – she has noted the strong reactions her body elicits in men and boys, and noticed both their sexual arousal and their exasperation or anger. Choosing her words carefully, she teaches the tutor and her brothers about being provocative and through that word choice about the proximity of their arousal to their anger, the blame they lay at her feet for their own frustrated desires. In the face of provocation, she remains unisingular, an autonomous entity not to be categorized by the surveillance of her body or by the ways that language mediates her gender, forcing it into one side of a binary divide they refuse. Rather, they draw attention to the epistemological uncertainty that the material body poses, the mediation of the physical through language. For while unique, they are also part of a collective of twenty-nine people whose gender has been inscribed as feminine but whose sense of themselves may span every color of a queer rainbow, whose symbolic significance has only recently caught up with Joyce's gender politics.

Issy shares their gender with twenty-eight rainbow friends. One way to understand this sense of embodiment is phenomenologically. Gender, for Merleau-Ponty, is completely individual rather than categorical. It is based not on the architecture of the body but on perception and experience. Merleau-Ponty offers a lovely metaphor for his very particular understanding of how perception or perspective operates:

> When I see the lamp on my table, I attribute to it not merely the qualities that are visible from my location, but also those that the fireplace, the walls, and the table 'see.' The back of my lamp is merely the face that it 'shows' to the fireplace. Thus, I can see one object insofar as objects form a system or a world, and insofar as each of them arranges the others around itself like spectators of its hidden aspect and as the guarantee of their permanence.[26]

In other words, we may see the object as if in a two-dimensional painting, but we experience it in its three dimensions as if seen from the perspective of other objects. More importantly, the lamp has its significance not in isolation but in the system or world in which it is arranged. Similarly, Issy, at play among twenty-nine rainbow friends, merges into the game and among its participants. The perspective of self is extended into the perspectives of the others like the lamp set amidst the walls and resting on the table. Even as they become themselves in concert with each other, the individual children emerge because of and are merged into the hues of the rainbow. More tragically, however, even as Issy resists their body's invasion by the tutor's touch and their brothers' surveillance, they become gendered in the experience of a body violated by touch and gaze. Thus for Issy in this scenario, as for Merleau-Ponty and other phenomenologists, the body is not an inert material object like a lamp but a physical entity that comes into being in its interaction with the world.

The body, then, to follow another illustrative scenario provided by Gayle Salamon, experiences thirst and moves an arm towards a water glass on a table. This gesture of extending the arm 'is not a matter of cognition, but of changing my comportment, my embodiment, my bodily being so that it encompasses the object of my desire and interacts with it. My body comes into concert not only with those objects in the world towards which my desire is intended but also with itself in that moment – it becomes purposefulness.'[27] In the gesture the body itself recedes from awareness as a singular entity and emerges into consciousness as an extension towards the object of its need or desire. In the lesson, Issy's body is not founded merely on its inert morphology but in its perception of invasion and its experience of resistance; their sense of the body and its gender is performed and perceived in the gesture of playing itself.

Gesture is crucial to Joyce's understanding of the embodied, communicative relations between people. One evening in *Stephen Hero*, Stephen Dedalus tells his confidant Cranly that 'there should be an art of gesture'. He explains that he does not 'mean art of gesture in the sense that the elocution professor understands the word. For him a gesture is an emphasis. I mean a rhythm' (*SH* 184). I'm not perfectly clear about what Stephen means by 'rhythm', but I am certain that this concept remains important to him, for Joyce repeats it years later while Stephen stumbles around the brothel and declaims, this time with Lynch in tow, 'So that gesture, not music not odour, would be a universal language, the gift of tongues rendering visible not the lay sense but the first entelechy, the structural rhythm' (U 15.105–7). Gesture is still about rhythm here, but crucially it is 'the first entelechy', the soul, the core principle that guides the person, the realization of potential. The source of being is located not within the body, but in its movement, in the gesture with which the body mediates conscious experience and the perspective outwards and into the world. Stephen's aspirations may be idealist, yet the body's gestures are not entirely free. Even in locating gender in the gesture, phenomenology accounts for the social and political contexts in which those gestures are performed. As Sara Ahmed cautions, 'Bodies are shaped by histories, which they perform in their comportment, their posture, and their gestures.' The horizons of our genders are mapped by these 'sedimented histories'.[28]

Perhaps we project our own ideas about gender onto Joyce's words like figures onto an ink blot. Perhaps Joyce was so open to possibility that he inscribed one hundred years of gender theory into his books as he buried conundrums to keep the professors busy. Or perhaps our ideas about gender change less than we think as we circle back to speech-act theory and phenomenology, to the truth of the body and the filtering of the cultures it inhabits. Where readers might seek clear political positions in the prose, in Joyce's fictions, as Karen Lawrence argues, the answers are indeterminate. This ambiguity remains the creative strength of the oeuvre, which may put political and social wrongs to right by witnessing to a long history of gender-based violence. But it may equally perpetuate them in the service of strange comedy. These texts place responsibility on the reader to make meaning and justice in the world. Without question, however, Joyce's words provide readers with more fluid possibilities to counter the old binaries of the sex/gender system.

Notes

1. Jeri Johnson, 'Joyce and Feminism' in *The Cambridge Companion to James Joyce*, 2nd edition, ed. Derek Attridge (Cambridge: Cambridge University Press, 2004), p. 196.
2. Traditionally, these shows were performed by white men with blackened faces, so the horrific description Joyce uses may have the kind of doubling effect Homi Bhabha described as mimicry, which circles back on white prejudice with dramatic irony. However, the prose is, nonetheless, startling in its ruthless, racist caricature: 'Tom and Sam Bohee, coloured coons in white duck suits, scarlet socks, upstarched Sambo chokers and large scarlet asters in their buttonholes,

leap out. Each has his banjo slung. Their paler smaller negroid hands jingle the twingtwang wires. Flashing white Kaffir eyes and tusks they rattle through a breakdown in clumsy clogs, twinging, singing, back to back, toe heel, heel toe, with smackfatclacking nigger lips' (*U* 15.412–18).

3. Elaine Unkeless, 'The Conventional Molly Bloom' in *Women in Joyce*, ed. Suzette Henke and Elaine Unkeless (Urbana: University of Illinois Press, 1982), p. 153.
4. Laura Doyle, *Bordering on the Body: The Racial Matrix of Modern Fiction and Culture* (Oxford: Oxford University Press, 1994), p. 136.
5. Susan Bordo, 'The Cartesian Masculinization of Thought', *Signs: Journal of Women in Culture and Society* 11.3 (1976): 439–56, 452.
6. Diana Fuss, *Essentially Speaking: Feminism, Nature and Difference* (New York: Routledge), p. 2.
7. Ibid., p. 2. 'For the essentialist, the natural provides the raw material and determinative starting point for the practices and laws of the social. For example, sexual difference (the division into "male" and "female") is taken as prior to social differences which mapped on to, *a posteriori*, the biological subject. For the constructionist, the natural is itself posited as a construction of the social. In this view, sexual difference is discursively produced, elaborated as an effect of the social rather than its *tabula rasa*, its prior object.' Ibid., p. 3.
8. Hélène Cixous, 'The Laugh of the Medusa', trans. Keith Cohen and Paula Cohen, *Signs: Journal of Women in Culture and Society* 1.4 (1976): 875–93, 884. Luce Irigaray introduced a variant on Cixous's ideal by arguing that because '*woman has sex organs just about everywhere*' her writing 'goes off in all directions in which "he" is unable to discern the coherence of any meaning'. Gayatri Spivak found these kinds of claims for avant-garde writing absurd, noting that 'there is something even faintly comical about Joyce rising above sexual identities and bequeathing the proper mind-set to the women's movement'. For Sandra M. Gilbert and Susan Gubar, the 'valorization of Joyce by feminists like Cixous' is completely unconvincing, as Molly and ALP are reduced to the language of the body, and Nora Barnacle was solicited to compose a 'calligraphy of shit'. See Luce Irigaray, *This Sex Which Is Not One*, trans. Catherine Porter with Carolyn Burke (Ithaca, NY: Cornell University Press, 1985), p. 103; Gayatri Spivak, 'French Feminism in an International Frame', *Yale French Studies* 62 (1981): 154–84, 172; and Sandra M. Gilbert and Susan Gubar, 'Sexual Linguistics: Gender, Language, Sexuality', *New Literary History* 16.3 (1985): 515–43, 523.
9. Marilyn French, *The Book as World: James Joyce's 'Ulysses'* (Cambridge, MA: Harvard University Press, 1976), p. 198.
10. Carolyn G. Heilbrun, 'Afterword' in *Women in Joyce*, ed. Henke and Unkeless, p. 215.
11. Fuss, *Essentially Speaking*, p. 2.
12. Virginia Woolf, *Three Guineas* (New York: Harcourt Brace, 1938), p. 80.
13. Kimberlé Crenshaw, 'Demarginalizing the Intersection of Race and Sex: A Black Feminist Critique of Antidiscrimination Doctrine, Feminist Theory and Anti-Racist Politics', *University of Chicago Legal Forum* 1989.1 (1989): 139–67.
14. Simone de Beauvoir, *The Second Sex*, trans. Constance Borde and Sheila Malovany-Chevallier (New York: Alfred A. Knopf, 2010), p. 293.

15. Judith Butler, 'Sex and Gender in Simone De Beauvoir's Second Sex', *Yale French Studies* 72 (1986): 35–49, 36.
16. Judith Butler, *Gender Trouble: Feminism and the Subversion of Identity* (New York: Routledge), p. 140.
17. Ibid., pp. 137, 33.
18. Ibid., p. 147.
19. Judith Butler provides a compelling account of Money's sexual reassignment research and medical practice, as well as its tragic results in *Undoing Gender* (New York: Routledge, 2004).
20. Toby Beauchamp, *Going Stealth: Transgender Politics and U.S. Surveillance Practices* (Durham, NC: Duke University Press, 2019), p. 139.
21. Gayle Salamon, *Assuming a Body: Transgender and Rhetorics of Materiality* (New York: Columbia University Press, 2010), p. 56.
22. Noting the extent to which Joyce explores the subsuming of human desire by consumer capitalism, Catherine Flynn argues that while the 'Circe' episode is aesthetically subversive, the desires and sexual exchanges described there are not: 'It is important to acknowledge that there is nothing uncommercial as such in Bloom's deviant activities: one can suppose that there are many brothels in which such doings are part of the standard bill of fare.' However, Bloom also presents a 'deviation from reproductive desire that undermines the conventional boundaries of the person, as well as the oppositions of subject and object', and 'Bloom is interested in an expansion of pleasure not through instrumentalizing women but rather through coming closer to their experience.' Catherine Flynn, *James Joyce and the Matter of Paris* (Cambridge: Cambridge University Press, 2019), pp. 156, 159, 160.
23. Leo Damrosch demurs that Swift was no Lewis Carroll, acknowledging that other biographers equate the two writers' sexual interests. He is more confident of Swift's amorous relations with another Esther, with the last name Vanhomrigh, who is referred to also as Vanessa in Swift's writings. Leo Damrosch, *Jonathan Swift: His Life and His World* (New Haven, CT: Yale University Press, 2014), pp. 50, 235, 327–8.
24. William York Tindall, *A Reader's Guide to 'Finnegans Wake'* (New York: Farrar, Straus, and Giroux, 1969), p. 4.
25. Many feminist scholars of Joyce have commented on this passage. Claudine Raynaud emphasizes the age difference in this pedagogical relationship. Claudine Raynaud, 'Woman, the Letter Writer; Man, the Writing Master', *James Joyce Quarterly* 23.1 (1986): 299–324. Kimberly Devlin notes that the book itself becomes an object of pandering or 'Galilleotto': 'In the hands of the lascivious teacher/toucher, Dante's text of moral instruction becomes a tool of sexual seduction.' Kimberly Devlin, *Wandering and Return in 'Finnegans Wake': An Integrative Approach to Joyce's Fictions* (Princeton, NJ: Princeton University Press, 1991), p. 46.
26. Maurice Merleau-Ponty, *Phenomenology of Perception*, trans. Donald A. Landes (New York: Routledge, 1974), p. 71.
27. Salamon, *Assuming a Body*, p. 53.
28. Sara Ahmed, 'Orientations: Toward a Queer Phenomenology', *GLQ: A Journal of Lesbian and Gay Studies* 12.4 (2006): 543–74, 552.

11

KATHERINE MULLIN

Sex and Sexuality

Writing to his brother Stanislaus on 12 August 1912, Joyce described a difficult conversation with his publisher. George Roberts was managing director of Maunsel & Co., the Dublin publishing house that had, in 1909, agreed to issue *Dubliners*. Yet, three years later, he was still quibbling about risky material: 'He asked me very narrowly was there sodomy also in "The Sisters" and what was "simony" and if the priest was suspended only for the breaking of the chalice' (*Letters II* 305–6). As Roberts's telling 'also' suggested, this was the latest of several skirmishes about *Dubliners*, which had already shipwrecked the collection's chances. In 1906, negotiations with Grant Richards had broken down when his printer had refused to typeset 'Two Gallants', objecting to Corley's account of his adventures with 'a fine tart': 'I was afraid, man, she'd get in the family way. But she's up to the dodge' (*D* 44). Rashly, Joyce had retorted that 'the more subtle inquisitor will denounce "An Encounter", the enormity of which the printer cannot see, because he is, as I said, a plain blunt man' (*SL* 83). Roberts, however, was the 'more subtle inquisitor' Joyce invoked, shrewdly decoding suspect nuances. 'Simony' – a theological term referring to the sale of sacred things – sounds like 'sodomy', which had a painful recent history in Irish literature after Oscar Wilde's 1895 conviction for homosexual offences. Roberts had already forced Joyce to remove a reference in 'Ivy Day in the Committee Room' to Father Keon's 'discreet indulgent velvety voice', speaking with a timbre, Joyce originally wrote, 'which is not often found except with the confessor or the sodomite'.[1] Roberts's questions were the last straw. Within weeks, Joyce was leaving Dublin for his home in Trieste, composing his scurrilous poem 'Gas from a Burner' as he travelled (*PSW* 261). Yet, ironically, Roberts was the very reader Joyce demanded: alert to references within and beyond the text, adept at detecting hidden meanings and distant echoes. His question registered the aural slippage between 'simony' and 'sodomy', whilst cross-referencing the clerical 'black sheep' Father Keon

Sex and Sexuality

and 'The Sisters''s Father Flynn. Moreover, Roberts detected the miasma of child abuse that taints the air of 'The Sisters' – and which has since fuelled a century of critical speculation.[2]

This chapter takes its cue from one of Joyce's earliest readers in recognizing sex as integral to his experiments in fiction. Roberts, like Richards before him, was anxious for the reputation and stability of his precarious firm.[3] In 1906, Richards had spelled out the stakes: 'If a printer takes that view you can be quite sure that the booksellers will take it, that the libraries will take it', and 'If a book is attacked as indecent the printer suffers also from the attack; and if it is sufficiently indecent he is prosecuted.'[4] Richards spoke 'commercially not artistically', he was at pains to explain, but Joyce failed to take seriously the threat of the 1857 Obscene Publications Act. 'You will not be prosecuted', he retorted, adding 'from the point of view of financial success it seems to me more than probable that an attack, even a fierce and organised attack ... would have the effect of interesting the public' (*Letters I* 62). From one perspective, Joyce's dismissal of Richards's concerns was naïve. In August 1912, Joyce's own solicitor, George Lidwell – directed to contest Roberts's assertion that 'certain paragraphs' in *Dubliners* would 'leave the Author and Printer and Publisher liable to a criminal prosecution' – advised bowdlerization since 'there is at present in this city a Vigilance Committee whose object is to seek out and suppress all writings of immoral tendencies' (*Letters II* 306).[5] Yet Joyce's sense that conflict, controversy, and condemnation meant fame, fortune, and favour was prescient. This chapter will outline how radical frankness was essential to his aesthetic purpose and eventual reputation. 'I seriously believe that you will retard the course of civilisation in Ireland by preventing the Irish people from having one good look at themselves in my nicely polished looking-glass' (*SL* 89–90), Joyce famously wrote to Richards in 1906 – but what was at stake was more than realism. Representing sexuality was vital to Joyce's creative method because it demanded strategies that would define his prose: ambiguity, ellipsis, opacity, and obscurity. Gaps and silences marked the emergence of an inchoate modernism that characterized Joyce's writing about sex – the subject in his fiction where form and content were most intimately entangled.

Dubliners opens with a freighted textual moment, added after the story's original composition: the narrator's observation that the word 'paralysis' 'had always sounded strangely in my ears, like the word gnomon in the Euclid and the word simony in the Catechism' (*D* 1).[6] Paralysis, gnomon, and simony have long been read as the collection's keynotes, but in focusing on simony, Roberts chased the wrong hare. Gnomon, Euclid's mathematical figure of a parallelogram with a smaller parallelogram cut from one corner, was defined by its missing piece, and missing pieces define how Joyce writes sex. They are, from the first page of 'The Sisters', distinctive of speech about what cannot be named. Old Cotter expresses his reservations about the boy-narrator's friendship with Father Flynn through ellipses: '—No, I wouldn't say he was exactly ... but there was something queer ... there was something uncanny about him. I'll tell you my opinion ...' (D 1). Yet Old Cotter cannot articulate his misgivings – 'I think it was one of those ... peculiar cases ... But it's hard to say ...' (D 1–2). His 'tiresome' ramblings tail off into a revealing idiom: '—I wouldn't like children of mine, he said, to have too much to say to a man like that' (D 2). The term 'to have too much to say', rather than the more usual 'to have anything to do with', presents impropriety as a matter of words not deeds. The narrator 'crammed my mouth with stirabout for fear I might give utterance to my anger' (D 3), in the first of many stifled back answers. Nonetheless, Old Cotter is correct in his suspicions about a relationship that has centred on conversation. Father Flynn's religious instruction has ranged from 'stories about the catacombs' to explanations of 'the secrecy of the confessional' (D 5), a reminder that the sacrament of confession is structured as confidential dialogue. Eliza's dark revelation of the symptoms of her brother's breakdown, 'sitting up by himself in the dark in his confession-box', 'Wide-awake and laughing-like to himself ...' indicates how 'there was something gone wrong with him ...' (D 10) and with the institution he serves. Confession – reliant upon secure and enclosed discursive exchange – has short-circuited, leaving blanks both Old Cotter and the boy struggle to fill. 'I puzzled my head to extract meaning from his unfinished sentences' (D 3), the narrator tells us – a blueprint for the experience of reading *Dubliners*.

'The Sisters' sets a mood where sexuality haunts silences. 'An Encounter' encodes the real 'enormity' of *Dubliners*, as Joyce put it: the queer old josser's retreat to a corner of the field to do something unspeakable. The old man has worked himself up through his repetitive, rhythmic monologue about boys and sweethearts, but the narrator flinches from recording its consequences:

> —I say! Look what he's doing!
> As I neither answered nor raised my eyes Mahony exclaimed again:
> —I say ... He's a queer old josser! (D 18)

Mahony's insistent 'I say' – first exclamation, then ellipsis – echoes Old Cotter. It suggests a fraught relationship between sex and words, otherwise implicit in the initial theme of 'An Encounter': the regulation of reading. Like Father Butler, who struggles to prevent the furtive circulation of *The Apache Chief*, the queer old josser assumes the role of censor, engaging the boy with 'talk of school and of books', before suddenly asserting that 'there were some of Lord Lytton's works which boys couldn't read' (D 17). Talk of books is a trap to trick the boy into self-incrimination – just as his refusal to answer Mahony or 'raise my eyes' condemns him. If we ask *why* the boy fails to respond, we might infer one answer: perhaps he *already knows* what the old man is up to, unlike his innocent comrade, to whom masturbation is still a novelty? Pregnant silences meanwhile attend *Dubliners*' young women, who are specially constrained by sexual mores. Eveline sits in silent reverie recalling the narratives of the two men in her life: Frank's beguiling 'tales of distant countries' and song 'about the lass that loves a sailor', and her father's cynical 'I know these sailor chaps' (D 32). As her mother's unintelligible deathbed babble of 'Derevaun Seraun!' (D 33) haunts her memory, Eveline cannot navigate these competing fictions of romantic opportunity and sexual peril. At the quayside, she retreats into a trance in which she can neither understand Frank 'saying something about the passage over and over again', nor respond: 'She kept moving her lips in silent fervent prayer' (D 34). Like Nannie in 'The Sisters', she is mute, 'passive, like a helpless animal', unable to give any 'sign of love or farewell or recognition' (D 34). Eveline's catatonia is a striking instance of *Dubliners*'s silence about what it cannot represent, and 'The Boarding House' is similarly costive, implying a sensational tale of sexual blackmail but withholding details. Polly's sexiness ('I'm a ... naughty girl' [D 57]) is the censored subject of the story, the focus of 'her mother's persistent silence', and the unreported 'talk' (D 58) of other borders. Her illicit relationship with Bob Doran is only glimpsed through his fleeting memory of 'her bath night' (D 62), and his confession, where 'the priest had drawn out every ridiculous detail of the affair' (D 60), remains confidential. Polly keeps 'secret amiable memories' to herself, as the story closes with our exclusion from her 'hopes and visions' (D 64). The story became Joyce's sticking-point: 'I shall delete the word "bloody" wherever it occurs except in one passage in "The Boarding House"' (SL 89), he protested to Richards in 1906. Yet ironically, its narrative mode is redaction, pushing scandal into its margins.

In 'Two Gallants', sex is similarly off-stage. As Corley squires his victim to Donnybrook, the narrative follows Lenehan's joyless perambulations around Dublin, glimpsing 'the pair of lovers' only '[i]n his imagination' (D 51) or through 'swift anxious scrutiny' (D 49). The perspective is tilted, and exploitation displaced onto the busker's harp, 'heedless that her coverings had fallen about her knees' (D 48). Corley's coarse boasts about his 'fine tart' prompted Grant Richards's printer's refusal, and the transparency of the harp symbol implies what cannot openly be written. But the narrator is seldom so frank. 'Two Gallants' describes a bleak inversion of the usual prostitution exchange, obliquely glossed through the curious information that Corley 'aspirated the first letter of his name after the manner of Florentines' (D 45), or 'Whorely'. This exotic detail is out of place in the grey Dublin mundane, naming Corley's 'whoredom' through elaborate circumlocution. Like 'The Boarding House', 'Two Gallants' piques prurience only to frustrate it – nowhere more starkly than in the final line, where exposure is supplanted by Corley's teasing revelation of the 'small gold coin' (D 55).

Later stories of disappointed celibates and unhappy spouses sustain this gnomic withholding. The most obvious instance is Maria's self-censoring performance of 'I Dreamt I Dwelt in Marble Halls' in 'Clay', which omits the verse beginning 'I dreamt that suitors sought my hand'. Other moments more subtly register disappointment. Farrington's explosive rage in 'Counterparts' is triggered when he is overlooked in Mulligan's pub by a young woman with an 'oblique staring expression' (D 91). In 'A Painful Case', Emily Sinico is similarly passed over, by a husband who has 'dismissed his wife so sincerely from his gallery of pleasures' (D 106) and by James Duffy, who refuses her love. Again, transgression is invoked only to be deflected: the 'paragraph in the evening paper', written by 'a reporter won over to conceal the details of a commonplace vulgar death' (D 111) is an exercise in tact. But Duffy's 'little sheaf of papers' (D 103), in which he writes 'from time to time a short sentence about himself' (D 104), may contain the most painful ellipsis of all. His observation, 'Love between man and man is impossible because there must not be sexual intercourse and friendship between man and woman is impossible because there must be sexual intercourse' (D 108), pivots, as Margot Norris suggests, on those 'musts': what if we read it 'as a revelation that James Duffy cannot give himself to this woman because if he could love, he would love a man'?[7]

'The Dead' discloses a different devastating secret. 'Moments of their secret life together' (D 214) fire Gabriel Conroy's anticipation of a rare night alone with his wife in a hotel. But this is Joyce, not D. H. Lawrence – and Gabriel, 'trembling with desire to seize her' but holding 'the wild impulse of his body in check' (D 217), is destined for deflation. Gretta's long-buried memories of her past romance with Michael Furey are prompted by a ballad about the gendered consequences of secrecy, 'The Lass of Aughrim', structured as a dispute with Lord Gregory, who has locked the Lass and their baby outside in the rain. She repeatedly pleads for admission ('My babe lies cold within my arms'), only to be denied through his demand that she 'Tell me the first token / That passed between you and me'.[8] The Lass belongs to the 'secret life' of Lord Gregory, and his refusal to acknowledge her condemns their child to death. The ballad prompts Gretta's thoughts of Furey, who similarly meets 'his death in the rain' (D 223). But it also shadows another young woman, 'Lily, the caretaker's daughter', employed that evening 'to scamper along the bare hallway to let in another guest' (D 175). Lily's peripherality is underscored when, in the privacy of the below-stairs pantry, Gabriel notes her 'slim, growing' figure and ventures flirtation: 'I suppose we'll be going to your wedding one of these fine days with your young man, eh?' (D 177). Her retort – '"The men that is now is only all palaver and what they can get out of you"' – caustically indicates bleak experience behind her 'great bitterness' (D 178), but it is a story that can only be echoed, faintly, in 'The Lass of Aughrim'. The men may be all palaver, but the narrator of 'The Dead' does not tell.

'I have just finished reading *Dorian Grey* [sic]', Joyce wrote to Stanislaus on 19 August 1906, adding, 'It is not very difficult to read between the lines' (SL 96). Joyce had completed all of the *Dubliners* stories save 'The Dead' and would soon begin to redraft *Stephen Hero* into *A Portrait of the Artist as a Young Man*. Reading between the lines was already the strategy *Dubliners* required to interpret its omissions and silences, and the ghost of Wilde was evident from the first page of the new novel (as John Paul Riquelme explores in Chapter 2). Listening to his father sing 'Lily Dale', Stephen does not realize that the song has been bowdlerized for a child's ear, 'little green grave' being changed to '*little green place*' (P 7), but he later recalls 'the song about the wild rose blossoms on the little green place' and wonders why 'you could not have a green rose' (P 12). A green rose is not a wild rose but a Wilde rose – for Oscar Wilde famously wore dyed green carnations as emblems of queer aestheticism – and Stephen's wish is ominous, as Joyce underlined in his March 1909 article on Wilde.[9] Citing his celebrated defence – 'What Dorian Gray's sin was no-one says and no-one knows. Anyone who recognises it has committed it' – Joyce presented Wilde as 'undoubtedly ... a scapegoat' (OCPW 150), and scapegoating informs Stephen's early understanding of sex. Christmas dinner is overshadowed by the fall of the leader of the Irish Parliamentary Party Charles Stewart Parnell, cited in the 1890 divorce of his lover Katherine O'Shea. The conflict between nationalism and morality catches fire in the dispute between Simon Dedalus, John Casey, and Dante Riordan, as Stephen looks on, 'terror-stricken' (P 39) into silence. The lessons of Wilde and Parnell, exposed and punished for sexual sins, are internalised when Stephen returns to school to find it in uproar. 'They were caught near the Hill of Lyons' (P 40), he hears, as if the runaway schoolboys were fugitive lovers, yet their flight is a mystery: 'What did that mean about the smuggling in the square?' (P 42). Readers may infer what Stephen cannot: the boys have been caught in (mutual?) masturbation. Indeed, Joyce hints that Stephen intuits more than he understands through his thoughts of Tusker Boyle's hands, 'always at his nails, paring them', and Eileen's 'long thin cool white hands' (P 42). When Father Dolan unjustly beats him: 'hand' or 'hands' occurs nine times in the space of a page, alongside several uses of 'arm', 'palm', and 'fingers' (P 49–51). Hands are the source of secret pleasure, pain, and disgrace, as Stephen's scapegoating is shadowed by the shades of Wilde and Parnell.

These anxieties, so ominous for Joyce's budding writer, escalate in puberty. Accompanying his father on a nostalgic visit to the lecture theatre of Queen's College Cork, Stephen reads 'the word *Foetus* cut several times in the dark stained wood. The sudden legend startled his blood' (P 89). His distress arises from discovering 'in the outer world a trace of what he had deemed till then a brutish and individual malady of his own mind' (P 90). The graffiti prompts thoughts not of an unborn child but instead of 'his own mad and filthy orgies' (P 91): insecurely anchored to its meaning, it 'capered before his eyes' (P 90) so that he 'could scarcely interpret the letters of the signboards of the shops' (P 92). This crisis of reading foreshadows how shame threatens to alienate Stephen not merely from his body but also from his control over language. Tellingly, he imagines a primal scene of inscription: 'A broadshouldered student with a moustache was cutting in the letters with a jackknife, seriously' (P 90). The vision is of his father's past and his own future, condemned to write abortively, and the struggle to reconcile bodily impulse with literary ambition is reprised when he uses 'the moneys of his exhibition and essay prize' (P 96) to visit the red-light district. Arousal is phrased as literary effusion: 'The verses passed from his lips and the inarticulate cries and the unspoken brutal words rushed forth from his brain to force a passage' (P 99). Desire is mediated discourse, 'the echo of an obscene scrawl which he had read on the oozing wall of a urinal' (P 100). The struggle to express sex in words builds to crisis when, traumatised by Father Arnall's hellfire sermons, Stephen resolves to 'murmur out his own shame' (P 126) through confession. As in 'The Sisters', what cannot be said falls into hesitation and ellipsis: 'I ... committed sins of impurity, father', 'And ... with others' (P 144). Stephen can barely speak his own sins but nonetheless considers becoming a priest himself and hearing the sins of others 'murmured into his ears in the confessional under the shame of a darkened chapel by the lips of women and of girls' (P 159). His understanding of confession as the only legitimate means through which sex can be articulated casts an ironic shadow over the predictable struggles of *Portrait* into print. (See also Finn Fordham on confession in Chapter 5.)

Joyce was writing *Portrait* alert to the problems likely to attend publication. He completed the novel whilst fielding Roberts's various demands for expurgation, even burning a manuscript 'in a fit of rage on account of the trouble over *Dubliners*' in 1912.[10] But both trouble and opportunity followed when, in December 1913, Ezra Pound wrote to introduce himself and to invite Joyce to contribute 'markedly modern stuff' to 'a new and impecunious paper' (*JJ* 349). The serialization of *Portrait* in *The Egoist* between February 1914 and September 1915 was impeded by the printer's refusal to typeset 'objectionable passages' and when, after various publishers' rejections, Joyce agreed to issue it in book form under the new *Egoist* imprint, a further seven printers declined. These difficulties anticipated the battle over *Ulysses*, first serialized in the New York magazine *The Little Review* in March 1918 (as discussed by Clare Hutton in Chapter 14) but subject to seizures and suppression. Nonetheless, Joyce's sexual frankness proved essential to his success. In January 1914, *The Egoist* had introduced him as 'an author of known and notable talents', printing Joyce's open letter 'A Curious History', which protested against the suppression of *Dubliners*.[11] Grant Richards finally published the collection that June. Meanwhile, *The Egoist's* championing of *Portrait* and, later, *Ulysses* had as much to do with content as it did with form. The journal had prided itself on 'unblushingness' since its inception, discussing 'sex loudly and clearly and repeatedly and in the worse possible taste'.[12] *Portrait* appeared alongside columns and extensive correspondence on masturbation, prostitution, homosexuality, and sexology.[13] *The Little Review* similarly paired sexual and aesthetic confrontation, summarized in its strapline 'MAKING NO COMPROMISE WITH THE PUBLIC TASTE'. When, six months before *Ulysses*'s debut, an issue was confiscated, editors Margaret Anderson and Jane Heap did not hide their delight: 'We had no hope that such a good piece of prose would gain the interest of the Postoffice for a moment. OBSCENITY!!!'[14] *Ulysses* was perfect for *The Little Review*, its daring confirming Joyce's rising position as modernism's *cause célèbre*.

Dubliners presented sex as omission, Euclid's gnomon acting as a metaphor for what could not be written. *Portrait* described how Stephen's tortuous negotiations with adolescence compromised his relationship with language, threatening his ambitions to write. In both texts, censorship informed content and form, as Joyce invited readers to fill in the gaps. *Ulysses* marked a shift consonant with his changes in fortune, since most was written after 1914, his '*annus mirabilis*' (*JJ* 353).[15] Joyce's audacity appalled *The Little Review*'s most influential patron, the New York lawyer John Quinn, who recoiled from Joyce's description of the 'scrotumtightening sea' (*U* 1.78) in the first instalment, but worse was to come in Bloom's thoughts of the Dead Sea as 'the grey sunken cunt of the world' (*U* 4.227).[16] Colloquial obscenities were integral to the text's realist experiment and were matched by representations of intimate bodily sensations. Contemplating a bath, Bloom foresees 'the dark tangled curls of his bush floating', his penis 'the limp father of thousands, a languid floating flower' (*U* 5.570–2). Passing through the National Library, he overhears Buck Mulligan's proposal for a new drama, 'Everyman His Own Wife, or, a Honeymoon in the Hand (a national immorality in three orgasms)' (*U* 9.1171–4), and, in 'Nausicaa', enjoys his own 'honeymoon in the hand' whilst watching Gerty MacDowell. Predictably, several numbers of *The Little Review* were suppressed before 'Nausicaa' precipitated the trial that would brand *Ulysses* legally obscene. As Joyce worked on, indecency escalated. In 'Circe', Stephen and Bloom meet in the fantasy kink space of Bella Cohen's brothel, and the novel culminates in Molly's monologue, where a flood of erotic reminiscences mingles with her menstrual flow: 'O patience above its pouring out of me like the sea' (*U* 18.1122–3).

The scandal of *Ulysses* was, however, in tension with the curious absence of actual sex. 'Ithaca' reveals that, for Bloom and Molly, 'carnal intercourse had been incomplete, without ejaculation of semen within the natural female organ' *(U* 17.2283–4) for over a decade. Although this definition does not preclude contraceptive *coitus interruptus* (and other more imaginative possibilities), it draws attention to a lack. Sex happens in fantasy, in memory, in conversation, and at a safe distance, but never in the moment on the page. Molly's liaison with Blazes Boylan is unrepresented save through her musings in 'Penelope' and through Bloom's voyeuristic cuckold fantasy in 'Circe'. Despite its brothel setting, even 'Circe' is strangely chaste: Stephen sings, dances, drinks, plays the pianola, and smashes the chandelier – but, like Bloom, fails to accomplish the expected object of his visit. These absences accord with *Ulysses*'s understanding of sexual modernity as serendipitous and impalpable. In 'Calypso', Bloom impatiently waits at the butcher's behind a young servant, eager 'To catch up and walk behind her if she went slowly, behind her moving hams' (*U* 4.171–2). He is alert to such chances: the 'Typist going up Roger Greene's stairs two at a time to show her understandings' (*U* 13.916) or a woman mounting a carriage outside the Grosvenor hotel. Bloom, attempting to catch a glimpse of her 'Wellturned foot' (*U* 5.118) and legs – 'Watch! Watch! Silk flash rich stockings white. Watch!' – is thwarted when 'A heavy tramcar honking its gong slewed between' (*U* 5.130–1). He immediately recalls another occasion, the 'Girl in Eustace street hallway Monday was it settling her garter', when his gaze was similarly impeded by 'Her friend covering the display' (*U* 5.133–4). *Ulysses* is full of attenuated opportunities, where sex is diffused into street glimpses, fleeting encounters, and fugitive sensations.

The word 'obscene' was derived from the Greek *ob scena*, or off-stage, and *Ulysses*'s obliqueness underscores its etymology. In 'Calypso', Molly is in the wings, heard as a 'sleepy soft grunt' (*U* 4.56) from the bedroom, her 'couched body' (*U* 4.306) shrouded. The letter she receives from Boylan is similarly half-seen, first legible through the 'Bold hand. Mrs Marion' (*U* 4.311) of its address, then hidden 'under the dimpled pillow' (*U* 4.08). Molly distracts Bloom with a question about *Ruby, Pride of the Ring*, which similarly doubles back on its promise. Despite racy illustrations – 'Fierce Italian with carriagewhip. Must be Ruby pride of the on the floor naked' (*U* 4.346–7) – Molly complains, 'There's nothing smutty in it' (*U* 4.355), requesting 'another of Paul de Kock's. Nice name he has' (*U* 4:358). *The Bath of the Nymph*, the 'splendid masterpiece in art colours' (*U* 4.370) framed over the marital bed, is similarly teasingly suggestive. It was 'Given away with the Easter number of *Photo Bits*' (*U* 4.369–70), a mildly pornographic and frequently suppressed magazine that, rather like *Ulysses* itself, subtended classicism and 'smut'.[17] Bloom uses *The Bath of the Nymph* to explain *metempsychosis* to Molly, but the picture implies another 'transmigration of souls' (*U* 4.341), since it shuttles between high and low culture, the permissible and the forbidden. 'Calypso' summarises *Ulysses*'s broader tendency to displace sex into suggestiveness: significantly, Bloom's two dalliances on 16 June 1904 are mediated rather than experienced. Gerty MacDowell models her high-kicking display on the 'Mutoscope pictures in Capel street: for men only' (*U* 13.794), which specialized in choreographed striptease.[18] Her limp, only revealed after her performance ends, exposes her distance from the image she cultivates. Bloom acknowledges the gap – 'See her as she is spoil all. Must have the stage setting, the rouge, costume, position, music' (*U* 13.855–6) – treating Gerty not as a sexual partner but as a pornographic stimulus to masturbation: 'Damned glad I didn't do it in the bath this morning over her silly I will punish you letter' (*U* 13.786–7). Martha Clifford is a similarly absent presence, since their anonymous intrigue is filtered through newspaper advertisement ('Wanted, smart lady typist to aid gentleman in literary work' [*U* 8.326–7]), Post Office collection boxes, and her typewriter. Her letter draws attention to its attenuated production through its mistakes: 'I do not like that other world' (for 'word'), 'my patience are exhausted', 'if you do not wrote' (*U* 5.250–5). The errors underline how typing, where metal rods strike whiteness to leave marks, is perfect for the flagellation narratives Bloom solicits.[19] The medium is the message, as sex is displaced into virtual reality.

To D. H. Lawrence, the final chapter of *Ulysses* amounted to 'the dirtiest, most obscene, indecent thing ever written'.[20] The eight long unpunctuated sentences of 'Penelope' promise the unfiltered thoughts of a woman of experience, as Molly's unblushing recollections suggest: 'He must have come 3 or 4 times with that tremendous big red brute of a thing he has' (*U* 18.143–4). Nonetheless, Molly's sexuality is far from organic but is channelled through borrowed sources. A performer by profession ('I could have been a prima donna only I married him' [U 18.896]), Molly's sense of theatre even informs her orgasm, when 'I gave my eyes that look with my hair a bit loose from the tumbling and my tongue between my lips' (U 18.592-4). She is explicit about how she assembles her masquerade, considering, for instance, the advantages of 'those kidfitting corsets I saw advertised in the Gentlewoman' (18.447). She compares herself to celebrity adulteresses – 'Kitty OShea in Grantham Street' (U 18.479), 'that Mrs Langtry the jersey lily' (U 18.481) – and muses wryly on Bloom's tastes in erotic literature – 'that Ruby and Fair Tyrants he bought me that twice' (U 18.492-3). She even compares herself to her husband's gallery of erotic images: 'would I be like that bath of the nymph with my hair down yes only shes younger or Im a little like that dirty bitch in that Spanish photo he has' (U 18.562-4). Ironically, Molly's status as gendered construct is most evident when her biology is most conspicuous. Menstruation could be read as somatic proof of the femaleness of a woman ventriloquised by a male novelist. But its status as a marker of authentic womanliness is undermined by her thoughts of bleeding as a sign to be faked:

> they always want to see a stain on the bed to know youre a virgin for them all thats troubling them theyre such fools too you could be a widow or divorced 40 times over a daub of red ink would do or blackberry juice no thats too purply O Jamesy let me up out of this pooh sweets of sin.   (U 18.1125-9)

Her glissade from menstrual to hymeneal blood as 'proof' presents her body as a site of tricksy inscription. *Sweets of Sin*, the erotic novel Bloom buys her (U 10.606), is similarly a story that will not tell since, unlike other allusions in Joyce's fiction, it appears not to exist.[21] The bloodstain of truth might be exchanged for the red ink of fabrication – red ink that leads, through *Ulysses* breaking the fourth wall ('O Jamesy let me up out of this'), to a direct appeal to her creator.

From the ellipses of *Dubliners* through Stephen's struggles to read, from Martha's flagellant typewriting to Molly's blood-feigning ink, Joyce's writing about sex repeatedly stresses the symbiosis of content and form. At its simplest, he exploits tensions between obscenity and obscurity, evident in his exasperated 1906 protest that a 'plain blunt man' would miss the 'enormity' of 'An Encounter'. To follow this logic is to understand how Joyce's 'difficulty' is entangled with his parallel reputation as the writer of a 'dirty book': one obvious response to censorship was to smuggle indecency past any 'plain, blunt' reader unable to detect it. The apotheosis of this strategy is *Finnegans Wake*, which pushed modernist difficulty beyond the limits envisioned by even Joyce's most ardent champions. After reading a draft in November 1926, Pound protested that 'Nothing short of divine vision or a new cure for the clapp can possibly be worth all the circumambient peripherization' (*Letters III* 145). Later that month, after fielding more genteel disappointment from Harriet Shaw Weaver, Joyce attempted to explain himself: 'One great part of every human existence is passed in a state which cannot be rendered sensible by the use of wideawake language, cutanddry grammar, and goahead plot' (*Letters III* 146). Joyce's 'book of Doublends Jined' (*FW* 20.15–16), written in its own dreamlanguage of polyglot portmanteau puns, lacks a plot that can be summarized. However, through the dynamic interrelationships of its five central characters, the patriarch Humphrey Chimpden Earwicker (HCE), his wife Anna Livia Plurabelle (ALP), their warring twin sons Shem the Penman and Shaun the Post, and their nubile daughter Issy, Joyce continued to explore now-familiar themes. Voyeurism, exposure, and punishment recur in *Dubliners*, *Portrait*, and *Ulysses*, with variations and embellishments so that, for instance, the queer old josser's enthusiasm for whipping is reprised in *Portrait*'s 'smugging' episode and in Bloom's enthusiasm for flagellation. *Finnegans Wake* unfolds a quasi-incestuous drama centred upon a shadowy crime, HCE's voyeuristic, possibly masturbatory, encounter with two girls in Dublin's Phoenix Park. This is the nub of any plot: HCE is accused, blackmailed, exposed through a trial, defended by his wife, written about by Shem, censored by Shaun, and made the subject of gossip and rumour, whilst his daughter Issy resembles the teasing, flirty temptresses of *Ulysses* – notably, Gerty MacDowell. Book 1, chapter five begins by proposing a list of potential titles for ALP's 'mamafesta' about her husband, including '*A New Cure for an Old Clapp*' (*FW* 104.22–3). The hat-tip to Pound acknowledges his grasp of a central truth: *Finnegans Wake* is as much 'about' sex and sexuality as it is about anything at all.

As in the earlier work, *Finnegans Wake* foregrounds confession as the formative experience of narrating sex. Stephen's sense of confession as licit erotica accords with Molly's memories of Father Corrigan:

> he touched me father and what harm if he did where and I said on the canal bank like a fool but whereabouts on your person my child on the leg behind high up was it yes rather high up was it where you sit down (*U* 18.107–10).

Molly reprises Bloom's speculations that 'Confession' is a 'Great weapon in their hands' (*U* 5.425–6): by this stage in the Joycean canon, confession has become sanctioned, ritualised pornography. *Finnegans Wake* presents Shaun the Post as censor-confessor, notably in the 'Jaunty Jaun' episode (book 3, chapter 2), where, floating in an empty Guinness barrel down the Liffey, he delivers 'many nuncupiscent words' (*FW* 432.10) to Issy and her fellow 'sinnerettes in silkettes' (FW 457.22–3). Issy is eager 'to flusther sweet nunsongs in his quickturned ear' (FW 457.27–9), elaborating Molly's recognition of Father Corrigan's priestly prurience: 'I'll strip straight after devotions before his fondstare' (FW 461.21–2). But earlier in the Shem chapter (book 1, chapter 7), Shaun's role as prurient confessor drives his attack on his brother's filthy life and art. Shem's sins of writing dirt are his creator's, as the first line proclaims: 'Shem is short for Shemus as Jem is joky for Jacob' (FW 169.01). His house, the Haunted Inkbottle, is 'persianly literatured with burst loveletters' (FW 183.10–11), an Arabian Nights of smut where he manufactures 'synthetic ink and sensitive paper for his own end out of his wit's waste' (FW 185.07–8). As in 'Penelope', ink and paper become bodily substances, as Shem generates 'from his unheavenly body a no uncertain quantity of obscene matter' (FW 185.28–9) and 'skrevened nameless shamelessness about everybody he ever met' (FW 182.14). Shaun's invective builds towards the confessional exchange of the chapter's final pages, introduced through his riff on the standard opening: 'Where have you been in the uterim, enjoying yourself all the morning since your last wetbed confession?' (FW 187.36–188.01). The confessional motif accords with a wider self-reflexivity, as the chapter confesses a secret: Joyce's reputation was enhanced rather than hindered by controversy. The paradox informs the tribute to Pound as 'Dr. Poindejenk, authorised bowdler and censor' of Shem's 'usylessly unreadable Blue Book of Eccles' (FW 179.26–8). Pound, as first champion and censor of *Ulysses*, personified the oxymoron of his writing life.[22]

Two intertextual moments in *Ulysses* underscore Joyce's understanding of the stakes. In 'Wandering Rocks', Bloom, browsing a second-hand bookstall for smut, 'turned over idly pages of *The Awful Disclosures of Maria Monk*' (U 10.584–5), a best-selling pseudo-memoir first published in 1836 and sensationally alleging systematic sexual exploitation of Catholic nuns by their confessors.[23] In 'Circe', the ghost of Bloom's grandfather presents himself as 'the Virag who disclosed the Sex Secrets of Monks and Maidens. Why I left the church of Rome. Read The Priest, the Woman and the Confessional' (U 15.2546–8). These books belong to an eccentric mid-Victorian sub-genre in which sectarian protests against priestly transgressions were disingenuously sold as pornography.[24] These slippery ephemera are thoroughly at home within Joyce's fiction, which routinely satirizes confession as an institution perversely inciting the 'sins' it regulates. But there is another reason for their presence. Confessional erotica acquired a place in legal history in 1868 when a startlingly explicit tract known as *The Confessional Unmasked* forced a definition that the 1857 Obscene Publications Act had declined to offer. Faced in 1868 with a publisher claiming religious freedom whilst energetically marketing a salacious shilling shocker to tens of thousands of readers, Lord Chief Justice Alexander Cockburn conceptualized a 'test of obscenity': whether the disputed work tended 'to deprave or corrupt those whose minds are open to such immoral influences, and into whose hands a publication of this sort may fall'.[25] The Hicklin test was adopted by the US Supreme Court in 1896, thereby enabling the suppression of *Ulysses*.[26] Joyce was famously litigious, and his knowledge of the backstory of obscenity's legal definition is confirmed through a dirty joke.[27] As he reads the death notices from *The Irish Independent* in the 'Cyclops' episode, the Citizen is interrupted when he comes to 'Cockburn, at the Moat House, Chepstow ...': '—I know that fellow, says Joe, from bitter experience' (*U* 12.231–2). The name of the architect of the Hicklin test becomes the 'burning cock' of a sexually transmitted infection and a jocose marker of Joyce's own 'bitter experience' of censorship. The satiric register of these allusions underlines what this chapter has shown: Joyce ultimately relished the possibilities, implications, and consequences of prohibition. Like the sectarian erotica *Ulysses* references, his fiction profited from controversy, both by bringing publicity and celebrity and by helping to generate innovations of literary style. *Finnegans Wake* confesses the value of its obscenscurity, becoming Joyce's scurrilously entertaining *mea culpa* about his emergence from 'an obscene coalhole' (*FW* 194.18) into the light of modernism.

Notes

1. Clare Hutton, 'Chapters of Moral History: Failing to Publish *Dubliners*', *The Papers of the Bibliographical Society of America* 97.4 (2003): 495–519, 509.
2. For a range of different readings of undertones of paedophilia in the story, see John Kuelh, 'a la joyce: The Sisters Fitzgerald's Absolution', *James Joyce Quarterly* 2.1 (1964): 2–6; Florence Walzl, 'Joyce's "The Sisters": A Development', *James Joyce Quarterly* 10.4 (1973): 375–421; Leonard Albert, 'Gnomonology: Joyce's "The Sisters"', *James Joyce Quarterly* 27.2 (1990): 353–64; and Margot Norris, *Suspicious Readings of Joyce's 'Dubliners'* (Philadelphia: University of Pennsylvania Press, 2003), pp. 16–29.
3. For a full account of the background to both Richards's and Roberts's refusals to publish *Dubliners*, see Hutton, 'Chapters of Moral History'.
4. Robert Scholes, 'Grant Richards to James Joyce', *Studies in Bibliography* 16 (1963): 139–60, 145, 150.
5. For Joyce's complex negotiations with this and other vigilance committees, see my *James Joyce, Sexuality and Social Purity* (Cambridge: Cambridge University Press, 2003).
6. The line does not appear in the first version of 'The Sisters', published under the pseudonym 'Stephen Daedalus' in the agricultural magazine *The Irish Homestead*, 13 August 1904, 676.
7. Norris, p. 166.

8. Ruth Bauerle, *The James Joyce Songbook* (London: Garland, 1982), pp. 177–8.
9. 'Oscar Wilde: The Poet of "Salomé"', *OCPW* 148–51. For a full account of Joyce's creative response to Wilde, see Joseph Valente, 'Thrilled by His Touch: The Aestheticization of Homosexual Panic in *A Portrait of the Artist as a Young Man*' in *Quare Joyce*, ed. Joseph Valente (Ann Arbor: University of Michigan Press, 1998), pp. 47–76.
10. Letter dated 6 January 1920 to Harriet Shaw Weaver and referring to a period 'about eight years ago', so c. 1912 (*Letters I* 136). Whether the draft Joyce refers to as 'the "original" original' was *Stephen Hero* or a version of *Portrait* is a matter for debate. See Hans Walter Gabler, 'The Seven Lost Years of *A Portrait of the Artist as a Young Man*' in *Approaches to Joyce's 'Portrait': Ten Essays*, ed. Thomas F. Staley and Bernard Benstock (Pittsburgh: University of Pittsburgh Press, 1976), pp. 25–60.
11. James Joyce, 'A Curious History', *The Egoist* 1.2 (15 January 1914): 27. *OCPW* 160–2.
12. Rebecca West, 'The Freewoman', *Time and Tide* (16 July 1926): 649.
13. See Katherine Mullin, 'Joyce through the Little Magazines' in *The Blackwell Companion to James Joyce*, ed. Richard Brown (Oxford: Blackwell, 2008), pp. 374–89.
14. *The Little Review* November 1917, rear flyleaf.
15. See Luca Crispi, 'Manuscript Timeline, 1905–1922', *Genetic Joyce Studies* 4 (Spring 2004) geneticjoycestudies.org/articles/GJS4/GJS4_Crispi.
16. See Paul Vanderham, *James Joyce and Censorship* (Basingstoke: Palgrave MacMillan, 1997), pp. 18–20.
17. See Jennifer Burns Levin, 'How Joyce Acquired "The Stale Smut of Clubmen": *Photo Bits* in the Early Twentieth Century', *James Joyce Quarterly* 46.2 (2009): 255–68.
18. See Mullin, *James Joyce, Sexuality and Social Purity*, pp. 140–70.
19. For an extended analysis of Martha as blackmailing typist, see Katherine Mullin, *Working Girls: Fiction, Sexuality, and Modernity* (Oxford: Oxford University Press, 2016), pp. 78–81.
20. See Rachel Potter, *Obscene Modernism: Literary Censorship and Experiment 1900–1940* (Oxford: Oxford University Press, 2013), p. 96.
21. The fruitless scholarly hunt for it has inspired the *James Joyce Quarterly* to offer its own serial version: for the first of several instalments, see 'Sweets of Sin, by A Gentleman of Fashion', *James Joyce Quarterly* 39.2 (2002): 348–56.
22. See Vanderham, *James Joyce and Censorship*, pp. 18–30.
23. See Sandra Frink, 'Women, the Family, and the Fate of the Nation in American Anti-Catholic Narratives, 1830–1860', *Journal of the History of Sexuality* 18.2 (2009): 237–64.
24. See Katherine Mullin, 'Unmasking *The Confessional Unmasked*: The 1868 Hicklin Test and the Toleration of Obscenity', *ELH* 85.2 (2018): 471–99.
25. Regina v. Hicklin (1868), *Law Reports 3: Queen's Bench Division 1867–1868*, 371.
26. Rosen v. United States, 161 U.S. 29 (1896), 43. The 'Hicklin test' remained the legal test for obscenity until Roth v. United States, 354 U.S. 476 (1957) – ironically

enough, a case precipitated by the actions of Samuel Roth, the notorious pirate publisher of *Ulysses* and the target of Joyce's successful 1927 injunction. See *JJ* 585–7.
27. *Every Man's Own Lawyer* (London: Crossby Lockwood, 1919), stamped 'J. J.', is listed in Richard Ellmann, 'Appendix: Joyce's Library in 1920' in *The Consciousness of Joyce* (Oxford: Oxford University Press, 1977), p. 108. For Joyce's litigiousness, see *JJ* 426–8, 440–1, 465–6.

12

SEAN LATHAM

Joyce and the Everyday

Art and Archaeology

Ulysses, Henri Lefebvre wrote, marked 'the momentous eruption of everyday life into literature', in which Joyce's sprawling prose 'rescues, one after the other, each facet of the quotidian from anonymity'.[1] In the book's 'Ithaca' chapter, for example, we find a list of all twenty-three books on Leopold Bloom's shelves (including those he hasn't even read) and the contents of a desk drawer containing everything from an old Christmas card to an abandoned workout diary. Seemingly random objects like a bar of soap or squeaky bedsprings assume outsize importance throughout the book, becoming leitmotifs, symbols, and even speaking characters. Famously, Joyce even risked censorship in order to drag into view details about the career of the human body that other novelists had ignored. Thus do we see Bloom graphically emptying his bowels on the toilet: 'hope it's not too big bring on piles again' (*U* 4.509–10). Stephen Dedalus lays 'dry snot picked from his nostril on a ledge of rock' (*U* 3.500), while Molly Bloom uses the chamber pot in the middle of the night as her period begins ('O patience above its pouring out of me like the sea' [*U* 18.1122–3]). This insistence on documenting the full range of human experience prompts critics like Lefebvre to celebrate the book's deep humanity. Even the judge who eventually admitted it to the United States nine years after its initial publication found that its attention to everyday detail formed an aesthetic structure that nullified any potential obscenity: 'Each word of the book contributes like a bit of mosaic ... to draw a true picture of the lower middle class in a European city.'[2]

The book's commitment to the 'rescue' of day-to-day life, furthermore, is evident not only in its swirling detail but also in its general indifference to the kind of plot that critics since Aristotle thought essential to narrative art.

For Declan Kiberd, that's exactly the point: 'The manifest content of Joyce's Homeric structure', he writes, 'must fall away to reveal the latent content beneath.'[3] And that content is the power, beauty, tragedy, and complexity of Irish life at the edge of modernity, a life that 'could be simultaneously cosmopolitan and supremely local'.[4] This way of understanding the novel, however, frustrated many of its earliest critics, who found themselves lost amid what seemed like a hodgepodge of people, locations, objects, streets, and local customs that seemed deliberately, even irritatingly obscure. We read *Ulysses* now, of course, with the aid of annotations, Google searches, and carefully drawn maps.[5] One wonders, however, what a reader in 1922 New York would have made of a chapter like 'Wandering Rocks', which interweaves an array of short narrative strands around the finest details of Dublin geography.[6]

Even those who knew the place well often recoiled from Joyce's detailed accounting of a city he both loved and despised. In a letter to Sylvia Beach declining to purchase a copy of *Ulysses*, George Bernard Shaw (while complaining about the price) called the book 'a revolting record of a disgusting phase of civilization'. It might, he admits, appeal to some as art, 'but to me it is all hideously real. I have walked those streets and know those shops and have heard – and taken part in those conversations.'[7] For Shaw, at least, there is simply too much of the everyday in the book and not enough art. Indeed, even one of the book's most influential early champions saw Joyce's obsession with the everyday as a problem to be solved. The book's epic structure, T. S. Eliot famously argues in '*Ulysses*, Order and Myth', is all that saves it from mere chaos, providing what he calls 'a way of controlling, of ordering, of giving shape and a significance to the immense panorama of futility and anarchy which is contemporary history'.[8]

This tension between art and the everyday is essential to Joyce's writing because he cannot settle it himself. He began his career as a fabulator – a maker of modern myths similar to W. B. Yeats. Steeped in the mysteries of a Catholicism he found both alluring and repulsive, he once believed the artist was a 'priest of eternal imagination, transmuting the daily bread of experience into the radiant body of everliving life' (*P* 221). This priestly urge, however, remained balanced by a courageous commitment to the materiality of the world around him: to the abject poverty that shattered his family, to the corrosive effects of British imperialism, and yet also to the communal buzz of a pub, the smell of lemon soap, and a stolen kiss among the flowers. He sought, as he writes in *Finnegans Wake*, 'to see life foully', that is, to witness both its fullness and its foulness (*FW* 113.13). The same Stephen Dedalus who imagined himself a priest of the imagination, after all, also grounded himself at a moment of crisis in the dirty alleyways of Dublin:

'That is horse piss and rotted straw.... It is a good odour to breathe. It will calm my heart' (*P* 86).

More than just a fabulator, Joyce also wrote as a kind of archaeologist, meticulously reconstructing a city that had literally been blasted by British gunboats and Irish revolutionaries. He created only four major works – *Dubliners*, *A Portrait of the Artist as a Young Man*, *Ulysses*, and *Finnegans Wake* – and used them first to build and then to keep rebuilding the city he fled as a young man. As Hugh Kenner argues, he took inspiration, in part, from Heinrich Schliemann's 1873 discovery of what appeared to be the remains of Troy. Suddenly, Homer's great battle before the walls of that ancient city changed from a fanciful romance to an event that had its roots in a real place and time. When the young Irish writer began to build his own city, Kenner writes, 'It seems clear that he was thinking of a Dublin one day gone the way of Troy, to be visited by some long future Schliemann, *Ulysses* in hand.'[9] In fact, while writing his masterpiece, Joyce read in a Zurich newspaper that Irish rebels had briefly seized the heart of Dublin only to be put down by British soldiers using rifles, artillery, and a gunboat. In that moment, imagining everyday Dublin in 1904 also meant preserving ruined streets and toppled buildings, transforming the rubble into the mythic markers that contemporary pilgrims still follow on the annual Bloomsday pilgrimage.

What Schliemann found as he dug through the dirt in what is now northwest Turkey was not the tomb of Hector but the bits and baubles of a long-vanished everyday life. There were fire pits and potsherds, jewellery and clothing, homes and hovels. A great battle (many, in fact) had been fought around the ancient city's walls, but mostly people had walked and cooked and tossed away their garbage. They mourned the dead and celebrated new life in ways that seemed momentarily to close the four-thousand-year gap between a vanished city and Ireland's colonized capital.

In his earliest surviving writings, Joyce set out to record the everyday life of his city in 'epiphanies', short sketches of daily life that might provoke 'a sudden spiritual manifestation, whether in the vulgarity of speech or of gesture or in a memorable phase of the mind itself' (*SH* 211), as discussed by Vicki Mahaffey in Chapter 6. As his writing became more experimental over the next decades, he never let go of this early insistence on the distinctive power of the everyday, though he could never quite define what it meant or why it mattered. This chapter analyzes Joyce's engagement with the everyday by focusing on scenes of mourning, when the everyday suddenly becomes at once visible and painfully fragile. These moments – funerals, wakes, and death rites – constitute a steady yet largely unexamined through-line running from Joyce's first story to his last novel. Death itself is at once the most common and the most shocking of experiences, an event that rends the fabric of our everyday life as we try to readjust our habits around an often abrupt and painful absence. Seen this way, Joyce's works become not only archaeological digs into the ever-vanishing everyday but also documents of human and cultural resilience amid the fury of modernity.

Gig Lamps, Improperly Arranged

The first and last pieces of fiction Joyce wrote were about funerals. He began with 'The Sisters', in which a young boy mourns the death of a priest with whom he has had a close, perhaps improper, relationship. We watch as he hears the news, reflects briefly on it, then goes to view the body that has been laid out in a formal sitting room. The adults have doubts about the priest's moral character but never address them directly, and the story's few pages are littered with ellipses like this one in which a gossipy character named Old Cotter announces the death: 'I have my own theory about it, he said. I think it was one of those ... peculiar cases. ... But it's hard to say...' (D 1–2). Because the narrative is focalized on the young boy, this puts us in a position commonly shared by children, who realize that adults use coded language to discuss delicate subjects like sex, violence, fear, or money. Such gaps are everywhere in this story, not only in the literal speech of the adults but also in the larger mystery of what exactly happened to this priest who had once dropped the chalice during mass and later was found 'sitting up by himself in the dark in his confession-box, wideawake and laughing-like softly to himself' (D 10). Such gaps, as Margot Norris provocatively argues, generate the art and pleasure of Joyce's stories since they encourage readers to fill them with what she calls a 'poisonous hermeneutic touch.'[10] Do we see an allusion here to sexual abuse? To apostasy or temptation? What, we ask, has the priest done, and what does his death actually mean?

Curiously, the boy at the centre of this story seems largely indifferent to such questions. He is neither overwhelmed with grief nor eager to unravel the adults' gossip. Instead, he spends much of the story fixating on the fine details of everyday life around him. The story begins with his comfortable daily habit of walking by the house where the priest lived with his two elderly sisters: 'There was no hope for him this time: it was the third stroke. Night after night I had passed the house (it was vacation time) and studied the lighted square of window: and night after night I had found it lighted in the same way, faintly and evenly' (D 1). The entire narrative unfolds in this same cold tone that Joyce called a style of 'scrupulous meanness' (SL 83). In scrutinizing the world around him, he discovers that we experience the death of another as a disruption of our regular habits: 'Had he not been dead

I would have gone into the little dark room behind the shop to find him sitting in his arm-chair by the fire, nearly smothered in his greatcoat. Perhaps my aunt would have given me a packet of High Toast for him and this present would have roused him from his stupefied doze' (*D* 4). He clearly expects death to be momentous, but it registers instead as a subtle yet powerful shift in the fabric of his own everyday life: 'I found it strange that neither I nor the day seemed in a mourning mood and I felt even annoyed at discovering in myself a sensation of freedom as if I had been freed from something by his death' (*D* 4). The freedom he experiences emerges from a newfound ability to change the everyday by reclaiming his own time for something other than his lessons with the priest. This too will likely harden into a new habit – a new iteration of the everyday – but for a moment he suddenly gains a new vantage on himself and the myriad of otherwise unconscious actions, dispositions, beliefs, pleasures, and frustrations that make up his habitus.[11]

As the story progresses, however, the everyday gradually washes back over the moment of rupture created by the death. In a scene that mirrors the conversation with Old Cotter, the boy visits the house of mourning and again finds himself trapped in an adult conversation that he can only partially understand. He listens carefully and, at the start, is sharply, even snobbishly, aware of a life he sees as dispiritingly shoddy. He takes careful note, for example, of 'how clumsily [Nannie's] skirt was hooked at the back and how the heels of her cloth boots were trodden down all to one side' (*D* 6). As the title characters discuss the dead priest, though, the narrator's consciousness largely fades from the diegesis, and any possibility of transforming the habitus gradually succumbs to a kind of narrative paralysis. In the end, the boy does not rage against the adult world as he did when he first learned of the death from Cotter. Instead, he joins the sisters themselves in listening to the quiet house, which brings with it the numbing effects of the everyday. Even the great mystery of what happened to the priest subsides into this creeping silence, lost in yet another enigmatic ellipsis that appears in the story's final line. For just a moment, death interrupts the everyday to reveal the structure of the habitus, potentially estranging the narrator and readers alike from the larger world to open the possibility of scandal, revelation, or change. This potential fades, however, beneath small talk, irresolution, and the stubborn power of the everyday to produce what Joyce called Dublin's 'paralysis' (*SL* 22).

One of the many curious things about *Dubliners* is that the first and last stories in the collection are symmetrical. The titles, in fact, could be switched, and the two protagonists, despite their difference in age, find themselves similarly disturbed by a moment when death interrupts the everyday. Unlike the boy in 'The Sisters', though, Gabriel Conroy in 'The Dead' does not look into the face of a corpse. Instead, after going through the highly ritualized performances of an annual holiday party, he returns to a hotel with his wife, expecting a night of lovemaking only to discover that she has been thinking of the tragic death of an old boyfriend: 'A shameful consciousness of his own person assailed him. He saw himself as a ludicrous figure, acting as a pennyboy for his aunts, a nervous wellmeaning sentimentalist, orating to vulgarians and idealising his own clownish lusts' (D 221). As was the case in 'The Sisters', this moment of rupture produces a lacerating self-awareness of the habitus as absurd, ritualistic, and even threatening to his sense of identity. It too is followed by an even more powerful assertion of the everyday as the diegesis abruptly pauses. After a small blank space on the page, we return to find Gabriel leaning against the window, his fiery moment of self-consciousness 'fading out into a grey impalpable world' (D 225). He watches the snow fall, the gently accumulating flakes a metaphor for the everyday that steadily covers everything, even moments of revelation, self-discovery, pain, and joy. Like the silence and ellipsis that concludes the story of the priest without resolving it, here the snow covers character and reader alike, leaving only a blank landscape that captures the ability of the everyday to submerge moments of profound shock in a blanket of familiarity.

Throughout *Dubliners*, Joyce treats the everyday as a frightening, intractable problem since even the shock of death cannot escape what Joyce called the 'hemiplegia' of habit (SL 22). Seen this way, the everyday is an illness infecting the colonized city of Dublin, and Joyce's next published work, *A Portrait of the Artist as a Young Man*, traces Stephen Dedalus's painstaking attempt to fashion a kind of cure for himself. Here again, Joyce uses a funeral to examine the power and potential limits of the everyday as Stephen imagines his own death after falling ill: 'He would have a dead mass in the chapel like the way the fellows had told him it was when Little had died. All the fellows would be at the mass, dressed in black, all with sad faces.... And they would carry the coffin out of the chapel slowly and he would be buried in the little graveyard of the community' (P 24). Far from seeing this as a disaster, the young boy instead imagines 'how beautiful and sad' the funeral and mourning rites would be (P 24). This is, in fact, the first story that the young Stephen actually tells, and he uses the youthful experiment with narrative as an attempt to see beyond the horizon of an everyday that has brought him misery and now sickness.[12]

Later in the book, a blistering sermon delivered at a retreat again causes him to reflect on his own death, and again he sees it as an opportunity to escape from a paralyzing habitus, this time through the steady mortification of the body. Initially, this process of alienation from taste, touch, and smell makes Stephen intensely aware of even his most familiar actions, ranging from what he wears to where he looks. These new behaviours, however, quickly morph into habits, so that the once fanatically faithful young man begins to imagine a new means of alienation and escape through apostasy: 'He would fall. He had not yet fallen, but he would fall ... and he felt the silent lapse of his soul' (*P* 162). Kenner argues that this cycle of revelatory transformation followed by disappointment defines the novel's core structure: 'The action of each of the five chapters is really the same action. Each chapter closes with a synthesis of triumph which the next one destroys.'[13] Stephen, at the end of *A Portrait*, in other words, is not much different than the boy struggling with that ellipsis in 'The Sisters' or Gabriel watching snow drift down over Dublin. Even the novel itself seems to succumb to the tidal pull of the everyday, sliding into an open-ended diary form most closely associated with the dull, day-to-day recording of what Walter Benjamin calls the 'empty time' of modernity.[14]

In an essay originally written in 1919 titled 'Modern Fiction', Virginia Woolf too confronted the problem and power of the everyday. 'Life', she laments in a pointed critique of realist fiction by writers like John Galsworthy and Arnold Bennett, 'is not a series of gig lamps symmetrically arranged.' Instead, it is 'a luminous halo, a semi-transparent envelope surrounding us from the beginning of consciousness to the end.'[15] Woolf, like Stephen in *A Portrait*, believes that life must be more than the dulling routines of the everyday – that a powerful enough imagination can take some measure of the 'luminous halo' and thus supercharge the world with meaning. Woolf called this space beyond the mere everyday 'life', and Joyce, in his earliest writings, sought to illuminate it through his epiphanies. Like many other modernists, they believed that a careful exploration of the everyday would allow us to discover a crack in the habitus through which revelation, even revolution, might be glimpsed. For Joyce, however, these efforts consistently end in failure, whether in the ellipsis at the close of 'The Sisters' or in *A Portrait*, a *Künstlerroman* (a narrative about an artist's growth to maturity) that simply trails off into a series of disjointed diary entries.

Resilience

At the end of *A Portrait*, Joyce had reached a limit. The power of plot – of an arc that might give shape and meaning to events – consistently failed in the face of the everyday and its ability to dissolve even death into mere routine. Eliot believed that he turned to Homer's *Odyssey* to resolve this problem, discovering in the order of the classical world a bulwark against the meaningless chaos of the everyday. Joyce's early notebook drafts for *Ulysses* show that he planned the book from the start around this epic structure, and he later shared with friends meticulous schemas and lists of correspondences. The problem, however, is that his novel only loosely tracks the *Odyssey*.[16] He adds, for example, an entire chapter called 'Wandering Rocks', named for a path not taken in the original. Stephen, the book's symbolic analogue for Telemachus, already has a father of his own and nonchalantly declines Bloom's offer of mystic adoption. Most significantly, of course, Bloom returns home to a decidedly unfaithful Penelope, leaving readers trying vainly to associate the epic slaying of the suitors with a mumbled conversation about breakfast. Critics like Eliot and Kenner have shaped our reading of the novel by arguing that Joyce used Homer in order to give structure to everyday life. It might just as easily be argued, however, that the current flows the other way: that Joyce's fascination with the dulling power of the everyday instead demolishes even the greatest of epic plots. As Schliemann discovered when poking around the remains of Troy, it's not Priam's treasury that endured, but potsherds, ash pits, and garbage tips.

This is not to say that the *Odyssey* isn't an essential structural device for Joyce's novel, but there are other plots at work in the events that unfold on the warm June day in 1904, almost all of which turn around death's interruption of the everyday. When we first meet Stephen in the novel, for example, he is dressed in black to mourn the death of his mother, May Dedalus, and tortured by unrelenting memories of her struggle with cancer. In glancing out at the sea, he sees a 'dull green mass of liquid' that evokes the bile she vomited (*U* 1.108). He then recalls a terrifying dream in which her corpse bent over him, 'her wasted body within its loose graveclothes giving off an odour of wax and rosewood' (*U* 1.270–1). This passage echoes the scene from the opening of 'The Sisters', since his mother carries with her the same ceremonial candles that the boy understood to be a sign of the priest's passing. In this case, however, May Dedalus appears not to be dead at all and becomes for Stephen a 'ghoul' and a 'chewer of corpses' that he drunkenly attacks at the end of 'Circe' (*U* 1.278; 15.4201–45).

May's brutal, intimate death creates a debilitating paradox for Stephen and his aspiration to become an artist. There is, after all, no Homeric analogue for his mother's death in the *Odyssey*. As the novel's graphic depiction of terminal cancer makes clear, there is nothing heroic, mythic, or redeeming about her agony. May, Stephen realizes, matters very little to anyone outside of his own family, and her death will go largely unremarked: one more life laid waste by poverty, misogyny, and brutal everyday existence in colonial Ireland. A distraught Stephen wonders what will happen to the remnants of her habitus: 'Her secrets: old featherfans, tasselled dancecards, powdered with musk, a gaud of amber beads in her locked drawer. A birdcage hung in the sunny window of her house when she was a girl' (*U* 1.255–7). The answer, of course, is that they will be lost, sunk into the relentless march of the everyday. At the start of *Ulysses*, then, Joyce recapitulates the challenge he faced at the end of *A Portrait*, and the death of May, it turns out, also becomes the death of Stephen and of his desire to impose some meaningful sense of plot or order on the everyday. Simply put, he cannot find a way to make a story of his mother's life or death. It's too painful to slide into the 'meanness' of mere ellipsis, but neither does it rise to the level of Aristotelian tragedy or Homeric epic.

Frustrated with Stephen as both a character and an implicit theory of what a novel should be, Joyce decided to start over again. 'Stephen no longer interests me', he wrote in a letter to Frank Budgen. 'He has a shape that can't be changed.'[17] In a series of carefully drawn parallels, therefore, he constructs Leopold Bloom, who also gets out of bed, plans his day, grabs a bit of breakfast, and dresses all in black – not in a show of prolonged mourning but in order to attend the funeral of a distant friend named Paddy Dignam. Just as Stephen finds images of his mother invading his thoughts, Bloom too thinks periodically about Rudy, his son who died in infancy. In 'Circe', Bloom even finds himself face-to-face with the child. Rather than striking out at him in terror, however, Bloom watches in wonder '*a fairy boy of eleven, a changeling, kidnapped, dressed in an Eton suit*' (*U* 15.4957–62, italics in original). As with May Dedalus, there is no Homeric equivalent for Rudy. Joyce, though, had watched his youngest brother George die of sepsis in 1902, and six years later his partner, Nora, suffered a miscarriage. Joyce examined the foetus and confessed his pain at the loss of this 'truncated existence' (*JJ* 268). Having experienced the tension between the sharp pain of grief and the dulling effects of the everyday, he built at least part of *Ulysses* around events that have no classical parallel. In Homer's epics, after all, death is harrowing yet glorious and thus set forever aside from the emptiness of the everyday. The deaths of May Dedalus, Rudy Bloom, and Paddy Dignam, however, exist fully outside the mythic schemas Joyce devised, and yet the book rotates fixedly around them.

Strangely, we never really learn *why* Bloom structures so much of his day around Dignam's funeral. There is scant evidence that the two men knew one another particularly well, and, even at the burial, Bloom spares almost no thought for the dead man. In fact, he seems to treat it as a conversation starter or even a social event. When he heads out for breakfast in the morning, for example, he passes a pub owner and thinks to himself, 'Stop and say a word: about the funeral perhaps. Sad thing about poor Dignam, Mr O'Rourke' (U 4.119).[18] Later in the day, when he runs into Mrs. Breen, he thinks 'may as well get her sympathy' (U 4.218–20) before explaining his mourning clothes. The stream-of-consciousness narrative even records a surprisingly callous train of thought as Bloom first creates a short musical mashup of songs about funerals before thinking 'that's quite enough of that' (U 8.226) and then steers the conversation towards a different topic. This is worlds removed from Stephen, who can't even look at the ocean without seeing an image of his mother's suffering.

The 'Hades' episode, in particular, reflects a radically different vision of death and its relation to narrative than in any of Joyce's early works. Despite its dreary setting, the chapter is filled with often comedic reflections on death, dying, and decomposition. While standing at the graveside, Bloom barely thinks of Dignam and instead takes note of those in attendance, wonders about the process of preparing a corpse for burial, and devises a plan for reusable coffins. We have come a long way from Stephen's bowl of bitter waters and Gabriel Conroy's swooning soul. Among other things, Bloom simply seems to possess a greater psychic resilience than Joyce's other characters, so that even after reflecting on the painful personal losses he has endured, he can emerge from Glasnevin Cemetery at the end of his episode and simply shake it off: 'Enough of this place', he decides, 'plenty to see and hear and feel yet' (U 6.996, 1003).

The episode, however, is about more than just Bloom since it also offers a way out of the tension between Woolf's insistence on the mystical power concealed within everyday life and Eliot's insistence on the need for classical order. The episode, in fact, appears to make fun of precisely this kind of search for symbolic meaning. As Bloom silently looks across the mourners, he sees a man wearing a macintosh. 'Where the deuce did he pop out of?' Bloom wonders, posing a question that has fascinated generations of critics who insist this unnamed man must mean something (U 6.826).[19] For those who believe that everything on the page must have some psychological or symbolic meaning, this remains one of the most diabolical 'enigmas and puzzles' Joyce placed in the book to 'keep the professors busy for centuries' (JJ 521). The fact that we cannot know the definitive answer to the question, however, is precisely the point. The man in the macintosh is not any one person, but the everyday itself. He is neither a deep symbol nor a luminous halo, but an escape hatch from the great modernist debate between plot and character. Like Paddy Dignam – indeed like Rudy Bloom and May Dedalus – he means nothing. Instead, he is a heartening, even comic, reminder, as Liesl Olson argues, that *Ulysses* 'comprehends the ordinary by keeping it open, by letting it go'.[20] In the graveyard, indeed in the novel as a whole, Joyce rejects mythic coherence in order to embrace the everyday as a source of strength and resilience, even in the face of death.

the...

After completing *Ulysses*, Joyce began work on *Finnegans Wake* by returning, once again, to the story of a funeral in order to explore the newfound richness and resilience of the everyday. Although he kept the title of this final work a closely guarded secret for fifteen years, it took early shape around a nineteenth-century comic ballad about a bricklayer named Tim Finnegan who shows up drunk to work and falls to his death. In place of the stately funerals afforded Father Flynn and Paddy Dignam, however, Tim is given an Irish wake, where the mourners drink, dance, and carouse around the body. In the midst of all this, a glass of whiskey splashes in the dead man's face, reviving him from what had merely been a drunken slumber. The riotous tune is a profane retelling of the gospels, and, in the *Wake*'s opening pages, Joyce's punning language riffs on the mysteries of both resurrection and transubstantiation: 'Hohohoho, Mister Finn, you're going to be Mister Finnagain! Comeday morm and, O, you're vine! Sendday's eve and, ah, you're vinegar!' (*FW* 5.10–11). Finn will be 'again' when he rises, but Joyce also returns here to Father Flynn, whose difficulties began when he dropped the chalice used at mass. His sisters believed that the accident began his ruin, even though 'it contained nothing' (*D* 10). The priest's problem was that he could not discern the difference between the sacred and the everyday, between the physical cup used in a ceremony and its miraculous contents: wine that had been transformed into the blood of Jesus. In this passage from the *Wake*, the sacred and the profane collapse into one another as Finn morphs from sacramental wine into mere vinegar. Just as Finn's wake is a mock resurrection, this scene too offers a blasphemous account of the Catholic eucharist, similar to the jokes about the 'white corpuscles' (*U* 1.23) Buck Mulligan makes atop the Martello Tower at the start of *Ulysses*. In that earlier novel, Joyce seemed determined to separate the sacred from the everyday, often scorning the former in order to elevate the beauty and the power of the latter. In the *Wake*, however, these two slide continuously in order to make everyday practices into sacred rites of their own.

To accomplish this, Joyce imbricates the everyday of the world he constructs with the habitus of the reader so that each word, phrase, and character becomes a compound of other times and places. Reading the *Wake* is thus like playing a game in which we, as readers, take an active part in the process of making meaning.[21] Finnegan is thus not just a profane analogue to Jesus but a compound of every human story about death and rebirth, from ancient Osiris to Ireland's own violent re-emergence as an independent state. This makes him a character of nearly infinite variety in the book and he typically appears as some variant of HCE, three letters that could be Humphrey Chimpden Earwicker, Haveth Childers Everywhere, or, simply, Here Comes Everybody. These characters, in turn, morph into others that encompass, at various times, Napoleon, Noah, Roderick (the last king of Ireland), Ivan the Terrible, the Duke of Wellington, and hundreds of others. His wife (ALP), sons (Shem and Shaun), and daughter (Issy/Maggie) similarly mutate into a cascade of different historical, fictional, and mythic characters. Even the book itself seems to follow this cycle, since it ends with ALP flowing out to sea in a sentence that abruptly ends 'A way a lone a last a loved a long the' (*FW* 628.15–16). It only makes sense if read as the start of the fragmentary passage that opens the book: 'riverrun, past Eve and Adam's, ... brings us by a commodius vicus of recirculation back to Howth Castle and Environs' (*FW* 3.1–3).

This process of condensation occurs in the language on the page as well, which Joyce overloads with puns, portmanteaus, homophones, and allusions in order to inject a sense of wonder and surprise into the everyday acts of speaking, reading, and communicating. The strange words on the page, in effect, insist on the historicity and plasticity of language itself, which not only bears the past into the present but opens up new possibilities for discovery or connection with an emerging future. In an attempt to rally support around a book that was being met with confusion and frustration, Samuel Beckett wrote that *Finnegans Wake* 'is not to be read – or rather it is not only to be read', by which he means that looking for character, plot, or even mythic structure will lead only to frustration and failure. The book, he contends, 'is not about something; it is that something itself'.[22] It is, in other words, an experience that the reader has in the course of everyday life rather than an attempt to record the plotted experiences of others. We too become characters in and even authors of the book, 'sentenced to be nuzzled over a full trillion times for ever and a night' (*FW* 120.12–13).

And this brings us back to the book's title and Joyce's decision to begin his last work exactly where he started the first one: at a funeral. The ellipses of 'The Sisters', however, give way in the *Wake* to a vast excess of concatenated plots, characters, and words that all mean too much rather than too little. Where Old Cotter carefully edited words out of his speech to obfuscate the mysterious details around Flynn's death, the *Wake* overwhelms us with detail. The fall of Tim Finnegan becomes the fall of man, the defeat of Napoleon, the comic shattering of Humpty Dumpty, the downfall of Parnell – all bitter deaths that should seemingly produce closure and thus create the basic element of a plot. Tim Finnegan, however, defies the plot set out for him by rising up from his deathbed and sparking a new round of celebration. He perpetually becomes 'Mister Finnagain', his funeral a 'funferall' (fun for all) that opens the way for another round of invention, improvisation, and discovery (*FW* 111.15).

As a young writer, Joyce believed that the most banal everyday experiences might hold the key to spiritual revolution and that 'it was for the man of letters to record these epiphanies with extreme care' (*SH* 211). His faith in the power of the everyday never left him, but, by the time he reached *Finnegans Wake*, he rejected the idea that such moments might be available exclusively to the elite 'priest[s] of eternal imagination' (*P* 221). The *Wake*'s seventh chapter focuses on what remains of Stephen Dedalus, an artist figure now called 'Shem the Penman', who, like Joyce, had written the 'usylessly unreadable Blue Book of Eccles' (*FW* 179.26–7). This artist lacks the snobbery of the boy in 'The Sisters', of Gabriel Conroy, and of Stephen from *Ulysses*. He lives in a 'Haunted Inkbottle', his workshop awash not in delicate epiphanies but in the accumulated mess of everyday life: 'burst loveletters, telltale stories, stickyback snaps, doubtful eggshells', and much more (*FW* 182.31, 183.11–12). (The full list stretches over a page.) Like Yeats, who wrote at the end of his career that poetry arose 'in the foul ragand-bone shop of the heart', Joyce here grounds his own artistic alter ego in the detritus of the everyday.[23] Where Yeats seems mournful (the poem, after all, is titled 'The Circus Animals' Desertion'), *Finnegans Wake* is shot through with humour and hope. The work of invention, after all, no longer falls solely to the over-burdened, even abject, artist, but instead courses through language itself, which explains why Joyce chose to the end his final book with the most everyday word he could imagine: 'the'. Rather than the climatic 'Yes' of *Ulysses*, Joyce uses the dullest of words here, but one that sparkles with promise. After all, it can never mark an end of a sentence, so must gesture always to the future, to what comes next – in this case, to all of *Finnegans Wake* itself, which spins out again when we turn from the last page to the first so that we, like Finn, can begin again.

To Be Continued

From the start of his career, Joyce set out to experiment with the mystery of everyday life – not just with the luminous halo of consciousness but with the actions, emotions, habits, and events that we otherwise ignore or forget. At times, the everyday seemed to offer an untapped reservoir of meaning, and he set out first to document it with the care of an archaeologist, hoping to preserve it against a series of titanic changes. These began with the collapse of his own family into poverty, a traumatic experience that left him painfully aware of the ways in which the everyday could simply, suddenly collapse. As Joyce wrote his way through the traumatic disordering of his family's everyday life, he watched the world plunge into the chaos of WWI. Suddenly caught behind enemy lines, the Joyce family scrambled to escape Trieste and just barely made it to Zurich, a city filled with equally bewildered refugees.[24] During these years, Joyce toiled away on *Ulysses*, attempting to preserve the vanishing everyday of the city that created him, even as the rest of the world bled and burned. And just as the guns went silent on the continent, Ireland fell into its own bloody turmoil, with the publication of *Ulysses* arriving on the cusp of a civil war that immediately plunged the newly liberated nation into more violence. Meanwhile, as Joyce became an international celebrity, his family life tilted again towards disaster. His beloved daughter, Lucia, showed signs of a severe mental illness that led the family to seek medical treatments that now seem barbaric. Amid it all, Joyce worked steadily to finish *Finnegans Wake*, completing the novel just before he had to flee yet another war. This time, he had to leave his daughter behind in a hospital as the Nazis entered France – bringing a regime that had been systematically slaughtering the mentally ill.

Joyce, the great artist of the everyday, in short, wrote amid its seemingly perpetual collapse. His personal, political, and even artistic life had been defined by trauma, failure, and flight from waves of violence and poverty. Olson writes that Gertrude Stein's aesthetic experiments with repetition grew out of a desire for survival: 'Only the repetition of the everyday remains during the war, and a hope that at least the everyday might continue.'[25] Joyce too shared this hope for the continuation of the everyday. Rather than seeking its radical disruption or looking on it with Eliot's jaundiced eye, Joyce saw instead a fundamentally human reservoir of connection, familiarity, and even community. For him, the everyday had only ever been a site of instability, which is why he turned so often to death and funerals as the largely unacknowledged wellsprings of his work. At those moments, the habitus both collapses and reasserts itself, wounding us even as it opens a pathway towards recovery. In pursuit of this mystery, Joyce set out not simply to document the everyday as a nineteenth-century novelist might but to reconstruct it as a site first of revelation, then of resilience, and finally of creation.

Notes

1. Henri Lefebvre, *Everyday Life in the Modern World*, trans. Sacha Rabinovitch (New York: Routledge, 2017), p. 2.
2. United States v. One Book Called 'Ulysses', 5 F. Supp. 182 (S.D.N.Y. 1933). See law.justia.com/cases/federal/district-courts/FSupp/5/182/2250768/.

3. Declan Kiberd, *'Ulysses' and Us: The Art of Everyday Life in Joyce's Masterpiece* (New York: Norton, 2009), p. 27.
4. Ibid., p. 22.
5. Don Gifford and Robert J. Seidman's *'Ulysses' Annotated* (Berkeley: University of California Press, 1989, revised and expanded edition 2008) was a landmark work of scholarship including around ten thousand entries. Vivian Igoe's *The Real People of Joyce's 'Ulysses'* (Dublin: University College Dublin Press, 2016) provides a catalogue of the hundreds of real people Joyce worked into the book, while Ian Gunn and Clive Hart, *James Joyce's Dublin* (London: Thames and Hudson, 2004), provide intricate maps that track characters' movements (sometimes to the second) and deduce the exact layout of the Blooms' bedroom.
6. Frank Budgen called Joyce an 'engineer' who worked out the details of 'Wandering Rocks' with a map and stopwatch. See *James Joyce and the Making of 'Ulysses'* (New York: Oxford University Press, 1989), pp. 124–5.
7. Sylvia Beach, *Shakespeare and Company* (New York: Harcourt, Brace, 1959), p. 52.
8. T. S. Eliot, 'Ulysses, Order and Myth' in *Selected Prose of T. S. Eliot* (London: Faber, 1975), pp. 177–8.
9. Hugh Kenner, 'Homer's Sticks and Stones', *James Joyce Quarterly* 50.1–2 (2013): 51–62, 56.
10. Margot Norris, *Suspicious Readings of Joyce's 'Dubliners'* (Philadelphia: University of Pennsylvania Press, 2003), p. 156.
11. Pierre Bourdieu uses the term 'habitus' to describe 'a whole system of predispositions inculcated by the material circumstances of life and family upbringing' that produce aesthetic, ethical, and practical orientations to the world that seem natural, familiar, and habitual. See Pierre Bourdieu, *Family and Society: Selections from the Annales, Économies, Sociétés, Civilisations*, ed. Robert Forster and Orest Ranum, trans. Elborg Forster and Patricia M. Ranum (Baltimore: Johns Hopkins University Press, 1976), p. 118.
12. Critics have long focused on Stephen's childhood experiments with language, but rarely have they looked at his early attempts to fashion basic narratives like this one.
13. Hugh Kenner, *Dublin's Joyce* (Bloomington: Indiana University Press, 1956), p. 129.
14. Walter Benjamin, 'Theses on the Philosophy of History' in *Illuminations*, ed. Hannah Arendt, trans. Harry Zohn (New York: Schocken, 1968), p. 261.
15. Virginia Woolf, 'Modern Fiction' in *The Common Reader* (San Diego: Harcourt, 1984), p. 150.
16. Joyce, in fact, depended heavily not on Homer's text but on a nineteenth-century version by Charles Lamb that he had read in school titled *The Adventures of Ulysses*.
17. Budgen, *James Joyce and the Making of 'Ulysses'*, p. 107.
18. In a further sign of his general lack of deep feeling about Dignam's death, Bloom actually decides not to comment on the funeral and opts instead to say something banal about the weather.
19. Vladimir Nabokov argued that he was a stand-in for Joyce himself, while others have suggested he might be Mr. Duffy (from *Dubliners*), Lazarus, or the Devil.

Vladimir Nabokov, *Lectures on Literature*, ed. Fredson Bowers (New York: Harcourt Brace Jovanovich, 1980), p. 320.
20. Liesl Olson, *Modernism and the Ordinary* (Oxford: Oxford University Press, 2009), p. 55.
21. For a longer argument about the *Wake* as a game, see Sean Latham, 'Playful Reading: *Finnegans Wake* I.6 and Game Theory' in *'Finnegans Wake': Polyvocal Explorations*, ed. Kimberly Devlin and Christine Smedley (Gainesville: University Press of Florida, 2015), pp. 90–114.
22. Samuel Beckett, 'Dante ... Bruno. Vico ... Joyce' in *Our Exagmination Round His Factification for Incamination of Work in Progress* (London: Faber, 1961 [1929]), p. 27.
23. William Butler Yeats, 'The Circus Animals' Desertion' in *The Collected Poems of W. B. Yeats* (London: Macmillan, 1982), p. 392.
24. Joyce's brother Stanislaus was not so fortunate. The one-time pillar of financial and emotional support for the family spent the duration of the war in a prison camp.
25. Olson, *Modernism and the Ordinary*, p. 28.

13

JIM FAIRHALL

Joyce and Nature

Ecocriticism has been catching up with James Joyce.[1] Moving beyond the heritage of Romanticism's binary opposition between human and nonhuman nature, contemporary critics (notably those in Robert Brazeau and Derek Gladwin's *Eco-Joyce*), have explored the entanglement of nature, culture, and the built environment in Joyce's works.[2] In this essay I will focus on Joyce's evolving presentation of the human body as a natural–cultural entity. His early fictions – *Stephen Hero*, *Dubliners*, and *A Portrait of the Artist as Young Man* – depict the body as a humbling counterweight to notions of transcendence, especially to Catholic ideas glorifying the spirit. The evolution of his thinking culminates in his portrayal of the body, in *Ulysses* and *Finnegans Wake*, as a site of constant transformation, where the human and the nonhuman interpenetrate and shape each other. In exploring this theme I will use a set of theories called, loosely, material ecocriticism, which lately has led to and overlaps posthuman ecocriticism.[3] Among the antecedents of these theories are feminism and ecofeminism, which share their concern with the body. An influential concept of material ecocriticism is Stacy Alaimo's 'trans-corporeality', which reveals the interlinkage and imbrication of our bodies with each other and 'more-than-human nature' (as opposed to the binary of 'nature').[4] Our imagined unitary selves arise through physical interactions with each other and 'the interconnections, interchanges, and transits between human bodies and nonhuman natures'.[5] Thus, in *Ulysses* and *Finnegans Wake*, even biologically dead bodies of the solar system intersect the characters' lives, both through their material environments and the senses, microbes, and atoms of their bodies.

Joyce's interest in the body as a natural–cultural phenomenon punctuates the surviving incomplete manuscript of his autobiographical novel, *Stephen Hero* (c. 1904–1906). It does so often in connection with mortality. The theme first appears indirectly when Stephen applies his theory of prosody to Byron's quatrain beginning, 'My days are in the yellow leaf' (*SH* 26).[6]

The theme's next emergence is also indirect: the scene of a dog baying in a park. The inexplicable baying, subliminally eerie, halts Stephen's normally hyper-analytic mind:

> Before the swampy beach a big dog was recumbent. From time to time he lifted his muzzle in the vapourous air, uttering a prolonged sorrowful howl ... People had gathered on the footpaths to hear him ... Stephen made one of them till he felt the first drops of rain, and then he continued his way in silence under the dull surveillance of heaven, hearing ... behind him the strange lamentation. (SH 38)

This passage implies the mortality and imperfection of the fallen world of nature although Stephen is too young and inexperienced to interpret it.[7] It presages his gradual rejection of Catholic supernaturalism and the death without transcendence of his younger sister, Isabel.[8]

In the lead-in to Isabel's fatal crisis (based on the death from typhoid fever in 1902 of Joyce's younger brother, George [JJ 44]), Stephen broods on unredeemed transience: 'Cemeteries revealed ... the lives of all those who ... had accepted an obvious divinity. The vision of ... congenital lives, shuffling onwards amid yawn and howl, beset him' (SH 162). He projects his mood onto nature: the 'rusty fires' of a 'dismal sunset', 'the decay of leaves and flowers' (SH 162). Then more-than-human nature – Isabel's haemorrhage – intervenes as a plutonic force uncontainable by culture. His mother asks: 'Do you know anything about the body? ... What ought I do? There's some matter coming away from the hole in Isabel's ... stomach' (SH 163). Mrs Daedalus's voice is that of a devout Catholic whose daughter's reduction to a dying body has collapsed, momentarily, her ideological framework for containing mortality. Later the hollow ceremony of Isabel's burial disgusts Stephen.[9] Not surprisingly, this no-exit view of nature and supernatural religion contributed to the reasons why *Stephen Hero* was for Joyce, in his early twenties, an artistic dead end. Years later, in *Ulysses*, he would fictionalize another family death, his mother's, within a still nonreligious but much richer artistic-philosophical framework.

The stories of *Dubliners*, unfolding from 1896 to 1904, overlap *Stephen Hero*. Unleavened by Stephen's energy, which only Molly Ivors matches in her cameo in 'The Dead', they depict the socio-political entrapment of a colonized city whose citizens are further entrapped by the operations of nature on their bodies. Many characters suffer from symptoms of paralysis, premature aging, senile decrepitude, and alcoholic disability. Although only two of them die, more-than-human nature intimates mortality in the form of darkness and unpleasant wet weather, enveloping Dublin like a hyperobject.[10] Individual natural bodies lack agency and suggest the futility of escape from cultural paralysis. The brief reprieve of the children's free play in 'Araby', under the 'ever-changing violet' of the 'space' of winter skies, ends with their being summoned indoors to the adult regime of 'sombre' (*D* 21) houses. For the adventure-seeking truants in 'An Encounter', the River Liffey fails as an escape route from the regimen of Catholic school because the boys, far from viewing it as wild nature, reduce it to 'the spectacle of Dublin's commerce' (*D* 15).[11] In 'Eveline' the Irish Sea becomes a dead end when the young protagonist, fleeing domestic entrapment, balks at boarding a ship to Buenos Aires as she equates elopement – 'All the seas of the world tumbled about her heart' (*D* 34) – with drowning. In 'A Painful Case' James Duffy stands alone under one of 'the gaunt trees' (*D* 113) in the Phoenix Park, his narcissism pierced for the first time by death as a felt reality.

The tree under which Duffy remembers his rejected lover is an ambiguous symbol, but it does not point to a realm of transcendence, any more than do images of nature in other stories. Neither do such images point, with one exception, to the real existence of more-than-human nature within or beyond Joyce's imagined Dublin, even though contemporary Irish naturalists were busy exploring it.[12] The exception is the ending of 'The Dead'. Falling asleep, Gabriel fleetingly transcends his patriarchal ego by surrendering to the more-than-human nature symbolized by the snow falling on 'the dark central plain, on the treeless hills, ... upon the Bog of Allen and, farther westward, ... into the dark mutinous Shannon waves' (*D* 225). This panorama is not only Gabriel's route to a reality larger than his self-conception but also the reader's route beyond Joyce's early, narrowly culture-centred conception of Dublin to turn-of-the-century Irish ecosystems – bogs and deforested hills – that helped shape Dublin's and Ireland's natural–cultural history.[13]

A Portrait of the Artist as a Young Man (1907–1916) advances its artist-hero from the stasis of *Dubliners* and *Stephen Hero* to a world, though still late Victorian and Edwardian, where transcending society and nature seems at least possible, even if always around the next corner. The earliest challenges to Stephen's felt apprehensions of reality are cultural. The claims of religious and social leaders to a morally authoritative, transcendent understanding of life are, as in Joyce's earlier fictions and his satirical poems, undermined by these agents' earthbound bodies.[14] The poems shame guardians of public morals by exposing their impurity in the form of waste-excreting body parts. Most often priests are the targets, like the officiant at Isabel's funeral: 'A priest with a great toad-like belly ... read the service rapidly in a croaking voice' (*SH* 167). Early in *A Portrait*, during the Christmas dinner debate over the Church's role in politics, Mr Dedalus rebuts Dante's admonition to revere priests by citing the Archbishop of Armagh's eating habits and corpulence: '—Tub of guts, said Mr Dedalus coarsely ... You should see that fellow lapping up his bacon and cabbage of a cold winter's day ... He twisted his features into a grimace of heavy bestiality' (P 33). At Belvedere College, Stephen's call to the priesthood is undermined by his vision of 'the raw reddish glow he had so often seen on wintry mornings on the shaven gills of the priests' (P 161). Later, at university, he dismisses the dean of studies, whose grey-haired 'aging body' (P 185), reminiscent of paralyzed Father Flynn's in 'The Sisters', is untouched by transcendence.

If one way to read Joyce's handling of nature in *A Portrait* is to focus on the tension between bodily lowliness and transcendence, another way is to examine the tension between Stephen's subjectivity and the incursions of more-than-human nature. The novel starts out in the aftermath of organic creation with a baby's sensory exploration of his newfound world. A naïve wish to marry a Protestant neighbour causes Stephen's fall from his natural Eden into cultural shame. Dante, a fervent Catholic, appropriates nature in threatening his body if he does not apologize: 'O, if not, the eagles will come and pull out his eyes' (P 8). Being shouldered at Clongowes Wood College into 'the square ditch', an outdoor cesspool, is another shameful, natural–cultural event imperilling Stephen's physical integrity: '(H)ow cold and slimy the water had been! And a fellow had once seen a big rat jump plop into the scum' (P 14). The rainwater–urine is a boundary-dissolving element associated with bodily lowliness and, through the rat, the culturally construed horror of nature feeding on human waste.

Later, as an adolescent visiting Cork with his father, Stephen feels a similar horror of breached natural–cultural borders. Maud Ellmann has brilliantly analyzed Stephen's shock on seeing the word '*Foetus*' carved into a desk in the 'anatomy theatre' (P 89) at Mr Dedalus's alma mater: 'This cut ... corresponds to the navel, which separates the foetus from the mother. A wounding anterior to naming, the navel testifies to the facticity of motherhood.'[15] In his psychic anatomy theatre, Stephen feels threatened by reabsorption into the womb and finds some phallic relief in peering at his father's initials on a desk. Identification with his bankrupt father, making a sentimental journey out of a mission to sell his last properties, is shameful, but identification with mother-as-nature entails engulfment. This episode looks back to Gabriel's vision of dissolution in 'The Dead' and forward to Stephen's dread of his dead mother in *Ulysses*, countered by Leopold Bloom's calm view of organic death as a reality that is part of nature's cycles.

In *Ulysses*, more-than-human nature radically differs from its counterpart in Joyce's earlier works. It is an energetic, transformative force that interpenetrates Dubliners and Dublin trans-corporeally. Organic substances and even material things become more alive than, say, the trees, birds, and other natural phenomena of *A Portrait*. Surf speaks; the Blooms' cat speaks; printing presses and other inanimate objects speak. Creatures and things metamorphose, sometimes into each other. Often these metamorphoses take place in a character's imagination, but often their causation is ambiguous, attributable to a narrator that channels the more-than-human world in ways the characters are not aware of nor would recognize as representing reality. This happens par excellence in the phantasmagoria of 'Circe' but runs throughout the novel, starting with the opening scene in which Buck Mulligan's bowl of shaving lather becomes a chalice of Communion wine transformed into Christ's blood.

Alaimo describes trans-corporeality as a 'sense of the human as ... perpetually interconnected with the flows of substances and the agencies of environments'.[16] In *Ulysses* Joyce's three main characters all embody interconnections with nature, especially fluid interconnections. Water in its various bodily forms – blood, semen, saliva, amniotic fluid – interacts in a trans-corporeal network with water outside the body: for example, the sea, the Liffey, the thundershower in 'Oxen of the Sun', the water conveyed from the Roundtree reservoir to the Blooms' kitchen tap, and Molly's recollections of 'that awful deepdown torrent' and 'the sea crimson ... like fire' (*U* 18.1597–8). These physical connections underpin metaphysical associations that Stephen, Bloom, and Molly make in their quests to fathom the impact on their lives of water and other forces of more-than-human nature.

Perhaps the least fluid character in *Ulysses*, except intellectually, is Stephen, whose intertextual counterpart had recently embraced, at the end of *A Portrait*, a would-be, fixed subject position as a masculine artist, the spiritual son of the artificer Daedalus. Now, spurred by his mother's death from cancer, Stephen grapples with the dissolving of that position as he newly experiences the world as being shaped by the unceasing transformations and interchanges of trans-corporeal bodies. In fact, the flow of his consciousness at once reflects on and embodies trans-corporeal flows. Shortly after Mulligan's mocking encomium to the 'snotgreen sea' – 'our great sweet mother' (*U* 1.78, 80) – Stephen gazes down from the tower: 'The ring of bay and skyline held a dull green mass of liquid. A bowl of white china had stood beside her deathbed holding the green sluggish bile which she had torn up from her rotting liver' (*U* 1.107–10). He recoils from the coughed-up fluid of his mother's dying body, yet as he regards her symbol, the sea, he unconsciously shares with her the element of water, which makes up about 60 per cent of an adult body. In the matrix of Dublin Bay he is linked trans-corporeally with both nature and her remembered body that bore him.

In 'Proteus', Stephen's brooding merges evolution (nature) with Catholic theology (a cultural artifact he cannot fully dismiss) when he imagines his tie, through the maternal body, to the biological chain of human beings extending back to Adam and Eve. He pictures two strollers on Sandymount Strand as midwives, one carrying in her bag a mis-birth with a trailing navel cord: 'The cords of all link back, strandentwining cable of all flesh' (U 3.37) Later he imagines the metamorphoses undergone by the corpse of a drowned man: 'A quiver of minnows, fat of a spongy titbit, flash through the slits of his buttoned trouserfly. God becomes man becomes fish becomes barnacle goose becomes featherbed mountain. Dead breaths I living breathe' (U 3.476–9). Here he recognizes his trans-corporeal kinship not just with his mother but with other human beings and with more-than-human nature.

The theme of trans-corporeal transformation ramifies in later chapters. At the National Library Stephen muses on the body's cellular flux: 'Molecules all change. I am other I now.' Characteristically, he draws a parallel with artistic transformation, but he replaces his paternal model Daedalus with a female one, the Celtic goddess of life and death, Danu: 'As we, or mother Dana, weave and unweave our bodies ... from day to day, their molecules shuttled to and fro, so does the artist weave and unweave his image' (U 9.205, 376–8). In 'Wandering Rocks' his dread of absorption into the feminized other of more-than-human nature, represented by his mother and the phallus-less drowned man, reawakens when he encounters his sister, Dilly: 'My eyes they say she has ... She is drowning ... She will drown me with her, eyes and hair. Lank coils of seaweed hair around me' (U 10.865, 875–6). Later, at the lying-in hospital, he intellectualizes the pregnant Mina Purefoy (unlike Bloom, who feels trans-corporeal empathy for her) as all-creating, all-destroying nature –'our mighty mother' (U 14.296), echoing Mulligan's epithet for the sea in 'Telemachus'. His gloomy rumination is washed away, however, by what Bloom describes as 'the discharge of fluid from the thunderhead ... a natural phenomenon' (U 14.426–8). The thunderstorm inundates Dublin in 'a swash of water flowing' from 'an infinite great fall of rain' and a 'cloudburst ... torrent' (U 14.491, 521–2, 1388–9) that, like heavenly semen, results in '(t)he air (being) impregnated with raindew moisture, life essence celestial, glistening on Dublin stone' (U 14.1407–8). Here human culture – the built city, along with Stephen's abstractions – undergoes a trans-corporeal sea-change, dissolved in the androgynous joining of water with air.

In 'Circe', Joyce's carnivalesque chapter of transmutations, people and things morph into other people and things in a prefiguring of *Finnegans Wake*. Outdoor Nighttown (about 40 per cent of the chapter) is a squalid, antipastoral cityscape where nature manifests itself, insofar as we can discern the 'realistic' narrative from the hallucinatory one, hardly more than in the close quarters of Bella Cohen's brothel. Unlike the realistic cat whose otherness and similarity Bloom recognizes at home in 'Calypso', canine spectres – variously a 'spaniel', a 'retriever', a 'wolfdog', a 'terrier', a 'setter', a 'mastiff', and a 'bulldog' (U 15.100/690, 357, 659, 663, 667, 673, 693) – materialize before him, harking back to Stephen's vision of the metamorphosing dog on the beach in 'Proteus'. Birds also appear fleetingly but are fantasies or memories, like the 'covey of gulls, storm petrels' (U 15.683), recalling the gulls Bloom fed in 'Lestrygonians'.[17] In 'Circe' Joyce no more differentiates material from organic things than he does literal actions from thoughts or imaginings. The material world here, bringing to a climax a tendency in earlier chapters, is alive and has agency along with the characters and their hallucinatory doppelgängers. Among many examples, a 'concave mirror ... presents to [Bloom] lovelorn longlost lugubru Booloohoom' (U 15.145–6). Then a maintenance tram – 'a dragon sandstrewer ... , its huge red headlight winking' – seems to regard him while its gong, sounding a warning, declines him: 'Bang Bang Bla Bak Blud Bugg Bloo' (U 15.184–9). Later, Bloom's soap from his morning bath takes on equal agential status with him, chanting, 'We're a capital couple are Bloom and I. / He brightens the earth. I polish the sky' (U 15.338–9).

Although the setting of 'Circe' is one of colonial and patriarchal degradation pervaded by the paralysis of mind and morale Joyce depicts in *Stephen Hero*, *Dubliners*, and to some extent *A Portrait*, it is marked by energy, metamorphosis, and bio-semiotic communication. Biological science shows that there are, as Timo Maran points out, 'countless organisms ... constantly interpreting and remaking the world they inhabit'.[18] Even nonorganic things, from the perspective of material ecocriticism, have agency and communicate interactively with each other and organic creatures. Serpil Opperman cites Karen Barad in arguing that 'not only biological organisms but also all material forms exhibit meaningful signs, making meaning "an ongoing performance of the world in its differential intelligibility"'.[19] Thus, in the carnival of things and creatures in 'Circe', both realistic and surreal, everything and everybody is imbricated in a dialogue of purposes and crosspurposes. Bloom, though a major generator and receiver of meaning (more so than drunken, exhausted Stephen), is only one player in this semiotic carnival. He doesn't catch all of the performance of meanings, which, of course, becomes the reader's task.

One set of meanings arises from the interplay of the binaries of waste/disease and purity/health, a motif reflecting a British–Irish material and cultural obsession. For example, the prophylactic sand that the 'dragon' tram strews, presumably to cleanse or otherwise keep the tracks in working order, is a natural substance. Here it is a human tool for maintaining built culture; at the same time it recalls Stephen's stroll on the unregulated sand of Sandymount Strand, whose natural properties cause it to capture the polluted waste of Dublin Bay, threatening the city's health and Dublin Corporation's civilizing mission. Culture can appropriate sand, as with the tram or Stephen's musing –'These heavy sands are language tide and wind have silted here' – yet sand remains one of 'Sir Lout's toys' (U 3.288–9, 291), an embodiment of more-than-human nature, retaining its agency even in an urban setting with rules, statutes, and offices dedicated to controlling nature. It interacts and 'speaks', presaging the gradual recognition by science of the agency of non-living things (a Cambridge physicist studying sand flows in 2020 describes 'sand dunes that communicate – inanimate objects communicating information').[20] Similarly, the organic ingredients of Bloom's speaking soap, such as fat and lemons, enable it to become a commodity and an emblem of civilization entangled with social injunctions of bodily purity whose ideological contradictions reveal themselves through physical human needs.[21] Bloom enacts this at Sandymount when desire spurs him to soil himself while he ogles Gerty MacDowell; his subsequent search inside his waistcoat for a 'Mansmell' (U 13.1036) leads to the lemon-scented soap, which he recalls guiltily not having paid for – his second soap-related violation of middle-class standards.

In Nighttown Joyce portrays the eruptions of the human sex drive as being perverted by the false consciousness of patriarchal sexual ideology, which bars unsanctioned enjoyment of sex and turns prostitutes' bodies into polluted receptacles of culture like the sand at Sandymount. The women themselves, in Dublin's socio-cultural economy, amount to waste products. Yet, having a fleshly as well as an ideological existence, they embody more reality than fantasy figures of sexual purity. Thus the personified magazine poster of the nymph above the Blooms' bed at 7 Eccles Street, who aligns herself with 'Only the ethereal', responds to Bloom's demystification by cracking amid 'a cloud of stench' (U 15.3437, 3469–70). Paralleling the cry of her counterpart, the madame Bella Cohen, she hails the police whose authority to quarantine women's bodies enables the '[r]ows of grimy houses with gaping doors' (U 15.3–4) that signal sexual fantasies and civic complicity in them. Only Molly Bloom, in 'Penelope', questions Dublin's patriarchal objectification and policing of women's bodies. She admires her lover Boylan's erect penis – a natural phenomenon – but also finds it a bit ridiculous because Boylan, the ne plus ultra of the culture of Dublin gallantry, is a bit ridiculous, too, like other male authority figures she muses on. She habitually fantasizes about escaping her physical subjection as a woman through experiencing sex as a male: 'always I wished I was one myself for a change' (U 18.1381).

But she doesn't imagine herself as transcending patriarchal culture, if not nature, through becoming someone like an educated New Woman, à la Molly Ivors. Fittingly, then, her double in Nighttown performs her entrapment in masculine fantasy as a fulsomely attractive Middle Eastern woman whose 'ankles are linked by a slender fetterchain' (U 15.313). Culture, not nature, limits her potential for transformation even in the shape-shifting carnival of 'Circe'. Instead, it is her husband's double – reflecting Bloom's status in *Ulysses* as a confounder of boundaries – who changes sex and even gives birth.

All the material, organic, and trans-corporeal energy in *Ulysses*, including the three protagonists' formidable mental energy, does not remove them (or the reader) from the glum realization that all individual beings must pay their debt to nature. In 'Circe' this necessity terrifies Stephen when Mrs Dedalus's ghost, announced by Mulligan as 'Our great sweet mother', reminds him of their trans-corporeal symbiosis: 'Years and years I loved you ... when you lay in my womb' (U 15.4180, 4203–4). Her insistence that he, too, must die –'All must go through it, Stephen' (U 14.4182–3) – and her metamorphosis into the green crab of cancer trigger his defiance of feminine more-than-human nature when he wields his phallic ashplant to banish her by smashing a chandelier.[22]

Who better to rescue Stephen from his masculine rigidity and fear than Leopold Bloom? A nonbinary 'new womanly man' (U 15.1798–9), Bloom, earlier at Paddy Dignam's funeral in Glasnevin Cemetery, has dismissed death's horrors by affirming the sensual present: 'Plenty to see and hear and feel yet. Feel warm live beings near you ... Warm beds: warm full-blooded life' (U 6.1003–5). Bloom does in fact rescue Stephen, saving him from arrest in Nighttown and leading him home to recuperate from his wild night. Yet the surrogate father–son relationship that the novel seemingly has been portending does not come to fruition; Stephen never warms to him and refuses lodging. Nevertheless, the two of them do enter into a communion – not only with each other but with other human beings and the more-than-human nature that threads their lives.

This communion occurs when they step out, just before parting, to urinate in the Blooms' half-wild back garden. As Bloom points out the constellations, the birth and death of celestial bodies frames them in a trans-corporeal relationship: Bloom–Stephen–humanity–nature. Stars wander 'from immeasurably remote eons to infinitely remote futures in comparison with which the years ... of allotted human life formed a parenthesis of infinitesimal brevity'; yet they die, too, emitting light from 'a past which possibly had ceased to exist as a present before its probable spectators had entered actual present existence' (U 17.1053–6, 1144–5). Just before the two men respond to the bodily cycle that has drawn them outside, 'each contemplat[es] the other in both mirrors of the reciprocal flesh of theirhisnothis fellowfaces' (*U* 17.1183–4). Although distinct and lonely in the world, as their desultory, unsatisfying interaction has shown, they are bodies whose inner universes 'of microbes, germs, bacteria, bacilli, spermatozoa [are] constellated with other bodies' (*U* 17.1060–1, 64–5).[23] Each has encountered the other's limitations as a potential friend, yet they are intimately connected in a transient, trans-corporeal web, including their own bodies (their eyes, their urinary flows), the planet Earth (Bloom's garden), and nonhuman celestial bodies (the sun, the moon, '[t]he heaventree of stars hung with humid nightblue fruit' [*U* 17.1039]). Amid wonder and pathos, the conclusion of their transitory union evokes the deep interconnectedness of human beings with each other – wandering entities, like the 'celestial sign' (*U* 17.1210) of a shooting star, which intersect and part.

More fully than *Ulysses*, *Finnegans Wake* elaborates all the strands of Joyce's thinking about the body, more-than-human nature, and human striving towards transcendence in a world of mortality and imperfection. His thinking is too rich to summarize here, as is the growing body of ecocritical studies of the *Wake*, such as Alison Lacivita's merging of genetic criticism with ecocriticism in *The Ecology of Finnegans Wake*, and Brazeau and Gladwin's *Eco-Joyce*, which addresses 'issues surrounding place and subjectivity, urban and rural landscapes, ecological degradation and … embodiment'.[24] Here I will focus on the entanglement and transformation into each other of human and more-than-human natural bodies, which Joyce presents as part of our world-historical drama, and on Joyce's evocation of our unique consciousness, in the natural history of organic creatures, of imperfection, tragedy, and the brevity of individual lives.

The opening/continuation of *Finnegans Wake* – 'riverrun, past Eve and Adam's, from swerve of shore to bend of bay, brings us by a commodious vicus of recirculation back to Howth Castle and Environs' (*FW* 3.01–3) – braids together several trans-corporeal flows and cycles. As the renewed river of time, the River Liffey, aka Anna Livia Plurabelle (ALP), carries a new cycle of history, reflecting Joyce's reading of Giambattista Vico's *New Science* (1725), in which ALP and her husband Humphrey Chimpden Earwicker (HCE, or Here Comes Everybody) are reborn as human actors. The river runs in tandem with the bloodstream and the digestive process, connoted by 'recirculation' and the commode or chamber pot in 'commodious'. Apart from trans-corporeal relations or the grand Viconian scheme of human historical cycles, the *Wake* is punctuated with expressions of Bergsonian *durée* – the individual's awareness of her life flowing through time, particularly ALP's awareness.[25] The melancholy of this awareness towards the end of life, when nature will reclaim the human subject, counterbalances the jouissance of the *Wake*'s seemingly pan-psychic energy – its depiction of the aliveness and agency of a world where 'every person, place and thing in the chaosmos of Alle [is] anyway connected' (*FW* 118.21–2).

Among the *Wake*'s four elements – air, earth, fire, water – water is the most transformative and hence closest to creation and destruction. Life emerges from the intercourse of the ocean and primeval lightning storms: '[c]umulonubulocirrhonimbant heaven electing, the dart of desire has gored the heart of secret waters' (*FW* 599.25–6). Like ALP, her husband HCE is inseparable from water, in his case the ocean or ocean-like bodies more than rivers. A foetus bathed in the amniotic fluid of his mother's womb, he is a fishlike 'waterbaby' floating on 'majik wavus' (magic waves) 'backtowards motherwaters' (*FW* 198.8, 203.31, 84.30–1), defined by his trans-corporeal relationship not just with maternal fluids but with the sea (he is 'a bairn of the brine' [*FW* 198.7]). 'Motherwaters' suggests the 'watery deep' of Genesis 1:2 – the primordial ocean where evolution began – and is the feminine obverse of the masculine sea invoked by ALP, at the end, as the destroyer of her individual life's flow. HCE's sperm, spilled into the maternal sea in a wet dream that may be of naked, newborn Venus, gives issue to Venus-like Issy, his 'deepseep daughter which was bourne up pridely out of medsdreams unclouthed when I was pillowing in my brime' (*FW* 366.14–15). In nature inbreeding is not uncommon, but as a human HCE is 'increaminated' (*FW* 366.17) by his incestuous desire for his daughter, a cultural violation of boundaries. As an old man he confesses to this 'Fall stuff' (*FW* 366.30), blaming humanity's fall from timeless Eden into guilty, cycle-driven nature.

Issy's trans-corporeal relationship with water also reflects her fallenness. Her narcissism and identification with desire – 'sensation that drives desire that adheres to attachment that dogs death that bitches birth that entails the ensuance of existentiality' (*FW* 18.26–28) – are both the source of the fall and the force of evolution. Issy's conflation with desire undermines her self-love because desire, leading to birth into a world of cycles, entails death. Her use of Pond's vanishing cream ('[t]hree creamings a day' – [*FW* 144.2–3]) suggests the Narcissus-like loss of her identity as she admires her image in a watery mirror: 'Sure she was near drowned in pondest coldstreams of admiration forherself ... making faces at her bachspilled likeness in the brook' (*FW* 526.28–31).[26] Like Narcissus, she identifies with her lovely reflection and rejects her trans-corporeal relationships with other people and more-than-human nature, thus risking being 'drowned' and missing the fullness of mortal life that ALP, flowing out to sea, has accepted. Biblically, Issy is implicated in the fact of mortality through her conflation with the serpent in Genesis (desire) and with postlapsarian Eve (humanity). As the feminine snake slipping down a tree of 'epples' and 'pommes' (*FW* 504.24, 33) – a 'downslyder in that snakedst-tu-naughsy whimmering woman't seeleib ... sinsinsinning since the night of time ... Evovae!' (*FW* 505.7–13) – she is the tempter responsible for Adam and Eve's Fall into nature. She is also human in having a conjoined soul and body ('seelieb'). Joyce here extends Stephen's meditation in 'Proteus' on Eve as generatrix, made immortal by the generational cycles of her descendants but marked by the Fall as having a '[w]omb of sin' (*U* 3.44). As evolution, Issy ushers in and embodies the new era, in earth's history, of natural–unnatural, fleshly–intellectual, self-regarding *Homo sapiens*. Being young and narcissistic, unlike her mother, she sees nature as an epiphenomenon of herself. Thus she is blinkered against the vanity of her efforts to achieve transcendence through self-enhancing artificial means (such as clothing and cosmetics) that will not keep her from vanishing, against the backdrop of geological time, as fast as Pond's cream or a reflection in water.

Anna Livia Plurabelle, like Molly Bloom in *Ulysses*, speaks the (temporarily) final monologue in *Finnegans Wake*, and is the centre of consciousness that represents adult human femininity. She also represents more-than-human nature's creative power in the form of the River Liffey. Margot Norris pinpoints her metamorphosis into the river in the washerwomen scene:

> The human dissolves into the natural; the female figure of [ALP] dissolves into the materiality of the river ... Her hair becomes the water's waves ... Her jewelry turns into the stones in the river ... Her costume falls apart as the flotsam and jetsam in the river.[27]

Like the Liffey and hundreds of other rivers that the *Wake* names or hints at, ALP, unlike the deep ocean, her 'cold mad feary father' (*FW* 628.2), nurtures the earth with her 'affluvial flowandflow' (*FW* 404.1). She is a 'safety vulve' and a 'constant of fluxion, Mahamewetma' (*FW* 297.26–7, 29–30) – references to the re-creation of the earth through the Vedic world cycle ('mahamavantara'), as John Bishop explicates, and to maternity and birth ('vulva', 'wet', 'ma(ma)').[28] Flowing unceasingly from source to mouth, rivers are also ancient metaphors for unbounded time; yet because they flow from beginning to end, they can stand as well for bounded human life.

These antithetical riverine metaphors point to a paradox of *Finnegans Wake*. When identified with the trans-corporeal fluxes and refluxes of more-than-human nature, human beings partake of their virtual immortality. Thus Anna Livia as the Liffey circulates as part of a perpetual cycle of discharge and replenishment. The cycle is beautiful and uplifting, as in the biologist

Tyler Volk's description of the trans-corporeal movement of carbon atoms as 'a grand chorus':

> Plant detritus is consumed by a worm, which releases carbon dioxide, which dissolves into groundwater that flows into river and then ocean, and from there diffuses as a gas back into the atmosphere. Then photosynthesis brings it back again into a plant's tissue ... A fallen leaf from this second plant is caressed and consumed by the searching hyphae of a fungus.[29]

In contrast, individual life experienced as *durée* – a 'funferall' of 'laugh-tears' (*FW* 13.15, 15.9) – flows one way, moving through happiness, troubles, and uncertainty to dissolution. A once-nubile, Issy-like temptress, ALP, in her incarnation as a descendant/alter ego of the first mother, rushes towards death as the consequence of desire and orgasm leading to conception: 'Die eve, little eve, die!' (*FW* 215.4).[30] She mingles memory with regret as she mourns HCE, herself, all humanity: 'First we feel. Then we fall ... My leaves have drifted from me. All' (*FW* 627.11, 628.6–7). Here she is not a river; she is not a plant caught up in the carbon cycle, painlessly yielding fallen leaves to nature for metamorphosis. The *Wakean* universe – irreligious, like all of Joyce's fiction – does not provide for transcendence through individual rebirth.

In closing, I quote an Irish naturalist's comments on the River Liffey as a trans-corporeal, more-than-natural entity:

> The water of the Liffey, even in its purest state before humans ever settled by its banks, has – like all rivers – always carried a substantial burden of organic material. Dead leaves, the excrement of fish and the last mortal remains of all kinds of animal life are carried downstream in suspension. In due course the human settlements added to the quantity and variety of this material. From the moment of death, plant and animal remains begin to be broken down by bacteria into simple chemicals.[31]

The Liffey is not a person, but Christopher Moriarty's sketch of its recycling of organic waste – a leitmotiv in the *Wake* – makes clear its trans-corporeal relationship to other entities, including people. The river's metamorphoses and its burden form a microcosm of the natural processes from which the *Wake*'s actors, in life, dissolution, or death, are inextricable.

Although Joyce never took much interest in the flora or fauna of more-than-human nature, he evolved over the course of his career from being a writer concerned with the human condition of bodily imperfection and mortality into something of a philosopher of nature. He became, in fact, a philosopher of the trans-corporeal interweaving (a continuous 'feminine' process rather than a fixed 'masculine' property) of human nature and more-than-human nature. Not just ecocriticism but science, on which it draws, has been bearing out his insights. It is no accident that this should be happening in the midst of a worldwide environmental crisis, caused less by fossil fuels than by the magical thinking underlying old binaries: humanity versus nature, masculinity versus femininity, autonomy versus connectedness. Joyce's critique of this ideology in the weird, beautiful, trans-corporeal art of *Ulysses* and *Finnegans Wake* is thus strikingly contemporary, and it points to the need to join to environmental action a re-envisioning of humans as hybrid, natural–cultural beings dwelling in a now endangered garden.[32]

Notes

1. Ecocriticism has many strands. All assume, as the European Association for the Study of Literature, Culture and Environment (EASLCE) states, 'that the ideas and structures of desire which govern the interactions between humans and their natural environment (including ... the very distinction between the human and the non-human) are of central importance.' EASLCE, 'What is Ecocriticism?' www.easlce.eu/about-us/what-is-ecocriticism.
2. Robert Brazeau and Derek Gladwin, eds., *Eco-Joyce: The Environmental Imagination of James Joyce* (Cork: Cork University Press, 2014).
3. Material ecocriticism is ramifying in many directions. See Serenella Iovino and Serpil Oppermann, eds., *Material Ecocriticism* (Bloomington: Indiana University Press, 2014), and Serpil Oppermann, 'From Material to Posthuman Ecocriticism' in *Handbook of Ecocriticism and Cultural Ecology*, ed. Hubert Zapf (Berlin and Boston: DeGruyter, 2016), pp. 273–94.
4. Alaimo has recently defined 'trans-corporeality' as 'a posthumanist mode of new materialism and material feminism'. Stacy Alaimo, 'Trans-corporeality' in *The Posthuman Glossary*, ed. Rosi Braidotti and Maria Hlavajova (London: Bloomsbury Academic, 2018), pp. 338–9.
5. Stacy Alaimo, *Bodily Natures: Science, Environment, and the Material Self* (Bloomington: Indiana University Press, 2010), p. 2. David Abram coined the term 'more-than-human world' in *The Spell of the Sensuous: Perception and Language in a More-than-Human World* (New York: Pantheon, 1996).
6. From Byron's poem 'January 22nd 1824. Messalonghi. On this Day I Complete My Thirty-Sixth Year', in George Gordon, Lord Byron, *The Complete Poetical Works*, vol. 7, ed. Jerome McGann (Oxford: Clarendon Press, 1993), p. 79.
7. Just before Stephen encounters the baying dog, he observes that often 'in the pauses of rapture Dublin would lay a sudden hand upon his shoulder' (*SH* 38). Clearly, however, what halts him is not Dublin but a feeling that implies, though he doesn't examine it, the larger natural–cultural world of mortality and loss.
8. 'If she [Isabel] lived she had exactly the temper for a Catholic wife of limited intelligence and of pious docility and if she died she was supposed to have earned for herself a place in the eternal heaven of Christians' (*SH* 126).
9. The fragment ends with another corpse, a 'long-looking green thing lying among the weeds' (*SH* 252) – a drowned woman, forerunning Stephen's imaginings of death as transformation in *Ulysses*.

10. See Timothy Morton, *The Ecological Thought* (Cambridge: Harvard University Press, 2010), and *Hyperobjects: Philosophy and Ecology after the End of the World* (Minneapolis: University of Minnesota Press, 2013).
11. In *Stephen Hero*, Stephen views downtown Dublin as a 'commercial prison' (*SH* 30).
12. Nathaniel Colgan's *Flora of the County Dublin* (Dublin: Hodges, Figgis, 1904) was only the most recent of several Irish naturalist books published before Joyce finished composing *Dubliners*.
13. See James Fairhall, 'The Bog of Allen, the Tiber River, and the Pontine Marshes: An Ecocritical Reading of "The Dead"', *James Joyce Quarterly* 51.4 (2016): 567–600.
14. See 'The Holy Office' (1905), 'Gas from a Burner' (1912), and 'Dooleysprudence' (1916), all in *PSE*.
15. Maud Ellmann, *The Nets of Modernism* (Cambridge: Cambridge University Press, 2010), p. 147.
16. Alaimo, 'Oceanic Origins, Plastic Activism, and New Materialism at Sea', in *Material Ecocriticism*, ed. Iovino and Oppermann, p. 187.
17. The 'storm petrels' signify to Bloom a bad omen, not another species accompanying the gulls. This is one of many transformations in *Ulysses* of more-than-human nature into language, part of a push-pull process in which language also points beyond itself to natural referents. Joyce appears to imply that we never escape either nature or language.
18. Timo Maran, 'On the Diversity of Environmental Signs: A Typological Approach', *Biosemiotics* 10 (November 2017), link.springer.com/article/10.1007/s12304-017-9308-5.
19. Serpil Opperman, 'How the Material World Communicates' in *Routledge Handbook of Ecocriticism and Environmental Communication*, ed. Scott Slovic, Swarnalatha Rangarajan, and Vidya Sarveswaran (New York: Routledge, 2019), p. 111. Opperman cites Karen Barad, 'Posthumanist Performativity: Toward an Understanding of How Matter Comes to Matter', *Signs* 28.3 (2003): 801–31, 821.
20. Paulina Firozi, 'Sand Dunes "Communicate" When They Move, Researchers Say', *Washington Post* 5 Feb. 2020, www.washingtonpost.com/science/2020/02/05/.
21. Yi-Peng Lai, *Eco-Ulysses: Nature, Nation, Consumption* (Berlin: Peter Lang, 2018), p. 72. Lai cites Anne McClintock's book *Imperial Leather* on 'Unilever's advertising campaign for *Imperial Leather* soap – with its slogan, "Soap is Civilisation"', quoted in Gillian Whiteley, *Junk: Art and Politics of Trash* (London: Tauris, 2011), p. 160.
22. Joyce undoubtedly knew of cancer's ancient identification as a fierce incarnation of nature, the crab, gnawing relentlessly on sufferers. 'Hippocrates (or one of his students) is thought to be the first to name the disease *karkinos*, or crab.' Ellen Wayland-Smith, 'This Ragged Claw', *Aeon* 26 Feb. 2020, aeon.co/essays/cancer-is-the-voracious-animal-that-early-moderns-imagined.
23. The biologist/philosopher Derek J. Skillings defines the neologism *holobiont* as 'a host, plus all of the resident microbes that live in it and on it'. Thus, humans are holobionts – trans-corporeal, multi-species entities who, as hosts, interact constantly with residents. Derek J. Skillings, 'I, Holobiont', *Aeon* 28 Feb. 2018, aeon.co/ideas/i-holobiont-are-you-and-your-microbes-a-community-or-a-single-entity.

24. Alison Lacivita, *The Ecology of 'Finnegans Wake'* (Gainesville: University Press of Florida, 2015). Brazeau and Gladwin, *Eco-Joyce*, p. 5.
25. Bergson argues that we err in defining our lives through quantitative time (clock time) in lieu of the qualitative time of human experience, *durée*, which flows from a constantly re-created past coterminous with the present. Intense moments of *durée* are transcendent in that they lift us from clock time. Examples in *Ulysses* are Bloom's and Molly's memory-reenactments of their tryst on Howth; an example in the *Wake* is ALP's memory of meeting her future husband: 'Where you meet I. The day. Remember! Why there that moment and us two only?' (*FW* 626.7–9). See Henri Bergson, *Time and Free Will*, trans. F. L. Pogson (New York: Humanities Press, 1971), pp. 100, 104–6.
26. Issy's reflection in the pond differs from the 'perfect forest mirror' of Thoreau's Walden Pond. His mirror, illuminating human nature through more-than-human nature, inspires understanding rather than narcissistic self-aggrandizement: 'A lake ... is earth's eye; looking into which the beholder measures the depth of his own nature'. See Henry David Thoreau, *Walden* (1854), pp. 209, 206–7, walden.org/work/walden/.
27. Margot Norris, 'Teaching *Finnegans Wake* between Domestication and Deconstruction', *James Joyce Quarterly* 39.1 (2001): 113–21, 118. See *FW* 206.29–30, 207.05–7, and 208.10–12.
28. John Bishop, *Joyce's Book of the Dark: 'Finnegans Wake'* (Madison: University of Wisconsin Press, 1986), p. 381.
29. Tyler Volk, *Metapatterns* (New York: Columbia University Press, 1996), p. 234.
30. In Shakespeare's plays, which Joyce knew well, to 'die' can mean to climax.
31. Christopher Moriarty, *Exploring Dublin* (Dublin: Wolfhound, 1997), pp. 39–40.
32. 'Emphasizing the material interconnections of human corporeality with the more-than-human world ... allows us to forge ethical and political positions that can contend with numerous late twentieth- and early twenty-first century realities in which "human" and "environment" can by no means be considered as separate.' Alaimo, *Bodily Natures*, p. 2.

CLARE HUTTON

Periodical Publication and Modernism

The Case of Ulysses

Encouraged by the energetic efforts made by both Ezra Pound and Harriet Shaw Weaver, Joyce arranged the serialization of *Ulysses* in August 1917. In order to preserve his copyright in the United States and internationally, and provide 'double fees', the work was scheduled to appear simultaneously in two periodicals: *The Egoist* in London and *The Little Review* in New York (*SL* 227). So far, so simple. But at this moment in 1917 Joyce had yet to write much of *Ulysses*, and those who agreed to publish it had little sense of the length and nature of what was to come. In the event, the plans for dual serialization did not come to be fully realized. In face of the intense conservatism of British printers (who were liable under the Obscene Publications Act), *The Egoist* only managed to publish a handful of instalments, these being chapters two, three, and six, and an excerpt from chapter ten.[1] They appeared in 1919 and were read with varying degrees of enthusiasm by subscribers to *The Egoist*, a journal that claimed to be for 'virile readers only' and aimed to 'secure a fit audience' for work 'bearing the stamp of originality and permanence' (see Figure 14.1).[2]

The serialization of *Ulysses* in New York proved to be more enduring. Thanks to the sustained efforts of Margaret Anderson and her partner Jane Heap, *The Little Review* serialized early versions of the first thirteen chapters of Joyce's work between March 1918 and December 1920. They also published the first instalment of chapter fourteen ('Oxen of the Sun') and would have been happy to continue publishing Joyce's text without alteration or deletion.[3] But it was not to be so. On 21 February 1921, the editors of *The Little Review* were successfully prosecuted in a New York court of Special Sessions. They were found guilty of publishing what was deemed an 'obscene' text: the third instalment of chapter thirteen ('Nausicaa') as it appeared in *The Little Review* of July–August 1920, the section in which Gerty MacDowell reveals her 'nainsook knickers' on Sandymount Strand as Leopold Bloom masturbates nearby.[4] The editors were ordered to stop

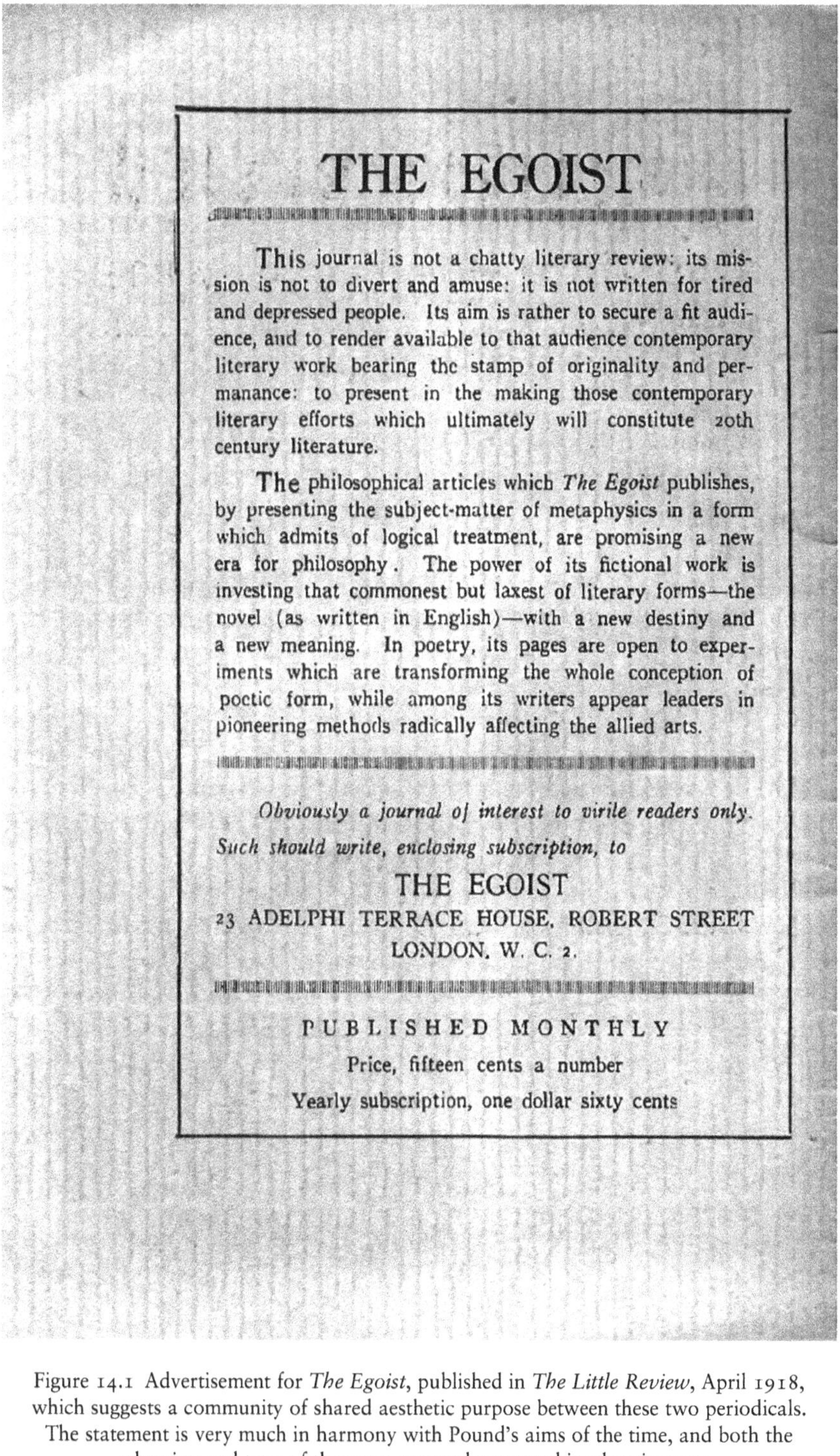

THE EGOIST

This journal is not a chatty literary review; its mission is not to divert and amuse: it is not written for tired and depressed people. Its aim is rather to secure a fit audience, and to render available to that audience contemporary literary work bearing the stamp of originality and permanance: to present in the making those contemporary literary efforts which ultimately will constitute 20th century literature.

The philosophical articles which *The Egoist* publishes, by presenting the subject-matter of metaphysics in a form which admits of logical treatment, are promising a new era for philosophy. The power of its fictional work is investing that commonest but laxest of literary forms—the novel (as written in English)—with a new destiny and a new meaning. In poetry, its pages are open to experiments which are transforming the whole conception of poetic form, while among its writers appear leaders in pioneering methods radically affecting the allied arts.

Obviously a journal of interest to virile readers only. Such should write, enclosing subscription, to

THE EGOIST
23 ADELPHI TERRACE HOUSE, ROBERT STREET
LONDON. W. C. 2.

PUBLISHED MONTHLY
Price, fifteen cents a number
Yearly subscription, one dollar sixty cents

Figure 14.1 Advertisement for *The Egoist*, published in *The Little Review*, April 1918, which suggests a community of shared aesthetic purpose between these two periodicals. The statement is very much in harmony with Pound's aims of the time, and both the phrasing and tone of the copy suggest he wrote this advertisement.

publishing *Ulysses*, fined five dollars each (the lowest possible tariff), and were not imprisoned, arguably a sign that the court did not regard their 'misdemeanour' as the most serious crime.[5]

Each and every issue of *The Egoist* and *The Little Review* in which *Ulysses* appears has a specific geography, cultural meaning, and temporality. Though there are overviews dealing with the whole process of serialization, the significance of the individual periodical issues in which *Ulysses* appeared has not been closely examined, particularly in respect of *The Egoist*. This omission has come about for several reasons. One is that the story of the first volume edition of *Ulysses* is a narrative that ends in triumph and was thus amplified more loudly by Joyce and early biographers than the more complicated backstory, particularly of *The Egoist*, which is all too easy to cast as a story of Joyce's genius being thwarted by Weaver's lack of temerity. *Ulysses* was first published in volume form in Paris on 2 February 1922 by the America-born Sylvia Beach, who willingly turned Shakespeare and Company, her English-language lending library and bookshop, into a publishing house specifically for the purpose of helping Joyce. Beach was a subscriber to *The Little Review* and made her agreement to publish *Ulysses* in April 1921, the month in which Joyce heard the outcome of *The Little Review* trial (*L1* 162). From that point on, Joyce worked feverishly on expanding *Ulysses*. He completed the final four chapters, and he added significantly to the fourteen chapters that he had prepared for serialization, often in haste and on the multiple proofs that Beach was generous enough to arrange and pay for. Thus the Parisian volume of *Ulysses* is very different to the unfinished serial text that was issued in London and New York. *The Little Review*, in particular, is full of textual corruptions. Based on typescripts that had been supplied by various willing but nonetheless amateur typists whom Joyce had befriended in Zurich and Trieste, *The Little Review Ulysses* was printed by Dushan Popovich, 'the cheapest printer in New York', according to Anderson.[6] Popovich was actually quite attentive to points of textual detail and nuance, but he was working with very little assistance and from bad copy, which had often been altered by Pound in advance of submission.[7] This is another reason for the relative critical neglect of the serial *Ulysses*. Why would one pay attention to an unfinished text that is full of obvious errors when the volume text is finished and (it would seem) so much more authoritative?

Then there is the problem of access. Periodicals are not designed to last, and generations of Joyce scholars had difficulty accessing *The Egoist* and *The Little Review*, even in specialist research libraries. The editors of *The Egoist* may have wanted to publish literature with a mark of 'permanence', yet they did so in a medium that is evanescent and fleeting. Beach ensured that the volume form of *Ulysses* was issued on high quality and durable paper, but both *The Little Review* and *The Egoist* were issued on cheap and highly acidic paper, which slowly turns brown, cracks, and crumbles to the touch in a process that conservationists dub 'slow fire'. Thanks to the affordances of the digital revolution, this is no longer an issue. The Modernist Journals Project has made high-quality digital facsimiles of both *The Egoist* and *The Little Review* available to all, online and for free.

Digital resources have renewed cultural and textual interest in the serial *Ulysses* and the process of what Jerome McGann terms 'radial reading' ('decoding one or more of the contexts that interpenetrate the scripted and physical text').[8] The contextual study of what Sean Latham has called 'moments of emergence' is also relevant.[9] Periodicals have an absolute and momentary historical specificity, being dateable to particular months. By looking at specific periodical issues in relation to particular events of that time, it is possible to identify new textual meanings. With the aim of demonstrating the significance of these approaches, this chapter close reads a small portion of *Ulysses* as it appeared in two specific contexts: *The Little Review* of April 1918, which published what was labelled as 'Episode II', the second chapter of the work ('Nestor'), and *The Egoist* of January–February 1919, where the same section of the text appeared, apparently in full but accompanied by a note demurely alluding to 'printing difficulties'.[10] These serial versions are an accessible glimpse of the work in progress, and reading that interim version – yet-to-be-finalised but intended for publication, and published alongside other literary works deemed to be important by Joyce's editors – is critically instructive.

Let's begin with a quick census of what is striking about *The Little Review* of April 1918, which ran to sixty-four pages and was priced twenty-five cents a copy. Under the banner 'The Magazine that is Read by Those who Write the Others', the contents page names Anderson as 'Editor' and Pound as 'Foreign Editor' (see Figure 14.2). May Sinclair's essay on 'The Novels of Dorothy Richardson' leads the issue. Sinclair made literary history by identifying, for the very first time, the prose style so closely associated with the modernist novel, the 'stream of consciousness', and by noting an affinity between Richardson and Joyce ('an extreme concentration on the thing felt or seen', which collapses the distinction between 'what is objective and what is subjective').[11] Beyond this essay, and the fourteen pages of *Ulysses*, very little of the content in this specific issue of *The Little Review* seems 'permanent', though Pound's editorial presence is evident in his essay on 'Unanimism' and two other contributions that he selected for the issue: Wyndham Lewis ('Imaginary Letters') and an excerpt of what was to become Ford Madox Ford's novel *Women and Men*.[12] Joyce, Ford, and

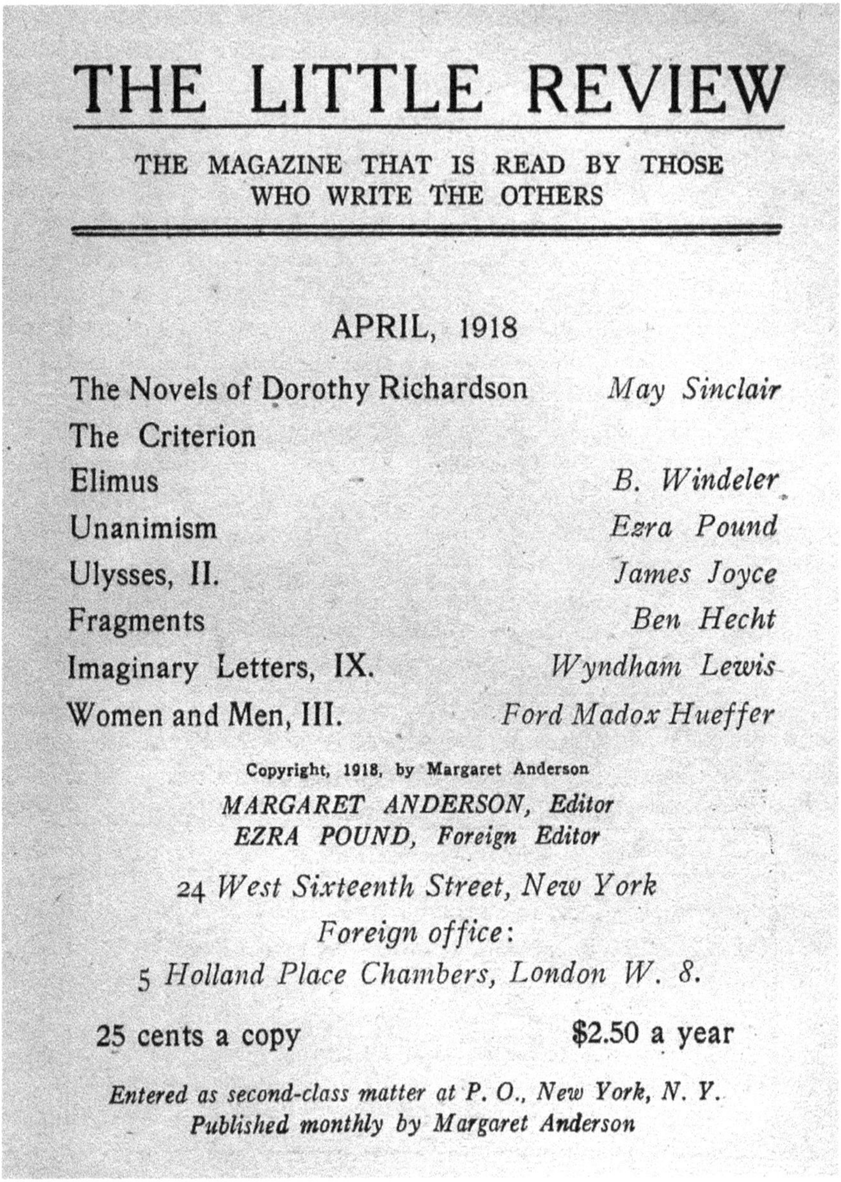

THE LITTLE REVIEW

THE MAGAZINE THAT IS READ BY THOSE
WHO WRITE THE OTHERS

APRIL, 1918

The Novels of Dorothy Richardson	May Sinclair
The Criterion	
Elimus	B. Windeler
Unanimism	Ezra Pound
Ulysses, II.	James Joyce
Fragments	Ben Hecht
Imaginary Letters, IX.	Wyndham Lewis
Women and Men, III.	Ford Madox Hueffer

Copyright, 1918, by Margaret Anderson

MARGARET ANDERSON, Editor
EZRA POUND, Foreign Editor

24 West Sixteenth Street, New York

Foreign office:
5 Holland Place Chambers, London W. 8.

25 cents a copy $2.50 a year

Entered as second-class matter at P. O., New York, N. Y.
Published monthly by Margaret Anderson

Figure 14.2 Contents page of *The Little Review*, April 1918. Pound lived at Holland Place Chambers in London at this time.

Lewis were paid for their contributions by Pound, who, for two years from May 1917, was paid a stipend of 750 dollars for his work on *The Little Review* by his friend John Quinn (1870–1924), a New York lawyer and patron of the arts.[13] (See Figure 14.2.)

Pound was based in London, and his role, with respect to *The Little Review*, was to round up what he perceived as the best 'European' talent and to arrange for those contributors to be paid from monies made available to him by Quinn. Meanwhile, it was left to the New York team to do everything else: finding copy from writers in the United States, finding advertisements, writing editorially, editing what came to hand, arranging for each issue to be printed, and arranging distribution. Anderson had started *The Little Review* in March 1914, but her enthusiasm for the practical labour involved in publication waxed and waned, and she was clearly helped a great deal by her partner Jane Heap, whom she met in February 1916, and who did the lion's share of the administrative and editorial work involved in production. A letter from Heap, which refers to Anderson as 'Mart', evokes the precarity, energy, and material economies at work behind the scenes:

> Such a week as we have had – up about 7.30 and at it until one and one thirty. We addressed, wrapped, and mailed the magazine here in my room – besides we got out 480 letters to prospective subscribers and pleas for renewals. ... [W]e only had 54 cents but there was a letter from Deansie in the mail with $5.00 in it for books ... We got out the magazine. We are going to do business with an agency about subs and circulation. We'll make this thing go – Mart had tantrums and almost 'hystics' with heat and weariness – and rage because we have to do the labour. And I had one of my fits of fatal patience – and we walked out hand in hand to our dinners and were good little things – [14]

Pound's parcel of cash was not shared with the American writers selected by Anderson (including Ben Hecht in the issue of April 1918), nor does it appear to have been paid to contributors who happened to be women. While Sinclair's essay on Richardson is notable, it is also notable that Richardson's work did not appear in *The Little Review* until after Pound's association with *The Little Review* had come to an end.[15] Sinclair, moreover, contributed her articles 'without payment', an arrangement that Pound described as 'very sporting', while cannily telling Anderson that 'we had better keep this to ourselves, for the present at any rate', an aside that reveals a tacit awareness of the cultural, real, and gendered economies at stake behind the scenes.[16]

That *The Egoist* sought 'virile readers' among those who read *The Little Review* is a desire that can be traced back to Pound. Writing to Quinn in 1915 about his plans to start a periodical, Pound had remarked that 'active America is getting fed up on gynocracy'. Thinking financially and in terms of his own immediate coterie, Pound wanted a periodical that 'could completely support Joyce, Eliot, Myself and asst-edtr.', a 'male review' for which 'no woman shall be allowed to write'.[17] Anderson may not have fully understood the extent of Pound's misogyny and cannily identified Pound's intervention as a means of keeping her impecunious venture afloat. It is also significant that Heap, who was doing so much of the practical work for *The Little Review*, was remarkably self-effacing. Some of her contributions are completely unsigned; others use only her italicized initials in lower case – '*jh*' – as though to emphasize, in typographical language, the insignificance of her role and to conceal her gender and identity more generally. Dora Marsden, founding editor of what would become *The Egoist*, was a militant suffragette who had a certain sense of Pound's attitudes. Acting against Weaver's wishes in March 1916, she turned down an offer of cash from Pound in exchange for control of her magazine. She felt that it would reduce 'our editorial powers to zero'.[18]

The extent to which her protest against Pound was effective is open to question, however. *The Egoist* of January–February 1919 was edited by Weaver, with the assistance of T. S. Eliot, who saw himself as a 'beneficial influence' to a journal 'run mostly by old maids', as he explained to his mother.[19] Marsden had been demoted to the position of mere 'contributing editor'. Her contribution, a lengthy and ponderous philosophical essay on 'The Science of Signs', was given a prominence that Eliot resented ('I wish Dora did not have to have the very front').[20] (See Figure 14.3).

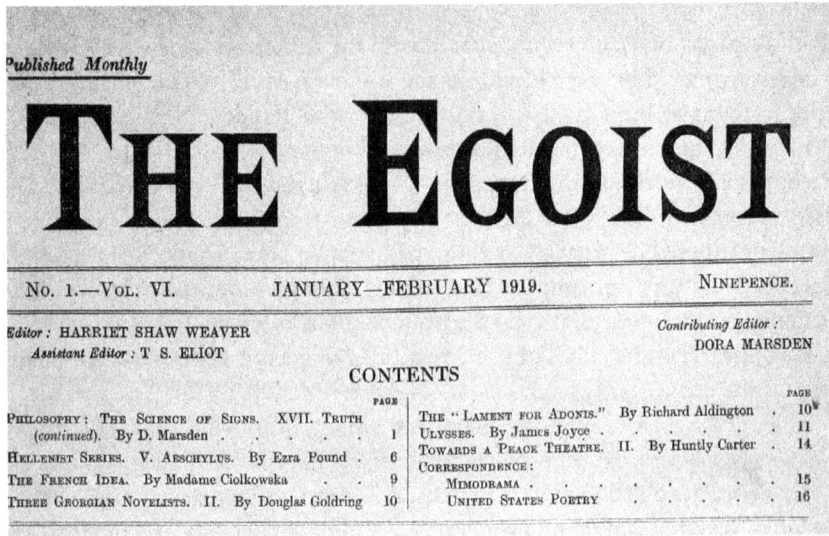

Figure 14.3 Masthead and contents of *The Egoist*, January–February 1919. Note Marsden's position as mere 'contributing' editor.

Periodical Publication and Modernism: *Ulysses*

In addition to 'The Science of Signs', contents include an essay by Pound on Aeschylus; a piece on 'Three Georgian Novelists' by Douglas Goldring; a poetry review by Richard Aldington; and a few pages of correspondence and advertisements, including advertisements for books published and financed by Harriet Weaver on behalf of *The Egoist*: Joyce's *A Portrait of the Artist as a Young Man* (1916), Lewis's *Tarr* (1919), and Eliot's *Prufrock and Other Observations* (1917). Both periodical issues being examined here – *The Little Review* of April 1918 and *The Egoist* of January–February 1919 – point to the powerful coterie politics, rifts, and dissonances of an emergent modernism, particularly in relation to gender. Weaver and Marsden found themselves at the helm of a periodical that Pound used to drive his cultural agenda. Similarly, Anderson and Heap, who declared themselves ardent feminists, allowed Heap's labour to be almost completely written out of the record and the literary energies of *The Little Review* to be dictated and directed by Pound and Quinn. All four of these women were in positions where their labour could be silently overlooked and undervalued. This is an important context for the first publication of *Ulysses*, and it is one that continued when Beach took up the cause of volume publication in Paris and found herself being disparaged as one of Joyce's 'flunkies' (according to Pound she was 'bone ignorant and lacking in tact').[21]

Given the thematic content of *Ulysses* – the way in which it represents women, its candour about the body and sexuality, and its troubled route to publication – it would certainly be possible to examine the serial *Ulysses* in relation to these tensions about gender and unacknowledged behind-the-scenes labour. But I want to turn instead to a more detailed consideration of the periodical reading experience. What kind of text did the very first readers of the second chapter of *Ulysses* encounter, and how did they make sense of that experience? For readers of *The Egoist*, chapter two, closely printed in two columns, would have presented particular challenges. Apart from a tiny footnote, hidden at the bottom of page 11, which refers to the difficulties of publishing *Ulysses* 'in full', there is absolutely no editorial attempt to introduce *Ulysses* (see Figure 14.4).

To use Sinclair's phrase, readers would have found themselves being 'plunged in' to a story that opens *in medias res*, with Stephen questioning Cochrane, Comyn, and Armstrong in his Dalkey classroom about the campaign of Pyrrhus against the Romans.[22] These readers would have had no sense of why *Ulysses* was suddenly being published, why they had missed the opening chapter, what they had missed in that chapter, and what was deemed too controversial for the printers employed by Weaver and Eliot, 'The Complete Press' in South London's West Norwood. In the determination not to be a 'chatty literary review', Eliot and Weaver had surpassed

> * As printing difficulties have made it impossible to publish *Ulysses* in full in serial form, a series of extracts from it will be printed in THE EGOIST during the next few months. The form in which the work is written—chapters for the most part complete in themselves—favours such a procedure.—EDITOR.

Figure 14.4 *The Egoist*, January–February 1919. This is how London readers were introduced to *Ulysses*. Note the emphasis on publishing difficulties, and the suggestion that the book is written in a form that favours being read in parts.

themselves, and presented readers of *The Egoist* with the enigma of Joyce's second chapter without any editorial commentary or interpretive rigging.

They had also assumed that chapter two of *Ulysses* would make sense to readers operating without any prior textual knowledge, and who tackled the work as a set of isolated chapters. *Ulysses* disdains readerly expectation and need in a classically modernist manner, but it is also true that the work refers back to itself through a structure of repeated phrases and citations, and that there is a plot that develops and makes more sense as the early chapters of the work progress. Readers of this issue of *The Egoist* might have got stuck on a few basic questions. Why is this work called *Ulysses*? What is the significance of the reappearance of Stephen Dedalus, last seen on the closing pages of *A Portrait of the Artist as a Young Man* packing his new second-hand clothes and preparing to leave Ireland? Where and when is the scene set? Why is Stephen teaching? Why does the text keep slipping from third to first person narration without warning? Who is Haines, and what is his chapbook? Why do these Irish schoolboys play hockey and recite *Lycidas*? Who are Stephen's 'literary friends', and why does Deasy insist on giving Stephen his letter on foot-and-mouth disease? Where does Deasy come from, and what is the significance of his political views more generally? How does his sense of Irish history differ from Stephen's?

The prose of chapter two demands concentrated attention, but its lyricism repays that effort. In essence this, the shortest chapter of *Ulysses*, contains four scenes. It opens with Stephen teaching his class; after the class leaves for hockey, Stephen helps Cyril Sargent, who is struggling with his sums; thereafter he goes to the study of the headmaster, Garret Deasy, to be paid; finally, after an intense set of exchanges with Deasy about money, Irish history, and politics, Stephen leaves the school and wanders 'down the gravel path under the trees, hearing the cries of voices and crack of sticks from the playfield'.[23] All four of these scenes are included in *The Little Review*, *The*

Egoist, and the volume version of the work, and in the transition between the versions nothing appears to have been significantly altered. This is the impression gained by carefully reading the text *in situ*, for example, in *The Egoist*, where, by printing in double columns, chapter two was accommodated on just four pages (see Figure 14.5).

It is worth looking at this particular page (Figure 14.5) in a bit more detail and considering the role that the typesetters have played in making choices about how to display Joyce's text. For such a complicated text, the interlinear spacing is too narrow and so is the column width: this is an obvious economy of form. In order to save paper costs – a particular consideration during WWI – the printer was aiming to get as many words on the page as possible. The other obvious typographical choice made here is the decision to use inverted commas as speech marks, rather than the em dash or tiret (—), which Joyce insisted on using: the form that he had used in his manuscript, that he had instructed his typist to use in the typescript, and that had been followed by Popovich in *The Little Review* publication of *Ulysses*. The tiret was non-standard in English language publications, but Joyce judged it to have considerable hermeneutic advantages for a novelist writing dialogue. Compared to sets of inverted commas, which have to open and close, it is more direct, fluent, and real. It suits Joyce's aesthetic because it leaves the page more uncluttered. The writer marks where a new speech begins, but does not mark the end point, thus leaving readers to do more of the work of figuring out where a voice or utterance is coming from. This is an important task on this page, which mixes the direct speech of two speakers (Deasy and Stephen), the voice of the narrator, and the voice of Stephen's interior monologue or stream of consciousness.

Chapter two gives a deeper sense of Stephen Dedalus, his psychology and preoccupations, and the nature of his sensibility. The streams of consciousness are particularly important in this regard. On this page, for example, we hear how Stephen feels about the routine of collecting his money from Deasy each month: 'That same room and hour, the same wisdom: and I the same. Three times now. Three nooses round me here.'[24] In response to Deasy's insistent *I owe nothing*, we hear the long list of Stephen's debts and his realization that the money he has been paid 'is useless': 'Mulligan, nine pounds, three pairs of socks, ties.'[25] Readers are also introduced to Stephen's predisposition as writer and thinker. In response to Deasy's mention of his ancestor, Sir John Blackwood, who voted 'against the union' between Britain and Ireland in 1800, and the story of him putting on 'his topboots' and riding to Dublin to do so, we are privy to a whole imaginative evocation of that scene, which describes how 'sir John' might have been greeted ('Soft day, your honour') and mixes citations from the song 'The

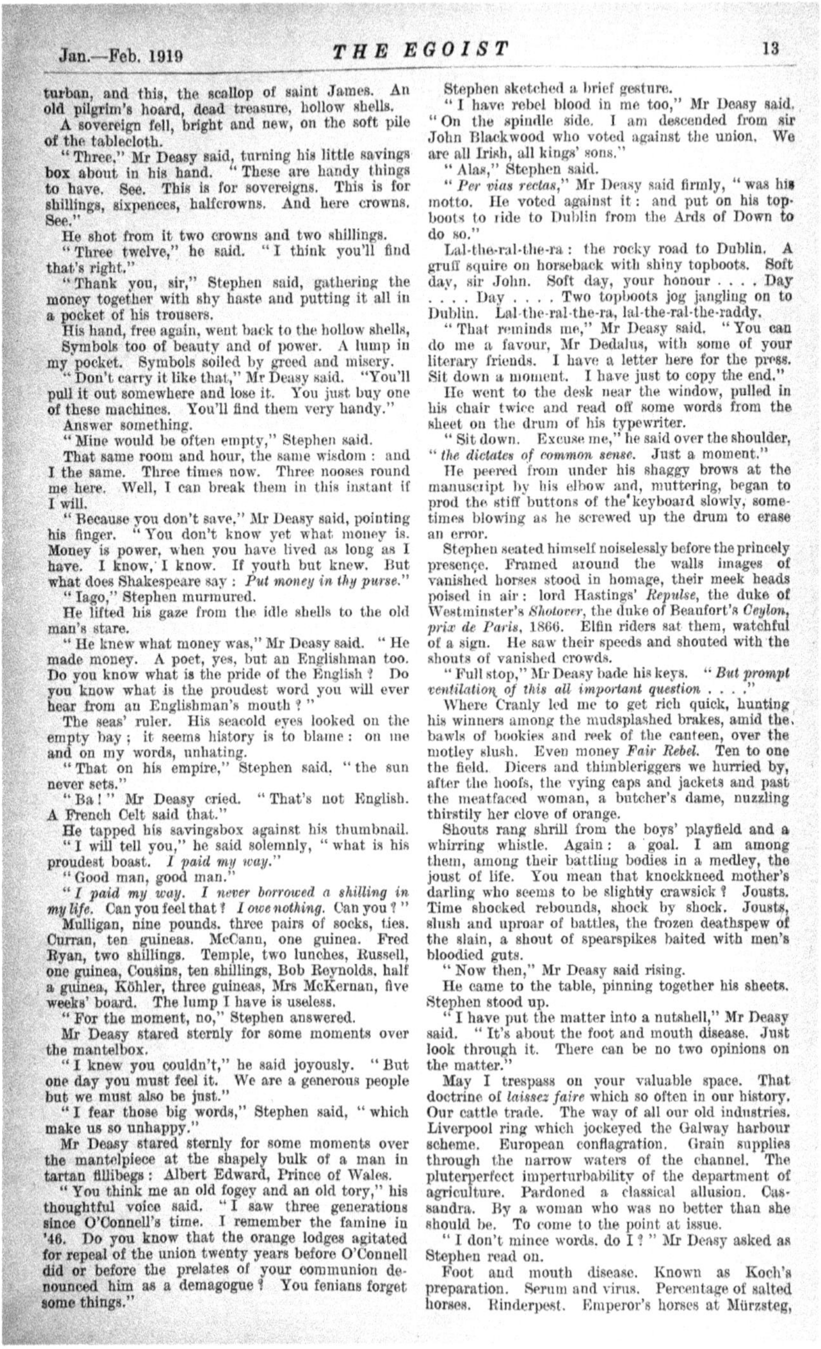

Figure 14.5 A full page of *Ulysses* as it appeared in *The Egoist*, January–February 1919.

Rocky Road to Dublin' ('Lal-the ral-the-ra, lal-the-lal-the-raddy').[26] The chapter also introduces the politics of the period, particularly through the character of Deasy, whose belief in the value of preserving political union between Britain and Ireland is made clear through details such as the display of a portrait of 'Albert Edward, Prince of Wales' and his characterization of Dedalus as a 'fenian'.[27] All of the conversational exchange between Deasy and Stephen is awkward, but this moment is perhaps the most awkward of all, and it merits further examination, specifically in the serial version.

The conversation has turned from money and debt to nationalism and politics. Having mentioned the English specifically, Deasy suddenly declares, 'We are a generous people but we must also be just', a *non sequitur* that elicits a terse but suggestive barb from Stephen: 'I fear those big words ... which make us so unhappy.'[28] This sets the scene for some big words from Deasy and a set-piece speech that expresses his lived experience of nineteenth-century Irish history:

> 'You think me an old fogey and an old tory,' his thoughtful voice said. 'I saw three generations since O'Connell's time. I remember the famine in '46. Do you know that the orange lodges agitated for repeal of the union twenty years before O'Connell or before the prelates of your communion denounced him as a demagogue? You fenians forget some things.'[29]

Discomfited by this tirade, which positions him rather too neatly, Stephen does not know what to say. He 'sketches a brief gesture'.[30] It is a gesture of resignation, of hopelessness, a realization that he has been mired yet again: because he needs Deasy's money, he is caught in Deasy's conversational noose, and cast aside glibly as a 'fenian', a potent word, used as a smear in this context and only once in *Ulysses*.[31] Before Stephen has had time to gather his thoughts, Deasy is ready with his next inconvenient fact: like Stephen (he assumes), Deasy has 'rebel blood'. He is descended from Sir John Blackwood 'who voted against the union', as already mentioned.[32] This is a moment of facticity, of the fiction being borne of real historical fact, though the facts in this case are quite obscure. Deasy's putative ancestor, Sir John Blackwood (1722–1799), had a long career as a member of Parliament and did, in fact, oppose the union of the British and Irish parliaments, though he died before he could get to Dublin to cast his vote.[33]

The very first readers of *Ulysses* – among them Pound, Virginia Woolf, Eliot, and Weaver – are unlikely to have unpicked this moment of the text in detail. In fact, there appear to be few recorded responses to the experience of reading this chapter serially. Weaver made very few comments on the *Ulysses* typescripts she was receiving; Pound was much more vociferous but thought chapter two 'inferior' to the opening chapter, which he described as 'corking' ('too serious for me to prattle into criticism. I think it is the only youth that has ever been written down').[34] Eliot was following *Ulysses* in *The Little Review* and, using very general terms ('superb', 'excellent'), commended it to a number of correspondents including Woolf, who turned down the opportunity to publish *Ulysses* at the Hogarth Press for complicated reasons, including the 'directness of language, and the choice of the incidents', which 'raised a blush even upon such a cheek as mine'.[35] *The Little Review* included an occasional column entitled 'The Reader Critic', which printed the queries and views of individual readers, including those who read *Ulysses*. This column began in May 1918 and includes the only recorded comments I have found that specifically respond to the second chapter of *Ulysses*. These praise Joyce's 'portrait of Cyril Sargent' as 'marvellous beyond words' and identify Joyce as 'the most sensitive writer alive'.[36]

No-one thought to read the politics of this chapter in relation to the evolving political situation in Ireland. In the weeks following the Rising of Easter 1916, attitudes to British rule were changing very quickly, particularly in response to the execution of the leaders, something that Yeats captures so exactly in 'Sixteen Dead Men' ('who can talk of give and take, / ... While those dead men are loitering there / To stir the boiling pot?').[37] Coming just after the end of WWI, the general election of December 1918 saw the Irish electorate return seventy-three seats for Sinn Féin, six for the Irish Parliamentary Party, and just twenty-six for the Unionists. This was a Sinn Féin landslide and a powerful vote in favour of an independent Irish state, to be achieved by physical force if need be; Unionism, while not quite a spent force, was suddenly far less powerful, and constitutional nationalism, of the kind that had been so powerfully advocated by John Redmond, had been thoroughly discredited by the many voters who thought that the British reaction to the Easter Rising was an unjust use of excessive force. After all, the Government of Ireland Act of 1914 had promised legislative independence, even if the issue of what would happen to Unionists like Deasy had never been satisfactorily resolved. Joyce may have been a world away from the electorate making these choices, but his very precise use of terms like 'tory' (used by Deasy to describe himself) and 'fenian' (used by Deasy to describe Stephen) signals his deep awareness of Irish politics in his own time. In fact, as Anne Marie D'Arcy has argued, Deasy is crucially representative of the fissures and displacements in Irish identity politics of the 1900s and 1910s, and may be read more interestingly as a Dublin Unionist (as he tells Stephen, 'We are all Irish, all kings' sons' [U 2.279–80]), and not an Ulsterman.[38] Dublin is the centre of his political universe, as it once was for his Blackwood ancestors, as D'Arcy argues in her thought-provoking analysis of Deasy's character. His political views serve to remind readers of 'the steadfast unionist sentiment among the Dublin bourgeoisie, which matched the royalism and pride in empire, if not the growing sense of isolated militancy, of their Ulster contemporaries'.[39]

In the period when Joyce was writing and then serializing the text of *Ulysses*, the cultural meaning of Irish nationalism was changing. In April 1918, when *The Little Review* first published the second chapter, a broad swathe of Irish political opinion was uniting in opposition to Lloyd George's proposed Military Service Bill, which threatened conscription for Ireland. Sinn Féin was gaining ground and was in a pivotally strong position by the Spring of 1919, when *The Egoist* published chapter two. What readers of either periodical would have found was a depiction of politics in stasis, with Deasy as 'an old fogey and an old tory' subtly gaining the stronger hand and Stephen sinking into disesteem. But what was happening on the ground was rather different. Irish nationalism was gaining power and organization. Dáil Éireann had met for the first time in April 1919, and the War of Independence was pressuring the British government to think differently about the future of the Irish state. Neither *The Little Review* nor *The Egoist* commented on politics of the period, something that Eliot particularly valued (silence of such a kind was a means to 'assert the perpetual importance of other things').[40] But a reader who read radially from the newspapers of the period could have identified a connection between the political situation depicted by Joyce and the deep tensions in Anglo-Irish relations.

In the latter half of 1921, when negotiators were working towards the Anglo-Irish Treaty, which created 'Saorstat Éireann' in January 1922, Joyce was at work revising *Ulysses*. With regard to the opening three chapters, Joyce does not appear to have made many revisions. He was building on the world of *A Portrait of the Artist as a Young Man* and had a very certain sense of the mental and cultural world in which Dedalus operates. Still, and with the certainty that a new Ireland was coming, Joyce took the opportunity to revise Stephen's exchange with Deasy. He changed the facts about Deasy's ancestor, Blackwood, who votes *against* the union in *The Little Review* and *The Egoist* but votes *for* the union in the volume edition issued by Beach in Paris on 2 February 1922.[41] As noted earlier, Deasy knows that Stephen thinks him 'an old fogey and an old tory' but attempts to claim an alliance with him by announcing, 'I have rebel blood in me too.'[42] In the 1922 version, Deasy recalls that 'I am descended from sir John Blackwood who voted for the union.' The exchange continues:

—*Per vias rectas*, Mr Deasy said firmly, was his motto. He voted for it and put on his topboots to ride to Dublin from the Ards of Down to do so.[43]

If Deasy wants to impress Stephen with his 'rebel blood', why is he pointing to an ancestor who voted in favour of the 1800 Act of Union between Great Britain and Ireland? This is exactly as one would have expected; the ancestor was not a rebel, and Deasy has simply inherited the political views of his forebears. In pointing to an ancestor who was clearly not a rebel, Deasy has shown himself to fit exactly the labels he has denied, both an old fogey (who cannot get his stories straight) and an old tory.

In response to a sense of the changing political possibilities for Irish nationalism, Joyce has taken the opportunity to weaken the force of Deasy's Unionism. In 1918, Deasy was a fogey and a tory with an upper hand; by 1922 he is being outwitted on the page by an individual who knows how to operate 'backstairs influence', another telling phrase that is added to the text post serially.[44] Deasy is trying to 'work up influence' with the department of agriculture but is finding it difficult. He needs Stephen's advocacy because he is 'surrounded by difficulties, by ... intrigues by ... backstairs influence by ...'.[45] The implication is that 'backstairs influence' is a crucial facet of Dublin's public and cultural sphere, which Deasy cannot access (but Stephen can), a point reiterated later in chapter seven, where Stephen is invited to write something for the newspaper and Deasy is derided by Crawford as 'that old pelters' and 'the bloodiest old tartar God ever made'.[46]

Of all the instructions and half-truths thrown out by Deasy in this highly charged scene, perhaps the most emotive is the statement that 'You fenians forget some things.' In revising the text post serially, Joyce inserts a mental riposte, a new paragraph, marked below in italics, that documents Stephen's stream of consciousness as he processes what Deasy has said:

> —You think me an old fogey and an old tory, his thoughtful voice said. I saw three generations since O'Connell's time. I remember the famine in '46. Do you know that the orange lodges agitated for repeal of the union twenty years before O'Connell did or before the prelates of your communion denounced him as a demagogue? You fenians forget some things.
>
> *Glorious, pious and immortal memory. The lodge of Diamond in Armagh the splendid behung with corpses of papishes. Hoarse, masked and armed, the planters covenant. The black north and true blue bible. Croppies lie down.*
>
> Stephen sketched a brief gesture.[47]

The insertion of this paragraph, along with the other post-serial changes already noted (adding 'backstairs' and changing the voting preferences of Sir John Blackwood) alters the power dynamic of the exchange. Deasy, who had been reasonably strong and assured in his exchanges with Stephen in *The Little Review* and *The Egoist*, is befuddled and confused by 1922. Stephen's voiced response to Deasy's barbs remains 'courteously recalcitrant,' but by 1922 his mental response to Deasy's polemic is much more than a 'brief gesture'.[48] That this may not be so readily apparent relates, in part, to the coded and ironic terms of the hastily added stream of consciousness. Every phrase of this dropped-in paragraph of interiority is replete with cultural and historical meaning, and needs annotation. 'Glorious, pious and immortal memory' is a reference to the Orangeman's toast to William ('To the glorious, pious and immortal memory of the Great and Good King William III, who saved us from popery, slavery, arbitrary power, brass money and wooden shoes').[49] 'Lodge of Diamond in Armagh' is a reference to the clashes between Catholics and Protestants in Armagh, which culminated in the Battle of the Diamond in 1795. The 'planters' covenant' is an Elizabethan initiative that consolidated control of land in Protestant hands in the 1590s. 'Croppies' is the name given to the Irish rebels in 1798.

Stephen is thinking about Irish history from Deasy's perspective, and has identified Deasy with Ulster Protestantism and the Orange Order. Other post-serial revisions, which remember Stephen's encounters with Deasy, position him as an Ulsterman from 'beyant Boyne water' and the six counties of the 'northeast corner'.[50] What Joyce has done is to change the position and possible genesis of Deasy's Unionism in anticipation of the partition of the island. As Andrew Gibson has argued, Stephen's imagination has also lingered on the barbarity of the English invasion of Ireland in the 1590s ('masked and armed'), as well as the violence of the nascent Orange Order in the 1790s ('behung with corpses of papishes').[51]

From the perspective of style, the way in which this passage works is particularly interesting. In a chapter that has a high level of repetition, with many words and phrases being repeated in close proximity ('blank', 'sir', 'fabled', 'pier', 'riddle', 'Kingstown', '*Weep no more*', 'history', 'nightmare', 'money', 'fight', etc.), moments of lexical variation stand out. 'Fenian', 'behung', 'papishes', and 'covenant' are only used once and insist on readerly attention. At the very moment when Stephen is accused of forgetting, this new paragraph directs readers to see what he is remembering. He professes that he is trying to wake himself from the nightmare of Irish history, but his consciousness refuses to forget.

That this kind of reading was not available to the very first readers and publishers of Joyce's text is obvious. Joyce's work was being published and read at considerable cultural distance from its setting and point of imaginative origin. But reading radially from the original points of publication in *The Little Review* and *The Egoist* can illuminate meanings and nuances that would otherwise remain obscure. In particular, there is value in reading the context and temporality of these publications, and in extending from there to questions of textual difference and variation that Joyce himself sanctioned. With respect to Deasy's characterization, Joyce changed the power dynamics of the scene playing out on the page to reflect the new and changed power dynamics of Irish politics. By reading radially from the serial texts of *The Little Review* and *The Egoist* to the handsome blue volume produced by Beach, it is possible to identify Joyce's creativity responding opportunely to a moment of emergence. If this leaves us foundering on a hermeneutic snare and wondering what a word like 'papishes' really means and why it is thought by Dedalus, it is perhaps as well to take solace in the view of the 'personality of the artist' expressed in *A Portrait of the Artist as a Young Man*. The writer is 'within or behind or beyond or above his handiwork, invisible, refined out of existence, indifferent, paring his fingernails' (*P* 215). It is up to readers to make sense of this handiwork, armed with whatever predisposition, preoccupation, hunch, or factual evidence they may bring to bear.

Notes

1. The chapters of *Ulysses* that appeared in *The Egoist* were two, three, and six, and an excerpt from chapter ten. These appeared in 1919 in the issues for Jan–Feb, March–April, July (ch. 6, part 1), September (ch. 6, part 2), and December, respectively. For all issues of *The Egoist* see the Modernist Journals Project, modjourn.org.
2. Advertisement for the *Egoist* included in *The Little Review*, April 1918 [verso of front cover], available at Modernist Journals Project, modjourn.org.
3. For all issues of *The Little Review* in which *Ulysses* appeared, see the Modernist Journals Project, modjourn.org.
4. *Little Review* 7.2 (July–August 1920), 43.
5. I discuss this trial and the textual and contextual significance of the *Little Review Ulysses* in detail in Clare Hutton, *Serial Encounters: 'Ulysses' and The Little Review* (Oxford: Oxford University Press, 2019).
6. Margaret Anderson, *My Thirty Years' War* (New York: Horizon Press, 1969), p. 157.
7. For Popovich and the issues of textual transmission and alteration in *The Little Review*, see Hutton, *Serial Encounters*, pp. 150–66.
8. Jerome McGann, *The Textual Condition* (Princeton, NJ: Princeton University Press, 1991), p. 119.
9. Sean Latham, 'Unpacking My Digital Library: Programs, Modernisms, Magazines' in *Making Canada New: Editing Modernism and New Media*, ed. Dean Irvine, Vanessa Lent, and Bart Vautour (Toronto: University of Toronto Press, 2017), pp. 31–60.
10. James Joyce, 'Ulysses', *Egoist* VI.I (Jan–Feb 1919): 11–14, 11n.
11. May Sinclair, 'The Novels of Dorothy Richardson', *Little Review* 4.12 (April 1918): 3–11, 6, 7, 9.

12. Ford Madox Ford, *Women and Men* (Paris: Three Mountains Press, 1923). Ford changed his surname from Hueffer in 1919 because Hueffer sounded 'too Germanic'.
13. Pound to Quinn, 8 February 1917, in *The Selected Letters of Ezra Pound to John Quinn, 1915–1924*, ed. Timothy Materer (Durham, NC: Duke University Press, 1991), p. 95. The financial arrangements are discussed in *Pound/The Little Review: The Letters of Ezra Pound to Margaret Anderson: The Little Review Correspondence*, ed. Thomas L. Scott and Melvin J. Friedman (New York: New Directions, 1988), p. 13n.
14. Jane Heap to Florence Reynolds (July 1917), in *Dear Tiny Heart: The Letters of Jane Heap and Florence Reynolds*, ed. Holly Baggett (New York: New York University Press, 2000), p. 51.
15. *The Little Review* began to serialize Richardson's *Interim* in June 1919 when Pound was no longer editor. Woolf is another prominent female novelist of the era who is notably absent from Pound's pantheon of markedly modern novelists.
16. Pound to Anderson (22 November 1917), in *Pound/The Little Review*, p. 161.
17. Pound to Quinn (26 August 1915, 13 October 1915, 8 September 1915), in *Selected Letters of Ezra Pound to John Quinn*, pp. 41, 53, 48.
18. Dora Marsden to Harriet Shaw Weaver (13 March 1916), Harriet Shaw Weaver Papers, British Library Ms. Add. 57354.
19. Eliot to his mother (13 May 1917), in *Letters of T. S. Eliot, 1898–1922*, ed. Valerie Eliot and Hugh Haughton (New Haven, CT: Yale University Press, 2008), 198.
20. Eliot to Pound (23 September 1917), in *Letters of T. S. Eliot*, p. 220. Writing to Quinn (9 July 1919), Eliot confessed that Marsden made him froth 'at the mouth with antipathy'. He thought *The Egoist* 'primarily a means for getting her philosophical articles into print', something that 'militated against the success of the paper' (*Letters of T. S. Eliot*, p. 375).
21. Pound to Quinn (21 February 1922), in *Selected Letters of Ezra Pound to John Quinn*, p. 205.
22. May Sinclair, 'The Novels of Dorothy Richardson', 4.
23. Joyce, 'Ulysses', *Egoist* (Jan–Feb 1919), 14.
24. Ibid., 13.
25. Ibid., 13
26. Ibid., 13
27. Ibid., 13
28. Ibid., 13
29. Ibid., 13.
30. Ibid., 13.
31. That 'fenian' is only used once can be ascertained by string searching the 1922 version of *Ulysses*, available from Modernist Versions Project, web.uvic.ca/~mvp1922/ulysses1922/. References to this edition are hereafter cited in text as *Ulysses 1922*.
32. Joyce, 'Ulysses', *Egoist* (Jan–Feb 1919), 13.
33. On Blackwood, see thepeerage.com/p13958.htm#i139573; Don Gifford with Robert J. Seidman, *'Ulysses' Annotated: Notes for James Joyce's 'Ulysses'* (Berkeley: University of California Press, 1989), p. 36.

34. For Weaver's response to *Ulysses*, see John Firth, ed., 'Harriet Weaver's Letters to James Joyce, 1915–1920' in *Studies in Bibliography* 20 (1967), pp. 151–88. Pound's responses are scattered. For the description of chapter two as 'inferior', see Pound to Quinn (22 February 1918), in *Selected Letters of Ezra Pound to John Quinn*, p. 144. See also Pound to H. L. Mencken (25 January 1918) in *The Letters of Ezra Pound, 1907–1941*, ed. D. D. Paige (London: Faber, 1951), p. 189; Pound to Joyce (19 December 1917), *Letters II*, 414.
35. For Eliot's advocacy of *Ulysses* in the *Little Review*, see his letters of 30 June 1918, 7 November 1918, and 9 July 1919 in *Letters of T. S. Eliot, 1898–1922*, pp. 236, 251, 314. Woolf's response to *Ulysses* cited here is recorded in a letter to Nicholas Bagenal (15 April 1918), in *The Question of Things Happening: The Letters of Virginia Woolf: Volume II: 1912–1922*, ed. Nigel Nicolson (London: The Hogarth Press, 1976), p. 231.
36. 'The Reader Critic', *The Little Review* 5.1 (May 1918): 62–4, 63.
37. 'Sixteen Dead Men', in *W. B. Yeats: The Major Works*, ed. Edward Larrissy (Oxford: World's Classics, 2008), p. 87.
38. Anne Marie D'Arcy, 'Dindsenchas, Mr Deasy, and the Nightmare of Partition in *Ulysses*', *Proceedings of the Royal Irish Academy: Archaeology, Culture, History, Literature*, 114C (2014): 295–325.
39. Ibid., p. 309.
40. Eliot to his mother, 14 October 1917, *Letters of T. S. Eliot, 1898–1922*, p. 224.
41. This is not a mistake. Joyce changed the text by simply changing 'against' to 'for'. All volume editions of *Ulysses* have Deasy's ancestor voting for the union.
42. Joyce, 'Ulysses', *Egoist* (Jan–Feb 1919), 13.
43. *Ulysses* 1922, p. 31.
44. Ibid., p. 33. See *Ulysses: A Critical and Synoptic Edition*, 3 vols., ed. Hans Walter Gabler (1984; London: Garland, revised ed., 1986), vol 1, p. 66.
45. *Ulysses* 1922, p. 33.
46. Ibid., p. 127.
47. Ibid., p. 31.
48. D'Arcy, '*Dindsenchas*, Mr Deasy, and the Nightmare of Partition in *Ulysses*', p. 299.
49. Gifford, *Ulysses Annotated*, p. 36.
50. *Ulysses* 1922, p. 182. Joyce added the phrase 'The northest corner' to the proofs, as well as the word 'beyant', which suggests someone identifying Deasy's accent as being from the North. *Ulysses: A Critical and Synoptic Edition*, vol. 1, p. 404.
51. Andrew Gibson, *Joyce's Revenge: History, Politics and Aesthetics in 'Ulysses'* (Oxford: Oxford University Press, 2002), p. 36.

15

DIRK VAN HULLE

Writing, Reading, Revising, Editing, Archiving

The Sociology of Joyce's Writing

Joyce's work has been paradigmatic in genetic criticism and scholarly editing. The facsimile edition of his manuscripts in the late 1970s (published as the *James Joyce Archive*) was instrumental in this process. This publication coincided with the coinage of the term 'genetic criticism' in France and enabled a lively discussion in Joyce studies between the so-called circumscribed and expansive approaches. The debate centred around the question whether knowledge about the writing process limits or, on the contrary, opens up the possibilities of interpretation. Meanwhile, the controversy around the *Ulysses* edition by Hans Walter Gabler, Claus Melchior, and Wolfhard Steppe sparked an interesting theoretical and methodological debate in textual scholarship and an exchange of ideas between the longstanding traditions of German *Editionswissenschaft* and Anglo-American copy-text editing. In the meantime, forty years after the publication of the Garland facsimile *James Joyce Archive*, the James Joyce Digital Archive offers transcriptions of most of the manuscripts online. In this case, the change of medium has not fundamentally changed the teleological way in which the material is presented (ordering it according to the episodes or chapters of Joyce's published books). Adopting a different approach, this essay also examines the less teleological aspects of Joyce's writing and revising process, including his reading and his notetaking habits, to work towards a digital library of James Joyce and an edition of Joyce's unpublished letters in a non-teleological, inclusive digital environment.

Writing

In his 1904 essay 'A Portrait of the Artist', Joyce initially saw his role as a writer as that of an 'alchemist', 'bringing together the mysterious elements, separating the subtle from the gross' (*PSW* 214). A. Walton Litz, however, suggested other metaphors, such as that of the mosaicist. When Litz published *The Art of James Joyce* in 1961, the academic study of Joyce's work had only just begun: Richard Ellmann's biography had been published two years before. The study of the writing process had been touched upon by friends of Joyce's such as Frank Budgen and Valery Larbaud, but their approach had been rather anecdotal. With its contemporary study of the genesis of *Finnegans Wake* by David Hayman (1963), Litz's study of the *Ulysses* and *Finnegans Wake* manuscripts took this enterprise to another, more scholarly level. Still, it seemed, for a long time, a sort of dead end. To some extent, Litz suggested as much himself in the introduction to his work, admitting in a rather gloomy tone that he had been 'lured by the multiple designs of [Joyce's] art into believing that somewhere there existed one controlling design which contained and clarified all the others'. From the very start of the book, he admits defeat. After having studied the writing process, he has not been able to find any such 'controlling design' and has therefore 'relinquished the comforting belief that access to an author's workshop provides insights of greater authority than those produced by other kinds of criticism'.[1] With hindsight, it has been a sobering but methodologically also healthy starting point for genetic Joyce studies to have accepted the fact that perhaps we should not be so intent on looking for the grand scheme but should focus instead on aspects of the writing process that are more modest in scope. Many small steps in scholarship can have a cumulative effect. In *Ulysses in Progress*, one of Litz's students, Michael Groden, suggested that the writing of the literary masterpiece consisted – broadly speaking – of three stages: the development of an interior monologue technique; the abandonment of experimentation with the monologue for 'a series of parody styles'; and the creation of several new styles, followed by the revision of earlier episodes.[2]

It is characteristic of the development of genetic criticism in the following decades that this three-phase process has been replaced by a five-phase scheme in Clare Hutton's *Serial Encounters*, importantly devoting a separate stage to the novel's serialization: '(i) conception, (ii) drafting, (iii) serialization, (iv) continued post-serial drafting, and (v) the formation of plans for publication in volume form'.[3] This new attention to serialization marks the more recent approach. What changed in the intermediate decades is an increased attention to the sociology of texts, to a large extent thanks to D. F. McKenzie's *Bibliography and the Sociology of Texts* (1986) and Jerome McGann's reflections on the 'socialization of the text' in *The Textual Condition* (1991).[4] As McKenzie noted, 'A book is never simply a remarkable *object*. Like every other technology it is invariably the product of human agency in complex and highly volatile contexts, which a responsible scholarship must seek to recover if we are to understand better the creation and communication of meaning as the defining characteristic of human societies.'[5] The increased attention to human agency beyond the myth of solitary authorship has had quite an impact on textual scholarship, also in Joyce studies.

Joyce was well aware of the 'human agency' involved in his literary enterprises. He had a knack for finding all kinds of textual agents to help him produce his works: typists such as Lily Bollach, benefactors and publishers such as Sylvia Beach, patrons such as Harriet Shaw Weaver, supporters such as the editors of *The Little Review* or *transition* and their printers, amanuenses such as France Raphael, secretaries such as Paul Léon, proofreaders and notetakers such as Samuel Beckett, champions and critics such as Ezra Pound, enemies such as Wyndham Lewis. In *Finnegans Wake*, Joyce seems to acknowledge their agency as that of 'anticollaborators' (*FW* 118.25) when a letter is being scrutinized in what can be read as a parody of a bibliographical analysis. The document is Anna Livia Plurabelle's (ALP's) letter in defence of her husband (HCE), who is being accused of having committed a crime in the park. In the pseudo-bibliographical lingo, this 'proteiform graph' is described as 'a polyexigetical piece of scripture' in a pre-book publication in T. S. Eliot's journal, *Criterion*: 'Closer inspection of the *bordereau* would reveal a multiplicity of personalities inflicted on the document.' The question therefore arises, 'who in hell wrote the durn thing anyhow?' – a 'whittlewit laden with the loot of learning?'[6] At some point, a common-sense voice suggests, 'Anyhow, somehow and somewhere somebody ... wrote it all down, and there you are, full stop.'[7] However, this is immediately nuanced with a 'yes, but ...', because a few circumstances need to be taken into account, such as 'the continually more and less inter misunderstanding minds of the anticollaborators' (*FW* 118.25).

The sociology of the text has been instrumental in the development of the discipline of book history, but it has also had (and is still having) an impact on genetic criticism, and I believe a rapprochement between both disciplines can be mutually beneficial. Joyce's works in progress serve as an excellent case study of this development. In the first few decades of genetic criticism, the discipline understandably had a tendency to distinguish itself from other textual disciplines, emphasizing the differences. Thus, it concentrated on the so-called 'avant-texte', the writing process preceding the 'bon à tirer', the moment the author decides the text is ready to be printed. Authorial post-publication modifications to the text are made 'in a public sphere', Pierre-Marc de Biasi argues, and therefore follow a logic that differs from prepublication variants or '*réécritures*'.[8] In the meantime, however, these post-publication modifications are being recognized as part of a work's epigenesis, the continuation of the genesis after publication.[9] For very often, as in Joyce's case, this publication is a pre-book serialization, and Joyce kept making changes to the texts after their journal publication.

From the perspective of book history, the McKenzian focus was originally mainly on the relatively 'public' aspect of book production, involving publishing houses. But it is also useful to apply this sociological focus to the writing process, which in genetic criticism is usually considered a more 'private' aspect of literary production. In the case of Joyce's later works, this so-called 'endogenesis' is often marked by an accretive tendency.[10] Joyce seldom threw away anything he had written. In his successive drafts, he may thus have been parsimonious in the way he economized on every passage he ever wrote, but the effect was one of generous abundance, or even overabundance. In his fable of 'The Ondt and the Gracehoper', the spendthrift Gracehoper is associated with the Penman. The fable was written in reaction to one of the most 'anti-' of all 'anticollaborators', Wyndham Lewis. Lewis had first asked Joyce for a contribution to his new journal *The Enemy*. Joyce submitted the piece, but, in the end, Lewis decided not to publish it and – to make matters worse – to publish his own 'Analysis of the Mind of James Joyce' in its stead. Joyce replied creatively, by writing a few fables as part of his 'Work in Progress'. One of them is 'The Ondt and the Gracehoper', loosely based on Aesop's fable of the ant who saves up for winter and the spendthrift grasshopper who is associated with the Penman, Joyce. The fable ends with a poem, which was fairly short in the earliest draft, only twelve lines. But it kept growing longer throughout the genesis. When it was first published in the magazine *transition* (March 1928), it had eighteen lines. The fable was subsequently published as part of *Tales Told of Shem and Shaun* in a deluxe edition by The Black Sun Press (1929), run by Harry and Caresse Crosby. At proof stage, it had ten extra lines, twenty-eight in total. And it would grow even further, resulting in thirty-four lines when the book came out. One of the instigators of this accretion was the printer. In her memoir, Caresse Crosby writes an anecdote about an 'unexpected incident' relating to the master printer Roger Lescaret during the production of *Tales Told of Shem and Shaun*:

> The pages were on the press and Lescaret in consternation pedaled over to the rue de Lilly to show me, to my horror, that on the final 'forme', due to a slight error in his calculations, only two lines would fall *en plaine* [sic] *page* – this from the typographer's point of view was a heinous offense to good taste.[11]

There was nothing to be done, because all the other *formes* had been printed and the type had been distributed for reuse since they only had enough type for four pages at a time. The printer therefore came up with the idea to ask Joyce if he would be willing to write a few extra lines – to which Caresse

Crosby reacted 'scornfully': 'What a ludicrous idea, when a great writer has composed each line of his prose as carefully as a sonnet you don't ask him to inflate a masterpiece to help out the printer!'[12] But that was exactly what Joyce did. Behind Crosby's back, the printer secretly went straight to the writer, asked him if he could write a few extra lines, and Joyce obliged. He produced the requested lines, masterpiece or not. Actually, to some extent one could say that if it is a masterpiece, that is partially due to the 'anticollaborators' and other agents of textual change such as the printer Roger Lescaret, who play a role in the sociology of writing.

As indicated above, the antagonism of this fable was instigated by Lewis, who had claimed that Joyce had basically nothing to say. According to Lewis, Joyce was only interested in 'ways of doing things' instead of in 'things to be done', and he did not have any 'special point of view, or none worth mentioning'.[13] Joyce did not allow himself to be tricked into a polemic. When Lewis dismissed *Ulysses* as 'a monument like a record diarrhoea', Joyce subsequently satirically presented his own work as written in an ink made from his own excrements.[14] And to crown the self-relativization, he remembered his old metaphors and satirized his pompous younger self as the 'alshemist' who 'wrote over every square inch of the only foolscap available, his own body' (*FW* 185.34–6). Everything, even the meanest criticism, could be useful for his literary project, which required a special receptiveness to whatever came his way. As Frank Budgen notes: 'He was always looking and listening for the necessary fact or word; and he was a great believer in his luck. What he needed would come to him.'[15]

Reading

Whatever came Joyce's way was jotted down in what Budgen describes as 'little writing blocks especially made for the waistcoat pocket': 'At intervals, alone or in conversation, seated or walking, one of these tablets was produced, and a word or two scribbled on it at lightning speed as ear or memory served his turn.'[16] What this passage does not mention is that many of these jottings are excerpts from books, newspapers, pamphlets, encyclopaedias, and magazines.

According to the tradition of genetic criticism, this sort of material belongs to the so-called 'exogenesis', the writer's interaction with external sources. Just like the Joycean endogenesis, this exogenetic aspect of the writing process is not always a matter of the solitary genius working in isolation. As indicated above, Joyce was receptive to anything that came his way, but especially when it concerned his own work. As John Nash has shown, he also inscribed versions of his own contemporary reception within his writing.[17] With the help of clipping agencies, Joyce collected all kinds of announcements and reviews of his previous works.[18] He thus made notes on a set of mostly negative reviews of *Ulysses* in a notebook (VI.B.06) that was used in *Finnegans Wake*. On page 116–9 of his notebook, he jotted down excerpts from almost a dozen clippings concerning *Ulysses*, written by Virginia Woolf in the *Times Literary Supplement* (10 April 1919), even before *Ulysses* had appeared as a book, and later by John Middleton Murry in the *Nation* and *Athenaeum* (April 1922), 'Aramis' in the *Sporting Times* (April 1922), Arnold Bennett in *Outlook* (April 1922), Ernest Boyd in the *New York Tribune* (May 1922), James Douglas in the *Sunday Express* (May 1922), Mary Colum in *Freeman* (July 1922), Edmund Wilson in the *New Republic* (July 1922), Margaret Maitland in *New Witness* (August 1922), and Stephen Gwynn in the *Manchester Guardian* (March 1923).[19] Especially such reviews as Aramis's 'The Scandal of *Ulysses*' were an enormous help in the marketing of the work. Joyce must have been one of the first modern writers who fully grasped and exploited the impact of bad publicity, not only in the promotion of his work but even in the creation of new work. The most negative criticism was repurposed to feature in chapter seven of *Finnegans Wake*, as part of the description of Shem the Penman, pejoratively presented 'amid the inspissated grime of his glaucous den making believe to read his usylessly unreadable Blue Book of Eccles' (*FW* 179.25–7).

Later in the writing process of *Finnegans Wake*, Joyce even outsourced his reading. Thus, he asked Beckett to read a book that was sent to him by Heinrich Zimmer, Jr., called *Maya: Der indische Mythos* (1938). Beckett made notes for Joyce on three pages, preserved at the University at Buffalo.[20] He also involved his friends in collective notetaking, as Stuart Gilbert's Paris journal entry on a reading session in preparation of *Haveth Childers Everywhere* shows: 'Five volumes of the Encyclopaedia Britannica on his sofa. He has made a list of 30 towns, New York, Vienna, Budapest, and Mrs. Fleischman has read out the articles on some of these.' Gilbert was pretty irritated by the way Joyce – 'curled on his sofa ... pondering puns' – shamelessly exploited his friends, such as Padraic Colum, Helen Fleischman, Paul Léon, Lucia Joyce, and Gilbert himself: 'I "finish" Vienna and read Christiania and Bucharest. Whenever I come to a name (of a street, suburb, park, etc.) I pause. Joyce thinks. If he can Anglicize the word, i.e. make a pun on it, Mrs. F. records the name of its deformation in the notebook.'[21] Gilbert gives the example of the word 'Slotspark', which became 'Slutsgartern' in *Finnegans Wake* (*FW* 532.22): 'Thus "Slotspark" (I think) at Christiania becomes Sluts' park. He collects all queer names in this way and will soon have notebooks full of them.' Gilbert's aggrieved reaction – 'With foreign words it's too easy. The provincial Dubliner. Foreign equals funny' – reveals the social tension involved in Joyce's self-styled literary manufactory, where he assumed the role of chief executive officer.[22]

Joyce was not just an omnivorous reader in general, he was also an avid reader of his *own* texts, which is a key element in the process of revision.

Revising

Joyce's modernist writing is duly recognized as paradigmatic of what David Herman has called modernists' capacity as '*Umwelt* researchers', their ability to depict the world *as perceived by* the characters in interaction with their cultural as well as material circumstances.[23] Leopold Bloom is probably one of the most empathetic characters in modern literature. From the very first episode in which he is introduced, he shows the ability to put himself into the position of other people and even other fellow beings, such as his cat. In the 'Calypso' episode, he famously wonders what he must look like to her. But this empathetic thought was a very late addition to the text. In the serialization in *The Little Review*, Bloom's reaction to the cat's 'Mrkgnao!' was: 'They call them stupid. They understand what we say better than we understand them. She understands all she wants to' (*U* 4.25–7). Only at the stage of the page proofs, when writers are supposed to just reread their work and make only minor corrections, did Joyce add the most remarkable demonstration of Bloom's empathetic mind. After the line 'She understands all she wants to', he added a superscript [A], corresponding to an addition in the bottom margin: '[A] Vindictive too. [B] Wonder what I look like to her. Height of a tower? No, she can jump me.' When he reread this line, he added the superscript [B] after 'Vindictive too', corresponding to yet another thought, leading from the minds of cats to the perceived world of mice: '[B] Cruel. Her nature. Curious mice never squeal. Seem to like it' (*JJA* 22.173). It is quite impressive to see how much Joyce's '*Umwelt* research' gained from these rereading and revising campaigns.

Especially in the early stages of the genesis, Joyce's typical unit of composition was the section or the episode, not the book as a whole, and consequently his process of revision is different in the episodes after the ones that were serialized in *The Little Review* (see Clare Hutton's discussion in Chapter 14). These episodes, up to and including 'Nausicaa', also received more *external* editing, 'sometimes of a censoring, excisive kind'.[24] Whereas, in the manuscript, Bloom 'felt full and heavy: then a gentle loosening of his bowels. He stood up, undoing the waistband of his trousers', this was reduced to, 'He felt heavy, full: then a gentle loosening. He stood up.' Similarly, 'the grey sunken cunt of the world' was changed to 'the grey sunken belly'.[25] This revision was the work of Pound in his capacity as the foreign editor of *The Little Review*. His way of pruning may have earned him the title of '*il miglior fabbro*' for his work on Eliot's *The Waste Land*, but here it was simply censorship, as Paul Vanderham has shown. It comes as no surprise, then, that Joyce started revising more 'when unshackled from the conventional requirements of print publishing', that is after the serialization.[26] From this perspective, the 1920 prosecution in the United States paradoxically appears to have had a liberating effect because it allowed Joyce to give free rein to his revisionary practice. Thus, the 'Eumaeus' episode accretes more pompous worn verbiage; 'Ithaca' becomes 'more insistently particular'; and the ending of 'Penelope' shows a quantitative increase of 250 percent, which necessitated no less than four sets of placard proofs.[27]

One of Joyce's techniques to create narrative coherence was to distribute references to newly added narrative elements over other episodes. But this was not always possible towards the end of the genesis of *Ulysses* because, from the early summer of 1921 until the end of January 1922, the production of the printed book was already underway while Joyce was still writing. As Luca Crispi has shown, it was only at a very late stage in the composition process that Joyce came up with the idea of introducing Molly's mother, Lunita Laredo.[28] Joyce might have wanted to insert a retrospective reference to her in, say, the earlier 'Calypso' episode, but that was impossible. By the time he was writing 'Penelope', almost all preceding episodes had already been printed and its type had been distributed for reuse. Nobody must have been more affected by this revision process than the printer of the first edition of *Ulysses*, Maurice Darantiere, to whom Joyce – after having added layers and layers of revisions to several sets of proofs – dictated yet more final revisions over the telephone.

Editing

There is a tradition of recognizing the textual imperfections of Joyce's works. As Georgina Nugent and Sam Slote note, the list of previous editions in most editions of *Ulysses* implicitly suggests that none of them is flawless, and this imperfect textualization was recognized from the very start with Sylvia Beach's apology (written by Joyce) that opens the first edition: 'The publisher asks the reader's indulgence for typographical errors unavoidable in the exceptional circumstances.' With the same statement, Ronan Crowley and Catherine Flynn duly open their essay on 'The Errata' in *The Cambridge Ulysses*.[29] The first edition by Shakespeare and Company (1922) was followed by a second edition in 1926. After that, the stemma forks, leading, on the one hand, to the pirate edition by Samuel Roth (1929) and, on the other hand, to the two-volume 1932 Hamburg Odyssey Press edition. The first printing of this fourth edition (December 1932) still features mistakes of a rather blatant type, such as 'LINKS TH BYGONE DAYS OF YOREWI' in the 'Aeolus' episode, several of which were corrected by the fourth impression in April 1939: 'LINKS WITH BYGONE DAYS OF YORE'. In the meantime, the first authorized edition after the book had been declared not to be 'obscene' in the trial United States v. One Book Called Ulysses, was published by Random House in New York (1934). One year later, the Limited Editions Club in New York published an edition of 1,500 numbered copies, illustrated and signed by Henri Matisse. The first edition to be printed and published in the UK was the 1936 Bodley Head edition. It was revised in 1960, after which the stemma forks again, leading to the 1961 Random House and the 1968 Penguin editions.

A special case is the 1984 Garland edition by Hans Walter Gabler, Claus Melchior, and Wolfhard Steppe, which was acknowledged as marking a paradigm shift in scholarly editing.[30] A most notable principle of this edition is that it contains only authorial variants, that is, only changes and additions to the typescripts and proofs that are either in Joyce's hand or can otherwise be shown to be authorial. The edition was hailed by textual scholars such as Jerome McGann, probably because it broke with the Greg-Bowers tradition of scholarly editing, against which McGann was writing his *Critique of Modern Textual Criticism* (1985). This is noteworthy, since Gabler's special focus on authorial variants does not quite accord with McGann's notion of the 'socialization of the text' or McKenzie's 'sociology of texts'. Given the 'exceptional circumstances' that caused the textual errors for which Beach asked the reader's indulgence, it made sense in 1984 to let authority reside with the author, not with other agents of textual change. The possibility that Joyce may have silently accepted a variant reading that is not in his hand – so-called 'passive authorization' – is ruled out in principle. Other voices in the United States, most famously John Kidd's, were more critical, although Kidd's attacks were not grounded in theoretical criticism. While at that moment, in the Anglo-American world, a new generation of textual scholars such as McGann, Peter Shillingsburg, Paul Eggert, David Greetham, and George Bornstein welcomed Gabler's innovations, in Europe, Gabler's edition was, remarkably, criticized by Paola Pugliatti precisely because it *adhered to* the 'traditional philological school' and 'completely neglected' 'the most important theoretical issues of recent textual criticism'.[31]

Gabler's edition endorses Hans Zeller's principle of avoiding 'contamination'. Zeller argued that the Greg-Bowers tradition of copy-text editing resulted in 'an eclectic (contaminated) text' because the 'eclectic editor contaminatingly synchronizes that which occurred diachronically', thus creating a text that has never existed before, 'in the name of authorial intention'.[32] But the result of Gabler's approach was also a text that had never existed before.

Jeri Johnson therefore edited an annotated Oxford 'World's Classics' edition (1993; updated 2022), which photographically reproduced the first edition (a copy held at the Bodleian Library). The rationale behind this editorial enterprise is McKenzian in nature in that it acknowledges and foregrounds the sociological fact that the first edition was the one that changed the literary world in 1922. While this edition meticulously reproduces the original edition, warts and all, at the other extreme on the spectrum is the 'Reader's Edition' edited by Danis Rose (1998), the most heavily edited text of *Ulysses* so far, which inserted punctuation marks in the 'Penelope' episode and was criticized on occasion because it did not provide readers with a justification for the many textual emendations. An alternative to the annotated edition by Jeri Johnson was the Penguin 'Annotated Students' Edition', based on the 1960 Bodley Head text with annotations by Declan Kiberd (1992). The more recent Alma Press edition (2012; 2015), annotated by Sam Slote, Marc A. Mamigonian, and John Turner, which Bill Brockman recommends as 'a text of choice for first-time and established readers alike', is based on the 1939 impression of the Odyssey Press edition, but it also includes page and line number references to the Gabler edition, thus acknowledging and confirming its status as the standard edition.[33] The revised annotations came out separately in 2022, on the occasion of the centenary of *Ulysses*, as did a whole range of new editions, such as the annotated Cambridge Centenary *Ulysses*, which follows the Oxford World's Classics tradition of using a facsimile of the 1922 first edition text (in this case a facsimile of copy nr. 876 held at the Bancroft Library, University of California, Berkeley).[34]

Archiving

In response to Richard Ellmann's praise of the Gabler edition's 'discovery' and insertion of the 'word known to all men' ('Love, yes.'), John Kidd had slightingly noted that 'the passage was actually uncovered and published by Clive Driver in 1975 in his facsimile of the Rosenbach Manuscript': 'Do you know what you are talking about? Love, yes. Word known to all men. *Amor vero aliquid alicui bonum vult unde et ea quae concupiscimus*' (*U* 9.429–31). It is interesting that Kidd's attack had the same title as Aramis's 1922 review, 'The Scandal of *Ulysses*', which Joyce – in sociological terms – 'recuperated' in *Finnegans Wake* to neutralize the criticism. For in Joyce criticism, Kidd's

'Scandal' seems to have undergone a similar fate, mainly because his announced new edition never materialized, while Gabler's edition recently received the honour of a critical retrospective.[35] Still, back in 1988, it did make sense to alert the Joyce community to the 1975 facsimile edition by Clive Driver. In 1978–9, another facsimile edition impacted on Joyce studies as it enabled and facilitated the then still quite new method of 'genetic criticism'. The *James Joyce Archive* gathers all the notes, manuscripts, typescripts, and proofs that were publicly available at the time. Although quite a few extra documents have surfaced since (notably the 2002 and 2006 acquisitions by the National Library of Ireland), and although the quality of the facsimile reproduction is not ideal, it is still a very valuable instrument. Inevitably, however, it is conditioned by the print medium. For pragmatic reasons, it is arranged according to the final structure of Joyce's works and is therefore partially organized according to a textual rather than a documentary orientation. In many cases, this is a useful arrangement, but it does disturb the integrity of the documentary evidence. If readers are interested, for example, in the writing process of *Finnegans Wake* Book I (chs. 1–8), they will find the earliest versions in the volumes devoted to these chapters. But because of this editorial choice, it will not be immediately clear to them that the earliest versions of chapters two, three, four, five, seven, and eight are in one single red-backed notebook, referred to as the 'Guiltless' copybook because that is the opening word on its first page. The very fragile, original document is kept at the British Library (BL Add. 47471b). To study the document in facsimile, one needs to scan or photocopy the relevant facsimiles in volumes forty-five through forty-eight of the *James Joyce Archive* and reconstruct the copybook's structure, which is necessary to see how all the different sections interacted. A good example to show this creative ecology at work is a passage in Book I, chapter five, about the hen and 'her genesic field':

> Lead, kindly fowl! They always did: ask the ages. What bird has done yesterday man may do next year, be it fly, be it moult, be it hatch, be it agreement in the nest. *For her socioscientific sense is sound as a bell, sir, her volucrine automutativeness right on normalcy: she knows, she just feels she was kind of born to lay and love eggs (trust her to propagate the species and hoosh her fluffballs safe through din and danger!); lastly but mostly, in her genesic field it is all game and no gammon; she is ladylike in everything she does and plays the gentleman's part every time. Let us auspice it!* Yes, before all this has time to end the golden age must return with its vengeance.   (FW 112.09–19; emphasis added)

Since the archive is arranged teleologically, it suggests an approach that starts from the published text and works backwards in time. This is also the arrangement applied in the James Joyce Digital Archive (2018), which chooses a textual approach (because it presents linearized transcriptions instead of facsimile images of the documents).[36] Thus, proceeding counterclockwise, as it were, the archive suggests the earliest occurrence of the paragraph is in the fair copy. This is where – for this particular passage – the teleological, textual approach, following the genesis 'upstream', strands.

Following the writing process 'downstream', however, the documents show that the earliest version of this passage occurs *before* the stage of the fair copy, in the 'Guiltless' copybook. It is a combination of two passages, one on folio 59v and one on folio 61v, the second of which (italicized in the quotation above) is 'inserted' in the middle of the first. One of the reasons why the two passages (combined into this one paragraph) are out of sight in the archives is that they were composed while Joyce was working on another chapter, chapter seven, devoted to Shem the Penman. The passage on folio 61v, for instance, is surrounded by unflattering portraits of Shem, such as 'One cannot even begin to imagine how really low such a creature really was', an addition meant to be inserted just before the following passage in the text on the facing recto page:

> Who knows how many unsigned first copies of original masterpieces, how many pseudostylous shamiana, how few of the most venerated public impostures how very many palimpsests slipped from that plagiarist pen?[37]

Passages from chapters five and seven thus share the same creative space on page 61 verso. As to the presentation of this kind of intersection in the genesis, the print paradigm has so far conditioned our editorial approaches, which have been aimed in the first place at disentangling the sections according to their teleology (the structure of the published text). This remains a necessary and valuable approach, but the digital medium offers us the opportunity to enrich it with other, less teleological approaches that focus precisely on the creative potential generated by the entanglement of various sections. To study this kind of *creative concurrence*, it would be useful to develop an infrastructure that accommodates a document-oriented approach in addition to the teleological, textual approach.

To do so, the print paradigm need not condition the (digital) editorial approach any longer. The current development of a digital library of James Joyce at the Centre for Manuscript Genetics and of a digital edition of Joyce's unpublished letters builds upon decades of genetic research as published in *Genetic Joyce Studies* and tries to offer digital tools for a next generation of Joyce scholars to examine not only the teleological development of Joyce's works but also the dysteleological dead ends, the 'vestigial'

Writing, Reading, Revising, Editing, Archiving

notes that did not make it into Joyce's published texts but nevertheless played a discreet, unobtrusive, but no less valuable role in the creative ecology of Joyce's writing practice.

Notes

1. A. Walton Litz, *The Art of James Joyce* (Oxford: Oxford University Press, 1961), v.
2. Michael Groden, *'Ulysses' in Progress* (Princeton, NJ: Princeton University Press, 1977), p. 4.
3. Clare Hutton, *Serial Encounters: 'Ulysses' and The Little Review* (Oxford: Oxford University Press, 2019), p. 74.
4. Jerome McGann, *The Textual Condition* (Princeton, NJ: Princeton University Press, 1992), p. 69.
5. D. F. McKenzie, *Bibliography and the Sociology of Texts* (Cambridge: Cambridge University Press, 1999), p. 4.
6. James Joyce, 'Fragment of an Unpublished Work', *Criterion* 3.12 (July 1925): 498–510, 498–9. See Dirk Van Hulle, *James Joyce's 'Work in Progress': Pre-Book Publications of 'Finnegans Wake' Fragments* (New York: Routledge, 2016), p. 26.
7. Joyce, 'Fragment of an Unpublished Work', 504–5.
8. Pierre-Marc de Biasi, 'What Is a Literary Draft? Toward a Functional Typology of Genetic Documentation', *Yale French Studies* 89 (1996): 26–58, 40–1.
9. See Dirk Van Hulle, *Modern Manuscripts: The Extended Mind and Creative Undoing from Darwin to Beckett and Beyond* (London: Bloomsbury, 2014).
10. Joyce's method was not always accretive. The revision of *Stephen Hero*, which resulted in the episodic *A Portrait of the Artist as a Young Man*, is a good counterexample.
11. Caresse Crosby, *The Passionate Years: An Autobiography* (New York: The Dial Press, 1953), p. 187.
12. Ibid., p. 187. See also *JJ* 614–5.
13. Wyndham Lewis, *Time and Western Man*, ed. Paul Edwards (Santa Rosa, CA: Black Sparrow Press, 1993), p. 88.
14. Ibid., p. 90.
15. Frank Budgen, *James Joyce and the Making of 'Ulysses'* (Oxford: Oxford University Press, 1972), pp. 175–6.
16. Ibid., p. 177.
17. John Nash, *James Joyce and the Act of Reception* (Cambridge: Cambridge University Press, 2006), pp. 103–30.
18. Van Hulle, *James Joyce's 'Work in Progress'*, pp. 9–10, 19–20, 33–4, 35–6, 44–5, 57–60, 62–4, 66–8, 69–70, 71ff; Dipanjan Maitra, '"Built with glue and clippings": Joyce, Clipping Bureaus, and the Art of Recycling', *James Joyce Quarterly* 57.1–2 (2019–2020): 135–140.
19. See Ingeborg Landuyt, *'Words in Distress': A Genetic Investigation into James Joyce's Early 'Work in Progress'*, Ph.D. diss. (University of Antwerp, 1999).
20. Dirk Van Hulle, 'Beckett, Mauthner, Zimmer, Joyce', *Joyce Studies Annual* (1999): 143–83.

21. Stuart Gilbert, *Reflections on James Joyce: Stuart Gilbert's Paris Journal*, ed. Thomas Staley and Randolph Lewis (Austin: University of Texas Press, 1993), pp. 20–1.
22. Ibid., pp. 20–1. 'The notebook' Gilbert referred to was probably *Finnegans Wake* notebook VI.B.24, which contains numerous notes derived from entries on cities in the *Encyclopaedia Britannica*. The other notebook used with the direct purpose of adding more cities to *Haveth Childers Everywhere* and thus making it a companion piece to *Anna Livia Plurabelle* was notebook VI.B.29. See Van Hulle, *James Joyce's 'Work in Progress'*, p. 163.
23. David Herman, 'Re-Minding Modernism' in *The Emergence of Mind: Representations of Consciousness in Narrative Discourse in English*, ed. David Herman (Lincoln: University of Nebraska Press, 2011), p. 266.
24. Hannah Sullivan, *The Work of Revision* (Cambridge, MA: Harvard University Press, 2013), p. 158.
25. Vanderham, Paul. 'Ezra Pound's Censorship of *Ulysses*', *James Joyce Quarterly* 32.3–4 (1995), 585.
26. Sullivan, *The Work of Revision*, p. 158.
27. Ibid., pp. 168, 179.
28. Luca Crispi, *Joyce's Creative Process and the Construction of Characters in 'Ulysses': Becoming the Blooms* (Oxford: Oxford University Press, 2015), p. 109.
29. Georgina Nugent and Sam Slote, *Ulysses Forty Years: A Critical Retrospective of Hans Walter Gabler's Critical and Synoptic Edition of Ulysses* (Liverpool: Liverpool University Press, 2024), p. 1. See also Wim Van Mierlo's contribution to this volume, pp. 17–36. Ronan Crowley and Catherine Flynn, 'The Errata' in *The Cambridge Centenary 'Ulysses': The 1922 Text with Essays and Notes*, ed. Catherine Flynn (Cambridge: Cambridge University Press, 2022), p. 940.
30. Geet Lernout, 'La critique textuelle anglo-américaine: une étude de cas', *Genesis* 9 (1996): 45–65, 56.
31. Paola Pugliatti, 'The New *Ulysses* between Philology, Semiotics and Textual genesis', *Disposito* 12.30/32 (1987): 113–40, 134. See also Pugliatti in Nugent and Slote, *'Ulysses' Forty Years*, p. 37–54.
32. Hans Zeller, 'A New Approach to the Critical Constitution of Literary Texts', *Studies in Bibliography* 28 (1975): 231–64, 237. Zeller, 'Structure and Genesis in Editing: On German and Anglo-American Textual Editing' in Contemporary German Editorial Theory, ed. Hans Walter Gabler, George Bornstein, and Gillian Borland Pierce (Ann Arbor: University of Michigan Press, 1995), p. 106.
33. William S. Brockman, 'Review of James Joyce, *Ulysses*: Based on the 1939 Odyssey Press Edition', *Variants* 12–13 (2016): 263–7, 267.
34. Sam Slote, Marc A. Mamigonian, and John Turner, *Annotations to James Joyce's 'Ulysses'* (Oxford: Oxford University Press, 2022); James Joyce, *The Cambridge Centenary 'Ulysses'* ed. Flynn.
35. Nugent and Slote, *Ulysses Forty Years*. For plans to turn it into a digital edition, see Hans Walter Gabler, 'Seeing James Joyce's Ulysses into the Digital Age: Forty Years of Steering an Edition through Turbulences of Scholarship and Reception',

Joyce Studies Annual (2018): 3–36. See also Ronan Crowley and Joshua Schäuble, 'Modernism on the Punch Tape: Editing the 1984 *Ulysses*', *Modernist Cultures* 15.1 (February 2020): 29–47.
36. The James Joyce Digital Archive: jjda.ie/main/JJDA/JJDAhome.htm.
37. James Joyce collection, British Library, Mss. Add. 47471b, 62r.

FURTHER READING

Compiled below are suggestions for further reading arranged under various subheadings, with brief annotations. This is a selection from an impossibly wide field that I hope will be a helpful, initial guide, as well as some indication of the scope of Joyce studies.

Titles listed under editions contain particularly helpful notes, introductions, and textual scholarship, and are restricted to English-language editions. As the Chronology at the front of this book implies, there was already a growing body of Joyce scholarship in his own lifetime, prior to the explosion of scholarly interest in his work in the 1960s and the celebration and critique of Joyce from various theoretical perspectives in the later twentieth century. Twenty-first century interest in Joyce, in many contexts, shows little sign of abating. The following selection focuses mainly but not solely on the last fifty years; within that period I have attempted to represent work from different eras and styles of scholarship. The lists are arranged under simple subheadings; readers who wish for more detail on a particular topic may want to consult in addition the 'Further Reading' in *James Joyce in Context*, edited by John McCourt. I have decided not to list individual essays or articles but to focus on books. All lists are in chronological order.

J.N.

Editions

Dubliners (1914)

John Kelly, ed. London: Everyman's Library, 1991. Introduction, with texts of the three *The Irish Homestead* stories and 'A Curious History'.

Terence Brown, ed. London: Penguin, 1992. Introduction, notes, and appendices by Brown. Text edited by Robert Scholes and A. Walton Litz, with further corrections by Robert Scholes based on suggestions by Jack P. Dalton (Viking Press edition of 1968).

John Wyse Jackson and Bernard McGinley, eds. *James Joyce's 'Dubliners': An Illustrated Edition*. London: Sinclair-Stevenson, 1993. Includes numerous photographs, newspaper clippings, drawings, and advertisements, giving a sense of the period. Short introduction to each story and marginal notes.

Hans Walter Gabler, with Walter Hettche, ed. New York: Garland, 1993. Reproduces the 'manuscript traces' that fed into the final stories. Introduction details history of composition and publication.

Margot Norris, ed. New York: Norton, 2006. Reproduces the Gabler text (above), with substantial contextual materials, including advertisements, maps, and songs, as well as a selection of criticism.

A Portrait of the Artist as a Young Man (1916)

The definitive text, corrected from the Dublin holograph by Chester G. Anderson and edited by Richard Ellmann. New York: Viking Press, 1964.

Seamus Deane, ed. London: Penguin, 1992. Introduction and notes by Deane; using the text established by Anderson and Ellmann (above).

Hans Walter Gabler, with Walter Hettche, ed. New York: Garland, 1993. The introduction details the history of composition and publication.

John Paul Riquelme, ed. New York: Norton, 2007. Reproduces the Gabler text (above), with substantial contextual and critical materials.

Ulysses (1922)

Hans Walter Gabler, with Wolfhard Steppe and Claus Melchior, ed. *Ulysses: A Critical and Synoptic Edition*, 3 vols. New York: Garland, 1984. A new 'critical edition' based on the idea of a 'continuous manuscript text' rather than on earlier published editions, making several thousand changes to previous versions. This three-volume edition has a 'new reading text' on the right hand page, while the history of Joyce's emendations is presented in the 'synoptic display' on the left hand page.

Hans Walter Gabler, with Wolfhard Steppe and Claus Melchior, ed. New York: Random House and London: Bodley Head, 1986. The most widely used text, with line numbering per episode.

Jeri Johnson, ed. *Ulysses: The 1922 Text*. Oxford: World's Classics, 1993. A reprint of the first edition text, therefore containing many errors, but has extensive endnotes.

Catherine Flynn, ed. *The Cambridge Centenary 'Ulysses': The 1922 Text with Essays and Notes*. Cambridge: Cambridge University Press, 2022. The first edition text; notable in that it contains an essay devoted to each of the eighteen episodes, thus constituting a huge volume.

Finnegans Wake (1939)

All printings use the same pagination and line count (36 lines per page). There have been three editions, incorporating Joyce's corrections. The most complete edition for readers is:

Robbert-Jan Henkes, Erik Bindervoet, and Finn Fordham, eds. Oxford: World's Classic, 2012. Contains a lucid introduction by Fordham plus a helpful synopsis of each chapter, along with a note on publication history and a list of variants.

Other Works

Richard Ellmann, ed. *Giacomo Joyce*. With an introduction and notes. London: Faber & Faber and New York: Viking, 1968.

Richard Ellmann, A. Walton Litz, and John Whittier-Ferguson, eds. *Poems and Shorter Writings*. London: Faber & Faber, 1991. Contains the Epiphanies, *Giacomo Joyce*, the essay 'A Portrait of the Artist', *Chamber Music, Pomes*

Penyeach, and all the uncollected poetry including 'The Holy Office', 'Gas from a Burner', and 'Ecce Puer'. Brief informative notes.
J. C. C. Mays, ed. *Poems and 'Exiles'*. London: Penguin, 1992.
Kevin Barry, ed. *Occasional, Critical, and Political Writing*. Oxford: Oxford World's Classics, 2000. Contains Joyce's journalistic articles and reviews, and his surviving Trieste lectures, with translations by Conor Deane. All relatively early career, and a fascinating insight into his thinking. An appendix contains the Triestine pieces in their original Italian. Informative notes.
Nicholas A. Fargnoli and Michael Patrick Gillespie, eds. *Exiles: A Critical Edition*. Gainesville: University Press of Florida, 2015. Useful essays and contextual material.
Sangam McDuff, Angus MacFadzean, and Morris Beja, eds. *Collected Epiphanies of James Joyce: A Critical Edition*. Gainesville: University Press of Florida, 2024.

Published Manuscripts and Early Versions

The James Joyce Archive. Eds. Michael Groden, Hans Walter Gabler, David Hayman, and Danis Rose, with John O'Hanlon. 63 vols. New York: Garland: 1977–1979. Although many early and interim drafts have come to light since publication, this colossal undertaking – facsimile reproductions of notebooks, galleys, and proofs – represents a major milestone in Joyce scholarship, setting out the compositional history of all the works.
The 'Finnegans Wake' Notebooks at Buffalo. Vincent Deane, Daniel Ferrer, and Geert Lernout. Eds. Turnhout: Brepols, 2001–2004. Twelve of the 'Work in Progress'/*Finnegans Wake* notebooks reproduced with transcriptions and identification of sources.
The Joyce Papers 2002, c.1903–1928. Held at the National Library of Ireland (NLI) and digitized at https://catalogue.nli.ie/Collection/vtls000194606. A wealth of material acquired by the NLI in 2002, including early drafts of eight episodes of *Ulysses*, as well as notes made by Joyce in 1903–4 and proofs of *Finnegans Wake*.
James Joyce Digital Archive: jjda.ie/jjdahome.htm. Makes it possible to view a substantial number of the compositional histories for *Ulysses* and *Finnegans Wake*.

Letters

Pound/Joyce. The Letters of Ezra Pound to James Joyce, with Pound's Essays on Joyce. Edited and with commentary by Forrest Read. New York: New Directions, 1965.
Letters of James Joyce. Ed. Stuart Gilbert and Richard Ellmann. 3 vols. New York: Viking and London: Faber & Faber, 1957 (vol. I), 1966 (vols. II and III).
Selected Letters of James Joyce. Ed. Richard Ellmann. London: Faber & Faber, 1975.

Bibliographies

John J. Slocum and Herbert Cahoon. *A Bibliography of James Joyce, 1882–1941*. Originally published by Yale University Press in 1953 and reprinted Westport: Greenwood, 1971. A full bibliography of Joyce's published work.

Thomas Jackson Rice. *A Bibliography of James Joyce Studies*. New York: Garland, 1982. An annotated bibliography of Joyce criticism up until 1981.
William S. Brockman. 'Current JJ Checklist' in each issue of the *James Joyce Quarterly*. Comprehensive lists of recent work in relation to Joyce studies.
Oxford Bibliographies, at oxfordbibliographies.com, includes annotated lists for James Joyce, modernism, and Irish modernism.
James Joyce Checklist. The most complete Joyce bibliography, easily searchable. Maintained by William S. Brockman, hosted by the Harry Ransom Centre in Austin, Texas, at norman.hrc.utexas.edu/jamesjoycechecklist/.

Reference Works

Ruth Bauerle. *The James Joyce Songbook*. New York: Garland, 1982.
Don Gifford. *Joyce Annotated: Notes for 'Dubliners' and 'A Portrait' of the Artist as a Young Man*. 2nd ed. Berkeley: University of California Press, 1982.
Robert H. Deming, ed. *James Joyce: The Critical Heritage*. 2 vols. London: Routledge, 1970. Excerpts from reviews and critical studies first published between 1907 and 1941.
Shari Benstock and Bernard Benstock. *Who's He When He's at Home: A James Joyce Directory*. Urbana: University of Illinois Press, 1980. Compendium of characters and people in Joyce's work, excluding *Finnegans Wake*.
Geert Lernout and Wim Van Mierlo, eds. *The Reception of James Joyce in Europe*. 2 vols. New York: Thoemmes Continuum, 2004. Twenty-nine essays, plus editorial matter, on translations and criticism of Joyce, arranged by country. Quotations translated with extensive footnotes in original languages. 'Europe' here excludes the UK, and Ireland is considered solely in relation to the Irish language.
Don Gifford, with Robert J. Seidman. *'Ulysses' Annotated: Notes for James Joyce's 'Ulysses'*. Revised and expanded edition. Berkeley: University of California Press, 2008. Probably the most widely used guide, covering a broad range of allusions, keyed to the Gabler edition line numbers.
Roland MacHugh. *Annotations to 'Finnegans Wake'*. 4th ed. Baltimore: Johns Hopkins University Press, 2016. Easy to use page-by-page correspondence, listing notes on specific 'words' and phrases, built from many more specialist reference works.
Sam Slote, Marc A. Mamigonian, and John Turner. *Annotations to James Joyce's 'Ulysses'*. Oxford: Oxford University Press, 2022. The most detailed and extensive annotations in a single volume.

General Critical Studies

Harry Levin. *James Joyce: A Critical Introduction*. New York: New Directions, 1941.
Hugh Kenner. *Dublin's Joyce*. 1955. Repr. New York: Columbia University Press, 1987.
J. Mitchell Morse. *The Sympathetic Alien: James Joyce and Catholicism*. London: Peter Owen Ltd. and Vision Press, 1959. Reclaims Joyce as an individual Catholic in the 'heretical tradition'.

William T. Noon. *Joyce and Aquinas*. New Haven, CT: Yale University Press, 1957.
Robert M. Adams. *Surface and Symbol: The Consistency of James Joyce's 'Ulysses'*. Oxford: Oxford University Press, 1962. Considers the relationship between realism and symbolism.
Bernard Benstock. *James Joyce: The Undiscovered Country*. New York: Barnes and Noble, 1978. Impact on his writing of Joyce's 'exilic condition'.
Colin MacCabe. *James Joyce and the Revolution of the Word*. London: Macmillan, 1979.
Dominic Manganiello. *Joyce's Politics*. London: Routledge, 1980. Study of Joyce's engagement with political ideas and movements, with focus on earlier career.
Mary T. Reynolds. *Joyce and Dante: The Shaping Imagination*. Princeton, NJ: Princeton University Press, 1981. How a deep knowledge of and appreciation for Dante shaped Joyce's aesthetic.
Suzette Henke and Elaine Unkeless, eds. *Women in Joyce*. Urbana: University of Illinois Press, 1982. Includes some groundbreaking essays on Joyce's depictions of women characters, such as that by Bonnie Kime Scott on Emma Clery.
John Paul Riquelme. *Teller and Tale in Joyce's Fiction: Oscillating Perspectives*. Baltimore: Johns Hopkins University Press, 1983.
Derek Attridge and Daniel Ferrer, eds. *Post-Structuralist Joyce: Essays from the French*. Cambridge: Cambridge University Press, 1984. Influential volume including essays by Jacques Derrida, Julia Kristeva, and Stephen Heath.
Zack Bowen and James F. Carens, eds. *A Companion to Joyce Studies*. Westport, CT: Greenwood Press, 1984. One of the first such volumes, wide-ranging (over 800 pages) and now dated, but much of interest including essays on *Dubliners* by Florence L. Walzl, on *Giacomo Joyce* by Vicki Mahaffey, and on the correspondence by Mary T. Reynolds.
Richard Brown. *James Joyce and Sexuality*. Cambridge: Cambridge University Press, 1984. Shows Joyce's engagement with contemporary debates concerning sexology, feminism, and marriage.
Beryl Schlossman. *Joyce's Catholic Comedy of Language*. Madison: University of Wisconsin Press, 1985.
Bonnie Kime Scott. *Joyce and Feminism*. Bloomington: Indiana University Press, 1984.
Fritz Senn. *Joyce's Dislocutions*. John-Paul Riquelme, ed. Baltimore: Johns Hopkins University Press, 1984. Collection of essays by a noted close reader of Joyce.
Cheryl Herr. *Joyce's Anatomy of Culture*. Urbana: University of Illinois Press, 1986. Joyce and social class in Dublin, mediated through institutions of church, theatre and newspaper.
Bernard Benstock, ed. *James Joyce: The Augmented Ninth: Papers from the Ninth Joyce Symposium*. Syracuse, NY: Syracuse University Press, 1988. Contains essays by Jacques Derrida and Julia Kristeva.
Vicki Mahaffey. *Reauthorizing Joyce*. Cambridge: Cambridge University Press, 1988. Different voices of authority in Joyce's texts, including notable analysis of Molly Bloom and clothing.
Suzette Henke. *James Joyce and the Politics of Desire*. New York: Routledge, 1990.
James Fairhall. *James Joyce and the Question of History*. Cambridge: Cambridge University Press, 1993. A 'new historical' analysis of important contexts.

Fritz Senn. *Inductive Scrutinies: Focus on Joyce.* Dublin: Lilliput Press, 1995. Collection of essays by a noted close reader of Joyce.
Vincent J. Cheng. *Joyce, Race and Empire.* Cambridge: Cambridge University Press, 1995. The first major study of race and seminal exploration of colonialism across Joyce's work.
Emer Nolan. *James Joyce and Nationalism.* London: Routledge, 1995. Joyce's deep engagement with debates in Irish nationalism.
Mark A. Wollaeger, Victor Luftig, and Robert Spoo, eds. *Joyce and the Subject of History.* Ann Arbor: University of Michigan Press, 1996. Essays on various historical questions in Joyce's work.
Robert Spoo. *James Joyce and the Language of History: Dedalus's Nightmare.* Oxford: Oxford University Press, 1994. Joyce's reading in the European historiography of his time, notably Ferrero, in writing *Portrait* and *Ulysses*.
Christine Froula. *Modernism's Body: Sex, Culture, and Joyce.* New York: Columbia, 1996. How issues in feminism are played out in Joyce's writing.
Karen R. Lawrence, ed. *Transcultural Joyce.* Cambridge: Cambridge University Press, 1998. Sixteen essays discuss influences in Latin American and South Asian fiction, in Ireland, and various European translations.
Garry Leonard. *Advertising and Commodity Culture in Joyce.* Gainesville: University Press of Florida, 1998. Follows from a *JJQ* special issue 30.4 (1993), edited by Leonard with Jennifer Wicke, on the same topic.
Joseph Valente, ed. *Quare Joyce.* Ann Arbor: University of Michigan Press, 1998. Essays from queer studies perspectives and studies of homosexuality in Joyce's work.
Marilyn Reizbaum. *James Joyce's Judaic Other.* Stanford, CA: Stanford University Press, 1999. Brings together theory and scholarship on race and ethnicity with Joyce's texts and knowledge of Judaism.
Willard Potts. *Joyce and the Two Irelands.* Austin: University of Texas Press, 2000. Study of the revival focusing on Joyce's early career, including a chapter on *Exiles*.
Derek Attridge. *Joyce Effects: On Language, Theory, and History.* Cambridge: Cambridge University Press, 2000. Related essays teasing out textual cruxes across Joyce's major works, including essays on 'Clay', Molly's 'flow', and the language of the *Wake*.
Derek Attridge and Marjorie Howes, eds. *Semicolonial Joyce.* Cambridge: Cambridge University Press, 2000. Significant collection addressing the national and colonial aspects of Joyce's writing, from a range of influential scholars.
Jean-Michael Rabaté. *James Joyce and the Politics of Egoism.* Cambridge: Cambridge University Press, 2001.
Michael Begnal, ed. *James Joyce and the City: The Significance of Place.* Syracuse: University of Syracuse Press, 2002. Essays not only on features and experiences of Dublin but also on topography and monuments.
Marian Eide. *Ethical Joyce.* Cambridge: Cambridge University Press, 2002. Joyce creates a literary ethics; reads Joyce alongside ethical philosophy, notably Levinas, Derrida, and feminism.
Tim Conley. *Joyce's Mistakes: Problems of Intention, Irony and Interpretation.* Toronto: University of Toronto Press, 2003.

Katherine Mullin. *James Joyce, Sexuality and Social Purity*. Cambridge: Cambridge University Press, 2003. Joyce's subversion of sexual policing.
Luke Thurston. *James Joyce and the Problem of Psychoanalysis*. Cambridge: Cambridge University Press, 2004.
Joseph Booker. *Joyce's Critics*. Madison: University of Wisconsin Press, 2004. Analysis of critical history of Joyce and development of Joyce studies.
Eric Bulson. *The Cambridge Introduction to James Joyce*. Cambridge: Cambridge University Press, 2006.
John Nash. *James Joyce and the Act of Reception: Reading, Ireland, Modernism*. Cambridge: Cambridge University Press, 2006. Joyce's responses, in his literary writing, to readers and critics.
John McCourt, ed. *Joyce in Context*. Cambridge: Cambridge University Press, 2009.
Geert Lernout. *Help My Unbelief: James Joyce and Religion*. London: Continuum, 2010. Situates Joyce amid Catholic doctrine and institutions as they were in his lifetime.
Andrew Gibson. *The Strong Spirit: History, Politics, and Aesthetics in the Writings of James Joyce 1898–1915*. Oxford: Oxford University Press, 2013. Close attention to Irish historical contexts as they informed Joyce's early career, up to and including *Exiles*.
Andrew J. Mitchell and Sam Slote, eds. *Derrida and Joyce*. New York: State University of New York Press, 2013. Collects Derrida's writing on Joyce, with critical essays addressing the Joyce–Derrida conjunction.
John Nash, ed. *James Joyce in the Nineteenth Century*. Cambridge: Cambridge University Press, 2013.
Robert Joseph Brazeau and Derek Galdwin, eds. *Eco-Joyce: The Environmental Imagination of James Joyce*. Cork: Cork University Press, 2014. The first collection of essays on ecological and environmental matters.
Luke Gibbons. *Joyce's Ghosts: Ireland, Modernism, and Memory*. Chicago: Chicago University Press, 2015. Links narrative modes to social and political conditions.
Michael Patrick Gillespie, ed. *Foundational Essays in James Joyce Studies*. Gainesville: University Press of Florida, 2017. Reprints a dozen essays by influential critics active in the 1960s and 1970s, with three essays on each of Joyce's principal fictions.
Cleo Hanaway-Oakley. *James Joyce and the Phenomenology of Film*. Oxford: Oxford University Press, 2017. Study of subjectivity and embodiment.
Catherine Flynn. *James Joyce and the Matter of Paris*. Cambridge: Cambridge University Press, 2019. The importance of French literature to the development of Joyce's aesthetics.
Leah Culligan Flack. *James Joyce and Classical Modernism*. London: Bloomsbury, 2020. Tracks Joyce's reading of classical texts and their influence on his developing aesthetic.
Keith Williams. *James Joyce and Cinematicity: Before and after Film*. Edinburgh: Edinburgh University Press, 2020. Pre-film technology in relation to Joyce's narrative methods.
Eric Bulson. *'Ulysses' by Numbers*. New York: Columbia University Press, 2021. Literary analysis based upon computational analysis, with visualizations.
Catherine Flynn. *The New Joyce Studies*. Cambridge: Cambridge University Press, 2022. Emerging and under-represented areas in Joyce studies.

Fran O'Rourke. *Joyce, Aristotle, and Aquinas.* Gainesville: University Press of Florida, 2022.
Daniel Ferrer. *Genetic Joyce: Manuscripts and the Dynamics of Creation.* Gainesville: University Press of Florida, 2023. Introduction to the 'genetic' study of Joyce's manuscripts and revisions for *Ulysses* and *Finnegans Wake*, with emphasis on 'Sirens' as an illustrative example.

Dubliners

Donald T. Torchiana. *Backgrounds for Joyce's 'Dubliners'.* London: Allen & Unwin, 1986. Analysis of each story.
Garry Leonard. *Reading 'Dubliners' Again: A Lacanian Perspective.* Syracuse, NY: Syracuse University Press, 1993.
Margot Norris. *Suspicious Readings of Joyce's 'Dubliners'.* Philadelphia: University of Pennsylvania Press, 2003. Inventive readings of each story with focus on slipperiness of narrative.
Vicki Mahaffey. *Collaborative 'Dubliners': Joyce in Dialogue.* Syracuse, NY: Syracuse University Press, 2012. Each short story addressed by two critics in varying modes of collaboration.
See also the Norton critical edition (in Editions, above) for essays and excerpts.

A Portrait of the Artist as a Young Man

Robert Scholes and Richard M. Kain. *The Workshop of Daedalus: James Joyce and the Raw Materials for 'A Portrait of the Artist as a Young Man'.* Evanston, IL: Northwestern University Press, 1965. Analysis of epiphanies and manuscripts.
Roy Gottfried. *Joyce's Comic Portrait.* Gainesville: University Press of Florida, 2000.
Mark A. Wollager, ed. *James Joyce's 'A Portrait of the Artist as a Young Man': A Casebook.* Oxford: Oxford University Press, 2003. Contains several important essays on aspects of narration, aesthetics, and cultural politics.
See also the Norton critical edition (in Editions, above) for essays and excerpts.

Ulysses

Stuart Gilbert. *James Joyce's 'Ulysses'.* First published 1930, revised and expanded London: Faber & Faber, 1952, and New York: Random House, 1955. Assisted by Joyce, this study was available while the US and UK bans on *Ulysses* were still in place.
William M. Schutte. *Joyce and Shakespeare: A Study in the Meaning of 'Ulysses'.* New Haven, CT: Yale University Press, 1957. Systematic explanation of allusions.
Harry Blamires. *The New Bloomsday Book: A Guide through 'Ulysses'.* 3rd ed. London: Routledge, 1996. Popular student guidebook originally published 1966.
David Hayman. *'Ulysses': The Mechanics of Meaning.* First published 1970, revised and expanded Madison: University of Wisconsin Press, 1982. The 1970 book introduced the idea of the 'Arranger' as guiding presence, somewhere between

author and narrators; the 1982 update contains an afterword that returns to the notion.

Marilyn French. *The Book as World: James Joyce's 'Ulysses'*. Cambridge, MA: Harvard University Press, 1976.

Michael Groden. *'Ulysses' in Progress*. Princeton, NJ: Princeton University Press, 1977. A foundational study of the redrafting process; although missing draft versions have subsequently been made public, this is still a compelling overview of the composition of *Ulysses*.

Hugh Kenner. *Ulysses*. 1980, rev. ed. Baltimore: Johns Hopkins University Press, 1987. Influential study of Joyce's language and narrative arrangement.

Karen Lawrence. *The Odyssey of Style in 'Ulysses'*. Princeton, NJ: Princeton University Press, 1981. Influential study of narrative technique.

Zack R. Bowen. *'Ulysses' as a Comic Novel*. Syracuse, NY: Syracuse University Press, 1989.

Mary Lowe-Evans. *Crimes against Fecundity: Joyce and Population Control*. Syracuse, NY: Syracuse University Press, 1989. Foucauldian study of matters affecting 'population control', including the Famine, Malthusian debates, and Catholic teaching.

Enda Duffy. *The Subaltern 'Ulysses'*. Minneapolis: University of Minnesota Press, 1994. Joyce's anti-colonial politics.

Richard Pearce, ed. *Molly Blooms: A Polylogue on 'Penelope' and Cultural Studies*. Madison: University of Wisconsin Press, 1994. Ranges widely beyond Molly and contains sections on the male gaze, identity as performance, colonialism, embodiment, and consumerism.

Maria Tymoczko. *The Irish 'Ulysses'*. Berkeley: University of California Press, 1994. Early Irish literature and mythology as sources and influences.

Mark Osteen. *The Economy of 'Ulysses': Making Both Ends Meet*. Syracuse, NY: Syracuse University Press, 1995. Financial matters elucidated in a novel analysis.

Paul Vanderham. *James Joyce and Censorship: The Trials of 'Ulysses'*. New York: New York University Press, 1998. An informative account of the parties and issues at stake leading up to Judge Woolsey's decision to overturn the ban in 1933.

Kimberley J. Devlin and Marilyn Reizbaum, eds. *'Ulysses': En-Gendered Perspectives: Eighteen New Essays on the Episodes*. Columbia: University of South Carolina Press, 1999. Significant reconsideration of *Ulysses* with an essay for each episode, focused on gender.

Andrew Gibson. *Joyce's Revenge: History, Politics and Aesthetics in 'Ulysses'*. Oxford: Oxford University Press, 2002. Places the episodes of *Ulysses* in particular Irish–British historical contexts.

Derek Attridge, ed. *James Joyce's 'Ulysses': A Casebook*. Oxford: Oxford University Press, 2004. Collection of influential essays.

Ian Gunn and Clive Hart. *James Joyce's Dublin: A Topographical Guide to the Dublin of 'Ulysses'*. London: Thames & Hudson, 2004. Contains street maps, calculation of walking times, timetable of implied events, and an interior layout for 7 Eccles Street.

Vincent Sherry. *James Joyce: 'Ulysses'*. 2nd ed. Cambridge: Cambridge University Press, 2004. Short, lucid introduction.

Sean Latham, ed. *The Cambridge Companion to 'Ulysses'*. Cambridge: Cambridge University Press, 2014.
Luca Crispi. *Joyce's Creative Process and the Construction of Characters in 'Ulysses': Becoming the Blooms*. Oxford: Oxford University Press, 2015. A study of the development of the Blooms' characterization applying 'genetic' methods.
Clare Hutton. *Serial Encounters: 'Ulysses' and 'The Little Review'*. Oxford: Oxford University Press, 2019. Thorough exposition of development of *Ulysses* in the context of its primary pre-book publication venue.

Finnegans Wake

Clive Hart. *Structure and Motif in 'Finnegans Wake'*. Evanston, IL: Northwestern University Press, 1962 and London: Faber & Faber, 1962. Recurrent elements in the *Wake* provide continuities and structure.
David Hayman. *A First-Draft Version of 'Finnegans Wake'*. Austin: University of Texas Press, 1963. Creates a draft text from the initial sketches that Joyce made.
Margot Norris. *The Decentered Universe of 'Finnegans Wake': A Structuralist Analysis*. Baltimore: Johns Hopkins University Press, 1976.
Adaline Glasheen. *Third Census of 'Finnegans Wake': An Index of the Characters and Their Roles*. Berkeley: University of California Press, 1977.
John Bishop. *Joyce's Book of the Dark*. Madison: University of Wisconsin Press, 1986.
Kimberly J. Devlin. *Wandering and Return in 'Finnegans Wake': An Integrative Approach to Joyce's Fictions*. Princeton, NJ: Princeton University Press, 1991.
Danis Rose. *The Textual Diaries of James Joyce*. Dublin: Lilliput, 1995. Orders the *Wake* notebooks into sequence in a precise and readable account of how Joyce composed his last work.
Vincent Cheng. *Shakespeare and Joyce: A Study of 'Finnegans Wake'*. Philadelphia: Pennsylvania State University Press, 2006.
Luca Crispi and Sam Slote, ed. *How Joyce Wrote 'Finnegans Wake': A Chapter by Chapter Genetic Guide*. Madison: University of Wisconsin Press, 2007.
Finn Fordham. *Lots of Fun at 'Finnegans Wake': Unravelling Universals*. Oxford: Oxford University Press, 2007.
Alison Lacivita. *The Ecology of 'Finnegans Wake'*. Gainesville: University Press of Florida, 2015. Joyce's attention to Irish landscape and ecology.

Shorter Works, including 'Exiles'

John MacNicholas. *James Joyce's 'Exiles': A Textual Companion*. New York: Garland, 1979. A substantial historical essay plus detailed textual and editorial information as background for his critical edition.
Louis Armand and Clare Wallace, eds. *'Giacomo Joyce': Envoys of the Other*. Prague: Litteraria Pragensia, 2007.
James Alexander Fraser. *Joyce & Betrayal*. London: Palgrave Macmillan, 2016. Contains a major chapter on *Exiles* and addresses its key theme more widely.
Katherine Ebury and James Alexander Fraser, eds. *Joyce's Non-Fiction Writings: 'Outside His Jurisfiction'*. London: Palgrave Macmillan, 2018.

Irish Literature and History

Terence Brown. *Ireland's Literature: Selected Essays*. Lanham, MD: Rowman & Littlefield, 1988.
John Wilson Foster. *Fictions of the Irish Literary Revival: A Changeling Art*. Syracuse, NY: Syracuse University Press, 1993.
Declan Kiberd. *Inventing Ireland*. London: Jonathan Cape, 1995.
Seamus Deane. *Strange Country: Modernity and Nationhood in Irish Writing Since 1790*. Oxford: Clarendon Press, 1997.
Gregory Castle. *Modernism and the Celtic Revival*. Cambridge: Cambridge University Press, 2001.
Emer Nolan. *Catholic Emancipations: Irish Fiction from Thomas Moore to James Joyce*. Syracuse, NY: Syracuse University Press, 2007.

Modernism

Kevin Dettmar and Stephen Watt, eds. *Marketing Modernisms: Self-Promotion, Canonization, Rereading*. Ann Arbor: University of Michigan Press, 1996.
Lawrence Rainey. *Institutions of Modernism: Literary Elites and Public Culture*. New Haven, CT: Yale University Press, 1998.
Mark S. Morrison. *The Public Face of Modernism: Little Magazines, Audiences, and Reception, 1905–1920*. Madison: University of Wisconsin Press, 2001.
Michael North. *Reading 1922: A Return to the Scene of the Modern*. Oxford: Oxford University Press, 2002.
Sean Latham. *Am I a Snob? Modernism and the Novel*. Ithaca, NY: Cornell University Press, 2003.
David Trotter, ed. *The Cambridge Companion to Modernism*. Cambridge: Cambridge University Press, 2011.
Abbie Garrington. *Haptic Modernism: Touch and the Tactile in Modernist Writing*. Edinburgh: Edinburgh University Press, 2013.
Victoria Bazin. *Modernism Edited: Marianne Moore and the 'Dial' Magazine*. Edinburgh: Edinburgh University Press, 2019.
Modernist Journals Project: modjourn.org.

Joyce's Life

Herbert Gorman. *James Joyce*. New York: Farrar & Rinehart, 1939. An update on Gorman's study *James Joyce: His First Forty Years*, New York: B. W. Huebsch, 1924.
J. F. Byrne. *Silent Years: An Autobiography with Memoirs of James Joyce and Our Ireland*. New York: Farrar, Straus and Young, 1953.
Mary Colum and Padraic Colum. *Our Friend James Joyce*. Garden City, NJ: Doubleday, 1958.
Stanislaus Joyce. *My Brother's Keeper: James Joyce's Early Years*. New York: Viking Press, 1958.
Constantine Curran. *James Joyce Remembered*. Oxford: Oxford University Press, 1968.

Jane Lidderdale and Mary Nicholson. *Dear Miss Weaver: Harriet Shaw Weaver 1876–1961*. London: Faber & Faber, 1970. Biography of Harriet Shaw Weaver in which Joyce is a major character.

Arthur Power. *Conversations with James Joyce*. Ed. Clive Hart. London: Millington, 1974, (repr. Dublin: Lilliput Press, 1999).

Richard Ellmann. *James Joyce*. New and Revised Edition. Oxford: Oxford University Press, 1982. Revision of the 1959 edition. Criticized for conflation of character and biography, and overlooking Joyce's Irishness, but also a widely lauded and hugely influential resource.

Brenda Maddox. *Nora: The Real Life of Molly Bloom*. Boston: Houghton Mifflin, 1988. Rescues Nora from marginalization as an 'unlikely' companion for Joyce, seeing her as sharp, witty, and influential.

E. H. Mikhail, ed. *James Joyce: Interviews and Recollections*. London: Macmillan, 1990.

Peter Costello. *James Joyce: The Years of Growth 1882–1915*. London: Kyle Cathie Ltd., 1992.

Stuart Gilbert. *Reflections on James Joyce: Stuart Gilbert's Paris Journal*. Ed. Thomas F. Staley and Randolph Lewis. Austin, TX: Harry Ransom Humanities Research Centre, 1993. Gilbert's journal, 1929–1934.

John McCourt. *The Years of Bloom: James Joyce in Trieste 1904–1920*. Dublin: Lilliput, 2000. Additional details on the Triestine years, making the case for their importance in Joyce's development and in shaping the character of Leopold Bloom.

Carol Loeb Shloss. *Lucia Joyce: To Dance in the Wake*. London: Bloomsbury, 2003. Joyce and Lucia's loving relationship; Lucia's quest to be a dancer in the twenties; her mental turmoil and hospitalizations.

Andrew Gibson. *James Joyce*. Introduction by Declan Kiberd. London: Reaktion, 2006. Focuses on the works in biographical context rather than a biography *per se*, with emphasis on Joyce's engagement with Irish history and politics.

Gordon Bowker. *James Joyce: A Biography*. London: Weidenfeld & Nicholson, 2011. Pays more attention than Ellmann to Joyce's life in the 1930s.

Journals, Book Series and Other Resources

James Joyce Quarterly. Known as the journal of record for Joyce studies: articles, letters, and bibliography ('checklist'), since 1963: jjq.utulsa.edu/.

Dublin James Joyce Journal. Started in 2008; emphasis of studies using resources at the NLI and elsewhere: ucd.ie/englishdramafilm/research/jamesjoyceresearchcentre/jjrc-dublinjamesjoycejournal/.

Genetic Joyce Studies. geneticjoycestudies.org/.

James Joyce Broadsheet. Short reviews and news items, since 1980, from Leeds University, UK.

James Joyce Literary Supplement. Reviews of recent Joyce-related material: english.as.miami.edu/publications/jjls/index.html.

Hypermedia Joyce Studies. hjs.ff.cuni.cz/.

European Joyce Studies. Book series of edited essay collections. Amsterdam: Rodopi.

Florida James Joyce Studies. Book series, mainly monographs. Gainesville: University Press of Florida.

James Joyce: Finnegans Wake. A Reading. By Patrick Healy. Dublin: Lilliput, 1992. The complete text: twenty hours across seventeen CDs. An abridged four-hour cassette version also available.

Joyce Images. joyceimages.com/. Created by Aida Yared to illustrate each episode of *Ulysses* using contemporary photographs, postcards, and other documents.

The Joyce Project. joyceproject.com/. An online copy of *Ulysses*, with various notes and resources such as annotations of characters and historical events.

James Joyce Online Notes. jjon.org. Notes on people, words, allusions, 'environs', and Joyce's Trieste and Paris libraries.

riverrun.org.uk/. Maintained by Ian Gunn for 'empirical' investigations. See the section 'Joyce Tools', in which may be found *Thom's Directory* 1904, various maps, and sundry quirky items.

INDEX

1798 Rebellion, 73–4

Abbey Theatre, 124
Act of Union, 1800, 73, 115, 127, 241, 246
Aesop's Fables, 69, 254
aestheticism, 32
Ahmed, Sara, 181
Alaimo, Stacy, 216
Aldington, Richard, 49–50, 54, 239
ALP (in *Finnegans Wake*), 85, 88, 176, 195, 211, 227, 253
  as Liffey, 225
Amis, Martin, 47
Anderson, Benedict, 165
Anderson, Margaret, 191, 232, 235, 237, 239
Anglo-Irish Treaty, 7, 245
Antient Concert Rooms, 74
Aquinas, 2, 6, 31, 35
'Aramis', 260
Argentina
  similarities to Ireland, 138
Aristotle, 6, 59
Arnold, Matthew, 162
Asquith, H. H., 114
Attridge, Derek, 9, 49, 51, 59
Aughrim, Battle of, 26
Augustine of Hippo, 94
Auschwitz, 136
Austen, Jane, 14, 78

Bakhtin, Mikhail, 58, 140–1, 148
Balfe, Michael William, 71
Barad, Karen, 222
Barnacle, Nora. *See* Joyce, Nora Barnacle
Beach, Sylvia, 148, 234, 239, 245, 248, 253
Beauchamp, Toby, 175
Beckett, Samuel, 75, 148, 211, 253, 256
Bell, Clive, 50

Benjamin, Walter, 206
Bennett, Arnold, 206
Bérard, Victor, 143
Bergson, Henri, 225
betrayal, 120, 128–30, 132, 134
Bildungsroman, 31, 40, 44
Bishop, John, 227
Blackwood, Sir John, 243, 245
Bloom, Leopold, 4, 6, 8, 57, 73, 110
  Boylan, and, 4–5
  on chamber music, 109
  on confession, 87–8, 96
  gender, and, 170
  Griffith, and, 145
  Jewish, 68, 172
  Jewishness, 143
  on justice, 161
  on love, 161
  modernity, and, 75
  mourning, and, 208
  political sympathies, 143
  relationship with Stephen Dedalus, 224–5
  sex and voyeurism, 193
  sexuality, 129
  transcorporeality, and, 221–2
  woman, as 171
Bloom, Molly, 4–5, 96, 145, 170–1, 223
  affair with Boylan, 5, 192
  confession, 91, 196
  menstruation, 194
  sex and performance, 193
  urinating, 109
Bloomsday, 202
body, 4, 216–18, *See also* trans-corporeality
  women's bodies, 223–4
Boer War, 162
Bollach, Lily, 253
Book of Job, 143

Book of Kells, 7, 85
Borach, George, 64
Borges, Jorge Luis, 138
Bourdieu, Pierre, 214
Brancusi, Constantin, 51
Brandes, Georg, 143
Brecht, Bertolt, 64
British Empire, 3, 20, 43, 67, 69, 73, 125, 146, 154, 156, 201, *See also* colonialism
  Leopold Bloom, and, 159
Bruni, Alessandro Francesco, 115
Bruno, Giordano, 145, 148
Budgen, Frank, 255
Bulson, Eric, 47
Burgess, Anthony, 65
Burke, Father Tom, 22
Butler, Judith, 172–4
Byron, Lord, 216

Caesar, Julius, 142
Camus, Albert, 99
Carleton, William, 121, 126
Castle, Gregory, 68
Cathleen Ní Houlihan, 29
Catholic Emancipation, 115
Catholicism, 2–3, 125, 128–31, 201
  blasphemy, 210
  body, and, 216
  British Empire, and, 21
  Church and colonialism, 156
  Church as empire, 67
  confession, 87–8, 91, 99–100, 186
  Confiteor, 92–3
  conversion to, 21, 33
  education, 31, 38, 138
  evolution, and, 221
  heresy, 130
  Jesuit order, 40
  Joyce as 'Catholic writer', 23
  laughter, and, 140
  modernism in Catholic Church, 144–5
  priest characters, 21
  protestantism, and, 95–6
  revival, and, 24
  social customs, and, 19–21
  social respectability, 68
  traditional beliefs, and, 22
  Trinity and Holy Family, 129–31
  Wilde, and, 121
Chamber Music, 102–3, 108, 110, 112
Cheng, Vincent, 26, 154, 164
Civil War, Irish, 7, 213
Cixous, Hélène, 171

class, 70–1, 79
  Irish language movement, and, 164
Clongowes Wood College, 114, 156
Collingwood, R. G., 76
colonialism, 26–8, 68–70, 72, 79
  Ceylon, 73
  class, and, 71
  education, and, 69
  colonial ambivalences, 72
  colonial subject, 68
  economic basis, 159
  Ireland compared with Egypt, 158
  Ireland's 'double status', 153
  ivory, and, 157
commodities, 2
  Pears' soap, 166
  Plumtree's potted meat, 4, 6
confession
  public admission, as, 88, 91–5
  sex, and, 190
Connor, Steven, 70
Crispi, Luca, 258
Croce, Benedetto, 76
Cromwell, Oliver, 139
Crosby, Caresse, 255
Culloden, Battle of, 73
Cumberland, Duke of, 73
Curran, Constantine, 127
Curtius, Ernst Robert, 138, 140

D'Arcy, Anne-Marie, 244
Dáil Éireann, 245
Dana, 144
Dante Alighieri, 79, 138
Darantiere, Maurice, 258
Davis, Thomas, 121
de Beauvoir, Simone, 172, 176
de Biasi, Pierre-Marc, 253
De Valera, Eamon, 7, 132, 147
Deane, Seamus, 25
death and mourning, 202–12
Dedalus, Simon, 67, 71
Dedalus, Stephen
  development from *Stephen Hero* to *Ulysses*, 38
  development of aesthetic theory, 107
  learning of, 126–7
  rejection of faith, 21
  Wilde, and, 31–4, 121
Dedalus, Stephen, in *Portrait*, 1–2, 4, 88, 113
  Catholic Church, and, 38, 96
  confession, 87
  cultural nationalism, and, 164

280

English language, and, 154
humiliation of, 94
irony, 41
mundane, and, 201
sex, and, 189
sex workers, and, 175
Dedalus, Stephen, in *Ulysses*, 57, 59, 76, 113, 129–30
  compared to Richard Rowan (*Exiles*), 115
  in drafts of 'Nestor', 241
  intellectual framework, 145
  on justice, 161
  Latin and Greek, 138
  on love, 161
  mother's death, 207
  natural world, and, 220–1
  on Shakespeare, 143
Deleuze, Gilles, 150
democracy, 142, 150
Derrida, Jacques, 9, 99
  'globalatinization', 140
Dickens, Charles
  parody of, 58
Doyle, Laura, 170
Doyle, Roddy, 49
Driver, Clive, 261
Dublin, 1–2, 9, 13, 79, 110, 124–7, 136, 147, 154
  compared to Troy, 202
  distinct from rest of Ireland, 125
  Dublin Bay, 220, 223
  Finnegans Wake, 133–4, 149
  immigration, 68–9, 77
  Irish ecosystems, and, 218
  Joyce's early life in, 20
  Phoenix Park, 133, 150
Dubliners, 6–8, 35–6, 38, 56, 77, 125, 145
  Catholic Church, and, 20–3
  composition and revisions, 14, 184–5
  Dublin, and, 125
  emotions, 19
  families, 20
  free indirect narrative, 15
  language, 18
  naturalism, 12–18
  realism, 38
  repetition, 18
  revival, and, 165
  sexual abuse, and, 177
  symbolism, 14, 26
  Ulysses, and, 19
Dubliners, stories of
  'After the Race', 15, 154–6

'Araby', 18, 218
'The Boarding House', 20, 187
'Clay', 14, 17, 188
'Counterparts', 3, 17
'The Dead', 17–18, 21, 24–7, 38, 141, 188–9, 205, 217–18
'An Encounter', 17, 184, 186, 218
'Eveline', 14, 17, 20, 187, 218
'Grace', 21
'Ivy Day in the Committee Room', 27, 184
'A Little Cloud', 15–16, 18, 24, 141
'A Mother', 24
'A Painful Case', 17, 27, 95, 188, 218
'The Sisters', 17, 21, 27, 84, 96, 184–6, 203–4
'Two Gallants', 184, 187
Duffy, Enda, 158
Dujardin, Edouard, 144

Easter Rising, 1916, 43, 74, 244
Eglinton, John (William Kirkpatrick Magee), 144–5
Egoist, The, 8, 191, 232, 240, 245–7
  Pound, and, 55
Eliot, T. S., 48, 57, 201, 206, 209, 239, 244
  Criterion, 253
  differs from Larbaud, 56
  differs from Lewis, 56
  The Egoist, and, 238
  'mythical method', 58
  response to *Ulysses*, 54–5
  The Waste Land, 258
Ellmann, Maud, 219
Ellmann, Richard, 27, 107, 252, 260
Emmet, Robert, 75, 130, 166
Empson, William, 76
environmental crisis, 229
epiphanies, 3, 35–6, 38, 102–3, 105–8, 112, 202
essays and lectures by Joyce
  'A Curious History', 191
  'Day of the Rabblement, The', 212, 239
  'Fenianism', 219
  'Home Rule Comes of Age', 219
  'Ireland at the Bar', 211, 219
  'Ireland, Island of Saints and Sages', 19, 226, 236, 263
  'Oscar Wilde: The Poet of Salome', 65
  'Home Rule Comet, The', 219
  'Shade of Parnell, The', 219
Exiles, 23, 176, 178, 193, 194–200, 233, 246
  and *Ulysses*, 178
  compared to *Giacomo Joyce*, 104
  composition, 113

Exiles (cont.)
  Irish historical context, 113–15
  on links Dublin and Europe, 146–7
  in performance, 115, 119
  sexual desire, 4
  Ulysses, and, 103

Fairhall, James, 77
Famine, 157
Fanon, Frantz, 34, 44–5
Fenian movement, 67, 77, 120, 127, 129, 131
Ferguson, Sir Samuel, 121
Ferrer, Daniel, 49
Ferrero, Guglielmo, 76, 149
  Joyce's reading of, 141–4
Finnegans Wake, 1, 8–9, 104, 122
  Aramaic sermons, and, 139
  Bakthin as framework for, 140
  ballad of Tim Finnegan, 148, 210
  betrayal, and, 132
  Buckley and Russian General, 85–6, 88, 90–1, 93, 99
  Caesar in, 142
  Chamber Music, and, 109
  chapter I.4, 89
  chapter I.5, 85, 195, 261
  chapter I.7, 88, 90, 196, 256, 262
  chapter I.8, 88
  chapter III.3, 89, 93–4, 98
  chapter III.4, 89
  colonialism, and, 162
  compared to shorter works, 102
  composition of, 89–90, 97–8
  criticism of *Ulysses*, and, 255–6
  Dublin in, 155
  ending compared to *Ulysses*, 212
  gender, and, 176–80
  'Here Comes Everybody', 92
  idea of Europe, and, 147–8, 150
  initial composition, 7
  Ireland, 8
  Irish language, and, 147
  language of, 92, 132
  music in, 73
  narrative, 86–7, 98
  notebooks, 97
  'The Ondt and the Gracehoper', 254–5
  performance, and, 97
  reception, 1
  transcorporeality, and, 225–8
  in *transition*, 89

  trials, 88, 94
  'Tristan and Isolde' episode, 110
  writing process, 261
Fitzpatrick, David, 80
Flaubert, Gustave, 49
Flotow, Friedrich von, 70
Flynn, Catherine, 77–8, 183
Forster, E. M.
  A Passage to India, 93
Foucault, Michel, 87, 99
Frank, Joseph
  spatial form, 55
Freeman's Journal, 76
French Revolution, 115
French, Marilyn, 171
French, Percy, 69, 72
Freud, Sigmund, 91, 113, 133, 174

Gabler, Hans Walter, 259
Galsworthy, John, 206
gender, 5, 67, 70–2, 112
  body, and, 179–81
  editing periodical magazines, and, 239
  education, and, 176–9
  grammar, and, 179
  performance, and, 174
  race, and, 172
  sex, and, 169–71
genetic criticism, 253–4
Giacomo Joyce, 102, 110–13
  Chamber Music, and, 111
  epiphanies, and, 103
  sexual desire, 4
  Ulysses, and, 103, 111
Gibson, Andrew, 114, 146, 247
Gifford, Don, 162
Gilbert, Stuart, 7, 52, 256
Gogarty, Oliver St. John, 110, 137
Goldsmith, Oliver, 124
  She Stoops to Conquer, 71
Gorman, Herbert, 110
Government of Ireland Act, 1914, 244
Greg-Bowers textual editing, 259
Gregory, Lady, 29, 124, 133
Griffith, Arthur, 127, 145
Groden, Michael, 53, 252
Guattari, Felix, 150
Guinness family, 75

Handel, George Friderich, 73
Hauptmann, Gerhard, 141
Haveth Childers Everywhere, 256
Hayman, David, 252

INDEX

HCE (in *Finnegans Wake*), 85–6, 88, 90, 92, 132, 195, 211, 226
  confession, 89, 99
  public shaming, 93
  stutter, 92
  water, and, 226
Heaney, Seamus, 63
Heap, Jane, 191, 232, 237–9
Heath, Stephen, 59
Hegel, Georg Wilhelm Friedrich, 150
Heilbrun, Carolyn G., 171
Hellenism, 129, 138
Henke, Suzette, 9
Herman, David, 257
Herr, Cheryl, 76–7
Hiberno-English, 67–8
Hicklin test (of obscenity), 197
historical materialism
  Joyce scholarship, and, 75–81
Hogg, James, 94
Hölderlin, Friedrich, 137
'Holy Office, The', 23, 96
Home Rule, 27, 32–3, 113–14, 120, 136, 146
Homer, 2, 133, 207
  battle of Troy, 202
homosexuality, 129–30
Howarth, Herbert, 110
Huguenots, 68
Hume, David, 75
Husserl, Edmund, 176
Hutton, Clare, 23, 49, 252
Hyde, Douglas, 164

Ibsen, Henrik, 124, 141
imagism, 103
Irish Agricultural Organisation Society, 27
Irish Free State, 153
Irish Homestead, The, 1, 12–13, 27
Irish language, 147
Irish Literary Theatre, 23, 29
Irish mythology, 2, 141
Irish National Theatre, 123
Issy (in *Finnegans Wake*), 176–7, 226

Jackson, Holbrook, 50
James Joyce Archive, 251
James, Henry, 50
Jameson, Fredric, 165
Jauss, Hans Robert, 47
Jewish people, 22, 73, 112
  anti-Semitism, 143
  Ferrero on, 143
  in *Giacomo Joyce* and *Ulysses*, 112

Semitic languages, 149
Stephen Dedalus on, 130
Veblen on, 138
Johnson, Jeri, 48, 260
Jolas, Eugène, 148
  revolution of the word, 145
Jolas, Maria, 148
Jousse, Marcel, 139
Joyce, George, 217
Joyce, Lucia, 213
Joyce, Nora Barnacle, 84, 113
Joyce, Stanislaus, 13, 102, 106
  on epiphanies, 107
Judaism, 129–30

Kafka, Franz, 145–6, 150
Kain, Richard M., 106
Kenner, Hugh, 6, 47, 49, 51–2, 56, 202, 206
Kiberd, Declan, 67, 69, 74, 201, 260
Kidd, John, 259–60
Kitcher, Philip, 48, 59
Kundera, Milan, 145–6, 150

Lacivita, Alison, 225
Larbaud, Valéry, 53–4, 148
  differs from Lewis, 56
Latham, Sean, 56, 235
Latin, 138–9
Lawrence, D. H., 193
Lawrence, Karen, 7, 66, 181
  on 'Sirens', 65
Lefebvre, Henri, 200
Léon, Paul, 253
Lescaret, Roger, 254–5
Levin, Harry, 47, 65
Levine, Caroline, 51
Lewis, Wyndham, 253–5
  response to *Ulysses*, 56–7
Liffey, River, 225, 227–8
Linati, Carlo, 52–3
Literary and Historical Society, 13
Little Review, The, 8, 47, 49, 191, 232, 241, 244–7, 253, 257
  obscenity, and, 191
  Pound, and, 236
  prosecution of, 258
  suppression of, 192
Litz, A. Walton, 52, 251
Lloyd George, David, 245

magazines, English fashion
  influence of, 67, 72

283

Mais, S. P. B., 50
Mangan, James Clarence, 120–4, 128, 130, 133
  influence on Joyce, 120–1
Maran, Timo, 222
Marsden, Dora, 238–9
Martin, Timothy, 80
Marx, Karl, 76, 143
Matisse, Henri, 259
Maunsel and Co., 23, 184
McCarthy, Tom, 47
McGann, Jerome, 235, 252, 259
McKenzie, D. F., 252, 259
memory
  cultural and historical, 37
Menasse, Robert, 136
Merleau-Ponty, Maurice, 176
  gender, and, 179
modernism, 7, 76, 78
  depictions of sex, and, 185
  gender, and, 239
  Irish modernism, 144
  popular culture, and, 4
Modernist Journals Project, 235
modernist magazines, 8
Money, John, 174
Monnier, Adrienne, 148
Moods, 108
Moore, George, 144
Moore, Thomas, 72–3
Moriarty, Christopher, 228
Moscow Show Trials, 94
Murry, John Middleton, 47, 49–50
musicals and opera, 70–2
musicals and operas
  The Bohemian Girl, 71
  The Daughter of the Regiment, 70
  Don Giovanni, 71
  Floradora, 70–1
  Martha, 70
  The Rose of Castile, 71
  La Sonnambula, 71

Nash, John, 255
National Library of Ireland, 261
nationalism, 34–5, 42–3, 73–5, 80, 127, 145–6, 150, 155, 162
  colonialism, and, 44–5, 157
  critique of violent nationalism, 160
  Joycean, 72–3
  in musical comedy, 72
  revival, and, 164
  Unionism, and, 244–7

naturalism, 1, 3–7
  in *Ulysses*, 56
Newman, John Henry, 94
Nietzsche, Friedrich, 76, 138, 144
Nolan, Emer, 157–9
Nordau, Max, 143
Norman, H. F., 27
Norris, Margot, 25–6, 188, 203, 227

O'Brien, William Smith, 114
Obscene Publications Act, 1857, 185, 196, 232
obscenity and obscurity, 194–5
Odyssey, 8, 39, 56, 206–7
Olson, Liesl, 209, 213
Opperman, Serpil, 222
Ormond Hotel, 68
Ovid, 150

Palmer, Geoffrey Molyneux, 110
Pappalardo, Salvatore, 149
Paris, 77, 131, 144, 147–8
Parnell, Charles Stewart, 20, 27, 40, 67, 114, 127, 129, 131, 189
  betrayal of, 120
  compared to Oscar Wilde, 33
Pater, Walter, 32, 35, 38
  influence on *A Portrait*, 34
  The Renaissance, 33
Peake, Charles, 66
Phelan, James Blackwell, 52
Piccolo della Sera, 149
Pinter, Harold, 115
Pius X, Pope, 21, 100
Platt, Len, 70, 72
Plunkett, Horace, 27
poems by Joyce. See *Chamber Music*, 'Gas from Burner', 'Holy Office, The', *Moods*, *Pomes Penyeach*, and *Shine and Dark*
Pomes Penyeach, 103, 108, 110–11
  'Nightpiece' and *Finnegans Wake*, 110
Popovich, Dushan, 234, 241
popular culture, 140
  advertising, 166
Portrait of the Artist as a Young Man, A, 1, 3, 7, 56, 77, 87, 150
  compared to *Stephen Hero*, 36, 106–7
  confession, and, 91
  as context for *Ulysses*, 245
  death, and, 33
  development of aesthetic theory, 33–41
  English language, 33

everyday, and, 205–6
influence of Oscar Wilde, 31–4
irony, and, 24
natural world, and, 218–19
non-linearity of, 41–5
politics of style, 34
quotation, and, 126
realism, and, 36
revival, and, 164
sectarianism, and, 156
sex and sexual desire, 4
'Portrait of the Artist, A', 94–5, 144, 251
Pound, Ezra, 9–10, 49, 55, 61, 148, 191, 195–6, 232, 253, 258
    contrast with Joyce, 150
    criticism of *Ulysses*, 57
    differs from Lewis, 56
    as editor of *Ulysses*, 61, 234
    at *Little Review*, 50, 235–9, 258
    misogyny of, 238
    on 'Nestor', 243
Prague, 146
Prezioso, Roberto, 113
Procter, Adelaide Anne, 71
Protestant Ascendancy, 153, 156
Proust, Marcel, 176
psychoanalysis, 96, *See* Freud, Sigmund

Quinn, John, 191, 236, 239

Rabelais, Francois, 148
race, 1, 9, 70–1, 139–40, 164, 166, 170
    racial othering, 72
Radstone, Susannah, 99
Raphael, France, 253
Read, Forrest, 51
Reformation, 95
Renan, Ernest, 139
Revival, Irish language, 25
Revival, Irish Literary, 1, 12, 24, 27, 123–4, 133, 163–5
    parody of, 58
Richards, Grant, 25, 125, 184–5, 187, 191
Richardson, Dorothy, 237
Roberts, George, 184–5, 190
Romanticism, 54, 145, 216
Rome, 141–2
Roosevelt, President, 142
Rose, Danis, 260
Rossetti, Christina, 179
Roth, Samuel, 259
Rousseau, Jean Jacques, 94–5

Rowan, Archibald Hamilton, 114–15
Russell, George, 12, 27

Salamon, Gayle, 175, 180
Schliemann, Heinrich, 202, 207
Schmitt, Ettore, 145
Scholes, Robert, 106
Schönberg, Arnold, 65
Senn, Fritz, 59
sex, 4–5
    confession, and, 195–6
    implicit, 185–90
sex work, 175–6
sexual abuse, 177–8
Shakespeare, William, 2, 4, 39, 80, 129, 131
    homosexuality, and, 130
    imperialism, and, 162
    Falstaff, 86
    Hamlet, 86, 129
    Richard III, 92–3
    The Tempest, 104
Shakespeare and Company, 258
Shaw, George Bernard, 123, 125, 201
Shem (in *Finnegans Wake*), 90, 92, 262
    as artist, 95
    confession, and, 99
    vs. Shaun, 93
Sheridan, Richard Brinsley, 124
Shine and Dark, 108
Sinclair, May, 235, 237
Sinn Féin, 127–8, 244
songs
    'The Croppy Boy', 70, 73–5, 160, 166
    'The Harp That Once Through Tara's Halls', 73
    'Johnny I Hardly Knew Ye', 73
    'The Lost Chord', 71
    'M'appari', 70
    'The Mountains of Mourne', 69
    'The Shade of the Palm', 70
Spoo, Robert, 76
St Lawrence, 94
St Patrick, 7
Stein, Gertrude
    Pound on, 57
Stephen Hero, 31, 33, 38, 107, 180, 217
    body, and, 216
    epiphanies, and, 105–7
    form of, 38
    gender, and, 174
    A Portrait of the Artist as a Young Man, and, 32

INDEX

Stirner, Max, 145
Stoppard, Tom, 146
Strauss, Richard, 32
structuralist narratology, 98
suffragism, 114, 146
Sullivan, Sir Edward, 85
Swift, Jonathan, 177
Swinburne, Algernon Charles, 130
Synge, J. M., 29, 133
   Playboy of the Western World, The, 123

Tales Told of Shem and Shaun, 254
Tandy, Napper, 115
Tindall, William York, 109, 178
Tolstoy, Leo, 78
Tone, Wolfe, 115
trans-corporeality, 216, 220
transition, 8, 145, 253
Trieste, 2, 32, 111, 138, 146
   dialect, 147

Ulysses, 54
   Chamber Music, and, 109–10
   comedy of language, 8
   compared to *Dubliners*, 131
   compared to *Finnegans Wake*, 98
   compared to shorter works, 102
   contemporary reception, 49–58
   death of May Dedalus, 217
   difference periodical and book publication, 245–6
   ending of, 27
   epiphanies, and, 38, 106
   final revisions, 258
   Gabler edition, 251, 259–60
   Homeric parallels, 52, 54, 56–7, 67, 201, 206–8
   idea of Europe, and, 141
   immigrant characters, 69
   interior monologue, 3
   length, 49
   memory, and, 38
   migration, and, 143
   national community, and, 165–6
   non-linearity, 56
   notebooks, 207
   obscenity trial, 200, 259
   schema, 51–4, 208
   serialization, 49, 232–5
   sex, and, 191–4
   styles of narration, 5–7, 34, 52–4, 56–9, 70
   Sweets of Sin, 5, 194

Ulysses, episodes of
   1. 'Telemachus', 3, 56–7, 122, 126
   2. 'Nestor', 56–7, 59, 160–1
     serialization of, 239–47
   3. 'Proteus', 37–8, 56–7, 59, 221
   4. 'Calypso', 56–7, 192, 222
     revisions to, 257
   5. 'Lotus-Eaters', 56–7, 170
   6. 'Hades', 56–7, 209
   7. 'Aeolus', 48, 57
   8. 'Lestrygonians', 57
   9. 'Scylla and Charybdis', 39–40, 57, 59, 80, 115, 129–30, 133, 143–4
   10. 'Wandering Rocks', 4–6, 57, 67, 157, 166, 196, 221
   11. 'Sirens', 57, 110
     and musical form, 65–7
     structure of, 70
   12. 'Cyclops', 57, 130, 158–61, 165, 197
   13. 'Nausicaa', 48, 57, 72, 111, 126, 192
     in *The Little Review*, 232
   14. 'Oxen of the Sun', 57, 66, 126, 221
   15. 'Circe', 5–6, 58, 88, 104, 169–75, 192, 196, 207, 221, 224
   16. 'Eumeaus', 68, 80, 258
   17. 'Ithaca', 6, 58, 200, 224, 258
   18. 'Penelope', 5, 9, 58, 91, 194, 258, 260
Unionism, 69, 146
United Irishmen, 120, 129
University College Dublin, 127–8
Unkeless, Elaine, 170

Valéry, Paul, 150
Vanderham, Paul, 258
Vaughan Williams, Ralph, 66
Vico, Giambattista, 133
   model of history, 137
Victoria, Queen, 71
Volk, Tyler, 228

Walton, William, 66
   Facade, 67
War of Independence, Irish, 133, 245
water, 220, 226
Waterloo, Battle of, 133
Weaver, Harriet Shaw, 64–5, 232, 234, 239, 243, 253
Wilde, Oscar, 34–5, 38, 40, 124, 128, 130, 138, 184, 189
   'The Critic as Artist', 37
   The Decay of Lying, 123
   Dorian Gray, 121
   English hypocrisy, and, 33

homosexuality, and, 130
importance for Joyce, 121–4
Picture of Dorian Gray, The, 33, 121–4
Salomé, 32
Ulysses, and, 122
Witen, Michelle, 78–9
Woolf, Virginia, 50, 209
  on everyday, 206
  gender, and, 172
  Hogarth Press, and, 244
  WWI, 213, 241
  Irish elections, and, 244
Wunderlich, Paul, 112

Xavier, St Francis, 156

Yeats, W. B., 10, 23, 29, 35, 43, 79, 108, 121, 124, 128, 201, 212
  aestheticism of, 32
  Countess Cathleen, The, 29, 41–2, 127
  Irish mythology, and, 144
  Joyce's praise for, 141
  Michael Robartes, 44
  national identity, and, 139
  as Nietzschean, 137
  'September 1913', 23
  'Sixteen Dead Men', 244
Young Ireland movement, 120

Zeller, Hans, 259
Zurich, 111, 148, 202, 213

Cambridge Companions to ...

AUTHORS

Edward Albee edited by Stephen J. Bottoms
Margaret Atwood edited by Coral Ann Howells (second edition)
W. H. Auden edited by Stan Smith
Jane Austen edited by Edward Copeland and Juliet McMaster (second edition)
James Baldwin edited by Michele Elam
Balzac edited by Owen Heathcote and Andrew Watts
Beckett edited by John Pilling
Bede edited by Scott DeGregorio
Aphra Behn edited by Derek Hughes and Janet Todd
Saul Bellow edited by Victoria Aarons
Walter Benjamin edited by David S. Ferris
William Blake edited by Morris Eaves
Boccaccio edited by Guyda Armstrong, Rhiannon Daniels, and Stephen J. Milner
Jorge Luis Borges edited by Edwin Williamson
Brecht edited by Peter Thomson and Glendyr Sacks (second edition)
The Brontës edited by Heather Glen
Bunyan edited by Anne Dunan-Page
Frances Burney edited by Peter Sabor
Byron edited by Drummond Bone (second edition)
Albert Camus edited by Edward J. Hughes
Willa Cather edited by Marilee Lindemann
Catullus edited by Ian Du Quesnay and Tony Woodman
Cervantes edited by Anthony J. Cascardi
Chaucer edited by Piero Boitani and Jill Mann (second edition)
Chekhov edited by Vera Gottlieb and Paul Allain
Kate Chopin edited by Janet Beer
Caryl Churchill edited by Elaine Aston and Elin Diamond
Cicero edited by Catherine Steel
John Clare edited by Sarah Houghton-Walker
J. M. Coetzee edited by Jarad Zimbler
Coleridge edited by Lucy Newlyn
Coleridge edited by Tim Fulford (new edition)
Wilkie Collins edited by Jenny Bourne Taylor
Joseph Conrad edited by J. H. Stape
H. D. edited by Nephie J. Christodoulides and Polina Mackay
Dante edited by Rachel Jacoff (second edition)
Daniel Defoe edited by John Richetti
Don DeLillo edited by John N. Duvall
Charles Dickens edited by John O. Jordan
Emily Dickinson edited by Wendy Martin
John Donne edited by Achsah Guibbory
Dostoevskii edited by W. J. Leatherbarrow
Theodore Dreiser edited by Leonard Cassuto and Claire Virginia Eby
John Dryden edited by Steven N. Zwicker
W. E. B. Du Bois edited by Shamoon Zamir
George Eliot edited by George Levine and Nancy Henry (second edition)
T. S. Eliot edited by A. David Moody
Ralph Ellison edited by Ross Posnock
Ralph Waldo Emerson edited by Joel Porte and Saundra Morris
William Faulkner edited by Philip M. Weinstein
Henry Fielding edited by Claude Rawson
F. Scott Fitzgerald edited by Ruth Prigozy
F. Scott Fitzgerald edited by Michael Nowlin (second edition)
Flaubert edited by Timothy Unwin
E. M. Forster edited by David Bradshaw
Benjamin Franklin edited by Carla Mulford
Brian Friel edited by Anthony Roche
Robert Frost edited by Robert Faggen
Gabriel García Márquez edited by Philip Swanson
Elizabeth Gaskell edited by Jill L. Matus
Edward Gibbon edited by Karen O'Brien and Brian Young
Goethe edited by Lesley Sharpe
Günter Grass edited by Stuart Taberner
Thomas Hardy edited by Dale Kramer
David Hare edited by Richard Boon
Nathaniel Hawthorne edited by Richard Millington
Seamus Heaney edited by Bernard O'Donoghue

Ernest Hemingway edited by Scott Donaldson
Hildegard of Bingen edited by Jennifer Bain
Homer edited by Robert Fowler
Horace edited by Stephen Harrison
Ted Hughes edited by Terry Gifford
Ibsen edited by James McFarlane
Kazuo Ishiguro edited by Andrew Bennett
Henry James edited by Jonathan Freedman
Samuel Johnson edited by Greg Clingham
Ben Jonson edited by Richard Harp and Stanley Stewart
James Joyce edited by John Nash (third edition)
Kafka edited by Julian Preece
Keats edited by Susan J. Wolfson
Rudyard Kipling edited by Howard J. Booth
Lacan edited by Jean-Michel Rabaté
D. H. Lawrence edited by Anne Fernihough
Primo Levi edited by Robert Gordon
Lucian edited by Simon Goldhill
Lucretius edited by Stuart Gillespie and Philip Hardie
Machiavelli edited by John M. Najemy
David Mamet edited by Christopher Bigsby
Thomas Mann edited by Ritchie Robertson
Christopher Marlowe edited by Patrick Cheney
Andrew Marvell edited by Derek Hirst and Steven N. Zwicker
Ian McEwan edited by Dominic Head
Herman Melville edited by Robert S. Levine
Arthur Miller edited by Christopher Bigsby (second edition)
Milton edited by Dennis Danielson (second edition)
Molière edited by David Bradby and Andrew Calder
William Morris edited by Marcus Waithe
Toni Morrison edited by Justine Tally
Alice Munro edited by David Staines
Nabokov edited by Julian W. Connolly
Eugene O'Neill edited by Michael Manheim
George Orwell edited by John Rodden
Ovid edited by Philip Hardie
Petrarch edited by Albert Russell Ascoli and Unn Falkeid

Harold Pinter edited by Peter Raby (second edition)
Sylvia Plath edited by Jo Gill
Plutarch edited by Frances B. Titchener and Alexei Zadorojnyi
Edgar Allan Poe edited by Kevin J. Hayes
Alexander Pope edited by Pat Rogers
Ezra Pound edited by Ira B. Nadel
Mary Prince edited by Nicole N. Aljoe
Proust edited by Richard Bales
Pushkin edited by Andrew Kahn
Thomas Pynchon edited by Inger H. Dalsgaard, Luc Herman and Brian McHale
Rabelais edited by John O'Brien
Rilke edited by Karen Leeder and Robert Vilain
Philip Roth edited by Timothy Parrish
Salman Rushdie edited by Abdulrazak Gurnah
John Ruskin edited by Francis O'Gorman
Sappho edited by P. J. Finglass and Adrian Kelly
Seneca edited by Shadi Bartsch and Alessandro Schiesaro
Shakespeare edited by Margareta de Grazia and Stanley Wells (second edition)
George Bernard Shaw edited by Christopher Innes
Shelley edited by Timothy Morton
Mary Shelley edited by Esther Schor
Sam Shepard edited by Matthew C. Roudané
Spenser edited by Andrew Hadfield
Laurence Sterne edited by Thomas Keymer
Wallace Stevens edited by John N. Serio
Tom Stoppard edited by Katherine E. Kelly
Harriet Beecher Stowe edited by Cindy Weinstein
August Strindberg edited by Michael Robinson
Jonathan Swift edited by Christopher Fox
J. M. Synge edited by P. J. Mathews
Tacitus edited by A. J. Woodman
Henry David Thoreau edited by Joel Myerson
Thucydides edited by Polly Low
Tolstoy edited by Donna Tussing Orwin
Anthony Trollope edited by Carolyn Dever and Lisa Niles

Mark Twain edited by Forrest G. Robinson
John Updike edited by Stacey Olster
Mario Vargas Llosa edited by Efrain Kristal and John King
Virgil edited by Fiachra Mac Góráin and Charles Martindale (second edition)
Voltaire edited by Nicholas Cronk
David Foster Wallace edited by Ralph Clare
Edith Wharton edited by Millicent Bell
Walt Whitman edited by Ezra Greenspan
Oscar Wilde edited by Peter Raby
Tennessee Williams edited by Matthew C. Roudané
William Carlos Williams edited by Christopher MacGowan
August Wilson edited by Christopher Bigsby
Mary Wollstonecraft edited by Claudia L. Johnson
Virginia Woolf edited by Susan Sellers (second edition)
Wordsworth edited by Stephen Gill
Richard Wright edited by Glenda R. Carpio
W. B. Yeats edited by Marjorie Howes and John Kelly
Xenophon edited by Michael A. Flower
Zola edited by Brian Nelson

TOPICS

The Actress edited by Maggie B. Gale and John Stokes
The African American Novel edited by Maryemma Graham
The African American Slave Narrative edited by Audrey A. Fisch
African American Theatre edited by Harvey Young
Allegory edited by Rita Copeland and Peter Struck
American Crime Fiction edited by Catherine Ross Nickerson
American Gothic edited by Jeffrey Andrew Weinstock
The American Graphic Novel edited by Jan Baetens, Hugo Frey and Fabrice Leroy
American Horror edited by Stephen Shapiro and Mark Storey
American Literature and the Body edited by Travis M. Foster
American Literature and the Environment edited by Sarah Ensor and Susan Scott Parrish
American Literature of the 1930s edited by William Solomon
American Modernism edited by Walter Kalaidjian
American Poetry since 1945 edited by Jennifer Ashton
American Realism and Naturalism edited by Donald Pizer
American Short Story edited by Michael J. Collins and Gavin Jones
American Travel Writing edited by Alfred Bendixen and Judith Hamera
American Utopian Literature and Culture since 1945 edited by Sherryl Vint
American Women Playwrights edited by Brenda Murphy
Ancient Rhetoric edited by Erik Gunderson
Arthurian Legend edited by Elizabeth Archibald and Ad Putter
Australian Literature edited by Elizabeth Webby
The Australian Novel edited by Nicholas Birns and Louis Klee
The Beats edited by Stephen Belletto
The Black Body in American Literature edited by Cherene Sherrard-Johnson
Boxing edited by Gerald Early
British Black and Asian Literature (1945–2010) edited by Deirdre Osborne
British Fiction: 1980–2018 edited by Peter Boxall
British Fiction since 1945 edited by David James
British Literature of the 1930s edited by James Smith
British Literature of the French Revolution edited by Pamela Clemit
British Romantic Poetry edited by James Chandler and Maureen N. McLane
British Romanticism edited by Stuart Curran (second edition)
British Romanticism and Religion edited by Jeffrey Barbeau
British Theatre, 1730–1830 edited by Jane Moody and Daniel O'Quinn

Canadian Literature edited by Eva-Marie Kröller (second edition)

The Canterbury Tales edited by Frank Grady

Children's Literature edited by M. O. Grenby and Andrea Immel

The City in World Literature edited by Ato Quayson and Jini Kim Watson

The Classic Russian Novel edited by Malcolm V. Jones and Robin Feuer Miller

Comics edited by Maaheen Ahmed

Contemporary African American Literature edited by Yogita Goyal

Contemporary Irish Poetry edited by Matthew Campbell

Creative Writing edited by David Morley and Philip Neilsen

Crime Fiction edited by Martin Priestman

Dante's 'Commedia' edited by Zygmunt G. Barański and Simon Gilson

Dracula edited by Roger Luckhurst

Early American Literature edited by Bryce Traister

Early Modern Women's Writing edited by Laura Lunger Knoppers

The Eighteenth-Century Novel edited by John Richetti

Eighteenth-Century Poetry edited by John Sitter

Eighteenth-Century Thought edited by Frans De Bruyn

Emma edited by Peter Sabor

English Dictionaries edited by Sarah Ogilvie

English Literature, 1500–1600 edited by Arthur F. Kinney

English Literature, 1650–1740 edited by Steven N. Zwicker

English Literature, 1740–1830 edited by Thomas Keymer and Jon Mee

English Literature, 1830–1914 edited by Joanne Shattock

English Melodrama edited by Carolyn Williams

English Novelists edited by Adrian Poole

English Poetry, Donne to Marvell edited by Thomas N. Corns

English Poets edited by Claude Rawson

English Renaissance Drama edited by A. R. Braunmuller and Michael Hattaway (second edition)

English Renaissance Tragedy edited by Emma Smith and Garrett A. Sullivan Jr.

English Restoration Theatre edited by Deborah C. Payne Fisk

Environmental Humanities edited by Jeffrey Cohen and Stephanie Foote

The Epic edited by Catherine Bates

Erotic Literature edited by Bradford Mudge

The Essay edited by Kara Wittman and Evan Kindley

European Modernism edited by Pericles Lewis

European Novelists edited by Michael Bell

Fairy Tales edited by Maria Tatar

Fantasy Literature edited by Edward James and Farah Mendlesohn

Feminist Literary Theory edited by Ellen Rooney

Fiction in the Romantic Period edited by Richard Maxwell and Katie Trumpener

The Fin de Siècle edited by Gail Marshall

Frankenstein edited by Andrew Smith

The French Enlightenment edited by Daniel Brewer

French Literature edited by John D. Lyons

The French Novel: From 1800 to the Present edited by Timothy Unwin

Gay and Lesbian Writing edited by Hugh Stevens

German Romanticism edited by Nicholas Saul

Global Literature and Slavery edited by Laura T. Murphy

Gothic Fiction edited by Jerrold E. Hogle

The Graphic Novel edited by Stephen Tabachnick

The Greek and Roman Novel edited by Tim Whitmarsh

Greek and Roman Theatre edited by Marianne McDonald and J. Michael Walton

Greek Comedy edited by Martin Revermann

Greek Lyric edited by Felix Budelmann

Greek Mythology edited by Roger D. Woodard

Greek Tragedy edited by P. E. Easterling

The Harlem Renaissance edited by George Hutchinson

The History of the Book edited by Leslie Howsam

Human Rights and Literature edited by Crystal Parikh

The Irish Novel edited by John Wilson Foster

Irish Poets edited by Gerald Dawe

The Italian Novel edited by Peter Bondanella and Andrea Ciccarelli

The Italian Renaissance edited by Michael Wyatt

Jewish American Literature edited by Hana Wirth-Nesher and Michael P. Kramer

The Latin American Novel edited by Efraín Kristal

Latin American Poetry edited by Stephen Hart

Latina/o American Literature edited by John Morán González

Latin Love Elegy edited by Thea S. Thorsen

Literature and Animals edited by Derek Ryan

Literature and the Anthropocene edited by John Parham

Literature and Climate edited by Adeline Johns-Putra and Kelly Sultzbach

Literature and Disability edited by Clare Barker and Stuart Murray

Literature and Food edited by J. Michelle Coghlan

Literature and the Posthuman edited by Bruce Clarke and Manuela Rossini

Literature and Religion edited by Susan M. Felch

Literature and Science edited by Steven Meyer

The Literature of the American Civil War and Reconstruction edited by Kathleen Diffley and Coleman Hutchison

The Literature of the American Renaissance edited by Christopher N. Phillips

The Literature of Berlin edited by Andrew J. Webber

The Literature of the Crusades edited by Anthony Bale

The Literature of the First World War edited by Vincent Sherry

The Literature of London edited by Lawrence Manley

The Literature of Los Angeles edited by Kevin R. McNamara

The Literature of New York edited by Cyrus Patell and Bryan Waterman

The Literature of Paris edited by Anna-Louise Milne

The Literature of World War II edited by Marina MacKay

Literature on Screen edited by Deborah Cartmell and Imelda Whelehan

Lyrical Ballads edited by Sally Bushell

Manga and Anime edited by Jaqueline Berndt

Medieval British Manuscripts edited by Orietta Da Rold and Elaine Treharne

Medieval English Culture edited by Andrew Galloway

Medieval English Law and Literature edited by Candace Barrington and Sebastian Sobecki

Medieval English Literature edited by Larry Scanlon

Medieval English Mysticism edited by Samuel Fanous and Vincent Gillespie

Medieval English Theatre edited by Richard Beadle and Alan J. Fletcher (second edition)

Medieval French Literature edited by Simon Gaunt and Sarah Kay

Medieval Romance edited by Roberta L. Krueger

Medieval Romance edited by Roberta L. Krueger (new edition)

Medieval Women's Writing edited by Carolyn Dinshaw and David Wallace

Modern American Culture edited by Christopher Bigsby

Modern British Women Playwrights edited by Elaine Aston and Janelle Reinelt

Modern French Culture edited by Nicholas Hewitt

Modern German Culture edited by Eva Kolinsky and Wilfried van der Will

The Modern German Novel edited by Graham Bartram

The Modern Gothic edited by Jerrold E. Hogle

Modern Irish Culture edited by Joe Cleary and Claire Connolly

Modern Italian Culture edited by Zygmunt G. Baranski and Rebecca J. West

Modern Latin American Culture edited by John King

Modern Russian Culture edited by Nicholas Rzhevsky

Modern Spanish Culture edited by David T. Gies

Modernism edited by Michael Levenson (second edition)

The Modernist Novel edited by Morag Shiach

Modernist Poetry edited by Alex Davis and Lee M. Jenkins

Modernist Women Writers edited by Maren Tova Linett

Narrative edited by David Herman

Narrative Theory edited by Matthew Garrett

Native American Literature edited by Joy Porter and Kenneth M. Roemer

Nineteen Eighty-Four edited by Nathan Waddell

Nineteenth-Century American Literature and Politics edited by John Kerkering

Nineteenth-Century American Poetry edited by Kerry Larson

Nineteenth-Century American Women's Writing edited by Dale M. Bauer and Philip Gould

Nineteenth-Century Thought edited by Gregory Claeys

The Novel edited by Eric Bulson

Old English Literature edited by Malcolm Godden and Michael Lapidge (second edition)

Performance Studies edited by Tracy C. Davis

Piers Plowman edited by Andrew Cole and Andrew Galloway

The Poetry of the First World War edited by Santanu Das

Popular Fiction edited by David Glover and Scott McCracken

Postcolonial Literary Studies edited by Neil Lazarus

Postcolonial Poetry edited by Jahan Ramazani

Postcolonial Travel Writing edited by Robert Clarke

Postmodern American Fiction edited by Paula Geyh

Postmodernism edited by Steven Connor

Prose edited by Daniel Tyler

The Pre-Raphaelites edited by Elizabeth Prettejohn

Pride and Prejudice edited by Janet Todd

Queer Studies edited by Siobhan B. Somerville

Renaissance Humanism edited by Jill Kraye

Robinson Crusoe edited by John Richetti

Roman Comedy edited by Martin T. Dinter

The Roman Historians edited by Andrew Feldherr

Roman Satire edited by Kirk Freudenburg

The Romantic Sublime edited by Cian Duffy

Romanticism and Race edited by Manu Samriti Chander

Science Fiction edited by Edward James and Farah Mendlesohn

Scottish Literature edited by Gerald Carruthers and Liam McIlvanney

Sensation Fiction edited by Andrew Mangham

Shakespeare and Contemporary Dramatists edited by Ton Hoenselaars

Shakespeare and Popular Culture edited by Robert Shaughnessy

Shakespeare and Race edited by Ayanna Thompson

Shakespeare and Religion edited by Hannibal Hamlin

Shakespeare and War edited by David Loewenstein and Paul Stevens

Shakespeare on Film edited by Russell Jackson (second edition)

Shakespeare on Screen edited by Russell Jackson

Shakespeare on Stage edited by Stanley Wells and Sarah Stanton

Shakespearean Comedy edited by Alexander Leggatt

Shakespearean Tragedy edited by Claire McEachern (second edition)

Shakespeare's First Folio edited by Emma Smith

Shakespeare's History Plays edited by Michael Hattaway

Shakespeare's Language edited by Lynne Magnusson with David Schalkwyk

Shakespeare's Last Plays edited by Catherine M. S. Alexander

Shakespeare's Poetry edited by Patrick Cheney

Sherlock Holmes edited by Janice M. Allan and Christopher Pittard

The Sonnet edited by A. D. Cousins and Peter Howarth

The Spanish Novel: From 1600 to the Present edited by Harriet Turner and Adelaida López de Martínez

Textual Scholarship edited by Neil Fraistat and Julia Flanders

Theatre and Science edited by Kristen E. Shepherd-Barr

Theatre History edited by David Wiles and Christine Dymkowski

Transnational American Literature edited by Yogita Goyal

Travel Writing edited by Peter Hulme and Tim Youngs

The Twentieth-Century American Novel and Politics edited by Bryan Santin

Twentieth-Century American Poetry and Politics edited by Daniel Morris

Twentieth-Century British and Irish Women's Poetry edited by Jane Dowson

The Twentieth-Century English Novel edited by Robert L. Caserio

Twentieth-Century English Poetry edited by Neil Corcoran

Twentieth-Century Irish Drama edited by Shaun Richards

Twentieth-Century Literature and Politics edited by Christos Hadjiyiannis and Rachel Potter

Twentieth-Century Russian Literature edited by Marina Balina and Evgeny Dobrenko

Utopian Literature edited by Gregory Claeys

Victorian and Edwardian Theatre edited by Kerry Powell

The Victorian Novel edited by Deirdre David (second edition)

Victorian Poetry edited by Joseph Bristow

Victorian Women's Poetry edited by Linda K. Hughes

Victorian Women's Writing edited by Linda H. Peterson

War Writing edited by Kate McLoughlin

Women's Writing in Britain, 1660–1789 edited by Catherine Ingrassia

Women's Writing in the Romantic Period edited by Devoney Looser

World Literature edited by Ben Etherington and Jarad Zimbler

World Crime Fiction edited by Jesper Gulddal, Stewart King, and Alistair Rolls

Writing of the English Revolution edited by N. H. Keeble

The Writings of Julius Caesar edited by Christopher Krebs and Luca Grillo

For EU product safety concerns, contact us at Calle de José Abascal, 56–1º,
28003 Madrid, Spain or eugpsr@cambridge.org.

www.ingramcontent.com/pod-product-compliance
Lightning Source LLC
LaVergne TN
LVHW040733250326
834688LV00031B/271